Turkey's Necropolitical Laboratory

For Max and Teo

Turkey's Necropolitical Laboratory

Democracy, Violence and Resistance

Edited by
BANU BARGU

EDINBURGH
University Press

Edinburgh University Press is one of the leading university presses in the UK. We publish academic books and journals in our selected subject areas across the humanities and social sciences, combining cutting-edge scholarship with high editorial and production values to produce academic works of lasting importance. For more information visit our website: edinburghuniversitypress.com

© editorial matter and organisation Banu Bargu, 2019, 2021
© the chapters their several authors, 2019, 2021

Edinburgh University Press Ltd
The Tun – Holyrood Road, 12(2f) Jackson's Entry, Edinburgh EH8 8PJ

First published in hardback by Edinburgh University Press 2019

Typeset in 10/13 Giovanni by
IDSUK (DataConnection) Ltd

A CIP record for this book is available from the British Library

ISBN 978 1 4744 5026 3 (hardback)
ISBN 978 1 4744 5027 0 (paperback)
ISBN 978 1 4744 5028 7 (webready PDF)
ISBN 978 1 4744 5029 4 (epub)

The right of Banu Bargu to be identified as the editor of this work has been asserted in accordance with the Copyright, Designs and Patents Act 1988, and the Copyright and Related Rights Regulations 2003 (SI No. 2498).

CONTENTS

Notes on the Contributors / vii
Acknowledgements / xii

ONE / Turkey's Necropolitical Laboratory:
Notes towards an Investigation / 1
Banu Bargu

PART ONE / Politicising Death: Sovereign Cartographies of Violence

TWO / 'These are ordinary things': Regulation of Death under
the AKP Regime / 25
Onur Bakıner

THREE / 'They wrote history with their bodies': Necrogeopolitics,
Necropolitical Spaces and the Everyday Spatial Politics of
Death in Turkey / 46
Lerna K. Yanık and Fulya Hisarlıoğlu

FOUR / Neither Civilian nor Combatant: Weaponised Spaces and
Spatialised Bodies in Cizre / 71
Haydar Darıcı and Serra Hakyemez

PART TWO / Negotiating Life: Resistance and Democracy

FIVE / The Necropolitics of Documents and the Slow Death of
Prisoners in Turkey / 97
Başak Can

SIX / Proper Subjects of Gendered Necropolitics: A Case of Constructed Virginities in Turkey / 118
Elif Savaş

SEVEN / Necropolitics, Martyrdom and Muslim Conscientious Objection / 139
Pınar Kemerli

EIGHT / The Use of Blood Money in the Establishment of Non-Justice: Necrodomination and Resistance / 160
Cem Özatalay, Gözde Aytemur Nüfusçu and Gülistan Zeren

NINE / Money for Life: Border Killings, Compensation Claims and Life-Money Conversions in Turkey's Kurdish Borderlands / 187
Fırat Bozçalı

PART THREE / Political Afterlives: Governing the Living and the Dead

TEN / Another Necropolitics / 209
Banu Bargu

ELEVEN / The Cemetery of Traitors / 232
Osman Balkan

TWELVE / Nightmare Knowledges: Epistemologies of Disappearance / 253
Ege Selin Islekel

Index / 273

NOTES ON THE CONTRIBUTORS

Onur Bakıner is assistant professor of political science at Seattle University. His research and teaching interests include transitional justice, human rights and judicial politics, particularly in Latin America and the Middle East. His book *Truth Commissions: Memory, Power, and Legitimacy* (University of Pennsylvania Press, 2016) has been awarded the Best Book Award by the Human Rights Section of the American Political Science Association. His articles have been published in the *Journal of Law and Courts*, the *International Journal of Transitional Justice*, *Memory Studies*, *Turkish Studies* and *Nationalities Papers*.

Osman Balkan is visiting assistant professor of political science at Swarthmore College. His research and teaching interests include migration and citizenship, religion and politics, and political identity, particularly in Europe and the Middle East. He is currently completing a book manuscript on the funerary practices and burial decisions of Muslims in Europe which draws on ethnographic fieldwork conducted in Berlin and Istanbul. His work has been published in journals such as *Studies in Ethnicity and Nationalism*, *Journal of Intercultural Studies* and *Contemporary French Civilization*, and in edited volumes including *Muslims in the UK and Europe* and *The Democratic Arts of Mourning*. He earned his BA and PhD in Political Science from Reed College and the University of Pennsylvania respectively.

Banu Bargu is associate professor in History of Consciousness, University of California in Santa Cruz. Her main area of specialisation is political theory, especially modern and contemporary political thought, with a thematic focus on theories of sovereignty, biopolitics and resistance. She is the author of *Starve and Immolate: The Politics of Human Weapons* (Columbia University Press, 2014), which received APSA's *First Book Prize* given by the Foundations of Political Theory section and was named an *Outstanding Academic Title* for 2015 by Choice. She is the co-editor of *Feminism, Capitalism, and Critique: Essays in Honor of Nancy Fraser* (Palgrave, 2017).

Fırat Bozçalı is assistant professor of anthropology at the University of Toronto. His research interests lie at the intersections of political and legal anthropology, political economy, transnational flows, and science and technology studies, with a focus on the modern Middle East. His writings have appeared in *Middle East Report, Arab Studies Journal, New Perspectives on Turkey, Toplum ve Bilim* and *Birikim*.

Başak Can has a PhD in anthropology from the University of Pennsylvania and is assistant professor at Koç University. She is a medical anthropologist with an interest in the intersections of human rights, state violence, gender, politics of care and the body. She is currently completing her book manuscript, titled *Documenting Bodies: Doctors and Human Rights in Turkey*. Her research has led to several publications in peer-reviewed journals including *Medical Anthropology, Medical Anthropology Quarterly, Reproductive Health Matters, New Perspectives on Turkey* and *Media, Culture & Society*. She has also published articles in peer-reviewed journals in Turkish such as *Toplum ve Bilim, Toplum ve Hekim* and *Moment Dergi*.

Haydar Darıcı is a postdoctoral fellow at the School of International Service in the American University at Washington DC. He received his BA in Turkish Language and Literature from Boğaziçi University, MA in Cultural Studies from Sabancı University, and PhD in the joint programme in Anthropology and History at the University of Michigan, Ann Arbor. He works on youth politics in Kurdistan and has published in journals such as *International Journal of Middle East Studies, Journal of Balkan and Near Eastern Studies*, and *New Perspectives on Turkey*.

Serra Hakyemez is lecturer of social anthropology at the University of Edinburgh and assistant professor of anthropology at the University of Minnesota (on leave). Her research concentrates on anthropology of law and politics, with a special focus on 'war on terror', state sovereignty and Kurdish political prisoners in Turkey. She is currently working on her book manuscript, *The Law's Enemy: Terrorism Trials in Turkey*. Her research has been published in *American Ethnologist, Anthropological Quarterly, Birikim, Dialectical Anthropology, Middle East Report* and *Political and Legal Anthropology*.

Fulya Hisarlıoğlu is assistant professor in the Political Science Department at Doğuş University. She received a bachelor's degree in international relations from Bilkent University. She completed her PhD research on Turkey's Europeanisation patterns at the Political Science Department of Bilkent University. Her research interests lie in the area of contemporary Turkish politics, identity politics, Europeanisation, Turkish–EU relations and Turkish foreign policy. She has contributed several chapters to edited books and published articles in academic journals including *Geopolitics* and *International Relations*.

Ege Selin Islekel is visiting assistant professor of philosophy at Loyola Marymount University. She received her PhD from the Philosophy Department at DePaul University in 2018. Her work lies at the intersection of social and political philosophy, critical theory, decolonial feminist theory and twentieth-century French philosophy. Thematically, her research analyses the political philosophy of death, investigating the ways in which death is implicated in contemporary biopolitics, and the resistant capacities of grief. Her articles in English and Turkish have appeared in journals and anthologies, such as *philoSOPHIA*, *Philosophy Today* and *Cinsiyeti Yazmak*.

Pınar Kemerli is clinical assistant professor in Global Liberal Studies at New York University. She specialises in modern political theory and comparative political thought, with a focus on theories of sovereignty and civil disobedience. She is currently completing a book project entitled *Muslim Conscientious Refusal: War and Dissent in Contemporary Turkey*. Her work has appeared in journals and anthologies including *International Journal of Middle East Studies* (IJMES), *Contested Spaces in Contemporary Turkey* and *The Oxford Handbook of the History of Terrorism*.

Gözde Aytemur Nüfusçu is a doctoral candidate at the Institut des Sciences sociales du Politique at École Normale Supérieure de Cachan and a research assistant in the Department of Sociology at Galatasaray University. Her doctoral dissertation is about the neoliberal transformation of judicial practices of prosecutors in Turkey. Her research interests are legal professions, the reconstruction of legal field in Turkey, institutional transformation, qualitative research methods and dangerous fieldworks. She is presently coordinator of the research project 'Corps ordonnés, la production des normes en Turquie et en France', created by junior researchers in Turkey and in France.

Cem Özatalay is a visiting research scholar at the New School for Social Research as IIE-SRF fellow and associate professor in the Department of Sociology at Galatasaray University. Özatalay completed his PhD at EHESS (Ecole des hautes études en sciences sociales) in 2010 with a thesis on *Diversity in Workers' Consciousness in the Age of Pragmatisms: 'Nation-State Worker' versus 'Glocalisation Worker'*. His research areas are social inequalities, social stratification, economic sociology of capitalism, neoliberalism, morality and economy, art and economy.

Elif Savaş is a PhD student in the Department of Political Science at University of Massachusetts Amherst, where she is also completing a graduate certificate programme in Women, Gender and Sexuality Studies. She received her MA degree in Politics from the New School for Social Research, New York, with a Fulbright scholarship, and her BA degrees in Political Science and International Relations and Philosophy from Boğaziçi University, Istanbul. Her MA thesis explored the conceptualisation of virginity and formation of different female subjectivities within and through medico-political assemblages of Turkey. Her research interests lie at the intersection of gender and sexuality studies, feminist theory and empirically informed political theory, with a focus on governmentality and financialisation of female sexual and reproductive health.

Lerna K. Yanık is professor in the Department of Political Science and Public Administration at Kadir Has University, Istanbul, Turkey. She received her BA from Boğaziçi University and her PhD from Georgetown University and has worked at Bilkent University in Ankara, Turkey, before joining Kadir Has University in 2011. She is the first prize winner of the 2006 Sakıp Sabancı International Research Award, has spent a semester at the City University of New York's Graduate Center as a visiting Fulbright scholar in 2009–10 and was Derek Brewer Visiting Fellow at Emmanuel College, University of Cambridge for Michaelmas Term 2017 and visiting scholar in the Department of Politics and International Studies, University of Cambridge in 2017–18. She specialises in non-Western international relations theory, history of Turkish foreign policy, politics of space and time in international relations, critical geopolitics as well as culture and politics. Her research has appeared in journals such as *Journal of International Relations and Development, Die Welt des Islams, Asian Journal of Social Sciences, International Journal, Turkish Studies, Uluslararası İlişkiler* (in Turkish), *Political Geography, Geopolitics, Middle East Journal of Culture and Communication, Human Rights Quarterly* and *Europe–Asia Studies*.

Gülistan Zeren is a graduate student at École Normal Supérieure de Lyon. Her master's thesis is about the neoliberal transformation of health care policies in Turkey. Her research is focused on institutional reconstruction of the medical field in Turkey and its effects on family physicians' professional identifications. She is presently a member of the research project 'Corps ordonnés, la production des normes en Turquie et en France', created by junior researchers in Turkey and in France. She is also a part of the internship programme in a NGO (Hakikat Adalet Hafıza Merkezi) aiming to uncover the truth concerning past violations of human rights, strengthen the collective memory about those violations and support survivors in their pursuit of justice.

ACKNOWLEDGEMENTS

This book was born from the intuition that in order to understand Turkey today, it is necessary to read its democracy from the point of view of its intimate relationship to violence, especially the kind of violence that renders life unliveable even when it does not directly result in death-making or long after it has wreaked death and destruction. Such violence, whose multiple modalities and operations this volume sets itself the task of investigating, insistently redraws the boundaries of life and death and, along with those boundaries, those of the political. It acts as an instrument of power as well as a means of resistance. Conceptualised under the rubric of necropolitics, the forms of violence that are traced and studied in this volume often remain in the long shadow cast by Turkey's democracy all the while they undergird its existence and condition its vicissitudes. Situating Turkey within a necropolitical problematic, therefore, promised a nuanced and original understanding of its recent past and its present.

However, the country's swift transformation in the present conjuncture and the increasing relevance of its necropolitical experiences have further compounded the need to look closely at the dark side of its democracy. Witnessing decline and decay brings forth the acute sense of loss, the withering away of a home to which the ones afar could have always imagined eventual return and the belonging of those already there would not have been subjected to recurrent questioning. These feelings of loss and homelessness come with a keen sense of intellectual urgency that leads one to the search for a community of interlocutors with whom one can commiserate, to be sure, but, more importantly, think together, in the best way one knows how to mourn loss, find hope and look forward.

If Turkey's present has thus fuelled the motivation for embarking on the project, however, that motivation was fortified upon reading the heartbreaking news of the passing of Dr Mehmet Fatih Traş, who committed suicide after being sacked from his position at Çukurova University for being a signatory of the well-known 'Peace Petition'. Even though I did not have the opportunity to meet Dr Traş, I consider him a kindred spirit whose immense despair must have been animated by the greatness of the passion we share – for the life of the mind and the future of Turkey. That passion is, I believe, shared by all the contributors of this volume, and our work is a small tribute to his life and what it could have been, as they have come to represent poignantly what trajectories of the future have been foreclosed in Turkey by the death-logics of what is and has been.

The rather uncommon approach of reading recent Turkish politics from a problematic of necropolitics, it turned out, resonated strongly among the authors to this volume, who without hesitation embraced my invitation to participate in this project. The resulting book comprises of original essays penned specifically in response to the call of the project from a wonderfully diverse group of scholars located in different disciplines, employing different methodologies and following a plurality of theoretical traditions, leading to a truly transdisciplinary and cutting-edge collection. I am further proud that this volume brings together scholars at very different stages of seniority in their academic lives and decisively tilts the gender balance with an amazing group of female scholars, who comprise the majority of the volume's contributors.

My biggest thanks go to the authors in this volume, in admiration of the way they enact scholarly ethics and uphold intellectual responsibility and for their commitment to advancing the critical–theoretical scholarship on Turkey. I am grateful to our editors, Jenny Daly and Adela Rauchova, and Edinburgh University Press, for enthusiastically taking on this project, concurring with us regarding the timeliness of its intervention and encouraging it throughout the process of its gestation. I wholeheartedly thank our anonymous reviewers who put immense trust in my scholarship and curation and insightfully indicated ways of making the project even stronger and more far-reaching. Sara Hassani, who is a doctoral candidate at the New School for Social Research, has my sincere thanks for her valuable research support in the planning stage of the book. I am thankful for the superb editorial assistance of Francesca Romeo, who is a doctoral candidate at the University of California, Santa Cruz. I thank James Martel and Kennan R. Ferguson, the co-editors of *theory and event*, for allowing me to reproduce my own essay, 'Another Necropolitics', for this volume, with minor modifications of format and style.

I want to end by expressing my loving gratitude for Massimiliano Tomba, who inspires me to embrace life, especially when I think and write about death and destruction. This book is dedicated to him and our son, Teoman, who came into the world as I was completing this project. Without their presence my life would be immeasurably, unconsolably less.

ONE

Turkey's Necropolitical Laboratory: Notes towards an Investigation

Banu Bargu

As the centennial of Turkey's republican founding approaches, there is great uncertainty about its democratic future. This uncertainty is not simply the product of a majoritarian democracy where the Justice and Development Party (AKP) has remained in government for nearly two decades, nor merely a function of recent events, especially the momentous failed coup of 2016, whose consequences are still acutely unfolding.[1] Without discounting the significance of either the authoritarian tendencies of majoritarian rule or the radical changes that have taken place, such as the shift to an executive presidency, during emergency rule following the failed coup, the chapters in this volume make a case that the uncertainty of Turkey's democracy is also a function of deeper and more longstanding facets of its political constitution. Of these, the focus of this volume is the presence and, indeed, intensification of a 'necropolitical undercurrent' that, sometimes loudly and at other times silently and subtly, flows below the surface of Turkey's political regime.

This 'necropolitical undercurrent' expresses the entanglement, indeed imbrication, of Turkey's democracy with violence. Necropolitics is best conceptualised as an undercurrent both because it often remains in the shadows, not visible to analyses that focus on electoral politics, constitutionalism and economic development, for example, and due to the acclamation and democratic legitimacy that sovereign violence often garners from large swathes of the population. Furthermore, while the most obvious exercise of violence is focused on death-making and creating physical harm and injury, many other forms of violence also readily belong to this repertoire, forms that are also less readily visible than death and destruction. Among these are symbolic forms, such as the popularisation and banalisation of martyrdom, as well as forms that take aim at cultural and religious values, such as the desecration of dead bodies and disruption of rituals around burial and mourning. There are also other, more subtle modalities of violence that operate not to kill or to injure but to render (some) lives unliveable, through the infliction of a myriad of psychic, symbolic and epistemic infringements and harms alongside the threat and deployment of deadly force. Together, these different forms of violence constitute the dark side of democracy and establish their reign over the forms and futures of political life.

Taking as our starting point Achille Mbembe's famous definition of necropolitics as the 'forms of subjugation of life to the power of death', the chapters in this volume aim to chart the contours of Turkey's democracy by mapping its 'necropolitical undercurrent' and investigating its multiple modalities and operations.[2] Building on the insights of critical and contemporary theory, these chapters address the multiple ways in which lives are brought into the fold of power and subjected to mechanisms of physical destruction and injury as well as logics of (infra)structural violence and exposure that produce new forms of vulnerability, impoverishment, inequality and disposability.

Bringing together historical, discursive and ethnographic approaches from multiple disciplines, including political theory, philosophy, anthropology, history, sociology, international relations, and gender and sexuality studies, this collection offers a sobering and original analysis of contemporary Turkey and its recent history. On the one hand, these chapters put forth provocative readings that present situated reflections to shed light on the contradictions of Turkey's democracy. On the other hand, they present theoretical insights that push back against and challenge the monolithic interpretation of necropolitics as limited to logics of pure destruction. Instead, they point us to a wide spectrum of violence that shows how life can be made to submit to death-logics without the manifest results of physical death and widespread destruction. These chapters thus aim to provide a new and rich lexicon that makes a sophisticated contribution to the growing research programme on violence in the critical humanities.

While registering the historically determined and context-bound characteristics of Turkey's necropolitics, these chapters also suggest that these modalities of violence are not necessarily unique or confined to Turkey. Recognising the fluent, dynamic and expansive character of the modalities of violence under investigation, this book approaches Turkey as a political laboratory in which a repertoire of necropolitics is in the making. This repertoire is one that is shared by and relevant to many countries other than Turkey. In this sense, the chapters in this volume offer a sense of the experimentation, flux and movement of this repertoire, which sustains and reproduces some of Turkey's most salient democratic contradictions and uncertainties, while also provocatively suggesting how these are constitutive features of sovereign states and are manifest in differing degrees based on historical and political dynamics specific to those states.

The Necropolitical Problematic

The book's primary aim is to make a case for the originality and theoretical resourcefulness of a *necropolitical problematic* for analysing Turkey specifically as well as politics more generally. At the most general level, this problematic is centred on the relationship between violence and power, viewing the sphere of the political, its limits and distinguishing characteristics, the subjectivities that are operative within it as well as pushed outside of it, as a function of this relationship. Accordingly, the main fault lines of political antagonism, the identities of the political actors in contention, and the determining issues of struggle become most evident when one focuses on how violence, especially but not only deadly violence, is deployed and mobilised. While this deployment often emanates from the repressive apparatuses of the state and is directed towards citizens, such violence can also be part and parcel of the repertoire of resistance among forces of political opposition. Furthermore, such violence can also imbricate political culture in a more diffuse way, becoming an ordinary mechanism of socialisation into and subjugation to dominant social norms, ensuring the conformity of social agents and the reproduction of hegemonic values. The necropolitical problematic, therefore, is an analytic that focuses on violent enactments within politics as a springboard to analyse political dynamics, delineate the characteristics of political regimes and explore the constituent contradictions of democracies.

Necropolitics directs our attention to violence that imbricates democracy and theorises it as the means and medium of its state sovereignty; its deployment makes manifest 'the power and the capacity to dictate who may live and who must die'.[3] As such, is necropolitics not simply another name for sovereign violence? Such an equivalence is reductive because it does not take into consideration the transformations in the nature of sovereignty as a power regime from its inception and especially the impact of the biopolitical modalities of power on the workings of sovereignty as such. The death-making power of absolute sovereignty in its early period is perhaps more total in its legitimation of rule and yet modern, democratic sovereignty for whose legitimacy the protection of life has become absolutely central has more instruments at its disposal to make life unliveable than simply the exercise of brute force. In other words, even when it does not exercise its death-making capacity, modern sovereignty has developed a spectrum of tools, of forms of political violence, whose exercise results in the instrumentalisation of human existence, differentiation of populations, and their selective management by which some are rendered closer, more exposed and vulnerable to death than others. If one difference between contemporary forms of sovereignty and their absolutist predecessors hinges on the rise of democracy, another crucial difference resides in large part on what Michel Foucault has famously theorised as the emergence of disciplinary power and biopower. The cumulative effect of the rise of these biopolitical modalities of power on sovereignty has not been its undermining and disappearance but, instead, the expansion of its purview, the increase in its efficiency, and the changing of its functions, as sovereignty has become more about the government of life than rule by the infliction or threat of infliction of death.[4]

In its initial formulation, Foucault's diagnosis had tended to stipulate a linear substitution among different modalities of power, embroiling itself in theoretical difficulties to explain the continuance of sovereign violence and the proliferation of its ways, as well as the increasing immensity of its might, reaching genocidal proportions. Even though the optimism of the initial biopolitical diagnosis was later moderated by Foucault himself, by the theorisation of 'racism' as the missing piece of the puzzle that enabled the coming together of sovereignty and biopolitics in ways that could finally account for widespread violence at a time when the political objects and objectives of life-making and life-enhancing should have long replaced those of death-making, this revision nonetheless left much to be desired in thinking about forms of violence that are not manifest in extraordinary moments of crisis or are not simply limited to the infliction of death.

Mbembe's intervention and theoretical contribution through the coinage of 'necropolitics' is a meaningful corrective to Foucault because it enables a conception of political violence emanating from sovereignty that is already biopoliticised and therefore more able to account for the ways in which the very boundaries of life and death are politically determined under the economies of management rather than laws of political rule. In other words, necropolitics helpfully designates the violence that emanates from a sovereign power that has already been permeated and modified by life-logics, leading to the reformulation of its strategic imperatives and their expansion much beyond the sphere of the law without, at the same time, forgoing the centrality of its former prerogatives that are now also transformed as a result of those life-logics. Hence, by pointing us to the concatenation of disciplinary, biopolitical and necropolitical registers of sovereignty, coalescing into a 'terror formation', Mbembe's 'necropolitics' enables us to theorise the new modalities and techniques of political violence that take life into its fold, not only by inflicting death but also by actively undermining, disabling, displacing forms of life that create living deaths that are unprecedented and largely irrelevant to power in the period of sovereignty's infancy.

Necropolitics, then, is the name that denotes the violence, or the wide spectrum of violence, of a particularly biopolitical and modern form of state sovereignty, one that is both governmentalised and democratised, and yet continues to exercise extra-legal, exceptional powers to eliminate threats that it perceives as detrimental to its survival, neutralise insurgents and manage populations based on the classification of their role as useful or inimical to the reproduction of sovereignty and its political objectives. Giorgio Agamben's conceptualisation of sovereignty as necessarily having the structure of the exception has enabled us to think about sovereignty's entwinement with violence towards an 'other' whose rights are always precarious as a permanent feature of its operation, even though his analysis does not offer the possibility of historicisation or an account of the historical transformation, either of sovereignty or of its violent tools.[5] Even though Agamben does not use the terminology of necropolitics, by equating the precarity of rights with having rights and insisting on the constitutive quality of this contradictory equation, thereby suggesting that every citizen is a potential target of sovereign violence, he arguably sets the ground for viewing modern sovereignty as thoroughly necropolitical. Thinking through a lineage of Foucault, Agamben and Mbembe, then, we can assume that necropolitics is the *permanent other of biopolitics*. Necropolitics is a common strategy and trope of biopolitical sovereignty that undergirds modern democracies and takes us well beyond the realm of rights and the law in charting how they really operate.

Pluralising Necropolitics

If the first aim of the volume is to situate Turkey within a necropolitical problematic defined by the aforementioned theoretical coordinates, the second aim is to build on the situated and empirically rich explorations offered by the contributors in this volume in order to investigate the plurality of forms that necropolitics assumes. The volume's chapters deal with a range of sites and spheres, including courts, prisons and political cemeteries, martyrdom, gender politics, social reproduction, military culture, armed insurgency, and counterinsurgency warfare, enforced disappearances, collective memory, and reparation claims. They focus on states and sites of exceptionality as well as the ordinary and routine aspects of political culture and everyday spaces. Based on the excavation of situated knowledges and explorations, the book thus aims to complicate the concept of necropolitics and suggest new and hitherto unthought dimensions of necropower, examining new areas in which it is operative and capturing a broader range of its manifestations.

What is the theoretical basis for the move to pluralise necropolitics? As is well known, necropolitics is often associated with a 'state of emergency' in which its deployment becomes most visible. These exceptional moments or political crises arise when the survival of sovereignty is presented as necessitating the abrogation of legality and as predicated on the elimination of those that are conceived as threats. In Mbembe's original formulation, the spatialisation of necropolitics in largely lawless sites, sites which are under siege and where the state of exception reigns instead, has led to the association of necropolitics with such spaces as the plantation, the colony, the territories under occupation and apartheid rule. On the other hand, Agamben's approach, which renders exceptionality constitutive of modern democracy, can be said to expand the sites of exception to encompass mundane spaces, such as stadiums and airports, that can easily be converted into lawless sites as a function of (in)security.[6] From this perspective, one can argue that insofar as the logic of security permeates modern sovereignty, democracy is always precarious and necropolitics lurks behind ordinary spaces, rendering them always-already convertible into sites of exceptionality where forms of death-making can be readily deployed.

However, even if one were to accept the assumption of the constancy of exceptionality as a latent formation of modern democracies and the broad recognition granted to it as unavoidable and often necessary, it would be an error to limit necropolitics to extra-legal forms of death-making. Jasbir Puar has recently argued against taking death as the only ultimate end point of biopolitics and showed how economies of injury and debilitation are integral components and distinct ends of biopolitics, especially in securitised practices of sovereignty that are predominantly shaped by settler colonialism. Differentiating the 'right to maim' from the 'right to kill', Puar shows how mechanisms of debilitation, the 'slow wearing down of populations', can be destructive for those who are racialised, subjugated and reduced to a state in which they can nevertheless be maintained as 'a source of value extraction' without being immediately disposable.[7] Indeed, forms of injury and debilitation can be frequently put to use in ordinary spaces, as a function of threat perception and expediency, but without the risk and burden of democratic delegitimation that comes with explicit exceptionality.

If this approach allows us to begin to pluralise necropolitics, discerning its different modalities, it also entails a greater recognition of how different tactics are selectively deployed according to the meaning and valorisation of its targets. In this sense, it must be noted that necropolitics is always discriminating: it works by defining which lives matter. It presupposes and performatively reproduces the differentiation of populations, particularly by way of racialisation and hierarchalisation, and becomes the instrument by which the existence of different populations is selectively managed. Through its operation, necropolitics divides the safe from the unsafe, the political from the criminal, the worthy from the unworthy. It therefore delineates not only what counts as political acts and public matters, but also who counts as political subjects, or the proper subjects of politics. Such violence produces some populations as outside of politics, and indeed, as outside of humanity *tout court* – as disposable, redundant and surplus populations that constitute a permanent excess, an excess that threatens democracy while also acting as its external support. Hence, the perpetuation and thriving of some lives depend on the creation of 'death-worlds' for others.

In these 'death-worlds', as Mbembe has put it, populations, when they are not direct targets of overt, physical violence, are subjected to multiple forms of indirect, slow and symbolic violence that destine them for lesser lives. Some lives are enabled and made to flourish, while others are either actively destroyed, debilitated or subtly made to wither away – in Foucault's words, they are 'disallow[ed] to the point of death'.[8] As Mbembe has maintained, this violence does not only destroy but creates 'new and unique forms of social existence in which vast populations are subjected to conditions of life conferring upon them the status of *living dead*'.[9] Hence, if massacres are performed in states of exception in order to decimate certain populations, the uses of political violence take different forms under more ordinary conditions or conditions in which exceptionality is more or less routinised. The longer temporality, lesser visibility and differential intensity of these other forms of necropolitics make them deployable with less political risk and greater economic benefit. The latter forms of violence produce what Eric Stanley has called 'near life' or a 'death-in-waiting'.[10]

Among these modalities of necropolitics, one can think of the deprivation of certain subjects from a properly human life through logics of exposure to risk, infrastructural disinvestment and strategic neglect, i.e., the purposeful engineering of the 'hollow[ing]' out of the land and its inhabitants.[11] These forms of violence correspond to everyday experiences, which include, in the words of Lauren Berlant, the 'physical wearing out of a population and the deterioration of people in that population that is very nearly a defining condition of their experience and historical existence'.[12] These forms of violence, which Berlant calls 'slow death', should also be considered integral to the necropolitical problematic as they are particularly relevant for understanding the internal limits of functioning democracies.

Those who are most affected by these modalities of violence and who are interpellated into experiencing these new forms of social existence are those structurally subaltern and marginalised populations defined by the intersection of race, class and gender. For Isabell Lorey, 'precarity' is what defines this position. Following Judith Butler's theorisation of precariousness as an ontological condition, she argues that precarity corresponds to the 'effects of different political, social, and legal compensations of a general precariousness'.[13] Thus, precarity names the differential distribution of vulnerability and its hierarchisation, distinctly exposing 'social positionings of insecurity' to different forms and intensities of violence. In what Henry Giroux has called the 'new biopolitics of disposability', the operation of sovereign violence is less by active destruction and the infliction of physical death than by the cessation of attention to those who are poor, sick, elderly, homeless or otherwise vulnerable, especially when they are non-white. The neglect of their lives is complemented by the invisibilisation of their existence. These populations are often locked into ghettos and prisons, criminalised, thus further marginalised, and thereby politically disqualified as subjects.[14] These subjects inhabit what Elisabeth Povinelli has theorised as 'zones of abandonment'.[15] The political economy of neoliberalism has particularly exacerbated the reduction of some populations into irrelevance, as recent scholarship has shown, and disposability, even death itself, has become integral to the crisis-prone operations of contemporary capitalism and its unevenness across the globe.[16]

If the politics of disposability is a more continuous and subtle form of necropolitics, it corresponds to 'everyday death worlds' that can be mundane and ordinary.[17] As Jin Haritaworn, Adi Knutsman and Silvia Posocco remind us in their analysis of 'queer necropolitics', a whole range of practices that target subjectification, especially on axes of gender and sexuality, can also be thought of as subject to a necropolitical logic in which the politics of inclusion often comes at the expense of complicity with dominant ideology.[18] As Puar has persuasively shown in her work on 'homonationalism', the trade-off between recognition and social death might entail the incorporation and co-optation of subjects (in this case, racialised queer subjects) otherwise at the receiving end of necropolitics into a sovereign project at the expense of others who are thereby produced as threats to security.[19] When the scope of necropolitics is broadened to encompass these complex interpellations, the political negotiations of identity and the contestations for recognition and inclusion, the modalities of violence are further proliferated, subjecting those who are pushed into alterity to forms of 'social death'.[20] Indeed, the more sovereignty is democratically legitimated on the grounds of life-logics, the greater the likelihood that necropolitical instruments approximating social death in place of actual death-making will be deployed in its service. Forms of social death can also be tracked by analysing how necropolitics infuses dominant culture, as chapters in this volume will show with respect to the centrality of martyrdom, for example. The deployment of necropolitics to shape subjectivities and define the boundaries of inclusion/exclusion within polities offers the implicit presuppositions that condition to what extent the political can find expression in genuinely democratic possibilities and shape what the internal limits of existing democracies look like.

Furthermore, as some of the contributions in this volume will make clear, there are still other modalities of sovereign violence that operate not as overt forms of death-making, destruction and debilitation, nor as techniques that destine subjects to forms of social death without largescale bloodshed, but as harms and infringements that take shape in the realm of the dead and as contestation over the signification of dead bodies.[21] These involve acts that are directed at the dead body, the rituals, cultural and religious traditions around death and burial, and the forms of mourning and commemoration. In a sense, they are what Stanley has called forms of 'overkill', namely, the 'violence that pushes a body beyond death'.[22] Enforced disappearances and mass burials should also be considered as part of this violence.[23] As physical as these acts of violence are, insofar as they mutilate, dismember, denude and desecrate dead bodies, destroy cemeteries, delay, interrupt or make impossible proper funerary rituals and mourning practices, their real work is symbolic. As I have argued in my own contribution to the volume, at issue is not the reduction of the living to 'the status of living dead',[24] but *'the dishonouring, disciplining and punishment of the living through the utilisation of the dead as postmortem objects and sites of violence'.*[25] In these modalities of necropolitics, while the realm of the dead is the immediate target of sovereign violence, it is actually transformed into the medium of disciplining other bodies and rendering them targets of further violence. In this sense, the entire ensemble of practices that targets the dead as a surrogate for, and means of, targeting the living is also part and parcel of a necropolitical repertoire.

Finally, but as importantly, are those forms of necropolitics that are not simply tools of sovereignty, emanating from the state towards its citizens, but the site and medium of resistance practices that take shape under biosovereign formations. On the one hand, the effects of necropolitics deployed by the state can become the grounds for a counter-politics that organises around human rights violations, seeking accountability, legal redress and reparations for the acts committed and to bring to justice those who are responsible for ordering and executing sovereign violence within and beyond the law. On the other hand, necropolitics can also be deployed by forces of opposition, either individually or as part of a collective and coordinated strategy. Whether in the form of hunger strikes or self-immolations, corporeal forms of self-harm and self-destruction can gain centrality as forms of political struggle, especially in those sites that Mbembe has identified as the exceptional spaces in which death-logics reign.[26] In these instances in which 'life is weaponised' as a tool of resistance, martyrdom often assumes great valence, furthering the centrality of death-logics within politics.[27]

Viewing Turkey from a necropolitical problematic that is delineated by way of these theoretical coordinates thus promises to analyse both the spectacular and extraordinary forms of violence, exercised to injure and kill as well as overkill, and their routinised, everyday, slow and subtle counterparts that make forms of hollowing out and social death constituent parts of the political landscape. By focusing on myriad forms of violence that manifest Turkey's democratic predicaments, these chapters thus go beyond conventional scholarly approaches to Turkey that emphasise such thematics as constitutionalism, parliamentary politics and established political parties, military-civilian relations or political ideologies. Instead, they creatively mobilise largely unexplored facets and sites of Turkish politics to track its 'necropolitical undercurrent'.[28] Not only explicit and physical forms of necropolitics, such as counterinsurgency warfare, enforced disappearances and postmortem violence, but also more insidious, invisible and diffuse forms, such as the infrastructural and wilful neglect of select populations, the popularisation of martyrdom, the instrumentalisation of formal and informal methods of monetary compensation to settle wrongful deaths and injuries beyond the law, are analysed as part of the rather expansive necropolitical repertoire in Turkey. Moreover, these chapters investigate both the forms of violence that emanate from the state and the ways in which necropolitics has also been appropriated by forces of opposition, as tools of negotiation, resistance and refusal. They look at how necropolitics can be a means of the furtherance of sovereign power as well as its contestation by insurgent politics and through individual negotiations and refusals of dominant norms.

Together, these chapters offer a much more nuanced and fine-grained tableau of the varieties of necropolitics than is generally available in the existing literature. While Turkey's necropolitics has taken a great multiplicity of forms across periods of monoparty, military and democratic rule, having its own ebbs and flows, it is particularly after the transition to democracy in the post-1980 coup d'état period that the angle between the state's biopolitical commitments and necropolitical practices becomes most acute. This is because the life-affirming and welfare-enhancing values that constitute the grounds of democratic legitimation (especially the state's investment in the nation's health, wealth and wellbeing) stand in strong tension with ongoing practices of violence that are justified on the grounds of security, order and unity. For this reason, in order to zoom in on this contradiction itself, the chapters in this volume focus primarily on the period after the 1980 coup d'état and in particular on the period of AKP rule, now approaching two decades.

Architecture of the Book

The book organises the investigation of Turkey's necropolitical repertoire in three parts: (1) politicising death, which analyses the emergent political cartographies as a result of the sovereign mobilisation of violence; (2) negotiating life, which looks at the ways in which different modalities of necropolitics are both deployed by the state and counter-deployed by forces of opposition; and (3) governing the living and the dead through postmortem forms of necropolitics that create political afterlives of the dead. The collection thus moves from the state's reliance on necropolitics, in both its discursive and widespread cultural forms and its overt and destructive applications, to the multiple uses and manifestations of necropolitics among different state institutions (prisons, forensics, courts, army) to govern select populations and the resistance carried out by forces of opposition, and finally, to the violent practices that target the realm of the dead and the forms of their contestation.

The first part tackles the ways in which death is both neutralised and pushed outside the boundaries of the political, on the one hand, and rendered ordinary and pervasive, even desirable, on the other hand. It focuses on the period of the AKP government, plotting the role death and martyrdom plays in official and public discourse while also delineating certain constants that have marked Turkish politics over time. It also looks at how the valorisation of martyrdom comes to define everyday urban spaces and is memorialised to interpellate subjects ready to die for the state. It deals with the deployment of violence as part of counterinsurgency warfare and the slippage between civilians and combatants in official discourse and how that slippage aids the legitimation of necropolitics. The chapters in this section speak to the construction of ideal citizens, on the one hand, and enemy subjects, both internal and external, on the other. The former construction is necessary for the maintenance of unity and support for the state. The latter is particularly crucial in order to justify the (selective) exercise of sovereign violence based on the discursive and practical sequestering of subjects.

Onur Bakıner's contribution opens the volume by offering a synoptic analysis of how Turkey's necropolitics has changed with the AKP regime against the background of the longitudinal features of state violence as exemplified in such tropes as martyrdom. Bakıner argues that while the management of death has been an important feature of various governments in Turkey, this way of exercising power has become central for the AKP regime, taking on stark qualities that reflect the country's transition to competitive authoritarianism. The most important shift that Bakıner tracks is the expansion of martyrdom, hitherto referencing the deaths of military, police and at times paramilitary forces in combat situations, into the civilian realm. If the state has long been a necropolitical agent responsible for managing deaths with political significance, the expansion of martyrdom entails the extension of its role as a necropolitical agent and its penetration into the private sphere. Bakıner delineates how the expansion of martyrdom into the civilian realm also comes with the normalisation and even banalisation of death. By positing death as an unavoidable, natural fact of life, especially attached to certain social, occupational and gender roles, the AKP seeks to depoliticise death and disqualify it as a means of citizens' demand-making, preventing efforts to hold the state accountable. Bakıner investigates how the AKP's conferral of martyrdom status on civilians, not only those victims of terrorist violence and those who become collateral damage in the hands of the state, but also those casualties in workplace accidents, highlights a collusion between state and capital. At the same time, the conferral of martyrdom becomes a way for the government to distribute material benefits and thereby enhance patronage relationships. The offer of material benefits leads to the important question of the political economy of necropolitics and is pursued in greater depth in the contributions of Cem Özatalay, Gözde Aytemur Nüfusçu and Gülistan Zeren, and Fırat Bozçalı (in the second part of the book). Overall, Bakıner's chapter puts into stark relief how the ruling party maintains strict discursive controls around how deaths are narrated, interpreted and commemorated as part of its necropolitical strategy.

Lerna K. Yanık and Fulya Hisarlıoğlu's chapter picks up on the theme of martyrdom and underscores its centrality for Turkey's necropolitics, especially in the aftermath of the failed coup of 15 July 2016. Their contribution demonstrates how martyrdom is exalted and popularised in ways that work to shape subjects who are ready to die for the state. The exaltation of martyrdom depends greatly on a politics of space, both at the domestic and the regional level. Domestically, Yanık and Hisarlıoğlu show, the government has adopted a policy of renaming streets, urban piazzas and important landmarks, such as the Bosphorus Bridge, after those who have been killed during the coup attempt while resisting the takeover in the streets. State authorities have erected statues and built mausoleums in places that blend into the background of everyday urban commutes. These practices spatialise necropolitics as an ordinary part of life, working to emphasise the importance and desirability of sacrificing one's life for the state in order to mould subjects predisposed to martyrdom. On a regional level, the authors argue, the construction of space takes the form of 'necrogeopolitics', a concept they coin to indicate how neighbouring states are constructed as unsafe places, as threats to Turkey's security and how, in turn, Turkey is constructed as a fatherland threatened geopolitically and in need of sacrifice from its citizens. Together, the domestic and international definition of space as worth dying for renders martyrdom and its memorialised spaces as central features of Turkey's necropolitics.

Haydar Darıcı and Serra Hakyemez turn to Turkey's ongoing ethnic conflict and focus on the recent instance of counterinsurgency warfare in the form of a highly televised security operation that took place in Cizre, leading to the destruction of urban neighbourhoods and residential areas, casualties in the hundreds, and the displacement of even greater numbers of Kurdish citizens from September 2015 to March 2016. Analysing the unfolding of this operation and the public discourse about the residents of Cizre, the authors problematise the instrumental, if opposing, use of the civilian-combatant distinction by both state officials and Kurdish politicians when that distinction was no longer stable or sustainable in the reality of urban warfare. The authors demystify the utility of this distinction, used on the part of the state to erase civilian casualties and transform the dead into combatants responsible for their own deaths, and on the part of the Kurdish movement to defend the right to life of citizens engaged in self-defence tactics in urban guerrilla warfare against the state and obtain humanitarian support and sympathy from national and international publics. As such, they critique the appeal to the figures of the civilian and combatant from both parties to the struggle in order to make claims about the identity of the dead, showing how this appeal worked to enhance the claims to legitimacy of necropolitical strategies in ethnic conflict.

The second part of the book turns to the analysis of the different forms of necropolitics experienced by differentiated populations, either at the hands of state institutions and dominant social forces or as forms of resistance, negotiation and refusal exercised by individuals and groups in opposition. Of significant interest to the chapters in this part is the mobilisation of necropolitics by and among different state institutions, ranging from the army and the judicial apparatus to prisons, from various ministries to hospitals and the state forensics institute. The chapters in this section show how creating hierarchies of life and negotiating the worth of life and death work to separate populations and subject them to differential tactics of power for their management. From decisions regarding whether the bodies in prison, allegedly under the state's care, deserve medical treatment, whether women are worthy candidates for marriage, whether the heirs and relatives of casualties of state violence or workplace accidents deserve monetary compensation to practices of resistance carried out by individuals and/or collective forces of opposition, such as human rights defenders and conscientious objectors, who contest their subjection to 'living deaths' and the determination of their worth, these chapters point us to a great plurality that marks necropolitics. They chart how necropolitics is perpetuated through forms that are not reducible to conventional forms of physical violence, focusing on techniques such as medical neglect, bureaucratic slow-down, the actuarial calculation of life, the monetisation of wrongful deaths through legal and extralegal compensation payments, social death and gendered ostracisation, among others. They also make visible the modalities in which necropolitics can be resisted, ranging from the seeking of legal redress and compensation to conscientious objection, from prisoners' rights mobilisation to hymenoplasty.

Başak Can looks at how temporality becomes an instrument of necropolitics by the state's slow management of prisoner illness. By focusing on the death fast (2000–7) in penal institutions and the biopolitical crisis the prisoners' self-starvation precipitated, Can not only examines how the state's resort to medicine was instrumental in solving the crisis, mainly by offering temporary reprieves or permanent amnesty to prisoners suffering from incurable conditions and thereby releasing them from prisons; she also demonstrates how this tactical resort to medicine opens a new path for the state by offering medico-legal documentation as an instrument of state violence and a technology of necropolitics that ensures the denial of timely health care. At the same time, Can argues, if medicalisation worked as part of the state's necropolitical repertoire, it also enabled human rights activists, Kurdish and leftist politicians to make political arguments in the public sphere based on the situation of ill prisoners. Can explores the illness clause in the law, allowing prisoners reprieve, as a field of contention in which the state can impose 'slow deaths' by dragging out medico-legal procedures and through the production and circulation of documents within a complex web of bureaucratic, legal and medical actors that are often contradictory with one another. As a result, she demonstrates how medico-legal processes necessary to make prisoner rights' claims are permeated by discretionary acts that enact sovereignty through 'slow' violence and yet how these processes provide the basis for biopolitical resistance by prisoners' rights and human rights organisations, to point us to the intertwined histories of sovereignty, biopolitics and necropolitics in Turkey.

Next, Elif Savaş turns to analyse the necropolitical tools of Turkey's gender regime and the infusion of violence in dominant cultural values, often with the explicit or implicit support of the state. Focusing on how virginity is exalted as the sign of a proper premarital female subjectivity, she shows how such subjectivity is upheld and reproduced by a range of disciplinary and violent tactics, ranging from the everyday inculcation of morals and medical virginity examinations imposed by parents and schools to honour killings when the hymen, which has come to signify virginity, is 'lost' improperly. Savaş discusses how physical violence deployed on women by families in the form of honour killings is often complemented by more subtle techniques of subjugation, such as social ostracisation and stigmatisation, in the service of ensuring a proper female subject, thereby bringing women into the necropolitical fold not necessarily of the state but of their own extended family and neighbourhood community. Savaş focuses on how, with the aid of modern medical technologies, hymen reconstruction surgeries have emerged as a way in which the hymen can be medically reconstructed, thereby enabling women to hide their sexual histories and perform virginity on their wedding night. Theorising hymenoplasty as a medico-political assemblage, Savaş explores how it becomes a site in which women can paradoxically reclaim some of their agency otherwise lost by their submission to the patriarchal regime. She argues that the possibility of remaking the hymen in its materiality empties virginity of content, thereby allowing women to resist the demand of virginity and become saboteurs of the necropolitical gender regime.

Pınar Kemerli returns us to the centrality of martyrdom as the discursive support of the institution of military conscription that plays a crucial role in the conflict between Turkey and the Kurdish liberation movement, a conflict that, as Darıcı and Hakyemez have also shown, is the site of multiple forms of necropolitical violence, from counterinsurgency warfare to the indiscriminate exposure of large segments of the Kurdish population to infrastructural harms. For Kemerli, the militaristic invocations of Islamic warfare and martyrdom in the conscript army have been deeply complicit in the legitimisation of necropolitical violence as well as in inspiring enthusiasm to participate in such violence as both a national and religious duty. By examining the perspective not of soldiers but, instead, of those who refuse to become soldiers, on account of their religious faith, she analyses how the resistance to participation in necropolitics takes shape. Working through their dissenting interpretations of Islamic martyrdom and refusal of the necropolitical uses of theological concepts and ideals, Kemerli shows how Muslim conscientious objectors transform Islamic martyrdom into a form of spiritual transformation to be pursued through the very refusal of necropolitical violence and as the peaceful acceptance of the punitive consequences of their refusal. Hence, Kemerli offers individual conscientious objection as a strategy for resisting necropolitics.

Cem Özatalay, Gözde Aytemur Nüfusçu, and Gülistan Zeren focus on 'blood money', or the financial compensation provided to surviving relatives upon the wrongful or accidental death of a person, as part of an increasingly pervasive form of necropolitics in Turkey, a form whose presence has been exacerbated as a result of neoliberal governmentality. They argue that blood money is put to use as a form of ethical and monetary bargaining among agents (with unequal powers), such as the state, capital and individuals, especially as individual contracts have increasingly replaced both collective agreements and the state's responsibilities towards its citizens with the ascendancy of neoliberalism. The authors focus on the compensation issued by the state or by private companies to dispense justice on the occasion of the deaths of security forces on duty, civilians as collateral damage, and employees in the course of their work. They thereby bring to the fore the use of such compensation as a tool of necropolitical domination that differentiates subjects on the basis of ethnic and class identity as well as proximity to political power. By looking at the kinds of deaths that get compensated monetarily and how compensation can become a means of silencing the weak and protecting the powerful from suffering the legal consequences of their actions, they chart the articulation of the state with neoliberal capitalism and show how the juridico-economic practice of 'blood money' becomes a legitimised and institutionalised form of subjugation of life to the power of death.

Pursuing the question of 'blood money' in the context of border killings, Fırat Bozçalı brings to the fore how the way in which the value of life is monetised is both connected to the state's necropolitical strategy for managing mobility across the Turkish–Iranian border and a new arena of contestation between the state and the Kurdish population. Looking at Kurdish smuggling economies that operate in the militarised borderlands near the eastern province of Van and the compensation claims that emerge around the deaths of smugglers at the hand of border patrols, Bozçalı analyses how compensation is either offered by the state in order to address casualties of state violence as a way to short-circuit the judicial process or pursued by citizens against the state in order to hold authorities accountable for borderland deaths. Taking us through the intricate procedures of compensation claims and the stipulations that apply to different kinds of military commands whose execution eventuates in borderland deaths, Bozçalı shows that it is legally possible to hold the state authorities financially accountable in civil courts even while individual perpetrators are often exonerated from criminal liability for smuggler deaths in criminal courts. Bozçalı thus argues that the political significance of compensation claims much exceeds their pecuniary value precisely because they offer a way to make state authorities indirectly take responsibility for the killings. At the same time, Bozçalı directs our attention to how the calculation of these compensation benefits, often based on counterfactual assumptions that do not reflect the complexities of smuggling economies, often falls short of desired amounts. The inadequacy of pecuniary support leads citizens to seek alternative means of compensation for the loss of their families' bread earners and engage in creative uses of the law in order to secure greater benefits. Overall, Bozçalı's chapter shows how the political subjugation of the living must be considered in tandem with states of precarity, by turning our attention to the economic underpinnings of states of exception, i.e., to how the restricted economic opportunities within those states create forms of subjugation that lead their inhabitants to engage in highly risky extra-legal activities, such as cross-border smuggling, in order to eke out a living.

Finally, the third part of the book turns to postmortem forms of violence, both physical and symbolic, to explore how they are used to perpetuate the necropolitical hold of the state over the living. The chapters in this part take us into the realm of the dead – funerals and cultural rituals of burial, graves and cemeteries, dead bodies, and in cases of enforced disappearances, the absence of a body or the surfaced material remains of the disappeared, as well as the counter-knowledges that emerge from the memories of the mothers and relatives of the disappeared about those they have lost to erasure by sovereign violence. Conceptualising forms of violence deployed in the realm of the dead departs from the mainstream use of the term 'necropolitics' that denotes how the living is subjugated by the logic of death. Instead, it brings into view how the realm of the dead can be a site of violence, a surrogate for the government of the living, a means of delineating the boundaries of political community and a conduit for the production of collective memory.

In my own contribution to the volume, I theorise the violence that takes as its object the realm of the dead as an explicit form of necropolitical violence by offering a reading of the image of the naked and bloody corpse of a woman leaked to the press and circulated in social media in the period of Turkey's hung parliament in the summer of 2015. I argue that the image of the denuded body, which belonged to Kevser Eltürk, also known as Ekin Wan, was a harbinger of the end of the peace process with the Kurds and the beginning of Turkey's new conjuncture of intensified authoritarianism.

By analysing the denuding, public display and desecration of Eltürk's body, who had allegedly been killed in combat with the state's security forces, alongside other forms of violence that target the realm of the dead, such as the destruction of local cemeteries, the delay, interruption or suspension of the conduct of funerary rituals, the imposition of mass or anonymous internment and the repression and dispersion of funeral processions for the newly dead, my contribution aims to underscore the role of violence on the dead as a distinctive and neglected form of necropolitics. In the production of some bodies as violable after death, one can find an absolutisation of enmity, the racialisation and alterisation of Kurdish identity, the derogatory sexualisation of the dead body and its production into a vehicle of both moralistic reprobation and humiliation. Highlighting how this violence is predicated on the centrality of chastity and the equivalence of the chastity of a woman and the honour of a nation, my chapter continues the exploration of a gendered necropolitics, exemplified earlier in this volume by Savaş's contribution. Overall, my chapter suggests how the desecration of the dead becomes a new site of articulating identity, of producing the ethnic, spiritual supremacy of the Turkish nation, and its dehumanised others. The chapter thus calls attention to an entire ensemble of practices that target the dead as a surrogate for, and means of, selectively governing the living.

Osman Balkan's chapter takes us to the curious 'Cemetery of Traitors', established after the failed coup attempt on 15 July 2016 and reserved for the enemies of the Turkish state (though with only one grave to date). Balkan takes up the cemetery not only as the material remnant of state violence towards those it deems its enemies but also as a tool of statecraft by which the dead become a means to govern the living and the boundaries of the political community are drawn. Comparing the funerals of soldiers and civilians who died in the coup attempt as part of the resistance with the denial of burial ground and funeral prayers to those who were considered perpetrators of the coup, Balkan shows how the treatment and commemoration of the dead produce the difference between those who belong to the nation and those who do not, rendering the former martyrs while the latter renegades. Balkan thus contends that the corpse is an important site of political contestation in which states and their challengers express, enact and contest the boundaries of national, political and moral communities. If the exaltation of martyrdom leads to mass funeral processions, visibility and public commemoration for the martyrs, the dehumanisation of the enemy leads to the denial of death rituals to the coup plotters. Through the denial of burial sites and rites, Balkan argues, state officials sought to push the perpetrators of the coup attempt not only out of the nation but also out of Islam. Rendered both renegade and infidel, the dead body was thus the site of postmortem symbolic violence for state-making.

Ege Selin Islekel theorises necropolitics as a power/knowledge assemblage, which produces knowledges that obey different rules than the normal biopolitical regimes of truth, knowledges that are generated around death and disappearance in Turkey. Focusing on mass graves where the dead have been buried anonymously, secret internments imposed by the state and the surfaced remains of enforced disappearances, as well as the more general condition of their absence, Islekel contends that sovereign erasure is not a complete elimination of the person but, rather, the production of what she calls 'nightmare knowledges'. These knowledges, which do not always make sense in conventional terms, arise from the fears, worries, dreams and investments of the families of the disappeared and build on the memories of the disappeared. They can work in ways similar to Foucault's 'subjugated knowledges' – insofar as they contradict the official narrative and are excised from it, or belong to those who are considered neither enjoying the epistemic status for producing knowledge, nor conforming to the boundaries of positive reason, they can be politicised against the dominant necropolitical episteme and its techniques of knowledge production. Islekel contrasts the epistemic work that necropolitics does, working through such techniques as silencing, gendered hystericisation, and invisibilisation, with the counter-knowledges of collective memory systems that can be mobilised as a site of resistance and resilience against necropolitics. By underscoring what is made invisible and what is repressed by necropolitics as also offering the possibility of politicisation against it, Islekel's contribution brings us full circle to the starting point of the book: namely, that the necropolitical is, much like the nightmare knowledges it produces as the undercurrent of established knowledges, the continuous undercurrent of Turkey's democracy, reminding us that our knowledge of Turkey's democracy would be radically incomplete if we did not attend to what is left in its shadows.

Notes

1. For a reconstruction of recent events and an assessment of the significance of the failed coup and its aftermath, see Banu Bargu, 'Year One'.
2. Achille Mbembe, 'Necropolitics', p. 39.
3. Ibid. p. 11.
4. Judith Butler, *Precarious Life*, pp. 50–100; Banu Bargu, *Starve and Immolate*, pp. 37–86.
5. Giorgio Agamben, *Homo Sacer*.
6. Ibid. pp. 174–5.

7. Jasbir Puar, *The Right to Maim*, pp. xiv, xviii.
8. Michel Foucault, *History of Sexuality*, p. 136, and *'Society Must Be Defended'*, pp. 240-1.
9. Mbembe, 'Necropolitics', p. 40.
10. Eric Stanley, 'Near Life, Queer Death', p. 1.
11. Eyal Weizman, *Hollow Land*.
12. Lauren Berlant, 'Slow Death', p. 755.
13. Butler, *Precarious Life*; Isabell Lorey, *State of Insecurity*, p. 17.
14. Henry A. Giroux, 'Reading Hurricane Katrina', p. 180.
15. Elizabeth Povinelli, *Economies of Abandonment*.
16. For an analysis of global capitalism that addresses the differentiation among populations through their racialisation, see Marina Gržinić and Šefik Tatlić, *Necropolitics, Racialization, and Global Capitalism*. For the argument that death itself has become a source of value within the uneven development of global capitalism, see Fatmir Haskaj, 'From Biopower to Necroeconomies'.
17. Jin Haritaworn, Adi Kuntsman and Silvia Posocco (eds), *Queer Necropolitics*, p. 2.
18. Ibid.
19. Jasbir Puar, *Terrorist Assemblages*.
20. Orlando Patterson, *Slavery and Social Death*.
21. Katherine Verdery, *The Political Lives of Dead Bodies*; François Debrix and Alexander D. Barder, *Beyond Biopolitics*; Thomas Gregory, 'Dismembering the Dead'.
22. Stanley, 'Near Life, Queer Death', p. 9.
23. Francisco Ferrándiz and Antonius C. G. M. Robben operate within forensic anthropology to explore the problem of state violence, especially enforced disappearances and mass killings, from the perspective of remains around the world in their *Necropolitics*.
24. Mbembe, 'Necropolitics', p. 40.
25. Banu Bargu, 'Another Necropolitics'.
26. Mbembe, 'Necropolitics', pp. 35-9; Stuart J. Murray, 'Thanatopolitics', pp. 193-9; Hamid Dabashi, *Corpus Anarchicum*, pp. 181-211.
27. Bargu, *Starve and Immolate*, pp. 223-70.
28. To date, there are few scholarly studies of Turkey that investigate the relationship between democracy, biopolitics and sovereign violence in light of the theoretical arsenal of the necropolitical problematic. For recent examples, see Cihan Ahmetbeyzade, 'Gendering Necropolitics'; Eylül Fidan Akıncı, 'Sacred Children, Accursed Mothers'; Bargu, *Starve and Immolate*; Josh Carney, 'Resur(e)recting a Spectacular Hero'; Ege Selin Islekel, 'Absent Death'; Sima Shakhsari, 'The Queer Time of Death'; and Aslı Zengin, 'Violent Intimacies'.

Bibliography

Agamben, Giorgio, *Homo Sacer: Sovereign Power and Bare Life*, trans. Daniel Heller-Roazen (Stanford, CA: Stanford University Press, 1998).

Ahmetbeyzade, Cihan, 'Gendering Necropolitics: The Juridical-Political Sociality of Honor Killings in Turkey', *Journal of Human Rights* 7 (2008): 187–206.
Akıncı, Eylül Fidan, 'Sacred Children, Accursed Mothers: Performativities of Necropolitics and Mourning in Neoliberal Turkey', in Sara Brady and Lindsey Mantoan (eds), *Performance in a Militarized Culture* (Oxford and New York: Routledge, 2018), pp. 47–65.
Bargu, Banu, *Starve and Immolate: The Politics of Human Weapons* (New York: Columbia University Press, 2014).
Bargu, Banu, 'Sovereignty as Erasure: Rethinking Enforced Disappearances', *Qui Parle: Critical Humanities and Social Sciences* 23, no. 1 (2014): 35–75.
Bargu, Banu, 'Another Necropolitics', *Theory & Event* 19, no. 1, January 2016.
Bargu, Banu, 'Year One: Reflections on Turkey's Second Founding and the Politics of Division', *Critical Times: Interventions in Global Critical Theory* 1, no. 1 (2018): 23–48.
Berlant, Lauren, 'Slow Death (Sovereignty, Obesity, Lateral Agency)', *Critical Inquiry* (Summer 2007): 754–80.
Butler, Judith, *Precarious Life: The Powers of Mourning and Violence* (London and New York: Verso Books, 2004).
Carney, Josh, 'Resur(e)recting a Spectacular Hero: Diriliş Ertuğrul, Necropolitics, and Popular Culture in Turkey', *Review of Middle East Studies* 52, no. 1 (2018): 93–114.
Dabashi, Hamid, *Corpus Anarchicum: Political Protest, Suicidal Violence, and the Making of the Posthuman Body* (New York: Palgrave Macmillan, 2012).
Debrix, François, and Alexander D. Barder, *Beyond Biopolitics: Theory, Violence, and Horror in World Politics* (Abingdon: Routledge, 2013).
Ferrándiz, Francisco, and Antonius C. G. M. Robben (eds), *Necropolitics: Mass Graves and Exhumations in the Age of Human Rights* (Philadelphia: University of Pennsylvania Press, 2015).
Foucault, Michel, *History of Sexuality, Volume I: An Introduction* (New York: Vintage Books, 1978).
Foucault, Michel, *'Society Must Be Defended': Lectures at Collège de France 1975–1976*, ed. Mauro Bentani and Alessandro Fontana, trans. David Macey (New York: Picador, 1997).
Giroux, Henry A., 'Reading Hurricane Katrina: Race, Class and the Biopolitics of Disposability', *College Literature* 33, no. 3 (Summer 2006): 171–96.
Gregory, Thomas, 'Dismembering the Dead: Violence, Vulnerability and the Body in War', *European Journal of International Relations* 22, no. 4 (2016): 944–65.
Gržinić, Marina, and Šefik Tatlić, *Necropolitics, Racialization, and Global Capitalism: Historicization of Biopolitics and Forensics of Politics, Art, and Life* (Lanham, MD: Lexington, 2014).
Haritaworn, Jin, Adi Kuntsman and Silvia Posocco (eds), *Queer Necropolitics* (New York: Routledge, 2014).
Haskaj, Fatmir, 'From Biopower to Necroeconomies: Neoliberalism, Biopower and Death Economies', *Philosophy and Social Criticism* 44, no. 10 (2018): 1148–68.

Islekel, Ege Selin, 'Absent Death: Necropolitics and Technologies of Mourning', *philoSOPHIA* 7, no. 2 (2017): 337–55.
Lorey, Isabel, *State of Insecurity: Government of the Precarious*, trans. Aileen Derieg, fw. Judith Butler (London and New York: Verso, 2015).
Mbembe, Achille, 'Necropolitics', trans. Libby Meintjes, *Public Culture* 15, no. 1 (Winter 2003): 11–40.
Murray, Stuart J., 'Thanatopolitics: On the Use of Death for Mobilizing Political Life', *Polygraph* 18 (2006): 191–215.
Patterson, Orlando, *Slavery and Social Death: A Comparative Study* (Cambridge, MA: Harvard University Press, 1982).
Povinelli, Elizabeth A., *Economies of Abandonment: Social Belonging and Endurance in Late Liberalism* (Durham, NC: Duke University Press, 2011).
Puar, Jasbir K., *Terrorist Assemblages: Homonationalism in Queer Times* (Durham, NC and London: Duke University Press, 2007).
Puar, Jasbir K., *The Right to Maim: Debility, Capacity, Disability* (Durham, NC: Duke University Press, 2017).
Shakhsari, Sima, 'The Queer Time of Death: Temporality, Geopolitics, and Refugee Rights', *Sexualities* 17, no. 8 (December 2014): 998–1015.
Stanley, Eric, 'Near Life, Queer Death: Overkill and Ontological Capture', *Social Text* 29, no. 2/107 (2011): 1–20.
Weizman, Eyal, *Hollow Land: Israel's Architecture of Occupation* (London and New York: Verso, 2007).
Verdery, Katherine, *The Political Lives of Dead Bodies* (New York: Columbia University Press, 1999).
Zengin, Aslı, 'Violent Intimacies: Tactile State Power, Sex/Gender Transgression, and the Politics of Touch in Contemporary Turkey', *Journal of Middle East Women's Studies* 12, no. 2 (July 2016): 225–45.

Part One

Politicising Death: Sovereign Cartographies of Violence

TWO

'These are ordinary things': Regulation of Death under the AKP Regime

Onur Bakıner

Turkey has climbed up numerous charts measuring state performance in the 2010s: it is the world leader in the number of jailed journalists[1] and academics[2] per capita and the erosion of fundamental freedoms.[3] Accompanying these trends is a rise in workplace deaths (third in the world and first in Europe)[4] and femicide.[5] The resumption of the internal armed conflict with the Kurdistan Workers' Party (*Partiya Karkerên Kurdistanê*, PKK) has claimed more lives since 2015 than any other period since the late 1990s.[6] Turkey is far from being the most violent place in the world, but for those who find themselves vulnerable due to their socioeconomic, political and gender identities/positions, death is an all-too-real possibility on a daily basis. This has led one scholar to question whether Turkey has become a necropolis, 'a state of the dead' for some social groups.[7]

This chapter examines the management of death under the Justice and Development Party (*Adalet ve Kalkınma Partisi*, AKP) regime (2002–present). The party's uninterrupted rule under the leadership of President Recep Tayyip Erdoğan has allowed it not only to govern state institutions, but also to consolidate its own brand of competitive authoritarian regime – hence the designation of its rule as a 'regime' throughout the chapter.[8] An integral element of this regime is to set formal and informal rules to sanction, narrate, commemorate and at times ignore the deaths of citizens. Large-scale death as a result of government action, complicity or inaction is nothing new in Turkey, but I argue that the AKP regime has enacted a remarkable shift in how courts and government officials address incidents resulting in death, what ordinary citizens are allowed to know and discuss about those deaths, and what kinds of demands for redress the relatives of the deceased can make. If sovereignty is about 'who may live and who must die',[9] the AKP regime has effectively consolidated its sovereignty in both discourse and practice.

I identify four strategies through which the AKP regime regulates death: (1) the *expansion of martyrdom*, a concept hitherto used as a religious justification for military casualties, into the civilian sphere, and the increasing distribution of material benefits through formal laws and informal government discretion regulating civilian and military conceptions of martyrdom; (2) the *normalisation of death* as an inherent feature of some citizens' occupational, socioeconomic and in some cases, gender position; (3) the *depoliticisation of death* to eliminate the risk of dissident mobilisation after deadly incidents; and (4) *controlling the narrative* around the news of death to maintain discursive hegemony.

These strategies should not be seen as premeditated action plans. Rather, the AKP regime has adopted elements of these strategies within an ongoing campaign of political violence and alongside the growth-at-all-cost economic model, especially from 2011 onwards. Instead of eliminating the underlying causes of deadly incidents, the AKP regime has chosen to treat death as an unavoidable, natural fact of political, economic and social life, and has instead set firm limits on how death would be addressed, narrated and commemorated. The increasing authoritarianism of the regime is both a cause and consequence of this approach to regulating death: the more opposition groups and the relatives of the deceased have asked for accountability after deadly incidents, the more the AKP regime has closed down the space for democratic demand-making; in turn, the more have democratic accountability mechanisms, such as judicial independence and free speech, been eroded, the more easily the regime has controlled the policies and narratives regulating death.

Most of the empirical observations for this chapter concern the period between 2011 and 2018, and focus on two issue areas: first, political violence in the form of clashes between the government and the PKK, the targeting of civilians by the government or the PKK, or targeting of civilians by other non-state actors, such as the Islamic State (IS); and second, workplace accidents resulting in death. These selective issue areas are pertinent because they have been at the centre of the AKP regime's regulation of death. In addition to political violence and workplace accidents, the chapter offers some observations on the regime's response to gender-based violence, and accidents due to infrastructure failure, but given the central position occupied by the expansion of martyrdom in the regime's regulation of death and life, these observations are limited in scope.

Expansion of Martyrdom

In the Islamic tradition, a person who has died for a religious cause is called a martyr (*şehit*). While interpretive disagreements abound in religious scholarship, there is broad-based agreement that martyrdom is among the highest honours a Muslim can attain after death. The Turkish state, nominally secular since the 1930s, has long granted martyr status to fallen members of the military and the police force[10] and promoted martyrdom in the context of international and internal conflicts.[11] Successive governments and media outlets have also referred to public servants who have died in the absence of violent conflict (like firefighters), as well as deceased paramilitaries with no official title (like village guards), as martyrs. What I call the expansion of martyrdom is the AKP regime's policy to confer martyr status to civilian victims of violent conflict, and to citizens who have died in work accidents, natural or human-made disasters, and so on.

'Civilian martyrdom' was first incorporated into the regime's vocabulary around 2012. It initially referred to unarmed civilians who had died during what the state labelled 'terror attacks',[12] but it has also been expanded to include civilians who have died as collateral damage during counterinsurgency operations. In 2012, the ostensible goal was to proffer state-sanctioned honour to the civilian victims of political violence. Arguably, a 2004 law that promised reparation for the relatives of the civilian dead during the internal armed conflict with the PKK would be amended to provide benefits for the more recent victims of both state violence and PKK attacks, but the government announced plans to legislate specifically for civilian martyrs.[13]

Numerous laws and regulations such as the pension law, the rules and regulations of the social security administration and the anti-terrorism law all set the framework to define martyr and veteran status and to assign rights and benefits to the families of martyrs and veterans. A July 2013 law (*Bazı Kanun ve Kanun Hükmünde Karanamelerde Değişiklik Yapılmasına Dair Kanun*) introduces the concept of the 'civilian martyr' and grants families of martyrs and wounded veterans benefits in the form of employment guarantees, low-interest mortgage credit and monthly income. In an interesting twist, the law agrees to pay monthly compensation to the relatives of victims who were killed during an Armed Forces airstrike in Uludere/Roboski[14] in December 2011.[15] Thus, the concept of martyrdom has been extended in an ad hoc manner to victims of state violence at a time when the state insisted that the airstrike was conducted in error.

The concept of civilian martyrdom underwent a major transformation in May 2014, when 301 miners died following an explosion at a coal mine in Soma, western Turkey. The mine was operated by a private company, but its sole buyer was the government; furthermore, it became apparent that work safety violations were enabled by lax inspection practices.[16] Thus, the government's failure to ensure work safety fuelled criticism in the early wake of the tragedy.[17] Government and opposition spokespersons debated over the correct labelling of the incident as an 'accident' or 'massacre'. Scholars and activists had been warning against the government's and businesses' desire to maximise production at the expense of work safety and environmental regulations for a long time; therefore, they were quick to point out that the Soma incident was inherent to the country's economic growth model, rather than an unlucky accident.[18] Faced with growing criticism, the government's first reaction was violent repression: surviving miners, miners' families and activists who were sympathetic to the miners suffered police violence, and a number of them were arrested.

After the violent repression of protesting families during the first week of the tragedy, however, the government changed its strategy and declared the miners who lost their lives civilian martyrs.[19] Although the media had named firefighters and other victims of non-violent incidents martyrs in the past, the inclusion of miners as martyrs represents a notable expansion of martyrdom outside the war and counterinsurgency context.[20] The mining tragedy, which took place three months before a presidential election, resulted in the quick adoption of a reparations programme for the families of the miners. The government's quick and positive response prompted reactions from the families of victims of earlier mining disasters, who had enjoyed no such privileged access to state resources. This opened a space of negotiation between government officials and victims' relatives over the visibility of death as a precondition for restitution. In the end, the government promised a further expansion of the martyrdom status to encompass victims of earlier work-related incidents.[21]

Civilian martyrdom elicited serious controversy in 2015, when bombings by IS took the lives of over one hundred peace activists and members of the Kurdish political movement in three attacks: Diyarbakır in June, Suruç in July and Ankara in October. The victims of these attacks definitely fit the definition of civilian martyrs adopted in 2012, but their dissident stance, as well as their relatives' and comrades' insistence that the state was negligent, if not complicit, in the IS attacks, made the government uneasy. The government granted civilian martyr status to the victims two weeks after the Ankara massacre.[22] Despite that, mainstream media refused to refer to the victims as martyrs; instead, the media still labelled them as people who 'have died' or 'have lost their lives' in the incident because acknowledging the martyrdom of peace activists, especially those who self-identified as members of the Left and the Kurdish political movement, would have jeopardised the dominant narrative of martyrdom as death in the service of the state.

Further controversy erupted in early 2017, when members of the main opposition, the Republican People's Party (*Cumhuriyet Halk Partisi*, CHP), claimed that the relatives of the Ankara victims were set to receive much less than what the relatives of other officially sanctioned martyrs did. In fact, no payment had yet been disbursed. When asked, government sources replied that the payments did not start because the judicial investigation had not yet been resolved.[23] This rather legalistic response highlights the extent to which the supposedly impartial regulation of martyrdom is in fact a smokescreen for the arbitrary implementation of the law and how the discourse of martyrdom is exploited to distribute symbolic and material rewards differentially.

The concept of civilian martyrdom was invoked once again in the wake of the failed coup attempt on 15 July 2016. The coup-makers, allegedly a branch of the military that was loyal to cleric (and former AKP ally) Fethullah Gülen, took over bridges, TV stations and other targets they deemed strategic, and bombed civilian targets, including the nation's parliament. The civilian victims of the attempt were those who were either actively resisting the coup or were caught in the crossfire. Of the 248 people who died on that day, 182 were civilians. This prompted the government to declare the fallen civilians martyrs.[24] Needless to say, after the putsch was crushed, the symbolism of martyrdom has been used to its fullest extent in the name of those who sacrificed their lives for the government:[25] Istanbul's main bridge has been renamed the 15 July Martyrs' Bridge, and commemorations have been held to honour the martyrs during the anniversaries of the coup attempt. Dissident voices blaming the government for allowing the infiltration of the military by what later turned out to be a coup coalition have fallen on deaf ears in the atmosphere of commemorating and celebrating martyrdom.

The expansion of martyrdom into the civilian sphere accompanies the expansion of martyrdom, both civilian and non-civilian, as a distributive mechanism. The symbolic implications of martyrdom (*şehadet*) have been written on extensively: such a designation may be said to present a degree of closure to the families of the dead and provide them with a sense of prestige. In material terms, martyrdom has now become an area of patronage distribution. While wounded veterans and families of the dead had been granted benefits historically, the expansion of martyrdom into the civilian sphere in the more recent past has also meant the transformation of distributive schemes.

The concept of martyrdom has, in the time span of five or six years, become widely acknowledged as among the chief mechanisms by which citizens are allowed to demand symbolic recognition and material benefits from the state. Martyrs' and civilian martyrs' families have organised across the country to ask for improvements to their pensions, education and employment benefits. The government amended civil and criminal codes numerous times between 2013 and 2018 in response to these demands. At a time when contentious demand-making has become increasingly delegitimised and criminalised, the state has allowed these citizens to voice their appeals.[26] In a way, being a civilian or non-civilian martyr's relative has helped to circumvent the regime's increasing authoritarianism.

Taking into consideration the fact that the expansion of martyrdom into the civilian sphere has to do with the increase in deaths resulting from violent political conflict and workplace deaths, it appears that the government's motivation is to preclude dissident mobilisation following lethal incidents and to stem the flow of potential lawsuits to government agencies and/or private actors responsible for the death. In other words, the families of the dead are provided with the Faustian if obvious choice of either drawing government hostility by publicly criticising the state and thus forgoing government compensation or accepting martyrdom for their fallen relative in order to receive restitution.[27] Acquiescence is thus ensured at a relatively cheap price for the regime.

However, the precondition for inclusion into this redistributive model necessitates having a relative die for the state (or at least for a reason that the state does not find objectionable), and subsequently, reproducing the state-sanctioned narrative of martyrdom. Failure to conform to governmental expectations around mourning leads to the immediate withdrawal of symbolic and material rewards. The most striking examples of non-conforming behaviour come from the period when the short-lived peace process between the Turkish state and the PKK came to an end in July 2015. As hostilities resumed, military casualties began to rise to levels not observed since the 1990s.[28] The government and Turkish nationalist groups wanted to capitalise on military martyrs' funerals to shore up support for the renewed war, but they found that not all relatives acquiesced to their narrative. Some relatives criticised the government for having stopped the counterinsurgency campaign in the first place, while others objected to the government's apathetic and half-hearted attitude during the peace process.

In one prominent example, Mehmet Alkan, himself an active-duty military officer, gave a speech on 23 August 2015 during the funeral of his brother, who died in a clash with the PKK. The speech criticised the government's handling of the peace process. Government response was quick: President Erdoğan attacked the officer verbally and Alkan was dismissed from the military soon afterwards. In fact, Alkan's speech conformed to nationalist tropes supporting violent counterinsurgency overall, but in a country where martyrs' relatives have historically affirmed their loved ones' death as a worthy sacrifice,[29] the subversive potential of his speech was not tolerated.[30] In the months that followed, government officials and the police watched soldiers' funerals closely to stop any anti-government mobilisation, and the media were instructed not to provide a platform for relatives who did not follow the official party line. Martyr status was allowed to empower fallen soldiers' relatives only to the extent that their agency did not threaten the regime's regulation of death and life in its aftermath.

Thus, relatives of deceased persons, civilian or not, are allowed to participate in the symbolic and material distribution of benefits as long as they conform to certain norms: the death should not occur while engaging in anti-government activity; the death should cause sufficient public outrage to warrant government attention; and grieving family members should not hold the government morally or legally responsible for the death. The regime has never revoked the martyr status of a dead person, but the way it has conferred upon, or withdrawn, the informal 'martyr's relative' status to citizens points to hierarchies in terms of what these relatives may receive as material compensation, and what kinds of demands they are allowed to make. Thus, the regime has been leveraging the distribution of martyrdom to differentiate among the dead, and, more importantly from the standpoint of necropolitics, among the living.[31]

Normalisation of Death

The tendency to naturalise and normalise death has become increasingly more common in official discourse in the recent past. To put it bluntly, the state has moved from expressing sorrow for death, which was typical of official discourse until the 2010s, to justifying why death is supposed to happen. Regardless of whether the cause of death is a military clash between government forces and insurgents, a work accident, or gender-based violence, government spokespersons have been quick to refer to the incident as somewhat inherent to one's occupational, socioeconomic or gender status. Sometimes the Islamic concept of *fıtrat*, referring to the God-ordained nature of socioeconomic and occupational roles in which people find themselves, is used to justify death.[32] The cause of death, accordingly, is the culmination of one's *fıtrat*: it is in a soldier's nature to face death, and it is in a miner's nature to risk death.

Erdoğan's rhetoric is emblematic of this shift. In 2006, while he was facing criticism for the counterinsurgency strategy that caused military casualties, he said: 'military service is not the kind of place to sit back and relax' (*askerlik yan gelip yatma yeri değildir*).[33] This statement caused a huge outcry; therefore, Erdoğan refrained from repeating such statements in the years that followed. However, as his power became more consolidated between 2006 and 2011, he went back to using language that normalised and relativised the experience of death.

On 28 December 2011, military jets killed thirty-four unarmed Kurdish civilians in the south-eastern town of Uludere/Roboski. The military chose to hide the incident at first and later declared that it had targeted suspected terrorists. Investigative journalists discovered that the victims were smugglers, many of them minors, who were crossing the Turkey–Iraq border at the time of the attack. The massacre and the lack of any mechanism of accountability in the aftermath were met with criticism, mostly coming from the Kurdish political movement.[34]

Erdoğan responded to criticisms in a speech on 26 May 2012, at the meeting of his party's women's organisation: 'I see abortion as murder, and . . . I say this to some groups that object to this statement of mine and the media . . . you [constantly talk about] Uludere. I say, every abortion is an Uludere.'[35] The main theme of that speech was that there was a global effort to reduce Turkish women's fertility through C-sections and abortions. The fact that Uludere was thrown into the speech as comparable to abortion served Erdoğan's short-term goal of generating controversy by shifting public discourse away from the massacre, while conveying an ultra-conservative message on women's reproductive rights. In a bitterly cynical twist, the prime minister acknowledged the massacre while denying it, or worse yet, implicated women having abortions in a massacre that the government denied. In addition, this speech has served as a model for Erdoğan's later justifications for those deaths that implicate the state: relativising death through comparison.

The relativisation of death through comparison as a tactic made a comeback in Erdoğan's first speech after the Soma tragedy. Rejecting the government's and employers' responsibility, Erdoğan stated that deaths in the mining sector were normal: 'Friends, let's not interpret the things that happen in coal mines as things that have never happened before. These are ordinary things. In the literature there is something called [a] work accident. These exist in [the job's] structure, in its inherent nature [*fıtrat*]. There is no such thing as "no accident". Of course, it has hurt us deeply that the scale of the thing is so big.' To support his argument, he gave examples of mining tragedies that produced large death tolls in England in 1862 and 1866, France in 1906, Japan in 1914 and 1963, the United States in 1907, China in 1942 and 1960, and India in 1975.[36]

The normalisation of death is not limited to Erdoğan's rhetoric, in large part because other AKP politicians and the pro-government media take Erdoğan's words as a call for action. In the days following Erdoğan's non-sequitur comments on abortion and Uludere/Roboski, public figures ranging from the Minister of Health to the President of the Directorate of Religious Affairs made anti-abortion statements. Daytime TV featured stories of women who had allegedly regretted having an abortion. While abortion is still legal in Turkey, Mor Çatı, a woman's organisation that is often critical of the government, called thirty-seven public hospitals operating in Istanbul and found that most hospitals have de facto stopped offering abortion services.[37]

The normalisation of death has likewise produced real consequences for the living: Turkey's workers endure some of the most dangerous and precarious conditions around the world.[38] As of this writing, the police were clamping down on a workers' protest for better work conditions at the construction site of Istanbul's new airport. In a rush to inaugurate the airport by the end of October 2018, the management ignored such basic demands as paying salaries on time, providing adequate food, and eliminating bedbugs in the workers' sleeping quarters. Official figures put the death toll due to accidents and health problems since 2015 at 27.[39]

The normalisation and banalisation of death produce contradictions inherent in the necropolitical discourse of the Turkish state. If certain forms of death happen everywhere and all the time, then it follows that the state should not be held responsible for not preventing them. But how is it possible to grant the deceased the special status of martyrdom in that case? Accompanying the normalisation of death is its fetishisation. Death does not just happen; it is supposed to happen! Militaristic nationalism accompanies the regulation of death in order to smooth out these contradictions. Accordingly, today's martyrs come from a long lineage of military and civilian warriors who have sacrificed themselves for the nation. Although the definition of citizenship as used by politicians in modern Turkey had always included the imagery of soldier-citizens intent on sacrificing themselves, arguably the post-2015 period stands out for the degree to which political discourse and media production converge on imagining Turkey as a martyr nation.[40]

Banu Bargu notes that the global transformation of warfare and the simultaneous adoption of a humanitarian discourse to regulate armed conflict have led to the use of 'collateral damage' as a category that expresses the symbiotic and complicit relationship between humanitarian discourse and the discourse of military necessity.[41] In the specific context of Turkey, the internal armed conflict had already normalised civilian casualties to some extent. The AKP regime employs the category of 'civilian martyrs' to deepen this normalisation; furthermore, it expands this category to other walks of life to claim that the risk of death is either inherent to one's position in society, or that it happens everywhere, so it is normal. The idea of martyrdom has even penetrated the economic sphere: although not as prominent as the lionisation of conflict-related martyrdom, the media have at times praised those who have died in the workplace as martyrs in Turkey's so-called 'economic war of independence'[42] – a thinly veiled euphemism for the country's crisis-prone, growth-at-all-cost development model that lies at the root of skyrocketing work-related accidents and environmental degradation in the past decade.[43]

The fetishisation of death has also enabled morbid performances. When a group of Erdoğan supporters first wore shrouds to signal that they supported him unto death in December 2013, the act was interpreted as a relatively fringe gesture. However, since then, public declarations of wanting to kill and die for the regime have permeated the public sphere.[44] Since the resumption of hostilities between the state and the PKK in July 2015, demanding the peaceful resolution of the conflict has become criminalised – to illustrate, the most spectacular example of this criminalisation is the case of a woman who has been sentenced to prison for saying 'children should not die' during a phone-in on a TV show.[45] While the advocacy of violent counterinsurgency tactics is not particularly novel, the post-2015 period is the first time when the government has altogether stopped promising an end to military casualties. The hope that violence could one day end, peacefully or otherwise, has been abandoned in favour of an endless war that has expanded from Turkey's southeast to northern Syria, and one in which martyrdom is expected of citizens, both as soldiers and as civilians.

Depoliticisation of Death

Depoliticising death has become yet another strategy for managing news of deadly incidents. To be more precise, depoliticising death refers to the AKP regime's efforts to stifle dissent fuelled by news of death. Fearing that reports of deaths might prompt protests from peace activists, women's and LGBTQ rights groups, citizens concerned with work safety or opposition parties, the regime's immediate reaction to any kind of public death is to criticise dissidents for politicising death. In the more recent past courts have imposed nearly blanket bans on publishing about any incident that has resulted in death.

Again, the tendency to depoliticise is not unique to the past decade: throughout the internal armed conflict, politicians and the media have chosen not to express the violence in terms of political incompatibilities, and instead have portrayed the PKK rebels as traitors and terrorists with a penchant for violence and treason. However, the degree to which exhortations not to politicise death pervade the public sphere and the expansion of this depoliticising language to other walks of life are novel phenomena. Government spokespersons have instructed the opposition not to politicise IS attacks, the resumption of violence with the PKK, workplace deaths, casualties from train crashes or gender-based violence, to name a few. The use of depoliticising language has infiltrated the mainstream to such an extent that in order to counter this hegemonic discourse, women's rights activists have adopted 'women's murders are political'[46] as their slogan, as labour activists have adopted 'workplace murders are political'[47] as theirs.

Needless to say, the tendency to treat death as apolitical reflects doublespeak on the part of the government because it has used death as a powerful tool for mobilisation when the occasion has called for it. Funerals of soldiers killed in clashes with the PKK are widely attended by government officials, including President Erdoğan. In fact, he has recently begun to use funerals as a platform to give political speeches – something that no politician had dared to do despite the longstanding tradition of using soldiers' funerals for nationalist mobilisation.[48] A funeral photo from 17 August 2015, where Erdoğan holds a microphone with one hand and leans on a flag-draped coffin with the other, stands out as one of the iconic images of the recent past.

The instrumental logic deployed in the attempted depoliticisation of death is obvious: the government does not want to face criticism concerning how it handles political affairs that result in death. In such cases, the government typically uses the language of leaving aside the partisan divide for the greater good. Accordingly, moments of national emergency call for the suspension of criticism because national unity trumps partisan interests. Deploying a normalising and relativising discourse serves to depoliticise as well: there is nothing politicians can or should do about things that happen everywhere all the time.

However, reducing the depoliticisation of death to this narrow instrumental logic misses an important point: government spokespersons sometimes react defensively about incidents of death even if government officials are not held to account for their criminal responsibility. The mere mention of government neglect is sufficient to draw negative reactions from them. In fact, hardly any low-level official has been asked to resign, let alone prosecuted, for incompetence or negligence in an incident resulting in death. Furthermore, instead of distancing themselves from private business owners who violate work-safety standards, or men who abuse and kill acquaintances, government spokespersons often take offense at the news of what appears to be lethal violence caused by non-state actors. Even when they have the option to not intervene in cases involving non-state victims and perpetrators, representatives of the regime go on the offensive.

I believe the AKP regime's extreme sensitivity to the implications of death as a political phenomenon reveals the extent to which its regulation of death is central to its regulation of life through social and political engineering. The regime embraces and embodies socioeconomic, political and gendered hierarchies: accordingly, employers rule over employees; the government rules over citizens; and men rule over women. Being ruled over means acquiescing not only to one's position in life, but also to the risk of death that comes 'naturally' with that subordinate position. Workers' acquiescence is necessary for high economic growth rates under conditions of physical and socioeconomic precariousness; citizens' acquiescence ensures the consolidation of a competitive authoritarian regime that promises no accountability for life-and-death decisions; women's acquiescence upholds conservative social norms that reproduce the social and political model for future generations. Thus, death in the hands of non-state perpetrators is not considered a private matter under this regime.

This does not mean that the regime actively supports certain forms of death. In fact, work-related deaths and accidents that reveal the deficiencies of physical infrastructure have been embarrassing for government officials. Rather, when an incident resulting in death happens, the regime sets rigid boundaries on the content and language of citizens' demands that arise in relation to such deaths. Ironically, their depoliticising stance affirms the political nature of these deaths all the more. Reforming or transforming Turkey's economic model, counterinsurgency model, political system or gender relations because they prove to be deadly simply remains outside the reach of citizens.[49] Instead, death should be acknowledged as an unavoidable, apolitical fact that sometimes, though not always, calls for a benevolent response from the state in the form of martyrdom benefits.

Controlling the Narrative

The AKP regime's obsession with controlling the narrative over death is likewise unprecedented. Blocking the public's access to any piece of evidence or opinion that contradicts the government's narrative about deadly incidents, corruption and other potentially scandalous news motivates numerous forms of official censorship.[50] The encroachment upon public media and the increasing concentration of private media in the hands of pro-government conglomerates,[51] combined with the courts' inability to serve as a check on government – a trend observed since 2010, and one that has become all the more prominent after the restructuring of the judiciary in 2014 – have facilitated the regime's control over such narratives.

For example, on 11 May 2013, two car bombs exploded in the southern town of Reyhanlı, killing over fifty people. Officials blamed the Syrian regime and its allies for the attack. A local court imposed a ban on all reporting of the incident. The ban not only set limits on gory images; it effectively banned all journalistic activity around the bombing. The judiciary was relatively more independent at the time, so another court lifted the ban five days later.[52] However, judicialised censorship became the model a couple of months later, when the fallout between the Gülen community and the regime was played out over their respective desires to control the judiciary. As Erdoğan's supporters consolidated their control over the judiciary between 2014 and 2016, court-imposed bans on reporting became standard practice for news about corruption allegations, terror attacks, the internal armed conflict, work-related accidents, natural disasters and cases of sexual violence involving minors or women. Combined with intermittent bans on popular social media sites,[53] these bans effectively control the flow of information in the immediate wake of an incident. This gives government officials extra time to produce their own narrative of events. Once people's outrage over a deadly incident begins to subside, the official narrative steps in to shape public discourse.

Another mechanism for controlling the narrative is the direct repression of academics and journalists who cover unpalatable issues like violent conflict, government corruption and the human and environmental cost of Turkey's economic model. Prosecution of academics and journalists with charges of aiding and abetting terrorism and exposing government secrets had been an ongoing practice since the AKP regime consolidated itself after the 2011 general election. The government's response to the failed coup attempt in 2016 intensified this form of repression: five days after the attempt, the government declared a state of emergency. During the nearly two years of rule by executive decree, newspapers, TV channels and radio stations were closed permanently under Erdoğan's directives and a record number of journalists and academics were prosecuted and forced into exile. Although eliminating a coup threat by dismantling the Gülen community was the explicit justification for the declaration of the state of emergency, many of the media outlets and individuals targeted by the regime are on the Left and often sympathetic to the Kurdish political movement.

The co-optation of the media and the repression of dissident voices produce an atmosphere in which the regime shapes the narrative of a deadly incident not only once, but as many times as political exigencies require. It is not uncommon for government spokespersons to attribute deadly incidents to one cause and completely discard their own initial explanation to support a contradictory hypothesis soon after. To give one prominent example: the regime has narrated the Uludere/Roboski bombing first as a non-existent event, then as a legitimate anti-smuggling operation, then as an unfortunate accident, and, finally, as a conspiracy by pro-Gülen intelligence officers.[54] The changing narratives have depended on the status of the government's fluctuating relationship with the Gülenists as well as its perceived need to provide a satisfactory answer to the Kurdish voters. From the downing of a Russian airplane in November 2015 to a deadly train accident in July 2018, the regime enjoys a near-total monopoly over narratives, including the privilege of contradicting earlier official narratives, in the absence of judicial independence and freedom of expression.

Conclusion

Different forms of lethal or near-lethal violence implicate state actors in different ways and at different levels of responsibility. State security forces take direct part in the internal armed conflict, including in the targeting of civilians. Work-related deaths take place in privately owned workplaces that should ideally be regulated by the state to ensure safety and security. Murders of women are usually instances of acquaintance or intimate partner violence, but the connivance, even complicity of the police, prosecutors and judges is well noted. In other words, even when the state is not the chief perpetrator of lethal violence, it plays a key role in regulating, allowing or disallowing, and ultimately legitimising or delegitimising it.

This chapter is an effort to explain the AKP regime's strategies for regulating information, demand-making and pecuniary distribution with regards to death. Although deaths that implicate state agents have always been central to politics in Turkey, the AKP regime has been employing novel discourses and practices (or using the existing ones with unprecedented intensity) to ensure that death serves as an area of patronage, while eliminating the risk that death may be the focal point of dissident mobilisation. In addition to the normalisation and fetishisation of death, these discourses and practices have resulted in the expansion of the regulation of death to what can be considered the 'private' sphere, where the penetration of the state as a necropolitical agent had been hitherto minimal. The AKP regime has intervened in public debates on any kind of deadly incident that could call into question the hegemonic political, economic and social hierarchies. Combined with the erosion of democracy and fundamental freedoms, this obsession with controlling the narrative around death has limited the ways in which citizens can mourn, talk about and protest death.

As of this writing, the Ministry of the Interior has declared a ban on protests by the Saturday Mothers (*Cumartesi Anneleri*), a civic initiative that brings together the relatives of persons who were disappeared during the internal armed conflict – in the 1990s in particular. The Mothers have met over 700 times since the mid-1990s to demand that the remains of their loved ones be found and the perpetrators punished. The AKP spokespersons had lent measured support for the Mothers when the party initially perceived and presented itself in conflict with the military establishment. As the AKP's grip on state institutions was consolidated, however, the limited criticism directed towards state perpetrators of human rights violations disappeared completely. Instead, the regime turned against the Mothers, whose rights to mourn and protest peacefully have been taken away. Since the deaths of their loved ones have become an inconvenient truth once again, the Mothers' activity is now characterised as politicising death and aiding and abetting terrorism. In a time span of four or five years, one of the oldest civic initiatives in Turkey has faced insurmountable challenges, given the AKP's intensified regulation of death.

The regime could not regulate death and life in such a meticulous fashion if it were not for the erosion of democratic accountability mechanisms – the AKP's control over the judiciary and the media are worth mentioning in particular. However, this particular form of necropolitics is not just another authoritarian intervention in a country known for its democratic openings and authoritarian reversals. It involves an intensified micro-level management of death, narratives around death and mourning. Akin to what Michel Foucault has called the 'capillary circulation' of power that produces identities in life and death, the AKP regime produces identities such as the 'civilian martyr' and 'martyr's relative', by which it represses certain forms of political action while creating an alternative, albeit controlled, space for the allocation of material resources through discursive practices around what death is and what it is not. This form of managing death has something to say and do about the announcement of every lethal incident, every funeral, every form of collective mourning and collective demand-making. The regime is paranoid about losing control over death, and consequently, life; therefore, it controls the narratives around death and regulates the distribution of symbolic and material resources in the wake of myriad forms of death.

Notes

1. Committee to Protect Journalists, '262 Journalists Imprisoned in 2017', p. 7.
2. Human Rights Watch, 'Turkey: Government Targeting Academics'.
3. Freedom House, 'Freedom in the World 2018: Democracy in Crisis'.
4. Behlül Özkan, 'Turkey's Choice', p. 37.

5. According to the We Will Stop Femicide Platform (*Kadın Cinayetlerini Durduracağız Platformu*), a civil-society initiative, 285 women were killed, mostly by family members and intimate partners, in the first eight months of 2018.
6. Official casualty figures are notoriously untrustworthy. An online journalism platform has recently published a comparative study of reported military, rebel and civilian casualties, using official and journalistic sources. 'Sayılarla', *140journos*, 24 March 2017.
7. Eylül Fidan Akıncı, 'Performativities of Necropolitics and Mourning in Neoliberal Turkey'.
8. Turkey had been considered a semi-democratic or competitive authoritarian regime, where relatively free and fair elections with serious restrictions on fundamental rights and liberties coexisted. Since the late 1990s the country's trajectory appeared to head towards greater recognition of civil and political rights, including during the first five years of the AKP government, but the AKP's consolidation of power between 2007 and 2011 led to another downward trajectory. By all qualitative and quantitative measures, Turkey's democracy has experienced a relatively quick decline by its own standards in the recent past, and by global standards. See Başer and Öztürk, *Authoritarian Politics in Turkey*.
9. Achille Mbembe, 'Necropolitics', p. 11.
10. Thomas W. Smith, 'Between Allah and Atatürk'.
11. Nadav Solomonovich, 'The Turkish Republic's Jihad?'; Kemerli, 'Religious Militarism and Islamist Conscientious Objection in Turkey'.
12. In Turkey's official and media discourse, the concepts 'terror' and 'terrorism' do not only refer to intentional acts of violence against civilian targets; non-state armed actors' attacks on military and police targets are also considered acts of terrorism. In addition, non-violent dissident activity has time and again been categorised as aiding and abetting terrorism by government spokespersons, courts and the media. Thus, descriptions of terrorism in government discourse reflect this extremely broad and tendentious definition.
13. 'İşte Sivil Şehit Yasası'nın detayları', *CNN Türk*, 21 March 2012.
14. Uludere is the official Turkish name for the district; Roboski is its Kurdish name.
15. 'Uludere Kurbanları Sivil Şehit', *NTV*, 23 March 2012.
16. Sinan Erensü, 'Powering Neoliberalization', p. 153.
17. Murat Yetkin, 'Analysis: Gov't ignored warnings, miners paid the bill with their lives', *Hürriyet Daily News*, 14 May 2014.
18. Fikret Adaman, Murat Arsel and Bengi Akbulut, 'Neoliberal Developmentalism, Authoritarian Populism, and Extractivism in the Countryside: The Soma Mining Disaster in Turkey'.
19. 'Soma'da ölen 301 madenci sivil şehit sayılacak', *Habertürk*, 18 May 2014.
20. In fact, the expansion of the martyr status has encouraged firefighters and peace officers to demand that their fallen members be officially recognised as martyrs, as well. 'Zabıta ve itfaiyeciler de gazi ve şehit sayılacak', *Milliyet*, 6 December 2016.

21. 'Maden şehitlerini ayıran yasa tasarısına tepki', *Hürriyet*, 11 February 2018.
22. 'Ankara'nın 'sivil şehitleri'ne 29 bin TL tazminat', *Habertürk*, 14 October 2015.
23. 'Şehitlikte Eşitlik', *Hürriyet*, 11 January 2017.
24. '15 Temmuz mağdurlarına ödenen tazminat miktarı açıklandı', *CNN Türk*, 2 March 2018.
25. Josh Carney, 'Resur(e)recting a Spectacular Hero'.
26. In May 2018, Minister of Labour and Social Security Jülide Sarıeroğlu announced extra payments to pensioners before religious holidays. The benefit would cover, among other pensioners, relatives of martyrs, veterans and retired village guards. The December 2017 and March 2018 amendments to the tax bill (*7061 & 7103 sayılı kanun*) are the latest regulations on the legal framework for addressing martyrdom. They extend benefits to the relatives of martyrs and civilian martyrs, as well as veterans.
27. It is worth noting that the relatives of the Soma victims have received generally favourable rulings in civil lawsuits. The criminal prosecution has resulted in prison sentences for some of the business owners; government officials have not been found guilty of any charges. The court's categorisation of the deaths as resulting from 'negligence' has drawn criticisms. 'Soma faciası davasının gerekçeli kararı açıklandı', *CNN Türk*, 29 August 2018.
28. For an analysis of the death toll between 2015 and 2016, see <http://www.crisisgroup.be/interactives/turkey/> (last accessed 28 May 2019).
29. Esra Gedik, 'Security of the Nation: Why Do We Need "Mothers of Martyrs" in Turkey?'; Senem Kaptan, 'Gendering Landscapes of War through the Narratives of Soldiers' Mothers'.
30. 'Şehit ağabeyi Yarbay Mehmet Alkan'dan sert sözler', *Hürriyet*, 11 May 2016.
31. Banu Bargu, 'Another Necropolitics'.
32. Sedef Arat-Koç, 'Culturalizing Politics, Hyper-Politicizing "Culture"'.
33. All translations mine. 'Askerlik yan gelip yatma yeri değil', *Hürriyet*, 4 September 2006.
34. 'TIMELINE: What Happened in Roboski?' *Bianet English*, 31 December 2012.
35. '"Her kürtaj bir cinayettir"', *Hürriyet*, 26 May 2012.
36. 'Erdoğan Soma'da konuştu: "Bunlar olağan şeylerdir"', *CNN Türk*, 14 May 2014.
37. Mor Çatı, 'Kürtaj Yapıyor musunuz? "Hayır Yapmıyoruz!"'
38. Özkan, 'Turkey's Choice'.
39. 'Turkish police detain hundreds of protesting airport workers', *Reuters*, 15 September 2018.
40. Carney, 'Resur(e)recting a Spectacular Hero'.
41. Banu Bargu, 'Human Shields', p. 286.
42. Murat Kazım Güney, 'Fatal Workplace Injuries in the İstanbul Tuzla Shipyards and the Obsession with Economic Development in Turkey'.
43. For a critical take on the increasing normalisation of gender-based violence, see Deniz Kandiyoti, 'Locating the Politics of Gender'.

44. Ibid.
45. 'Tahliye edilmişti: Ayşe öğretmen altı ay sonra yeniden cezaevine girecek', *Diken*, 7 May 2018.
46. For an illuminating account of the history behind the slogan, see Ebru Yıldırım, 'Kadın Cinayetleri Politiktir', *Bianet*, 10 July 2010.
47. Three days after the Soma incident, LuBUnya, an LGBTI group based in Boğaziçi University, organized a march under the slogan 'the murders of workers and LGBTI people are political', <http://www.kaosgl.org/sayfa.php?id=16606> (last accessed 28 May 2019).
48. Arzu Kibris, 'Funerals and Elections'.
49. Some (but by no means all) non-state perpetrators, like business owners operating coal mines and men who kill women, have received prison sentences, but these punishments are typically lenient, as they take into account mitigating circumstances, are delivered years after the initial outrage over the deadly incident and fail to prompt a public debate over the broader system of injustice and oppression that produces death.
50. A list of court bans (in Turkish) can be found at <https://www.rtuk.gov.tr/mahkeme-yayin-yasaklari-5320> (last accessed 28 May 2019).
51. Berk Esen and Sebnem Gumuscu, 'Building a Competitive Authoritarian Regime'.
52. 'Reyhanlı'ya yayın yasağı kalktı', *Hürriyet*, 16 May 2013.
53. Popular social media platforms and information websites, such as Twitter, Wikipedia and YouTube, have been banned time and again in the 2010s.
54. Examples of these explanations can be found in pro-government media: 'Turkey deeply saddened by Uludere incident', *Anadolu Agency*, 25 May 2012; 'Gülenists attempted to create chaos in Turkey through Uludere incident, analysts claim', *Daily Sabah*, 27 July 2016.

Bibliography

'15 Temmuz mağdurlarına ödenen tazminat miktarı açıklandı', *CNN Türk*, 2 March 2018, <https://www.cnnturk.com/turkiye/15-temmuz-magdurlarina-odenen-tazminat-miktari-aciklandi> (last accessed 28 May 2019).

Adaman, Fikret, Murat Arsel and Bengi Akbulut, 'Neoliberal Developmentalism, Authoritarian Populism, and Extractivism in the Countryside: The Soma Mining Disaster in Turkey', *The Journal of Peasant Studies*, 24 October 2018, DOI: 10.1080/03066150.2018.1515737.

Akıncı, Eylül Fidan, 'Performativities of Necropolitics and Mourning in Neoliberal Turkey', in Sara Brady and Lindsey Mantoan (eds), *Performance in a Militarized Culture* (New York, NY: Routledge, 2017).

'Ankara'nın 'sivil şehitleri'ne 29 bin TL tazminat', *Habertürk*, 14 October 2015, <https://www.haberturk.com/gundem/haber/1139818-ankaranin-sivil-sehitlerine-29-bin-tl-tazminat> (last accessed 28 May 2019).

Arat-Koç, Sedef, 'Culturalizing Politics, Hyper-Politicizing "Culture": "White" vs. "Black Turks" and the Making of Authoritarian Populism in Turkey', *Dialectical Anthropology* (March 2018): 1–18.

'Askerlik yan gelip yatma yeri değil', *Hürriyet*, 4 September 2006, <http://www.hurriyet.com.tr/gundem/askerlik-yan-gelip-yatma-yeri-degil-5029543> (last accessed 28 May 2019).

Bargu, Banu, 'Human Shields', *Contemporary Political Theory* 12, no. 4 (November 2013): 277–95.

Bargu, Banu, 'Another Necropolitics', *Theory & Event* 19, no. 1, January 2016.

Carney, Josh, 'Resur(e)recting a Spectacular Hero: Diriliş Ertuğrul, Necropolitics, and Popular Culture in Turkey', *Review of Middle East Studies* 52, no. 1 (April 2018): 93–114.

Committee to Protect Journalists, '262 Journalists Imprisoned in 2017', <https://cpj.org/data/imprisoned/2017> (last accessed 28 May 2019).

'Erdoğan Soma'da konuştu: "Bunlar olağan şeylerdir"', *CNN Türk*, 14 May 2014, <https://www.cnnturk.com/haber/turkiye/erdogan-somada-konustu-bunlar-olagan-seylerdir> (last accessed 28 May 2019).

Erensü, Sinan, 'Powering Neoliberalization: Energy and Politics in the Making of a New Turkey', *Energy Research & Social Science* 41 (July 2018): 148–57.

Esen, Berk, and Sebnem Gumuscu, 'Building a Competitive Authoritarian Regime: State–Business Relations in the AKP's Turkey', *Journal of Balkan and Near Eastern Studies* 20, no. 4 (November 2018): 1–24.

Freedom House, 'Freedom in the World 2018: Democracy in Crisis', <https://freedomhouse.org/report/freedom-world/freedom-world-2018> (last accessed 28 May 2019).

Gedik, Esra, 'Security of the Nation: Why Do We Need "Mothers of Martyrs" in Turkey?' *DisClosure: A Journal of Social Theory* 22 (2013): 24–50.

'Gülenists attempted to create chaos in Turkey through Uludere incident, analysts claim', *Daily Sabah*, 27 July 2016.

'"Her kürtaj bir cinayettir"', *Hürriyet*, 26 May 2012, <http://www.hurriyet.com.tr/gundem/her-kurtaj-bir-cinayettir-20632631> (last accessed 28 May 2019).

Human Rights Watch: 'Turkey: Government Targeting Academics', <https://www.hrw.org/news/2018/05/14/turkey-government-targeting-academics> (last accessed 28 May 2019).

'İşte 'Sivil Şehit Yasası'nın detayları . . .' *CNN Türk*, 21 March 2012, <https://www.cnnturk.com/2012/turkiye/03/21/iste.sivil.sehit.yasasinin.detaylari/654069.0/index.html> (last accessed 28 May 2019).

Kandiyoti, Deniz, 'Locating the Politics of Gender: Patriarchy, Neo-Liberal Governance and Violence in Turkey', *Research and Policy on Turkey* 1, no. 2 (July 2016): 103–18.

Kaptan, Senem, 'Gendering Landscapes of War through the Narratives of Soldiers' Mothers: Military Service and the Kurdish Conflict in Turkey', *Journal of Middle East Women's Studies* 13, no.1 (March 2017): 47–68.

Kemerli, Pınar, 'Religious Militarism and Islamist Conscientious Objection in Turkey', *International Journal of Middle East Studies* 47, no. 2 (May 2015): 281–301.

Kibris, Arzu, 'Funerals and Elections: The Effects of Terrorism on Voting Behavior in Turkey', *Journal of Conflict Resolution* 55, no. 2 (October 2010): 220–47.

'Maden şehitlerini ayıran yasa tasarısına tepki', *Hürriyet*, 11 February 2018, <http://www.hurriyet.com.tr/maden-sehitlerini-ayiran-yasa-tasarisina-tepki-40738295> (last accessed 28 May 2019).

Mbembe, Achille, 'Necropolitics', trans. Libby Meintjes, *Public Culture* 15, no. 1 (Winter 2013): 11–40.

Mor Çatı, 'Kürtaj Yapıyor musunuz? "Hayır Yapmıyoruz!"', <https://www.morcati.org.tr/tr/290-kurtaj-yapiyor-musunuz-hayir-yapmiyoruz> (last accessed 28 May 2019).

Özkan, Behlül, 'Turkey's Choice: Is There a Way Out for Erdoğan?' *Political Insight* 5, no. 3 (November 2014): 34–7.

'Reyhanlı'ya yayın yasağı kalktı', *Hürriyet*, 16 May 2013, <http://www.hurriyet.com.tr/gundem/reyhanli-ya-yayin-yasagi-kalkti-23293233> (last accessed 28 May 2019).

'Sayılarla 1984'ten bu yana pkk ile çatışmalardaki ölümler', *140journos*, 24 March 2017, <https://140journos.com/sayilarla-1984ten-bu-yana-pkk-ile-catismalardaki-olumler-5ce123d214be> (last accessed 28 May 2019).

Smith, Thomas W., 'Between Allah and Atatürk: Liberal Islam in Turkey', *The International Journal of Human Rights* 9, no. 3 (2005): 307–25.

Solomonovich, Nadav, 'The Turkish Republic's Jihad? Religious Symbols, Terminology and Ceremonies in Turkey during the Korean War 1950–1953', *Middle Eastern Studies* 54, no. 4 (March 2018): 592–610.

'Soma faciası davasının gerekçeli kararı açıklandı', *CNN Türk*, 29 August 2018, <https://www.cnnturk.com/turkiye/soma-faciasi-davasinin-gerekceli-karari-aciklandi> (last accessed 28 May 2019).

'Soma'da ölen 301 madenci sivil şehit sayılacak', *Habertürk*, 18 May 2014, <https://www.haberturk.com/gundem/haber/949279-somada-olen-301-madenci-sivil-sehit-sayilacak> (last accessed 28 May 2019).

'Şehit ağabeyi Yarbay Mehmet Alkan'dan sert sözler', *Hürriyet*, 11 May 2016, <http://www.hurriyet.com.tr/gundem/sehit-agabeyi-yarbay-mehmet-alkan-dagdaki-teroru-sehre-indirenler-bu-akan-kanlarin-sorumlusudur-40102494> (last accessed 28 May 2019).

'Şehitlikte Eşitlik', *Hürriyet*, 11 January 2017, <http://www.hurriyet.com.tr/gundem/sehitlikte-esitlik-40333665> (last accessed 28 May 2019).

'Tahliye edilmişti: Ayşe öğretmen altı ay sonra yeniden cezaevine girecek', *Diken*, 7 May 2018, <http://www.diken.com.tr/tahliye-edilmisti-ayse-ogretmen-alti-ay-sonra-yeniden-cezaevine-girecek/> (last accessed 28 May 2019).

'TIMELINE: What Happened in Roboski?' *Bianet English*, 31 December 2012, <https://bianet.org/english/human-rights/143200-timeline-what-happened-in-roboski> (last accessed 28 May 2019).

'Turkey deeply saddened by Uludere incident', *Anadolu Agency*, 25 May 2012.

'Turkish police detain hundreds of protesting airport workers', *Reuters*, 15 September 2018.

'Uludere Kurbanları Sivil Şehit', *NTV*, 23 March 2012, <https://www.ntv.com.tr/turkiye/uludere-kurbanlari-sivil-sehit,RZimXD3meEG1z2Y9O2NV4A> (last accessed 28 May 2019).

Yetkin, Murat, 'Analysis: Gov't ignored warnings, miners paid the bill with their lives', *Hurriyet Daily News*, 14 May 2014, <http://www.hurriyetdailynews.com/opinion/murat-yetkin/analysis-govt-ignored-warnings-miners-paid-the-bill-with-their-lives-66441> (last accessed 28 May 2019).

Yıldırım, Ebru, 'Kadın Cinayetleri Politiktir', *Bianet*, 10 July 2010, <http://bianet.org/biamag/kadin/123086-kadin-cinayetleri-politiktir> (last accessed 28 May 2019).

'Zabıta ve itfaiyeciler de gazi ve şehit sayılacak', *Milliyet*, 6 December 2016.

THREE

'They wrote history with their bodies': Necrogeopolitics, Necropolitical Spaces and the Everyday Spatial Politics of Death in Turkey

Lerna K. Yanık and Fulya Hisarlıoğlu

In this chapter, through an alternative reading of biopolitics and by way of merging the literature on necropolitics with critical geography, we develop the concepts of necrogeopolitics and necropolitical spaces. We argue that the Turkish sovereign has very little difficulty in making death and self-sacrifice a desired behaviour by spatialising necropolitical power domestically and internationally. Necrogeopolitics emerges as a discursive practice that conditions the subject to die for the geopolitical and security interests of the sovereign; necropolitical spaces, on the other hand, are both material and discursive spaces that aim for the same goal at the domestic level. Both spaces condition the subjects to believe that death should be the appropriate response if/when the state is under attack. This modification of social behaviour is engineered by the Turkish state in a very subtle, silent and everyday manner. We discuss these instances of intervention through the necrogeopoliticisation of Turkey's territorial self, as well as the specific necrospatial changes that took place in the aftermath of the 15 July 2016 coup attempt.

When on the night of 15 July 2016 the first tanks appeared on what was then called the Bosphorus Bridge, blocking the traffic flowing from the Asian side of Istanbul to the European city, most citizens of Turkey thought that this was yet another security measure taken to foil a potential terrorist attack or, perhaps, some sort of a military drill. But when the news of low-flying F-16s, coupled with gunfire inside the headquarters of the Chief of Staff in Ankara, reached various media outlets, either possibility was quickly discarded. The tanks over the bridge were the sign of a military coup led by putschist soldiers with ties to the cleric in self-imposed exile – Fethullah

Gülen. As the coup attempt unfolded, accompanied by what were unusually timed *sala* prayers (such prayers are normally reserved for calling the *umma* to gather for funerals or Friday prayers), President Erdoğan's call to the public to take to the streets and resist the putschists was duly obeyed by the people. Yet those who resisted the coup – both civilians and soldiers – were attacked by the putschist soldiers, which, according to initial counts, resulted in 246 deaths (later updated to 250) and thousands of wounded.[1] A couple of days after the coup attempt, both the civilians and soldiers who were killed while standing up to the putschists during the coup attempt were given the title of *şehit* (martyr), while the wounded were declared *gazi* (veteran), and families of the dead and those who were wounded were awarded compensation.[2] Because, according to President Recep Tayyip Erdoğan, the *şehit*s and the *gazi*s had 'written history by using their bodies as a shield against tanks, planes and bullets'.[3]

This appreciation of the dead and the wounded for resisting the coup attempt did not end here. It was followed by the creation of what we call 'necropolitical spaces', a variety of spatial changes that altered the character of public spaces in Turkey. These changes ranged from constructing '15 July Martyrs' Monuments' to renaming public landmarks such as the Bosphorus Bridge and streets or stations/stops in the public transportation network (mostly in Istanbul and Ankara) either with the date of the failed coup attempt, or after those who were killed while resisting the coup attempt.[4] The aim was, to quote the TRT, Turkey's state news channel, commenting on the opening of one such monument, 'to make sure that "heroism" would not be forgotten'.[5]

In this chapter, we argue that the creation of these necropolitical spaces possesses an intent that surpasses the rationale offered by the TRT. Rather, the necropolitical spaces that came to life after the failed coup attempt in Turkey are a testament to the sovereign's desire to declare that death is necessary for the maintenance of the state, and that death was, has been, and will remain a necessary condition that is deemed a desirable and appropriate form of behaviour. It is through the establishment of necropolitical spaces that the sovereign unleashes its necropolitical power to govern the masses and furthers the interests of the ruling elite by encouraging the masses to die for the sovereign state.

Necropolitical spaces rest at the top of a hierarchy of necropolitical power, or the 'subjugation of life to the power of death',[6] in several different ways. First, the element of everydayness pervades necropolitical spaces. As Sharp argues, 'hegemony is constructed not only through political ideologies but also, more immediately, through detailed scripting of some of the most ordinary and mundane aspects of everyday life'.[7] The sheer inescapability of these necropolitical spaces and the embedding of these spaces as the 'ordinary and the mundane', to quote Sharp, into the field of vision and within the cityscape, impose these spaces upon the daily lives of Turkish citizens whose daily routines and commutes traverse such spaces, thereby normalising such exceptional spaces as unexceptional and part of the regular landscape. Second, by conditioning the masses to die for the sovereign, the sovereign's overt 'right to kill' transforms itself into a covert 'encouragement to die'. The sovereign becomes an entity that does not kill, but one that is died for and whose subjects are encouraged to do so. Third, the 'selectivity' or 'disposability'[8] that is usually attached to necropolitical power and necropolitical boundary-making is reversed. Necropolitical spaces work to naturalise necropolitical power by celebrating death. Such 'honourable' deaths are reserved for the select few who are 'lucky' enough to serve the nation through the sacrifice of their lives. So, through the creation of necropolitical spaces in the mundaneness of the everyday, it is the act of the dying that is turned into an exception. We argue that necropolitical power in Turkey is being formed in contrast to Achille Mbembe's conceptualisation of necropolitics. In Mbembe's description of necropolitics, killing enacted by the sovereign is inflicted on the 'dehumanised other' and occurs in a space defined by the state of exception. Through our conceptualisation of necrogeopolitics and necropolitical spaces, we propose a modification to the literature on necropolitics. We argue that death is not the result of being 'other' but rather becomes a benchmark of the 'real' self and that space acts as an exceptional yet everyday conduit that works to naturalise death. Overall, necropolitical spaces communicate a covert message to citizens: namely, that making the ultimate sacrifice for the sovereign is something that only a select few can do or are entitled to do. Necropolitical spaces are spaces in which the masses are both reminded and conditioned to accept death as an everyday condition of patriotism, such that death itself becomes desirable and life is simply a burden – a necessity that one has to go through before the *real* life, which can only begin after death. Space, put differently, is a means by which the state can constitute ideal forms of citizenship that are compliant with the sovereign's security interests. Finally, this conditioning and constitution, we argue, are done in the absence of the dead body, or when burials and even cemeteries – the usual components of necropolitical power – are non-existent.

This chapter unfolds in three sections. First we present an overview of the literature concerning necropolitics and develop our concept of necropolitical spaces. Even though we began with a discussion of the necropolitical spaces that emerged from the spatial changes following the 15 July 2016 coup attempt, necropolitical spatialisation is not something new to Turkey. This shift has occurred at both the domestic and international levels. In order to examine the roots of the necropolitical spaces that formed in the aftermath of the failed coup, the second section analyses the construction of what we call 'necrogeopolitical space' that Turkey has developed at the international level over the course of the years. Necrogeopolitical space is based on the extremely securitised territorial assumptions that feed Turkish geopolitical imaginations. With the term necrogeopolitical space, we argue that the sovereign legitimates its claims to territory by making death an object of implied desire, conditioning the masses to view death as an inevitable reality through the concept of fatherland (*vatan*). Following this analysis, we turn to necropolitical spaces at the domestic level and extrapolate how such spaces came into existence to 'remind' the living that the sacrifices of a 'select few' made during the 15 July 2016 coup attempt were necessary to secure and maintain the integrity of the nation and the state. In the conclusion, we reiterate our argument and discuss the potential implications of necropolitical spaces and necrogeopolitics for the future of democracy in Turkey.

From Necropolitics to Necropolitical Spaces and Back

The emerging literature on necropolitics, or, as defined by Achille Mbembe, 'new and unique forms of social existence in which vast populations are subjected to conditions of life conferring upon them the status of living dead',[9] has mostly focused on the act of death through the sovereign's right to kill.[10] This categorisation includes the sovereign's means of death (such as drones)[11] and post-death related practices (such as funeral processions, commemorations, burials and reburials) and spaces (such as cemeteries) as the major building blocks of the sovereign's exercise of its necropolitical power.[12] In all instances, the sovereign's necropolitical power is made omnipresent through the body of the dead and the living. But is it possible for the sovereign to maintain its necropolitical power over the living beyond the dead body or beyond the cemeteries by exercising such power in an everyday manner?

The ultimate focus of this study is to develop an alternative understanding of necropolitical power that operates beyond the 'political lives of dead bodies'[13] that 'have barely been extended beyond the living' through space.[14] Based on the existing literature on necropolitics, we introduce a conceptual toolkit that consists of modern practices of necropolitical control; namely, forms of inclusion/exclusion and boundary-making that support our argument concerning necrogeopolitics and necropolitical spaces.

In her seminal study entitled *Precarious Life*, Judith Butler claims that an obituary –the public announcement and notice of death – is an act of nation-building.[15] The notification of death is a form of necropolitical recognition and inclusion, a discursive realisation that some lives deserve mourning because they are worthy parts of the collective body of the nation. Thus the 'selective mourning for the death'[16] is a post-mortem necropolitical boundary-making practice that discursively dissociates the 'loyal subject' from the 'other'. Butler argues that the extensive reporting that emerged concerning the last minutes of the lives of the victims of 9/11 not only establishes a bond between victim –individual body – and the survivor – collective body – but that it also humanises the victim by nominalisation, inclusion and remembrance.[17] In this context, noticing and remembering the bodily existence of a loyal subject as the average citizen structures the political-normative ground that recognises some lives as more vulnerable than others.[18] From the perspective of the sovereign, the vulnerable subject is a figure whose ontological existence and corporeality can justly be expelled from society. According to this necropolitical imaginary, the putative subject's vulnerability is not a concern, since their bodily and social existence is vindicated. Far from espousing a humanist and ethical perception of the subject, the sovereign articulates and justifies hierarchies of vulnerabilities as a means of necropolitical power projection through its biopolitical control over life and death.

This (de)humanising discourse on vulnerability is a symbolic communicative practice consolidating the norm-making character of the sovereign. Based on Giorgio Agamben's notion of the sovereign as the exception and norm-maker,[19] Mbembe discusses how asymmetries of power structure the actual and political death of the 'Other'. To put it differently, 'power (and not necessarily state power) continuously refers and appeals to exception, emergency, and a fictionalised notion of the enemy'.[20] At the domestic level, dead bodies are strategically and hierarchically categorised by inclusionary and/or exclusionary discourses that draw the boundaries of both citizenship and the nation-state, thus re-energising the authority of the sovereign.

Necropolitical boundary-making goes hand in hand with necropolitical remembrance and identity politics. 'The core meaning of any individual or group identity, namely a sense of sameness over time and space, is sustained by remembering; and what is remembered is defined by the assumed identity.'[21] Based on this constructivist assumption, national identity is an institutionalised form of the 'lies of the old man'[22] combined with repetitive narratives about the past becoming a tradition.[23] Necropolitical communication over dead bodies provides political elites with a convenient political order in which national identity and collective memory are constantly being reconstructed. The dead body with its symbolic function is more than a physical object. 'A body's materiality can be critical to its symbolic efficacy: unlike notions such as "patriotism" or "civil society", for instance, a corpse can be moved around, displayed, and strategically located in specific places.'[24] Although corpses cannot speak for themselves, they do have agency. They communicate the messages and expectations of the sovereign to the subjects who outlive them.

In this sense burial and reburial ceremonies are more spectacular ways of communicating this message in which the politics of remembering and forgetting are (re)articulated by repeated narratives about the death of a loyal subject, a war hero or a founding father.[25] Verdery in her study on necromobility argues that the reburial of Hungarian Prime Minister Imre Nagy, who was executed and buried in an unmarked grave by the Soviet regime, represents Hungary's break with state socialism and transition to democracy in post-communist Hungary.[26] In the same vein, Young and Light study the mobility of the corpse of Petru Groza, the contested political leader of Romania, and illustrate how post-communist Romania necropolitically co-opted Groza's body.[27] Both examples illustrate how necropolitical boundary-making occurs through selective remembering and forgetting that operates to reframe post-Soviet foreign policy and its democratic transitions. Parallel to these examples, Carney discusses how hundreds of Turkish soldiers entered Syria in order to transfer the tomb of Suleiman Shah – the grandfather of the founding father of the Ottoman Empire (Osman I), who died in the thirteenth century – in the middle of the Syrian civil war. For Carney, the government's decision to move the remains of a symbolic historical figure, on the eve of local elections, is a necropolitical performance in which the neo-Ottomanist political agenda of the political elites dovetails with the government's interest in the tomb of a long-dead war hero.[28]

The hyper-nominalisation[29] and politicisation of the dead body of a martyr have a special place in necropolitical boundary-making. The discourse on martyrdom for a sacred and higher purpose creates an alternative necropolitical reality. In this logic of self-sacrifice 'the body duplicates itself and, in death, literally and metaphorically escapes the state of siege and occupation'.[30] Accordingly, the predominant motivation for martyrdom is the individual's claim and will to attain eternity through weaponising their body.[31] Here, the central focus is not the sovereign's right and power to kill but the individual subject's willingness and commitment to sacrificing their life for a sacred higher cause coequal with the protection of the national collective body. Although the individual body of the dead departs from this life, the soul survives if the collective body of the nation remains intact.

According to its religious version, to become a martyr is to attain a supreme level of spiritual awareness reinforced by one's full commitment to God. Raja, in his study examining the Muslim imagery of martyrdom, conceptualises the term as 'a special death or more precisely, a "non" death'.[32] In religious discourse this special form of death offers individuals eternal rewards including 'the continuance of a martyr's life after death (a master of time), their place of glory in the eyes of God and the rewards of their sacrifice for their loved ones'.[33] To Değirmencioğlu, this religious-political framing of martyrdom serves to reinforce its image as a sacred and special duty that can only be performed by a handful of privileged people who are rewarded with post-mortem advantages. Such a conceptualisation of the martyr thus creates an alternative image of death that extends beyond the finality implied by the corpse. Through the commemorative vigilance of the political elites, self-sacrifice for the nation (death) becomes a *desideratum* for every loyal subject.[34]

Although martyrdom is originally a religious concept, it has been utilised by a range of political elites in the service of emerging nation-states since the early nineteenth century.[35] From a biopolitical/necropolitical perspective, martyrdom operates in a way that frames the individual's sacrifice for the nation as a natural and instinctual characteristic of the common citizen. Death for what is deemed a sacred cause – defense of the nation – is projected as the duty of every citizen who takes part in a social contract established with the sovereign, thus normalising its occurence. The corporeality of the dead body of a war hero, accompanied by society's affection and gratitude, is instrumentalised by the nation-state to stimulate national honour and a sense of belonging. Through several spatial and narrative arrangements, the political lives of martyrs continue to serve the nation-state. The hyper-nominalisation of the martyr and the spectacular memorial gatherings dedicated to martyrs are reinforced by narratives that detail the post-human characteristics of war heroes[36] as well as their honourable sacrifice for the sovereign, all of which works to maintain the integrity of the national body. Değirmencioğlu argues that martyrdom is depicted as a transcendental struggle for the nation, homeland, freedom, humanity and peace in the Turkish context.[37] To him, martyrs symbolise the honour and dignity of the Turkish people who have been waging a war against injustice and oppression for centuries. Thus, the eternal body of the martyr functions to construct a transcendental notion of Turkishness as well as to depict the Turkish nation as a credible moral power that effectively rescues the oppressed citizenry.

The specific sites of memory – necropolitical spaces – reserved for martyrs and commemorative innovations representing their eternity energise the necropolitical discourse on martyrdom. As Pierre Nora underlines, these sites are not a natural part of the landscape; instead, they have to be designed in a way that tells the 'official' and thus fabricated and distorted representation of the past.[38] Therefore, sites of memory reflect a cultural and political hegemony that make particular collectivities by erasing alternative ones.[39] Savage argues that this new spatial awareness, reflecting cultural hegemony, started in the late nineteenth century in order to nationalise memory by inscribing it on the landscape itself.[40] To him, monuments, especially those exhibiting national(ised) characteristics, serve to anchor collective memory and national identity. Monuments heroising soldiers have spread sporadically throughout Europe in the post-World War I era and served as forms of national boundary-making. The figure of the war hero 'who is always erect and unwounded' represents the 'image of bodily continuity that seeks to displace and overcome the memory of the bodies violated and destroyed'.[41] Thus the exhausted but victorious posture of the unknown war hero and their forward-looking gaze are parts of a spatialised necropolitical communicative strategy. This strategy aims to move beyond mere expressions of respect and gratitude and actively works to shape the character of national boundaries. Laqueur also considers World War I as an important turning point for the emergence of necropolitical sites of mourning. He underlines that with the establishment of the British Grave Registration Commission, mass war graves, decorated with uniform scripts and stones, were built to nationalise mourning practices. These places that commemorate the war also institutionalise its memory and remind visitors that the body in the symbolic or actual grave 'may belong to me'.[42] Thus modern memorials are designed to involve their visitors as participants in the construction of reality.

Turkey's necrogeopolitics at the international level and necropolitical spaces at the domestic level, especially the spatial changes that took place after the 15 July 2016 coup attempt, show how citizens as subjects become an active part of constructed reality – a spatial reality that encourages and normalises the death of the subject for the sovereign in an everyday manner. What is more, the everydayness of necropolitical space invests the sovereign's necropolitical power with an omnipresence that extends itself over the bodies of the living and the dead, even when the latter are long gone and out of sight. Put differently, necropolitical spaces expand the reach of the sovereign's necropolitical power and condition the masses for death. Beyond cemeteries and funerary practices, necropolitical spaces in the form of domestic monuments and daily infrastructure exist in conjunction with broader necrogeopolitical spaces.

Turkey's Necrogeopolitical Power

The creation and the production of necropolitical spaces or using space for political ends is not a novelty for Turkish politics. As any critical geographer would argue, space is political, and more so in Turkey. Space, or how it is governed – both discursively and materially – has been an integral part of the ways in which politics has been conducted in contemporary Turkey. Through the production and the reproduction of space, Turkish politicians and bureaucrats are able to govern masses, shape public opinion and justify their policy decisions. For example, while early republican architecture was an ideological tool employed in the Kemalist period to show Turkey's modern face,[43] the so-called neo-Ottomanist architecture has left the ideological imprint of the AKP's neo-Ottomanist, neo-Islamist ideology throughout Turkey.[44] Again at the domestic level, renaming urban and rural spaces has been a common practice since the early days of the Republic. In order to consolidate power and realise the full Turkification of modern Turkey, the state has renamed villages, cities, streets and even regions in order to erase the 'Other' – the non-Muslims, the Kurds and the Ottoman Empire – not only physically but discursively as well.[45] Renaming cities, villages and localities was a powerful tool for Muslim Turks to ensure that they could emerge as the real owners of these territories.[46] More recently, however, after the victory of pro-Kurdish parties in municipal government elections, a variety of localities and street names were re-Kurdified in eastern Turkey, thus repeatedly making space both a scene and a means of counter-hegemony.[47]

Internationally, the renaming practices of the space that Turkey occupies on the world map have been subtler. Given the difficulty of changing international names, the Turkish state has used metaphors or analogies that redefine Turkey and its surrounding territories. For example, one such choice was when Turkey's politicians metaphorically likened Turkey's territory to a 'bridge.' In order to be able to make a case for its strategic value and thus to increase its allure to the West, Turkey's politicians started portraying Turkey as a 'bridge' between the East and the West, the Middle East and Europe, and finally between Christianity and Islam, both textually and visually.[48] The bridge metaphor was so useful that it found resonance beyond Turkey's politicians and became embedded in the everyday as well.[49] The 'bridge' metaphor was not the only such attribute associated with Turkey. One other less frequently used metaphor likened Turkey to an 'island of stability.'[50] This analogy of an 'island of stability' implied that Turkey is surrounded by instability, and yet possesses the superiority that enables it to survive amidst such chaos. Hence, Turkey's neighbours are automatically relegated to an inferior status while Turkey becomes elevated to a superior status by way of implication.

In addition to exalting the country's strategic value with such positive metaphors, Turkey's politicians used metaphors that perpetuated the debasement of neighbouring regions. The Middle East, for example, was likened to a 'swamp'.[51] Especially after the 1960s, as a result of the Arab-Israeli conflict in the Middle East, Turkey's politicians preferred to have limited engagement with several countries in the region. After all, as Benli Altunışık argues, 'the Middle East represented what Turkey was and not what Turkey wanted to be.'[52] The message that underlay the 'swamp' metaphor was quite clear: 'let's not get drawn into these unending conflicts in the Middle East, for like a swamp it will suck us down and kill us'. Overall, geopolitically, the space that Turkey occupied was imagined to be a versatile and multipurpose one. By associating a neighbouring region with death, Turkey's politicians were indeed creating geopolitical pockets of necropolitical spaces to justify their foreign policy goals and decisions.

The designation of the Middle East as a 'swamp' and thus as a necropolitical space would have multiple consequences during the Justice and Development Party (AKP) period. The AKP, without paying sufficient detail to the nuances that took place in Turkey's engagement with the region before it came to power, would collapse the pre-AKP period into a uniform narrative and accuse the Kemalist regime of utter disengagement from the region. In parallel, the 'swamp' metaphor was replaced with metaphors such as 'backyard' and, as the grand strategist of the AKP, Davutoğlu, put it, the Middle East was destined to become Turkey's 'hinterland'.[53] All in all, this metaphorical spatial (re)production was executed in a schizophrenic manner. In some cases, the space that Turkey occupied was elevated to a superior status vis-à-vis its neighbours through a set of positive metaphors. Yet, at other times, Turkey's spatial self was equated with danger and death, making Turkey the perfect example of necrogeopolitics.

The concept of fatherland (*vatan*) plays a crucial role in the construction of this Turkish necrogeopolitical discourse. Partly as a result of Turkey's militaristic culture and partly as a result of its political worldview, embedded in the rhetoric of 'fatherland first' (*önce vatan*) or 'so there can be fatherland' (*vatan sağolsun*), the Turkish fatherland has been narrated as a place that supplants everything of political importance, including human life. This rhetoric is coupled with a siege mentality or the 'Sèvres Syndrome' concept, which argues that Turkey is surrounded by external enemies that are collaborating with its internal ones with the intent to divide Turkey into pieces. This perspective not only normalises a sense that there is a perpetual state of emergency, but also quells dissent that might question the

Figure 3.1 'Önce Vatan' on the outskirts of Diyarbakır. (Source: Lerna K. Yanık.)

legitimacy and validity of the claims made by those who run Turkey.[54] After all, as Bilgin has argued, highlighting geopolitical exigencies has become one of the most important excuses for those who have governed Turkey for many years, slowing down or curbing the democratisation of the country.[55] As can be seen in Figure 3.1, it is very common to write the slogan 'fatherland first' (*önce vatan*) on the barren hills of Turkey, but more so in the Kurdish populated areas of eastern Turkey.[56] The fatherland, therefore, is a concept that seeks to perpetuate the notion that inhabitants of Turkey should sacrifice themselves without question. It is, in other words, the spatialisation of necropolitical power geopolitically, or, a form of necrogeopolitics par excellence.

Furthermore, in combination with the concept of fatherland, the concepts of 'martyrdom' and 'blood' further intensify the necrogeopoliticisation of Turkey and, as the Değrimencioğlu volume shows, combining the elements of fatherland, blood and martyrdom is hardly new. Just to cite one example, the full version of the Turkish national anthem written by Mehmet Akif Ersoy contains two stanzas[57] that (in very rough translation) say that 'Turkish soil is unlike any other soil because Turks are sons of martyrs ... and if one squeezes Turkish soil nothing but martyrs' blood would come out.' However, since the 1980s, and even more so in the AKP period, these themes of fatherland, martyrdom and blood have not only become more frequently invoked by the ruling elite but have also become everyday themes for other strata of the society as well.[58] For example, President Erdoğan frequently refers in his speeches to two lines of a poem written by Mithat Cemal Kuntay that says 'what makes a flag a flag is the blood on it; earth can only become a fatherland (*vatan*) when there are those willing to die for it'.[59] In 2008, this analogy was adopted by a group of high school students who sent a Turkish flag made of their blood to then Chief of Staff Yaşar Büyükanıt.[60]

Overall, necrogeopolitics, or the spatialisation of necropolitical power geopolitically, works in a perverted way in Turkey. At certain times, Turkey is presented as a country that is an object of desire and envy amidst a 'rough and rowdy neighbourhood'. In these instances, Turkey is portrayed as a secure territory that harbours the potential to be coveted by its neighbours that are themselves hotbeds of death and instability. At other times, Turkey is presented as surrounded by insecurity. Though Turkey's rulers exploit Turkey's spatiality to offer two contradictory messages, these messages both convey a single conclusion; namely, that Turkey's territory is a source of envy that necessitates that Turkish subjects should be willing to die for this space. This was exactly the underlying message that propelled the spatial changes or the formation of necropolitical spaces that took place throughout Turkey in the wake of the 15 July coup – with one difference, however: the everydayness embedded in the necropolitical spaces not only repeatedly produces necropolitical boundary markings but also operates subconsciously to bring about the active participation of the subjects in the sovereign's message.

Everyday Spatialisation of Necropolitical Power

The formation of *necropolitical spaces* around Turkey in the aftermath of 15 July happened in two different ways. First, street names and station names in the public transport network and several important landmarks were renamed. Second, monuments were constructed around Turkey and named after the date of the failed coup. In the first case, the names of the people – the 'martyrs' – who were killed during the attempted coup were given to streets, parks and stations within the public transport network, with a martyr (*şehit*) prefix before their names. Alternatively, the date '15 July' was given to a variety of landmarks, mostly in Istanbul and Ankara, and in other cities around Turkey as well. In Nevşehir, for example, not only were the streets given the names of 'martyrs', but, in addition, these acts of renaming were accompanied by plaques that detailed how a specific subject 'became a martyr' – something which the state-owned news agency, Anadolu Ajansı, evaluated as '15 July Martyrs' Names are Being Immortalised'.[61] Almost every city in Turkey devoted a monument to the 'martyrs' of the coup, so as to 'immortalise their memory', to quote the pro-government newspaper *Sabah*.[62] In Balıkesir, for example, the mayor of the city prided himself on erecting the first such monument in the country. The mayor Zekai Kafoğlu stated that 'we are saying that we will not forget and we will not let it be forgotten, and how are we going to do this? We are going to erect monuments and statues, we are going to name institutions after our Martyrs of 15 July.'[63]

Interestingly enough, 'martyrdom' was not the only adjective that accompanied the date of 15 July. A variety of concepts were associated with the date of the coup attempt including 'democracy' and 'national will'. The subliminal message that was given by equating these concepts with 'martyrdom' was that 'martyrdom' was the price that needed to be paid for democracy and national will. This message was possible because Turkish politicians and bureaucrats (re)narrativised the coup as not simply an attempt to topple the government, but, rather, as an 'invasion' of the fatherland by traitors[64] trying to 'redesign the region and world politics'.[65] Thus, the narrative about those who were killed 'resisting' the coup attempt was reimagined as those 'martyred' while 'saving the fatherland', allowing one to 'feel both sorrow and pride' for them, to quote President Erdoğan, who spoke on the second anniversary of the coup attempt.[66]

The spatial end result of countering the coup attempt with 'martyrdom', but also with 'democracy' and 'national will', was a frenzy of renaming major landmarks mostly in Istanbul and Ankara and in greater Turkey as well. The intercity coach station in Esenler, Istanbul, for instance, was renamed as 'Istanbul 15 Temmuz Demokrasi Otogarı' (Istanbul 15 July Democracy Coach Station); Kısıklı Square near President Erdoğan's private residence in Istanbul, where people also gathered on the night of the coup attempt, was renamed as 'Milli İrade Meydanı' (National Will Square).[67] Similarly, in Ankara, several different places were renamed: the well known Kızılay Square was renamed '15 Temmuz Kızılay Milli İrade Meydanı' (15 July Kızılay National Will Square); the street in front of the Headquarters of the Chief of Staff where the highest number of deaths in Ankara occurred was renamed '15 Temmuz Şehitler Kavşağı' (15 July Martyrs' Cross) and the name of Ömer Halisdemir, who was a member of the Turkish Armed Forces killed by putschist soldiers while resisting the coup (and who, according to the 'official' narrative, played a crucial role in the failure of the coup), was given to a street that previously carried the name of another soldier, İrfan Baştuğ – one of the key players in the 1960 military coup.[68] Even the newsroom of the state TV channel TRT, where the putschists made their live coup declaration, was renamed '15 Temmuz Millet Stüdyosu' (15 July Nation Studio).⁶⁹ The message that can be derived from the equation of the date of the coup attempt with 'democracy', the 'national will' and the 'immortalisation of the martyrs' is that in order to celebrate 'democracy' and the 'national will', it is the duty of the sovereign's subjects to become 'martyrs'. Only then can one be truly immortalised. Thus death and life become interchangeable with one another. The sovereign sends the message to its subjects that life after death is more worthy than life itself.

The most prominent and symbolic renaming in the creation of necropolitical space was that of the Bosphorus Bridge. The bridge was renamed as 15 Temmuz Şehitler Köprüsü (15 July Martyrs' Bridge) because the Asian side entrance of the bridge was the site of the killing of thirty-four civilians by putschist soldiers. For many years, the Bosphorus Bridge had been the symbol of Istanbul as a city that connected East and West and of Turkey as a country that connected Europe and Asia. The fact that it was renamed within ten days of the coup attempt was an official cabinet decision.⁷⁰ But what topped even that decision was the creation of a monumental complex named Şehitler Makamı (roughly translated as The Martyrs' Respected Post [hereafter MRP], as there is no one English phrase that corresponds to the word 'makam', which signifies a respected position of higher authority). This monumental complex is worthy of discussion because of its complexity and everydayness.⁷¹

MRP is a complex, complete with a monument, a museum, a mosque and a park named Şehitler Parkı (Martyrs' Park). While President Erdoğan officially opened the monument on the second anniversary of the coup attempt, the mosque and the museum were still being constructed at the time of writing. Those who would like to visit the monumental complex have to get off at the metrobus stop renamed '15 July Martyrs' Bridge' where the passengers on board the metrobus are reminded that 'those who would like to visit MRP should get off' via an automated voice system.

This monumental complex is exemplary of the spatialisation of necropolitical power, starting with the way that it was named. Şehitler Makamı (The Martyrs' Respected Post) is a name that, by default, contains an element of respect and deference to the martyrs by elevating them to a position of authority. Second, the semi-spherical shaped monument is strategically positioned just above one of Istanbul's major highways. Though the monument is not atop a hill, it is still situated in a way that enables its visitors to have an all-encompassing view of the Bridge, the European side of Istanbul and its surrounding areas. Overall, even if one were to miss the frequent signposts marking the direction towards the MRP erected all the way from Beşiktaş to the Asian side entrance of the 15 July Martyrs' Bridge, once in proximity to the Asian side of the Bridge, one cannot miss the monument

Figure 3.2 A view from the MRP Complex: path lined with cypress trees and the dome-shaped monument at the end. (Source: Lerna K. Yanık.)

because of its sheer magnitude and highly visible location. Put differently, the everydayness of the monument (and thus its message) stems from its embedded position within the cityscape. With such positioning and visibility, one cannot escape being reminded of the coup attempt and the people who were killed because the monument and its surroundings are a part of the daily commutes of Istanbulites. The renaming of the bridge, the bus stop near it and the new monument are all silent, everyday reminders of the coup attempt, urging the public to martyr themselves in order to sustain the sovereign.

While the strategic positioning of this landmark ensures the everydayness of the monumental complex, the design details further intensify the necropolitical message of the sovereign. For example, the names of the 250 'martyrs' (even those that did not die near the area where the monument is constructed) inscribed on the inner walls of the MRP are accompanied with verses from the Qur'an praising martyrdom. The *sala* prayers that are recited twenty-four hours a day and the fountain inside the dome-shaped monument add an element of serenity to the environment. Visitors to this monument are bombarded with the message that if such an act is ever repeated again, they will need to sacrifice themselves just as the 250 'martyrs' did that night. Martyrdom is the only way to ensure that their name will be inscribed and revered for protecting the sanctity of the state in service of the national will, thus reaching serenity in the afterlife.

Figure 3.3 Fountain and martyrs' names inscribed on the wall inside the dome. (Source: Lerna K. Yanık.)

Figure 3.4 Skyline and verses from the Qur'an as seen from inside the dome. (Source: Lerna K. Yanık.)

The architect of the monument, Hilmi Şenalp, interpreted these details of the monument to the pro-government *Sabah* newspaper as follows:

> The dome, in its totality, represents the universe and eternity; it means in reality that martyrs are not dead, they have been granted divine blessing along with an eternal life. The arms that are formed of stripes and that hold the transparent dome, show the nation's unity (*milli birlik*) and the unison (*beraberlik*) against the (coup) attempt.[72]

This 'national unity' is an important symbolic theme that is repeated throughout 15 July monuments elsewhere in Turkey.[73] Necropolitical boundary-making is very much at work in this 'national unity' insofar as 'national unity' is owed to the martyrs who were 'chosen' to prevent the 'invasion of the fatherland' (*vatan*). According to the then mayor of the Greater Municipality of Istanbul, Kadir Topbaş, martyrs 'were chosen people'.[74] Linking the necrogeopolitics of Turkey with this necropolitical space, through the concept of fatherland (*vatan*), he argued:

> There are so many different stories . . . . It is because of these heroes that we are still here today and our flag is still flying. The Republic of Turkey will live forever and we, as a nation, will walk towards the future in unity. We remember these heroes with benevolence and want them never to be forgotten.'[75]

Finally, despite its spherical shape intended to symbolise national unity, the monument also exhibits a series of pentagon-shaped connections which give the impression of a hybrid post-modern mausoleum, imparting upon it a sense of cemetery with a considerable degree of sanctity. The dome looks like a shrine that incorporates the architectural elements of the Seljukid kümbet-style and Ottoman türbe-style tombs, where one expects to find the grave of a sultan or other highly respected religious person.

Yet the monument is not wholly emblematic of either style, because there are no bodies buried at the complex. This concept of a burial ground devoid of bodies can also be found in the way that the Marytrs' Park around the monument is designed. This park is envisioned as a virtual cemetery or burial ground where each of the 250 'martyrs' is represented with a plate bearing their names alongside a cypress tree and a rose. The calligrapher Hüseyin Kutlu, who decorated the inner walls of the monument with verses from the Qur'an, explains the choice of the cypress tree and rose for the garden: 'Cypress tree means *elif* (the first letter of the Arabic alphabet), *elif* is the symbol of Allah's name and it means Tevhid, i.e., unity. The roses represent our Prophet.'[76] While the metal plates substitute for graves, the cypress trees and roses are traditional landscaping elements drawn from the cemeteries of Turkey. What is more, the metal plates also include a QR code that when scanned by a mobile device reveals the biography of the 'martyr' and how, when, and where they were 'martyred'. By using QR codes, a virtual yet interactive cemetery is created, thus actively engaging the visitors.

Google Maps imparts the final touch of virtual sanctity to the monumental complex. When one Googles the MRP, one encounters several things: directions to the site, a photo from the complex, a map detailing its location and a brief description of the site – 'a sacred place in Istanbul'. In this way, the MRP is endowed with a virtual sanctity that nourishes the necrogeopolitics of Turkey and further adds to the everydayness of the monument and its message. Overall, the MRP reshapes our regular understanding of necropolitics by showing that necropolitical power is not solely dependent upon killing, but that it can also operate through the cultivation of necropolitical spaces that use both physical and virtual means to memorialise the dead even in the absence of dead bodies and in an everyday manner.

Conclusion

Mbembe has argued that 'under the conditions of necropower, the lines between resistance and suicide, sacrifice and redemption, martyrdom and freedom are blurred'.[77] Mbembe's argument is to a large extent verified by Turkey's relationship to sacrifice as an integral part of its politics and the ongoing substitution of freedom and democracy with martyrdom and resistance with death. In this chapter we highlighted the necrospatial changes that have taken place in the aftermath of the failed coup attempt in 2016, exemplified by the renaming practices throughout Turkey. We focused on a particular monument – the MRP – in Istanbul, connecting it to the already existing necrogeopolitical discourse in Turkey that necessitates the death of the subjects for the survival of the fatherland. It is through such necropolitical spaces in differing scales that the Turkish sovereign has been empowered to make death and self-sacrifice a desired behaviour even in the absence of dead bodies or cemeteries. In this way, necropolitical spaces become not only about those who have died in the (near or distant) past, but also about those living in the present, enmeshed in the 'now' of a politics that provokes them to consider their future as potential martyrs. What is more, as the case of Turkey shows, this power is exercised in a subtle, silent, ordinary and hence, everyday manner. With this everydayness, and through the spatial practices in Turkey, the sovereign makes its subjects believe that it is possible to 'write history with their own bodies' and to reach 'democracy' and express the 'national will' –as defined by the sovereign – at the same time. Death is not something that belongs to the 'Other', as is the case with a more traditional understanding of necropolitics. Rather death becomes the one and only condition to become 'oneself', shifting our understanding of necropolitical boundary-making.

In this process of becoming the 'Self', changing (necro)geopolitical imagination(s) of the region, the Turkish fatherland and the discourse on martyrdom play an important role in necropolitical boundary-making. The long-term cartographic anxieties and ontological concerns of the nation are reflected through the necropolitical spatialisation of the Turkish homeland and its neighbourhood. This spatialised necropower also operates at the international level and has been instrumentalised by political elites to justify the pre-set principles, traditions, goals and practices of foreign policy.

The discourse on martyrdom and the process of hyper-nominalising martyrs through spatial arrangements, such as the MRP and other spatialisation practices, reminds the public of the 15 July coup attempt and acts as a subtle yet everyday mode of necropolitical communication between the state and the subject. As this chapter shows, the coup attempt is a critical juncture not only for the overall state of politics in Turkey, but also for its necropolitical discursive, material and spatial inventions. The post-mortem commemorative performances, spectacular forms of memorialisation, and, more importantly, necrospatial arrangements have enriched the necropolitical agenda and representational practices of Turkey's political elites. In deconstructing these spatialised practices, our chapter offers an alternative reading of current scholarship by bringing together the literatures on biopolitics, necropolitics and critical geography. This alternative conceptual framework allows us to read the operation of power through necropolitical spaces and post-mortem figurative meaning-making practices not only in Turkey but for every state that constitutes its ideal forms of citizenship that are compliant with its security interests through the everyday spatial politics of death.

Notes

1. This number does not include the putschists' deaths. For a timeline of the coup in a brochure prepared by the Office of the President of Turkey, please see Ali Osman Mert, *15 July Coup Attempt and the Parallel State Structure 2016*.
2. 'İşte Şehit ve Gazilere Verilecek Haklar', *Sözcü*, 17 August 2016.
3. Recep Tayyip Erdoğan, 'Türkiye, 15 Temmuz Gecesi Tüm Farklılıklarını Geride Bırakarak Birleşti'.
4. Hacı Bişkin, '15 Temmuz Sonrası Nerelerin Adı Değişti?'
5. 'Saraçhane 15 Temmuz Anıtı Açıldı'.
6. Achille Mbembe, 'Necropolitics', p. 39.
7. Joanne P. Sharp, *Condensing the Cold War*, p. 31.
8. Henry A. Giroux, 'Reading Hurricane Katrina', p. 175.
9. Mbembe, 'Necropolitics', p. 40.
10. Ibid.
11. Jamie Allinson, 'The Necropolitics of Drones'.
12. Judith Butler, *Precarious Life*; Banu Bargu, *Starve and Immolate*; Eylül Fidan Akıncı, 'Sacred Children, Accursed Mothers'.
13. Katherine Verdery, *Political Lives of Dead Bodies*.
14. Craig Young and Duncan Light, 'Corpses, dead body politics', p. 136.
15. Butler, *Precarious Life*, p. 34.
16. Bargu, 'Another Necropolitics', p. 7.
17. Butler, *Precarious Life*, p. 38.
18. Bargu, 'Another Necropolitics'.

19. Giorgio Agamben, *Homo Sacer*, pp. 15–25.
20. Mbembe, 'Necropolitics', p. 16.
21. John R. Gillis, *Commemorations*, p. 3.
22. Thomas W. Laqueur, 'Memory and Naming', p. 160.
23. Edward Said, 'Invention, Memory, and Place'.
24. Verdery, *Political Lives of Dead Bodies*, p. 27.
25. Young and Light, 'Corpses, dead body politics', p. 140.
26. Verdery, *Political Lives of Dead Bodies*, p. 29.
27. Young and Light, 'Corpses, dead body politics'.
28. Carney, 'Resur(e)recting a Spectacular Hero'.
29. Laqueur, 'Memory and Naming', p. 160.
30. Mbembe, 'Necropolitics', p. 37.
31. Bargu, *Starve and Immolate*.
32. Masoof Ashraf Raja, 'Death as a Form of Becoming', p. 12.
33. Ibid. p. 13.
34. Serdar Değirmencioğlu, *Öl Dediler Öldüm*.
35. Bircan Düzcan, 'Çanakkale İçinde Kurdular Beni'.
36. Ibid.; E. Zeynep Güler, 'Bir Ulusal Hafıza Mekanı Olarak Gelibolu Yarımadası'.
37. Değirmencioğlu, *Öl Dediler Öldüm*, p. 180.
38. Pierre Nora, 'Between Memory and History'.
39. Gillis, *Commemorations*; Benjamin Forest and Juliet Johnson, 'Unraveling the Threads of History'.
40. Kirk Savage, 'Politics of Memory'.
41. Ibid. p. 131.
42. Laqueur, 'Memory and Naming', p. 157.
43. Sibel Bozdoğan, 'The Predicament of Modernism in Turkish Architectural Culture: An Overview', pp. 133–40.
44. Jeremy Walton, 'Practices of Neo-Ottomanism'; 'AKP'nin Osmanlı Mimarisiyle İmtihanı'; 'Kamuda Neo-Osmanlı Modası'; 'Ankara'nın Kimlik Bunalımı'.
45. Joost Jongerden, 'Crafting Space, Making People'; Kerem Öktem, 'The Nation's Imprint'.
46. Sezgi Durgun, *Memaik-i Şahane'den Vatan'a*, p. 214.
47. Jongerden, 'Crafting Space, Making People'; Öktem, 'The Nation's Imprint'.
48. Lerna K. Yanık, 'The Metamorphosis of Metaphors of Vision'; Lerna K. Yanık, 'Of Celebrities and Landmarks'; Lerna K. Yanık, 'Constructing Turkish "Exceptionalism"'.
49. Çağrı Yalkın and Lerna K. Yanık, 'Entrenching Geopolitical Imaginations'.
50. See for example, Süleyman Demirel, '1995 Yılının Gelişmeleri ve 1996 Yılı Hedefleri, 20 Ocak 1996', p. 297; Ahmet Davutoğlu, 'Türkiye Bölgenin İstikrar Adası'; Numan Kurtulmuş, 'Türkiye Bölgede Bir İstikrar Adası'.
51. Mufti Malik, 'From Swamp to Backyard', pp. 81, 93.
52. Benli Altunışık, 'Worldviews and Turkish Foreign Policy in the Middle East', p. 175.
53. Davutoğlu, *Stratejik Derinlik*, p. 129.

54. Behlül Özkan, *From the Abode of Islam to the Turkish Vatan*, pp. 9, 11.
55. Pınar Bilgin, 'Only Strong States Can Survive in Turkey's Geography'.
56. Ibid. p. 8.
57. These two stanzas are: 'Bastığın yerleri 'toprak' diyerek geçme, tanı! Düşün, altında binlerce kefensiz yatanı. Sen şehit oğlusun, incitme, yazıktır atanı; Verme, dünyaları alsan da bu cennet vatanı'. 'Kim bu cennet vatanın uğruna olmaz ki feda? Şüheda fışkıracak toprağı sıksan, şüheda! Canı, cananı, bütün varımı alsın da Hüda, Etmesin tek vatanımdan beni dünyada cüda'.
58. See for example Düzcan, 'Çanakkale İçinde Kurdular Beni'.
59. Metin Münir, 'Bayrakları Bayrak Yapan Nedir Usta'.
60. Düzcan, 'Çanakkale İçinde Kurdular Beni', p. 119.
61. '"15 Temmuz" Şehitlerinin İsimleri Ölümsüzleşiyor'.
62. Y. E. Kavak, 'Türkiye'nin 15 Temmuz Anıtları'.
63. '15 Temmuz Şehitler Anıtı Yeniden Düzenlendi'.
64. See for example the statements of the Prime Minister Binali Yıldırım, 'Başbakan Yıldırım'dan 15 Temmuz Mesajı: Milli İradeyi Hiçe Sayan Gafiller, Hak Ettikleri Cevabı Almışlardır'; 'Başkan Erdoğan Sabah İçin Kaleme Aldı: 15 Temmuz Ruhu Hiç Sönmeyecek'.
65. 'Saraçhane 15 Temmuz Anıtı Açıldı'.
66. '15 Temmuz, Türk Milleti'nin Yeniden Dirilişinin ve Şahlanışının Adıdır'.
67. Bişkin, '15 Temmuz Sonrası Nerelerin Adı Değişiti?'
68. 'Kızılay Meydanı'nın İsmi "15 Temmuz Kızılay Milli İrade Meydanı" oldu'.
69. 'Darbecilerin Dokunduğu Yerin Adı Değişiyor'.
70. 'Boğaziçi Köprüsü'nin Adı Değişti, İşte Yeni İsmi'.
71. There are several necropolitical spaces devoted to 15 July in Istanbul: in Saraçhane, above the hills of Ortaköy overseeing the European side of the '15 July Martyrs Bridge', and two different forests were created for 15 July martyrs. See for example, 'Saraçhane 15 Temmuz Anıtı Açıldı'.
72. 'İşte Türkiye'nin 15 Temmuz Anıtları'.
73. The monument built in Ankara to commemorate the 15 July coup attempt is described as a 'monument that would consolidate feelings of national unity and unison (*milli billik ve beraberlik*); aims simultaneously to transmit and to represent the one nation, one flag, one vatan and one state feeling to next generations'; see for example, 'İşte Türkiye'nin 15 Temmuz Anıtları'.
74. 'Başkan Topbaş '15 Temmuz Şehitler Abidesi'ni İnceledi'.
75. Ibid.
76. İşte Türkiye'nin 15 Temmuz Anıtları'.
77. Mbembe, 'Necropolitics', p. 40.

Bibliography

'15 Temmuz' Şehitlerinin İsimleri Ölümsüzleşiyor', *Anadolu Ajansı*, <https://www.aa.com.tr/tr/15-temmuz-darbe-girisimi/15-temmuz-sehitlerinin-isimleri-olumsuzlesiyor≥ (last accessed 8 August 2018).

'15 Temmuz Şehitler Anıtı Yeniden Düzenlendi', *Milliyet*, 31 May 2018, <http://www.milliyet.com.tr/15-temmuz-sehitler-aniti-yeniden-duzenlendi-balikesir-yerelhaber-2834820/≥ (last accessed 30 September 2018).

'15 Temmuz, Türk Milleti'nin Yeniden Dirilişinin ve Şahlanışının Adıdır', Turkiye Cumhuriyeti Cumhurbaşkanlığı, <https://www.tccb.gov.tr/haberler/410/94898/-15-temmuz-turk-milleti-nin-yeniden-dirilisinin-ve-sahlanisinin-adidir-≥ (last accessed 3 October 2018).

Agamben, Giorgio, *Homo Sacer: Sovereign Power and Bare Life* (Stanford, CA: Stanford University Press, 1999).

Akıncı, Eylül Fidan, 'Sacred Children, Accursed Mothers: Performativities of Necropolitics and Mourning in Neoliberal Turkey', in Sara Brady and Lindsey Mantoas (eds), *Performance in a Militarized Culture* (New York and Oxford: Routldege, 2017), pp. 47–65.

'AKP'nin Osmanlı Mimarisiyle İmtihanı', *Sol*, <http://haber.sol.org.tr/devletve-siyaset/akpnin-osmanli-mimarisiyle-imtihani-haberi-57625> (last accessed 30 April 2016).

Allinson, Jamie, 'The Necropolitics of Drones', *International Political Sociology* 9, no. 2 (2015): 113–27.

'Ankara'nın Kimlik Bunalımı', *Radikal*, <http://www.radikal.com.tr/kultur/ankara-nin-kimlik-bunalimi-1212815/> (last accessed 30 April 2016).

Bargu, Banu, *Starve and Immolate: The Politics of Human Weapons* (New York: Columbia University Press, 2014).

'Başbakan Yıldırım'dan 15 Temmuz Mesajı: Milli İradeyi Hiçe Sayan Gafiller, Hak Ettikleri Cevabı Almışlardır', *Hürriyet*, 15 July 2017, <http://www.hurriyet.com.tr/basbakan-yildirimdan-15-temmuz-mesaji-milli-i-40521040≥ (last accessed 3 October 2018).

'Başkan Erdoğan Sabah İçin Kaleme Aldı: 15 Temmuz Ruhu Hiç Sönmeyecek', *Sabah*, 15 July 2018, <https://www.sabah.com.tr/onbes-temmuz-ihaneti/2018/07/15/15-temmuz-ruhu-hic-sonmeyecek≥ (last accessed 3 October 2018).

'Başkan Topbaş '15 Temmuz Şehitler Abidesi'ni İnceledi', *Istanbul Buyuksehir Belediyesi*, <https://www.ibb.istanbul/News/Detail/34107> (last accessed 30 September 2018).

Benli Altunışık, Meliha, 'Worldviews and Turkish Foreign Policy in the Middle East', *New Perspectives on Turkey*, no. 40 (2009): 171–94.

Bilgin, Pınar, '"Only Strong States Can Survive in Turkey's Geography": The Uses of "Geopolitical Truths" in Turkey', *Political Geography* 26, no. 7 (September 2007): 740–56.

Bişkin, Hacı, '15 Temmuz Sonrası Nerelerin Adı Değişiti?' *Gazete Duvar*, 15 July 2017, <https://www.gazeteduvar.com.tr/gundem/2017/07/15/15-temmuz-sonrasi-nerelerin-adi-degisti≥ (last accessed 8 August 2018).

'Boğaziçi Köprüsü'nin Adı Değişti, İşte Yeni İsmi', *Internethaber.com*, <www.internethaber.com/bogazici-koprusunun-adi-degisti-iste-yeni-ismi≥ (last accessed 8 August 2018).

Bozdoğan, Sibel, 'The Predicament of Modernism in Turkish Architectural Culture: An Overview', in Sibel Bozdoğan and Reşat Kasaba (eds), *Rethinking Modernity and National Identity in Turkey* (Seattle and London: University of Washington Press, 1997), pp. 133-56.

Butler, Judith, *Precarious Life: The Powers of Mourning and Violence* (London and New York: Verso, 2004).

Carney, John, 'Resur(e)recting a Spectacular Hero: Diriliş Ertuğrul, Necropolitics, and Popular Culture in Turkey', *Review of Middle East Studies* 52, no.1 (2018): 93-114.

'Darbecilerin Dokunduğu Yerin Adı Değişiyor', *Sonhaberler.com*, <https://www.sonhaberler.com/gundem/darbecilerin-dokundugu-yerin-adi-degisiyor-h139621.html≥ (last accessed 30 September 2018).

Davutoğlu, Ahmet, *Stratejik Derinlik: Türkiye'nin Uluslararası Konumu* (Istanbul: Küre Yayınları, 2001).

Davutoğlu, Ahmet, 'Türkiye Bölgenin İstikrar Adası', *A Haber*, <https://www.ahaber.com.tr/webtv/gundem/turkiye-bolgenin-istikrar-adasi≥ (last accessed 30 September 2018).

Değirmencioğlu, Serdar, 'Kurgunun Deşifresi: Şehitlik Söylemini Anlamak', in Serdar Değirmencioğlu (ed.), *'Öl Dediler Öldüm' Türkiye'de Şehitlik Mitleri* (Istanbul: İletişim, 2014), pp. 177-202.

Değirmencioğlu, Serdar (ed.), *'Öl Dediler Öldüm' Türkiye'de Şehitlik Mitleri* (Istanbul: İletişim, 2014).

Demirel, Süleyman, '1995 Yılının Gelişmeleri ve 1996 Yılı Hedefleri, 20 Ocak 1996', in Cengiz Ergen (ed.), *Cumhurbaşkanı Süleyman Demirel'in Söylev ve Demeçleri* (n.p.: 2002), pp. 296-307.

Durgun, Sezgi, *Memalik-i Şahane'den Vatan'a* (Istanbul: İletişim, 2011).

Düzcan, Bircan, 'Çanakkale İçinde Kurdular Beni: Şehitlik İmgesi Üzerinden Toplumsal Bedenin İnşası' in Serdar Değirmencioğlu (ed.), *'Öl Dediler Öldüm' Türkiye'de Şehitlik Mitleri* (Istanbul: İletişim, 2014), pp. 111-32.

Erdoğan, Recep Tayyip, 'Türkiye, 15 Temmuz Gecesi Tüm Farklılıklarını Geride Bırakarak Birleşti', Turkiye Cumhuriyeti Cumhurbaşkanlığı, 24 July 2016, <https://www.tccb.gov.tr/haberler/410/49741/turkiye-15-temmuz-gecesi-tum-farkliliklarini-geride-birakarak-birlesti> (last accessed 8 August 2018).

Forest, Benjamin, and Juliet Johnson, 'Unraveling the Threads of History: Soviet-Era Monuments and Post-Soviet National Identity in Moscow', *Annals of the Association of American Geographers* 92 (2002): 524-47.

Forest, Benjamin, and Juliet Johnson, 'Monumental Politics: Regime Type and Public Memory in Post-Communist States', *Post-Soviet Affairs* 27, no. 3 (2011): 269-88.

Gillis, John R. (ed.), *Commemorations* (Princeton: Princeton University Press, 1994).

Giroux, Henry A., 'Reading Hurricane Katrina: Race, Class and the Biopolitics of Disposability', *College Literature* 33, no. 3 (Summer 2006): 171-96.

Güler, E. Zeynep, 'Bir Ulusal Hafıza Mekanı Olarak Gelibolu Yarımadası', in İnci Özkan Kerestecioğlu and Güven Gürkan Öztan (eds), *Türk Sağı: Mitler, Fetişler, Düşman İmgeleri* (Istanbul: İletişim, 2012), pp. 307-44.

'İşte Şehit ve Gazilere Verilecek Haklar', *Sözcü*, 17 August 2016, <https://www.sozcu.com.tr/2016/gundem/iste-sehit-yakinlari-ve-gazilere-verilecek-haklar-1355056/≥ (last accessed 29 September 2018).

'İşte Türkiye'nin 15 Temmuz Anıtları', *Sabah*, 23 July 2017, <https://www.sabah.com.tr/pazar/2017/07/23/iste-turkiyenin-15-temmuz-anitlari≥> (last accessed 30 September 2018).
Jongerden, Joost, 'Crafting Space, Making People: The Spatial Design of Nation in Modern Turkey', *European Journal of Turkish Studies* (2009), <https://journals.openedition.org/ejts/4014≥> (last accessed 3 August 2018).
'Kamuda Neo-Osmanlı Modası', *Radikal*, <http://www.radikal.com.tr/hayat/kamuda-neoosmanli-modasi-1145889/> (last accessed 30 April 2016).
Kavak, Y. E., 'Türkiye'nin 15 Temmuz Anıtları', *Sabah*, 23 July 2017.
'Kızılay Meydanı'nın İsmi "15 Temmuz Kızılay Milli İrade Meydanı" oldu', *BBC*, <http://www.bbc.com/turkce/haberler-turkiye-37020466> (last accessed 8 August 2018).
Kurtulmuş, Numan, 'Türkiye Bölgede Bir İstikrar Adası', *Yeni Dünya Gündemi*, <http://yenidunyagundemi.com/haber/turkiye-bolgede-bir-istikrar-adasi-9264.html≥> (last accessed 30 September 2018).
Laqueur, Thomas W., 'Memory and Naming in the Great War', in John R. Gillis (ed.), *Commemorations* (Princeton: Princeton University Press, 1994), pp. 150–67.
Mbembe, Achille, 'Necropolitics', trans. Libby Meintjes, *Public Culture* 15, no. 1 (Winter 2013): 11–40.
Mert, Ali Osman, *15 July Coup Attempt and the Parallel State Structure 2016* (Cumhurbaşkanlığı Yayınları: n.p., 2016), <https://www.tccb.gov.tr/assets/dosya/15Temmuz/15temmuz_en2.pdf> (last accessed 8 August 2018).
Mitchell, Katharyne, 'Monuments, Memorials, and the Politics of Memory', *Urban Geography* 24, no. 5 (2003): 442–59.
Mufti, Malik, 'From Swamp to Backyard: The Middle East in Turkish Foreign Policy', in Robert O. Freedman (ed.), *The Middle East Enters the 21st Century* (Gainsville: University Press of Florida, 2002), pp. 80–110.
Münir, Metin, 'Bayrakları Bayrak Yapan Nedir Usta', *T24*, 29 September 2015, <http://t24.com.tr/yazarlar/metin-munir/bayraklari-bayrak-yapan-nedir-usta,12829≥> (last accessed 30 September 2018).
Nora, Pierre, 'Between Memory and History: Les Lieux de Mémoire', *Representations* 26 (Spring 1989): 7–24.
Öktem, Kerem, 'The Nation's Imprint: Demographic Engineering and the Change of Toponymes in Republican Turkey', *European Journal of Turkish Studies* (2008), <https://journals.openedition.org/ejts/2243> (last accessed 8 August 2018).
Özkan, Behlül, *From the Abode of Islam to the Turkish Vatan: The Making of a National Homeland in Turkey* (New Haven and London: Yale University Press, 2012).
Piehler, G. Kurt, 'The War Dead and the Gold Star: American Commemoration of the First World War', in John R. Gillis (ed.), *Commemorations* (Princeton: Princeton University Press, 1994), pp. 168–87.
Raja, Masood Ashraf, 'Death as a Form of Becoming: the Muslim Imagery of Death and Necropolitics', *Digest of Middle East Studies* 14 (2005): pp. 11–26.
Said, Edward, 'Invention, Memory, and Place', *Critical Inquiry* 26, no. 2 (Winter 2000): 175–92.

'Saraçhane 15 Temmuz Anıtı Açıldı', *TRT*, <www.trthaber.com/haber/gundem/sarachane-15-temmuz-aniti-acildi> (last accessed 8 August 2018).

Savage, Kirk, 'Politics of Memory: Black Emancipation and the Civil War Monument', in John R. Gillis (ed.), *Commemorations* (Princeton: Princeton University Press, 1994), pp. 127–49.

Sharp, Joanne P., *Condensing the Cold War: Readers' Digest and American Identity* (Minneapolis: University of Minnesota Press, 2000).

Till, Karen, 'Places of Memory', in John Agnew, Katharyne Mitchell and Gerard Toal (eds), *A Companion to Political Geography* (Oxford: Blackwell Publishing, 2003), pp. 290–301.

Verdery, Katherine, *Political Lives of Dead Bodies: Reburial and Post-Socialist Change* (New York: Columbia University Press, 1999).

Walton, Jeremy, 'Practices of Neo-Ottomanism: Making Space and Place Virtuous in Istanbul', in Deniz Göktürk (ed.), *Orienting Istanbul: Cultural Capital of Europe?* (Oxford: Routledge, 2010), pp. 88–103.

Yalkın, Çağrı, and Lerna K. Yanık, 'Entrenching Geopolitical Imaginations: Brand(ing) Turkey through Orhan Pamuk', *Journal of International Relations and Development* (2018): 1–20.

Yanık, Lerna K., 'The Metamorphosis of Metaphors of Vision: "Bridging" Turkey's Location, Role and Identity after the End of the Cold War', *Geopolitics* 14, no. 3 (2009): 531–49.

Yanık, Lerna K., 'Constructing Turkish "Exceptionalism": Discourses of Hybridity and Liminality in Post-Cold War Turkish Foreign Policy', *Political Geography* 30, no. 2 (2011): 80–9.

Yanık, Lerna K., 'Of Celebrities and Landmarks: Space, State and the Making of "Cosmopolitan" Turkey', *Geopolitics* 22, no. 1 (2017): 176–203.

Young, Craig, and Light, Duncan, 'Corpses, dead body politics and agency in human geography: following the corpse of Dr Petru Groza', *Transactions of the Institute of British Geographers* 38 (2016): 135–48.

FOUR

Neither Civilian nor Combatant: Weaponised Spaces and Spatialised Bodies in Cizre

Haydar Darıcı and Serra Hakyemez

On 13 December 2015, the Directorate of National Education sent a text message to all schoolteachers in Cizre, and *only* in Cizre, asking them to attend a compulsory in-service training seminar that would start the following day. The text message informed teachers that they would attend the seminars in their hometowns. This whole arrangement seemed odd, as it disregarded the usual procedure in that such seminars are always held in the summer, not in the middle of school year, and teachers across the country are usually asked to go back to the city where their school is located, not to leave it. Receiving this message amid low-intensity clashes between the Turkish security forces and the Kurdish youth, which had culminated with intermittent curfews being imposed four times since September 2015, the teachers took it as an encrypted order from the government requesting that they leave town immediately if they wanted to save their lives.

Within a couple of hours after the spread of this news, the members of the Revolutionary Patriotic Youth Movement (YDG-H) – designated by the Turkish state as a subgroup of the outlawed Kurdistan Workers' Party (PKK) – erected barricades in the main streets to keep out the Turkish security forces, using any large objects available, including large trash containers and even cars parked on the streets. Meanwhile, many teachers, if not all, bought tickets and rushed to the bus station with large suitcases that they dragged through half-finished barricades. All bus tickets were sold out in the blink of an eye and a long line of hitchhiking teachers appeared on the sidewalks ahead of the barricades in the late afternoon. This scene generated a profound sense of abandonment on the part of Cizre residents, who feared the scale of violence that would befall them in the absence of the 'real' Turkish citizens who could serve as eye-witnesses.

The so-called seminars were never held, but the military operation did occur with a death toll of approximately 350 people.[1] If the teachers exercised the disciplinary power of the Turkish state over the Kurds, their departure indicated the culmination of the racialised biopower of the state. As would soon become clear, this departure also marked the transformation of this biopower into a necropower exercised in the form of actual death.[2] Due to the definition of Turkish citizenship since its inception, the Kurds have never been granted full citizen status.[3] They are rather viewed as potential citizens whose passage to actual citizenship is predicated on their incorporation into Turkishness through exposure to disciplinary state institutions, ranging from schools to the army on the one hand, and to biopolitical interventions carried out by administrative and medical institutions on the other. Where such institutions fail to produce docile subjects and governable populations, military operations follow suit, corroborating the discourse of national security against the Other with the human security of the Other.[4] The relation between the biopower and necropower of the state is, therefore, not one of opposition. While the former aims at eliminating aspects of the culture associated with Kurdishness, the latter eliminates the bodies marked as Kurdish.

This chapter focuses on the latest military operation conducted in Cizre which destroyed its four neighbourhoods, set fire to residential areas, killed hundreds of residents and displaced thousands from September 2015 to March 2016. It has been a common practice among state officers to burn human settlements (villages in particular) and to deny responsibility for the killings since the beginning of the PKK's anti-colonial guerrilla war in the mid-1980s. What distinguishes this latest operation from the previous ones is that it unfolded *not* in the form of terror, which produces unknown spaces of death that give birth to subversive necropolitics.[5] During the latest Cizre operation, the dead were neither forcefully disappeared nor buried in unmarked mass graves (as they were in the 1990s when paramilitary forces like JITEM and Hizbullah carried out extrajudicial executions).[6] Beyond any uncertainty, the killings of Cizre residents were openly supported by state officers and nearly live streamed, hour by hour, minute by minute and second by second. While Cizre residents, both armed and unarmed, attempted to prove to the death that they were civilians, the state remade their dead bodies in the aftermath of the operation into those of combatants.

What kind of work does the categorical distinction between combatant and civilian do in the interplay of the necropolitics and biopower of the Turkish state? This chapter argues neither that the state killed only civilians, nor that the only lives to be protected during the Cizre operation were those of civilians. Instead of taking the distinction between civilian and combatant for granted, we examine what it means for that distinction to be no longer operable as the war tactics of the Kurdish movement shift from guerrilla attacks of hit and run in the mountains to the self-defence of residents in urban centres. In this chapter, we deploy the term 'resident' not as a referent of the individuals' civilian or combatant status but as a marker of their native status, relying on which they pursued self-defence. Despite this change in war tactics, both the Kurdish politicians and state officials kept using the categories of civilian and combatant to promote the right to life and exercise the right to declare war respectively. Nevertheless, we argue that, just like the infinite malleability of terrorism discourse, which has been well documented, the discourse of the civilian-combatant mystifies rather than illuminates political happenings.[7]

Using data from ethnographic fieldwork in Cizre,[8] review of newspapers, forensic and legal documents and reports by the Peoples' Democratic Party (HDP), this chapter investigates the myth of a civilian-combatant distinction to reveal, first, the limits of inciting compassion through the figure of the civilian who is assumed to entertain a pre-political life that is directed towards mere survival. Second, we explore how the government reconstructed the dead bodies using forensics and techno-science in order to portray these figures as combatants exercising necroresistance. As long as the civilian-combatant distinction remains and serves as the only episteme of war and to defend the right to life, we argue that the state is enabled to entertain not only the right to kill, but to turn the dead into the perpetrators of their own killing. Finally, this chapter argues that law and violence on the one hand, and the right to life and the act of killing on the other, are not two polar opposites but are mutually constitutive of each other in the remaking of state sovereignty put in crisis by the Kurdish movement's self-defence practices.

Of the City and the Mountain

On the border of Syrian and Turkey's Kurdistan, Cizre is a valley located near the mountains of Cudi and Gabar, which harbour a significant number of guerrilla camps. There has been a constant flow of bodies, weapons and intelligence between Cizre and its surrounding mountains since the beginning of PKK's guerrilla war. Despite their spatial proximity, the city and the mountain are discursively separated for the distinct symbolic value and political promise that each carries. The distinction denotes more than a rural–urban dichotomy. The mountains stand symbolically for a space outside the state law, kinship norms and the capitalist mode of production. It promises freedom from the predicaments of urban life afflicted by police violence and poverty. By joining the guerrillas, Kurdish youth envision that they 'make an exit' (*çıkış yapmak*) from economic deprivation, domestic violence, gender and age-based hierarchies and the unending threat of arrest, even as they take on the immanent risk of untimely death.[9]

Since the launch of the recent struggle for democratic autonomy in 2006 and of self-defence in 2013, the discursive difference between Cizre and its mountains has begun to fade away. The leader of the Kurdish movement, Abdullah Öcalan, envisioned democratic autonomy as primarily bottom-up governance, enabling all social, political and religious groups to 'express themselves directly in all local decision-making processes'.[10] This participatory system of direct democracy is based on the creation of neighbourhood and city councils, which would collectively forge new institutions in the domains of law, education, economy, health, self-defence and the like. Although democratic autonomy has been experimented with in several Kurdish cities and towns simultaneously since 2006, it has found its most radical and controversial form in Cizre.

Of all the emergent institutions of democratic autonomy, self-defence has played the most significant role in collapsing the discursive distinction between the city and the mountain by investing the former with the symbolic value and political promise of the latter. Self-defence undermined the previous division of labour between Cizre residents who had occasionally staged intifada-like uprisings and the guerrillas who had contained the war in the mountains. The presumption that PKK guerrillas serve as the people's army was revised in that Kurds were encouraged to defend themselves in their neighbourhoods and cities. With this new model of defence, urban centres were transformed into main battlefields where it would be difficult, if not impossible, to tell the difference between combatants and civilians – the terms derived from conventional wars whose application to guerrilla wars has always been problematic.

The introduction of this new war strategy based on democratic autonomy altered the promise of the mountain. As opposed to the previous context where new recruits had to complete a long-term training programme in guerrilla camps, the youth went to the mountain only for a short period to attend a crash programme of military and ideological training in preparation for the defence of their neighbourhoods. Having returned from training, they improvised a new mode of defiance by digging deep, explosive-laden trenches alongside the entrances to their neighbourhoods located on the eastern and western sides of Nusaybin Avenue.

Nur, Cudi and Sur neighbourhoods are located on the west side of the avenue resided by peasant (*gundi*) and nomad (*koçer*) populations. These neighbourhoods came into existence in the early 1990s when a large rural population was displaced from Gabar and Cudi with the evacuation of mountain villages and the imposed ban on the use of pastures. The displaced population built shanty houses in these three neighbourhoods where there used to be empty land at the margins of the city skirting the surrounding hills. On the east side of the avenue, however, are located the neighbourhoods of Yafes, Kale, Dağkapı, Şah, Dicle and Alibey, which, except for Yafes, are populated mainly by Turkish civil servants and the Kurdish urbanites (*bajari*).[11] Most of the politically active youth involved in self-defence came from the displaced families living in Nur, Cudi, Sur and Yafes, where they dug trenches and set up barricades.

As the armed conflict moved from rural to urban areas after the summer of 2015, the tenured guerrillas located in the mountains also descended to the urban centres for support.[12] Greeting the guerrillas' arrival, families, neighbours and teenagers came and sat beside them for hours. The number of Cizre residents paying visits to those defending the neighbourhoods increased day after day, as did the duration of their visits – to the extent that some spent the entire day by the trenches. Besides the youth, other members of the Kurdish movement also participated in self-defence in different capacities. Some, for example, provided food for the fighters, while others supported them by refusing to leave their neighbourhoods despite the declaration of an indefinite curfew on 14 December 2015.

Towards a Humanitarian Crisis: Indefinite Curfew

The first curfew was declared by the Şırnak governor in September 2015 and lasted for eight days while claiming the lives of twenty-two residents.[13] Because the residents were not allowed to step outside at any time during those eight consecutive days, even the dead body of a ten-year-old girl who had been killed by a sniper's bullet could not be removed and was placed by her family in a deep freezer to prevent from rotting.[14] In support of this outrageous curfew, President Erdoğan warned Cizre residents from a televised broadcast: 'The governor has the authority to declare curfew. Those who breach the curfew are terrorists. If my citizens demand peace, they shall let the operation be conducted with ease.'[15] Until December 2015, the Şırnak governor declared intermittent curfews three more times, each of which lasted for less than twenty-four hours. Yet, as the text message sent by the Ministry of National Education indicated, the fifth and final curfew would be quite different.

In a classified document sent by the then Prime Minister Ahmet Davutoğlu to the Şırnak Governor on 13 December 2015, the former named the operation that would start in the next twenty-four hours in Cizre 'The Peace and Freedom Operation' (*Huzur ve Özgürlük Operasyonu*). The names assigned to large-scale military operations give insight into the role the state takes upon itself when repressing uprisings in urban neighbourhoods, prisons and rural areas. Similar to the operations undertaken by the colonial forces in Afghanistan, Iraq and lately Syria, the Cizre operation's name implied that the Turkish security forces would carry out a 'humanitarian' mission to bring peace and freedom to the territories that have already been under the jurisdiction of the Turkish state.[16] In compliance with the Provincial Administration Law, Davutoğlu's letter laid out all the measures the governor was permitted to take including the declaration of an indefinite curfew, the closure of all schools and the transfer of healthcare personnel and medical equipment to local hospitals. The next night at eleven p.m., the governor barred Cizre residents from leaving their homes until further notice.[17]

On the same day that the operation was launched to 'clean' Cizre neighbourhood by neighbourhood, house by house and street by street, the prime minister clarified his intentions with a declaration. 'There is not a single house,' he said, 'not a single neighbourhood where [weapons] are not stored up.'[18] Cizre, with a population of over 130,000, was thus turned into a battlefield where the residents could neither take to the streets nor stay at home since the 'clean(s)ing' was occurring (as in the settler colonial regime of Israel–Palestine)[19] in both public and private spaces all at once. If the struggle for democratic autonomy had mobilised Cizre's four neighbourhoods, its repression would entail nothing less than a war between the state and these neighbourhoods. The destruction of this space inhabited by displaced populations who were deemed ungovernable was necessary for the Turkish state to re-establish its territorial and popular sovereignty. If territoriality and necropower are counterparts,[20] the Turkish state was going to subject those who insisted upon residing in the curfew site to death so as to reconstruct Cizre as a territory of the Turkish nation.

In a document submitted by the government to the European Court of Human Rights (ECtHR) responding to the latter's concerns about the curfew, the former noted: 'The terrorist organisation tried to make its members *look like civilians*[21] in order to receive the public's support.'[22] This note admits, albeit indirectly, that distinguishing civilians from combatants in the absence of a visible difference between the two was not so easy, given that the operation unfolded in the midst of human settlements. A combatant could easily pass for a civilian, and, though never admitted by the government, a civilian for a combatant. The aforementioned statement's emphasis on the *look* was premised upon the assumption that human sight was prone to error and should not be trusted to inhibit security forces from conducting a cleansing operation.

Initially, the Turkish security forces positioned themselves on top of the hills around the neighbourhoods of Yafes, Nur, Cudi and Sur. On 14 December 2015, tank fire and artillery began to hit Yafes from Hastane Tepesi, Nur from Aşk Tepesi, Cudi from Caferi Sadık Tepesi and Sur from Şahin Tepesi. The first phase of the operation, which took over a month, mainly comprised such attacks from the hills, complemented with shootings by snipers placed on top of high buildings and some incursion attempts by troops on the ground. During this time, the security forces indiscriminately shelled four neighbourhoods and randomly hit residential buildings and people on the streets. Afterwards, the security forces gradually climbed down and entered the neighbourhoods. Having repressed the resistance in Yafes, they seized control of Nusaybin Avenue and encircled Nur, Cudi and Sur. The second neighbourhood to fall was Nur, where the security forces advanced by widening the streets and destroying shanty houses. As they encircled Cudi and Sur, many residents took shelter in the basements of random buildings to protect themselves from continuous tank fire and artillery. Among several basements where people were stranded at the time, three of them attracted the special attention of humanitarian campaigns and became the grim symbol of state terror, which claimed the lives of more than 120 people.

The Spaces of Death

The general public first heard about the basements on 23 January 2016 through a social media post by Faysal Sarıyıldız, an HDP deputy and Kurdish local in Cizre. With the announcement of the curfew, journalists were forbidden to enter Cizre unless they were embedded with the Turkish security forces and reported news from their armoured military vehicles. The Turkish government had also declined the request of Human Rights Watch and Amnesty International to access curfew sites to probe the allegations of massacre.[23] Public intellectuals who had condemned the Cizre operation faced smear campaigns and prosecutions on the grounds of 'aiding and abetting terrorists'.[24] The HDP deputies, protected at the time by parliamentary immunity, were thus the only ones who could release information about the extent of the violence that Cizre residents were exposed to in the areas inaccessible to independent journalists and external observers.

'There are thirty-one people,' Sarıyıldız's social media post noted, in a basement of a half-destroyed building in the Cudi neighbourhood.[25] Most of the individuals were severely injured and in need of urgent medical assistance. When Sarıyıldız exhausted all channels of communication with local state officers, other Kurdish deputies located in Ankara contacted the Prime Minister, the Ministry of Interior and the Ministry of Health to find a way to rescue the injured individuals entrapped in this basement.[26] As they were exchanging phone calls and making official visits, news circulated on social media on 26 January that three people had already lost their lives in this basement. In the following days, it turned out that at least ninety more people were similarly stranded in two other basements in the vicinity of the first one. It had been almost forty-five days since the beginning of the operation, which over time destroyed the urban infrastructure, including water and sewage systems, electricity and landlines. With no way of having their most basic needs met, the injured individuals surrounded by their friends' dead bodies were waiting for their own death.

Upon the failure to stop security forces in Cizre, three HDP deputies embarked on a sit-in and hunger strike at the office of the Ministry of Interior on 27 January. They demanded that the dead bodies be transferred to a morgue, the injured be transferred to a hospital, and their right to health and life be respected.[27] This protest succeeded in compelling government officials to allow ambulances to enter the Cudi neighbourhood. Yet the health personnel could not reach the basements due to heavy shelling.[28] While the HDP deputies believed that it was the security forces that were targeting these ambulances, state officials placed the blame on 'terrorists'. Amid the dissonance between Cizre and Ankara as well as amongst the HDP deputies and state officials, both the President and the Prime Minister refused to acknowledge that people were dying in the basements, and they speculated that nobody was even injured.[29]

The Turkish state conceived of those in the basements as sovereign subjects risking the lives of others along with their own[30] and exercising what Banu Bargu would call 'necroresistance'.[31] The institutions within the Kurdish movement, ranging from pro-Kurdish news channels to local municipalities, however, refused to frame the injured as sovereigns. By avoiding any mention of that which had kept these individuals in the Cudi neighbourhood – namely their faith and/or participation in the struggle for autonomy – the Kurdish deputies, for example, tended to draw attention to the humanitarian crisis that the injured were facing in the basements instead. Where the state presumed necroresistance as a way of justifying its necropower, Kurdish political activists and human rights advocates resorted to the universalising language of humanitarianism, which, following Didier Fassin,[32] we describe as an affective movement drawing humans towards their fellows on the basis of a shared humanity. It was no longer the radical politics of autonomy through the self-defence of entrenched territories, but rather a claim to humanitarian ethics with the purpose of inciting a sense of compassion among the international and national audience that they pursued.

Upon the refusal of the President and Prime Minister to acknowledge that there were injured individuals in the basements, the latter sent pictures of themselves and their deceased friends from these very same basements. By revealing the interiors of the basements, these pictures aimed at reversing their portrayal as a storehouse of weapons and explosives as had been characterised by government sources. In these pictures, some bodies were tightly covered by blankets indicating that they were already dead, while others seemed to be immobilised, lying down on the ground. The latter with extremely pale and skinny faces looked neither fully alive nor entirely dead. Not every picture of human suffering incites the same feeling of compassion amongst its audience, though. As has been noted in the context of Israel–Palestine and anti-black police brutality in the US, a racialised structure of feelings invests the picture of the Other with the suspicion that it might be fake, or justifies the violence thereby recorded.[33] Likewise, the basement pictures posted on social media could not clear the air of doubt about whether the individuals in the picture had *really* been injured and whether or not they were civilians or combatants.

The visual materials that the injured shared to produce the effect of reality were corroborated with text messages and a teleconference. The main contact that served as an unofficial spokesperson of the basements was Mehmet Tunç. He was the co-chair of the People's Assembly established in Cizre to establish democratic autonomy through mobilising residents to take initiative in the governance of their neighbourhoods. Since the declaration of the curfew, Tunç had stayed in the besieged neighbourhoods and recounted what they were experiencing to the HDP deputies via mobile phones. The text messages he sent from the basements to the HDP deputies were frequently shared on social media to underline that the people injured in the basements had proper names, families, jobs and feelings. In these messages, Tunç mentioned their thirst, hunger, pain and fear while also describing the sound of gunshots and explosions fired in the vicinity. One of the last text messages he sent to Sarıyıldız read as follows:

> A mortar shell hit the chimney. We got scared to death. Thankfully it exploded on the third floor. All the dust came down to the basement. They (security forces) are now firing at the building. Very badly. There is an injured

girl named Soltan [here]. She is always telling me: 'Father, do not leave me here.' This makes me aggrieved. She keeps asking for water. There is another kid who keeps asking for water. She has internal bleeding. We cannot give her water.

Among all those injured and dead, it was not a coincidence that the only name Tunç mentioned was that of Soltan, who was afraid of being left alone in the basement, given the role that the figure of children plays in humanitarian campaigns to mobilise moral sentiments. The other vignette he provided belonged to another child asking for water on her death bed. As Liisa Malkki reminds us, the figure of children 'tends to be identified as apolitical, even suprapolitical; yet the forms in question have political effects'.[34] In the discourse of humanitarianism, which, despite its Western genealogy, has prevalence across the world, children are considered innocent victims of wars whose causes they cannot comprehend. It is noted by anthropologists that this humanitarian imaginary does not always map onto the actual experience of these children, which varies to a great extent based on how their age intersects with other identities.[35] In his work on the stone-throwing children in Adana, Haydar Darıcı shows how childhood is turned into a signifier of revolutionary politics (as opposed to adulthood, which is associated with parliamentary politics), becoming a category with which urbanised and displaced Kurds began to identify, irrespective of their age.[36] In the context of the Cizre operation, however, the mentioning of the singularities of different forms of childhood would have only exacerbated the already isolated condition of the injured. Hence, Tunç resorted to the universal language of 'innocent children' with the hope that he would speak to the feelings of the outside world and convince them to stand against the rise of fatalities.

In addition to the pictures and text messages sent by the injured that were shared on social media and in the parliament, a brief teleconference with Mehmet Tunç was arranged with the HDP deputies attending the Annual Conference on the European Union, Turkey, the Middle East and the Kurds on 27 January 2016 at the European Parliament. Amidst gunfire, Tunç attempted to describe the indescribable to the European audience. Struggling to find a proper name with adequate force to describe what they were exposed to in the basements, he enlisted, one after another, the terms that would ring a bell for his audience: tragedy, massacre, genocide. Before hanging up the phone he directly addressed what he called 'our friends there', and made the following plea: 'Please stop this atrocity. You have the power to stop this massacre in Cizre. You have the power to lift the siege by pressuring the AKP government. Otherwise you will have been considered by us complicit in the massacre.'[37]

In this brief teleconference, which lasted for less than two minutes, Tunç acknowledged, on the one hand, the relation of inequity between him and his European audience, which was the precondition to making a plea for compassion.[38] On the other hand, he envisioned a morally higher ground that both him and the others stranded in the basements would occupy in the future anterior, when they would be dead if the EU did not stop the Turkish government. If the lives of those in the basements were at the mercy of the EU's intervention in the here and now, Tunç argued, the EU's moral standing would be at the mercy of the judgement of the dead in the future. Put differently, Tunç stressed that the suffering they were going through was temporary. His living body was not that of a sovereign carrying out a self-destructive resistance. His death would nonetheless pass a sovereign judgement on the living with regard to the moral and political principles the latter claimed to stand for.

All these humanitarian efforts resulted in the ECtHR's acceptance of the initial requests of the five applicants for interim measures.[39] The ECtHR asked the Turkish government to take all measures in its capacity to protect the lives and physical integrity of these individuals injured in the basements and waiting to be taken to hospitals.[40] In the following days, however, the ECtHR declined the requests of other applicants based on a decision given by the Turkish Constitutional Court on 29 January 2016.[41] The latter's decision centred on the ambiguities they detected in the information submitted to the Constitutional Court[42] on behalf of the injured. The Court was not convinced that the medical conditions of the injured required immediate intervention since their political and legal representatives had failed to provide the applicants' proper names, home addresses and family records.

The Kurdish lawyers and HDP deputies explained the difficulty of locating the injured in a definite space given that the Cudi neighbourhood had become unrecognisable over the course of the operation. The security forces had destroyed many buildings by tank fire and artillery, both to make new roads and to avoid the explosives planted in the streets. The residents had built internal roads by breaking the walls between buildings. Hence it was almost impossible to describe a location with street names and apartment numbers, let alone situate the injured in this destroyed space. For the proper identification of the injured, the Court also demanded that official identification documents be provided with detailed information about the applicants' family records. Yet the only institution that could issue family records was the Cizre Population Directorate, which had been shut down due to the curfew. Furthermore, the lawyers had difficulty in acquiring even the names of the injured due to the lack of efficient communication. Not to mention that many Cizre residents use both a Kurdish and a Turkish name, and that the latter is employed exclusively in official settings and might not be known even by one's own close friends. Finally, some were so seriously injured that they could not even say their names.

Without such identification markers, the Court denied recognition to the injured as legally legible subjects in need of urgent medical assistance. If the applicants had really been injured, the Court argued, they would not have changed their locations. If they changed their locations amid armed clashes, they must have been connected to the combatants who were assumed to have total control over the Cudi neighbourhood. The Court also asked why the injured had called the HDP deputies instead of state officials for help. Their unwillingness to surrender to security forces was another indication of their 'subversive' character. As the biopower of the state failed to produce felicitous subjects with proper names, permanent home addresses and records of family history, its necropower would be unleashed beyond its official boundaries.

With the refusal of the Court to grant innocence and extend compassion to the injured, the basements were transformed into spaces of death. The limited communication that the HDP deputies had entertained for a brief period until the end of January abruptly ended. No pictures were uploaded to social media; no text messages were sent from the basements; no voice recordings circulated. Human rights advocates hoped that the batteries of the cellular phones that the injured were using had died and nothing worse. With the completion of the Cizre operation on 14 March 2016, however, it became obvious that everyone in the basements had died. According to a UN report, more than 200 residents were killed throughout the operation.[43] An HDP report suggests that the number of residents killed was about 280, among whom eighteen were burnt so badly that they could not even be identified and were thus buried in a potter's field.

Reconstructing the Dead

When the injured were still alive, the Court considered them unidentifiable despite the efforts of their political and legal representatives to provide as much information about their identities as possible. Upon their death, however, public defenders in collaboration with cartographers and forensic experts reconstructed the dead bodies, which were by then unidentifiable to the naked eye. In his exploration of the power of the dead, Achille Mbembe refers to a number of skeletons preserved in a visible state in the aftermath of the Rwandan genocide so as to underline 'the tension between the petrification of the bones and their strange coolness on one hand, and on the other, their stubborn will to mean, to signify something'.[44] What skeletons signify is not inherent to what they consisted of but is contingent upon the political atmosphere within which they are unearthed. With the rise of transnational human rights activism in post-conflict countries, exhumation sites are valorised as the sites of political truths.⁴⁵ Focusing on the exercise of necropower in relation to bodily remains exhumed from mass graves, Francisco Ferrándiz and Antonius C. G. M. Robben highlight 'the increasing dominance of a high-tech logic in the production of scientific and legal evidence – the mass grave as crime scene and the body as criminal evidence – as a preamble to the desired prosecution and conviction of war criminals'.⁴⁶

The forensic regime of truth does not necessarily have politically subversive effects or justice securing outcomes, however. Instead of the prosecution and conviction of war criminals, it may end up justifying war crimes, as different technologies of power are assembled to reconstruct the dead bodies. In the aftermath of the Cizre operation, the government resorted to forensic reports to invalidate the legal struggle of the families of thirty-four of the dead who filed a lawsuit with the ECtHR on the grounds that the government violated the right to life, the prohibition of inhuman and degrading treatment, and the right to liberty and security during the curfew in Cizre.⁴⁷ In response to the allegations, the government presented two dossiers consisting of aerial and on-the-ground images, forensic and intelligence reports and repentant testimonies to assert that the security forces had not killed any civilians but had rather protected the lives of the civilians at the expense of their own. With the help of these dossiers, it constructed a new cartography of Cizre in which the dead bodies acquired not only proper names and family records but also definite home addresses, which were now their graveyards.

By utilising a combination of techno-science and forensic science, the government 'produced' two different bodies, the civilian that is in need of protection and the combatant that is a threat to be 'neutralised'. Following Michel Foucault, Crystal Parikh calls the human body 'a hybrid biopolitical subject, at once the created object *and* the political agent of state power'.⁴⁸ Prior to any claim that secures the right of some human bodies to life, the government had to produce other bodies that were visible only to the bird's-eye view of techno-science and the microscopic view of forensic science. Like a magician that creates the illusion of control, these lenses rendered the present bodies of the security forces absent while making the absent bodies of the Cizre residents present.⁴⁹

In the ECtHR report of the government, the civilian became an empty placeholder who was ascribed shifting and conflicting roles. This category was sometimes invoked to refer to those who left their homes upon the declaration of the curfew, as advised by the governor. Other times, civilians were referred to as the ones who remained in the curfew site and were allegedly forced to serve as human shields for those fighting against the security forces. Still other times, the government argued, they were the direct targets of the 'terrorist' organisation. What was common amongst the various iterations of the term 'civilian' was that anyone who was supportive of and/or participated in self-defence failed to qualify as such.

Imaging satellites took aerial pictures of Cizre, which reordered the disorder of the operation by identifying every building with a code number and matching each ditch, barricade and explosive with a street name. The most pronounced part of the aerial map were the streets coloured in purple-blue, resembling a wide vein pumping blood to the heart of a body. The cartographers inserted icons rendering visible what used to be invisible to the security forces. Thin red rectangles represented trenches placed along the main streets that opened up to smaller side streets. Thin yellow rectangles became the icons of barricades. On either side of these rectangular icons, a yellow circle with an exclamation mark at its centre was placed to indicate that explosives were laid underground. Cables connected to these explosives were marked on the map with red circles. Rectangles, circles and exclamation marks were the graphic referents of the lawlessness that was allegedly carried out by those the government called 'terrorists'.

In addition to the imaging satellites, the security forces used manual cameras to give depth of vision to the operation site. From the corner of these picture frames, blue heavy-duty tarps and colourful large blankets became evident, for they had served as curtains for Cizre residents to hide from the security forces at the time of the operation. The tarps and blankets were now wide open, yet there was no-*body* hidden behind them. The pictures walked the viewer through the basements where the applicants' relatives had died. Smoke from the fire, which had blazed within the buildings and had killed the bodies trapped inside, was still hanging in the air. Plaster on the walls was peeled off, exposing steel and bricks. The floor was covered with ashes and charred human remains. Like criminals caught red-handed, three and a half rifles were pictured in an upright position at the corner of a basement with a yellow paper beside them that served as their identification card.

The government introduced these images with the following sentence: 'Some photographs showing the houses where the bodies were found, the ammunitions in the houses and the members of the terrorist organisation are annexed to this document [sic].'[50] Dead bodies were nowhere and everywhere at the same time – fingerprints on the weapons, personal items beneath the barricades, bodily remains on the floor. The dead bodies and the spaces they inhabited were inextricable from each other. The spatial images indexed the bodies whose labour produced such a space. The bodily images indexed the space that produced these bodies. If the aerial and on-the-ground images conjured up an embodied space, the forensic reports produced spatialised bodies. While the former moved from the outside in, the latter moved from the inside out, to reconstruct the dead as combatants.

The ambiguity that had evolved around the names, addresses and family records of those in the basements was resolved by resorting to the forensic regime of 'truth'. The public defender's office carried out post-mortem examinations and autopsies to identify the dead bodies and determine the cause of their death. Some bodies were so severely damaged that an autopsy could not produce any results. In other instances, bullets and other metal fragments removed from the bodies helped reconstruct how and when internal organs had failed. Tissue samples were sent out to forensic institutes in Gaziantep and Istanbul for toxicological and molecular-genetic analysis.[51] Upon the families' application to the Cizre public defender's office, their DNA samples were compared to the samples removed from the unidentifiable dead bodies.

Once the identities of the dead were determined, their bodies were handed over to their families for immediate burial. If the families did not claim the dead bodies within three days of identification, local state authorities were given permission to bury them in a potter's field, based on the law concerning burial proceedings, which the government amended amid the Cizre operation on 7 January 2016.[52] Consequently, the governors across Turkey's Kurdistan proceeded with the burials without giving any formal notice to, or enough time for, the families of the dead to come to the morgues.[53] In some instances, the families were given a plastic bag of bones weighting five kilos in the place of their loved ones.[54] With the purpose of preventing the dead from disrupting the symbolic order of the nation,[55] the Şırnak governor banned the families from holding funeral ceremonies with mass participation. While the cemeteries at the city centres were to be avoided, the families were commanded to carry out their burials at either dusk or dawn.

Forensic reports made the deceased identifiable and yet left the identity of the perpetrator(s) unclear. The ballistic examination of the bullets removed from the dead bodies remains inconclusive. In contrast to the large number of visuals captured by imaging satellites and hand-held cameras, which pictured Cizre as a space of visibility, the public defender in Cizre argued that no image of the basements existed from the time of operation. Hence the investigation results reiterated the same conclusion time and again: 'in the absence of any camera recording of the incident scene, and in the absence of any witnesses who could identify perpetrator(s) of the incident, the perpetrator(s) could not be identified, and that the work to identify and arrest perpetrator(s) is ongoing'.[56] These results should not be taken to imply that the government did not know which security forces were deployed in the Cizre operation. Rather, they suggest that the security forces were considered 'legitimate defenders' of the lives of civilians insofar as the bodies found in the operation site were assumed to belong to combatants. With the legislation of a new impunity law in June 2016, the government confirmed that security forces undertaking counterterrorism operations cannot be held responsible for the crimes of torture, execution and mistreatment.[57]

In his search for the 'real' perpetrators, the public defender thus turned to the bodies of the dead. He requested that the chemistry specialisation unit of the Forensic Institute report if any residue of gunpowder or explosives (TNT, HMX) were detected on the clothes and skin of the dead. The reports submitted to the ECtHR convey that it was impossible to extract swab samples and perform other forensic tests on some bodies due to their severe damage. However, two out of twenty-six dead bodies found in a basement reportedly carried such residues. Based on this report, the public defender claimed that these bodies must have belonged to combatants. In line with the public defender's claims, the government went a step further and asserted:

> The Government would like to underline that in the examination carried out on the body of [name undisclosed], TNT and HMX were found, and that gunpowder residues were found on the swabs taken from [name undisclosed]. In addition, the Government considers that the fact that swabs could not be taken from other deceased persons on the ground because the physical condition of their bodies was unsuitable does not mean that they had not used weapons.

This counterfactual argument was corroborated by the public defender's findings based on the previous intelligence and court reports retrieved from the files on the dead. From the moment of complete uncertainty about their innocence, the government moved to that of complete certainty about their guilt. The Security Directorate presented the existing court cases (which were dropped upon the death of the accused) as evidence of the connection between the accused to the PKK and YDG-H. In violation of the presumption of innocence, charges ranging from terrorist propaganda to membership in a terrorist organisation were treated as if they were final court verdicts. Anonymous witnesses who resorted to the Repentance Law to evade punishment testified that the ECtHR applicants' relatives had served as combatants during the Cizre operation. Finally, the Security Directorate notified the public defender that the pro-PKK websites declared the applicants' relatives to be 'martyrs'.

Nothing remained opaque in the reconstruction of the dead bodies in the aftermath of the Cizre operation. The dead were made criminals first and then reconstructed as the perpetrators of their own death. The temporal invisibility of the operation site from where Mehmet Tunç had pleaded for humanitarian aid was rendered prosecutable. Street numbers, building names, family histories and proper names were collected not to save lives but to refuse the recognition of their murder. The categories of civilian and combatant, which had been in flux at the time of operation, were re-ordered in its aftermath by exploiting the optics of techno-science and forensic science.

Conclusion

The popular uprisings and corresponding military operations carried out in the Middle East and beyond liberally deploy the categories of civilian and combatant. The struggle for autonomy waged in Cizre along with forty-eight other districts in Turkey's Kurdistan is not an exception. This chapter took issue with the impasse that these categories produce when the warring parties, as well as human rights advocates, deploy such terms to either legitimise the necropower of war or dispatch the biopower of humanitarian aid. We demonstrated how the line between civilian and combatant became increasingly blurred with the shift in Kurdish politics from guerrilla warfare to popular self-defence, which ultimately resulted in the replacement of mountains with cities as a totalising space of death. We also showed how the Turkish state represented the residents who were entrapped in this space as un-identifiable during the operation and, after literally rendering them un-identifiable, reconstructed the charred bodies to generate the figure of the combatant. As for the Kurdish movement, their preference for the language of innocence over that of necroresistance rendered their struggle for autonomy unspeakable. Upon the destruction of Cizre's neighbourhoods and killing of their 'subversive' residents, the Turkish state seemed to reclaim the city as a territory of the nation in which its disciplinary institutions and biopolitical interventions would operate again until the return of the power of the dead.

Notes

1. The total death toll during this period in all the urban centres of the province of Şırnak including Cizre is 990. For a detailed breakdown of the numbers, see <http://www.crisisgroup.be/interactives/turkey/> (last accessed 28 May 2019).

2. Achille Mbembe, 'Necropolitics', and Michel Foucault, *Society Must Be Defended*.
3. Mesut Yeğen, *Müstakbel Türk'ten Sözde Vatandaşa*.
4. Banu Bargu, *Starve and Immolate*; Paul Amar, *The Security Archipelago*; Eyal Weizman, *The Least of All Possible Evils*.
5. Ömer Özcan, *Waiting as a Way of Life in a Kurdish Border Town in Turkey*; Hişyar Özsoy, 'The Missing Grave of Sheikh Said'; Isaias Rojas-Perez, *Mourning Remains*; and Diana Taylor, *Disappearing Acts*.
6. Özgür Sevgi Göral, Ayhan Işık and Özlem Kaya, *Unspoken Truth*; Özlem Biner, 'Documenting "Truth" in the Margins of the Turkish State'; Mehmet Kurt, *Kurdish Hizbullah in Turkey*; Duygu Şendağ, *State Violence and Human Rights*.
7. Cynthia Keppley Mahmood, 'Terrorism, Myth, and the Power of Ethnographic Praxis'; Deniz Yönücü, 'The Absent Present Law'; Julia M. Eckert (ed.), *The Social Life of Anti-Terrorism Laws*; and Richard Ashby Wilson (ed.), *Human Rights in the 'War on Terror'*.
8. Ethnographic fieldwork and interviews were conducted by Haydar Darıcı. While data from fieldwork concern the period between 2013 and the breakout of urban war in 2015, interviews were conducted during and after the war.
9. Most of the guerrillas lose their lives before reaching the age of thirty.
10. Abdullah Öcalan, *Democratic Confederalism*, p. 26.
11. Cizre residents use the term neighbourhood (*mahalle*) to refer merely to the neighbourhoods on the west side of Nusaybin Avenue, while employing the terms 'centre' (*merkez*) or 'Old Cizre' (*Eski Cizre*) for the eastern side.
12. The number of youth fighters behind the trenches was much larger than that of tenured guerrillas.
13. '16 Ağustos 2015 – 21 Ocak 2016 Tarihleri Arasında Sokağa Çıkma Yasakları ve Sivillere Yönelik Yaşam Hakkı İhlalleri', TIHV, 23 January 2016.
14. Aslı Zengin, 'Cemile Çağırga'.
15. For Erdoğan's call to Cizre, 'Erdoğan: Sokağa çıkma yasağı ilan edildi; belli saatler arasında sokağa çıkılmaz, çıkan teröristtir', *T24*, 16 September 2015.
16. Derek Gregory, *The Colonial Present*.
17. For the original announcement, see the Governorate's website: <http://www.sirnak.gov.tr/basin-duyurusu-14122015> (last accessed 28 May 2019).
18. From a mainstream television channel, Davutoğlu commented on the declaration of curfew. For his comments, see 'Davutoğlu: O ilçeler gerekirse ev ev temizlenecek', *Evrensel*, 14 December 2015.
19. Areilla Azoulay, 'When a Demolished House Becomes a Public Square'; Daniel Bertand Monk, *An Aesthetic Occupation*; and Eyal Weizman, *Hollow Land*.
20. Antonius C. G. M. Robben, 'Exhumations, Territoriality, and Necropolitics in Chile and Argentina'.
21. Emphasis ours.
22. *Halil Yavuzel and others v. Turkey* and two other applications.
23. These organisations prepared their reports on Cizre and other curfew sites on the basis of the interviews they conducted with the residents who had managed

to escape. See Amnesty International's 'Briefing: End abusive operations under indefinite curfews in Turkey' and Human Rights Watch's 'Turkey: State blocks probes of Southeast Killings'.
24. One of the targets of the Turkish government was Academics for Peace, who signed a petition to condemn the state massacres in Kurdish cities. For more information, see <https://barisicinakademisyenler.net/English> (last accessed 28 May 2019). A group of artists and writers also made a call to the government to stop the civilian death in Cizre; see 'Aydın ve sanatçılardan Cizre çağrısı: Siz kurtarmazsanız biz kurtarmaya hazırız', *Diken*, 2 January 2016.
25. 'The Anatomy of Brutality'.
26. For more details on the meeting of three HDP deputies with the Prime Minister, see 'HDP'li vekiller Davutoğlu ile Cizre'yi konuştu', *Ihlas Haber Ajansı*, 26 January 2016.
27. For the HDP's press release about the hunger strike, see 'HDP milletvekilleri İçişleri Bakanlığı'nda açlık grevine başladı', *T24*, 27 January 2016.
28. For the then Interior Minister Efkan Ala's press conference on 2 February 2016, see 'Bakan Ala'nın "algı yönetimi": Cizre'deki yaralılara giden ambulanslara ateş açıldı', *Diken*, 2 February 2016.
29. 'Başbakan: Cizre'de bodrum katında muhtemelen hiç yaralı yok, getirilen yaralı olmadı', *T24*, 3 February 2016.
30. Mbembe, 'Necropolitics'.
31. Bargu, *Starve and Immolate*.
32. Didier Fassin, *Humanitarian Reason*.
33. Judith Butler, *Frames of War*; Judith Butler, 'Endangered/Endangering'; and Rebecca Stein, *Digital Militarism*.
34. Liisa Malkki, 'Children, Humanity and the Infantilization of Peace', pp. 58–9.
35. Gill Valentine, 'Angels and Devils'.
36. Haydar Darıcı, '"Adults See Politics as a Game"'.
37. See the full script of his speech: Nurcan Baysal, 'Avrupa Parlamentosu'na açık mektup', *T24*, 9 February 2018.
38. Fassin, *Humanitarian Reason*.
39. Based on Rule 39 of the Rules of the Court, the ECtHR may request a state party to take urgent measures should there be an imminent risk of irreparable harm.
40. See ECtHR's press release concerning the complaints about curfew measures in Turkey, 'Curfew measures in south-eastern Turkey: Court decides to give priority treatment to a number of complaints', ECtHR, 5 February 2016. Within less than twenty-four hours of the ECtHR's decision, four of the injured had nonetheless died. See 'European Court of Human Rights looks into complaints about curfew measures in Turkey', ECtHR, 15 December 2016.
41. See its decision, 'Curfew measures in south-eastern Turkey: Court decides to give priority treatment to a number of complaints', ECtHR, 5 February 2016.
42. Hereafter, 'the Court' refers to the Turkish Constitutional Court.
43. Report on the human rights situation in south-east Turkey by Office of the United Nations High Commissioner for Human Rights, February 2017.

44. Mbembe, 'Necropolitics', p. 35.
45. Özcan, *Waiting as a Way of Life*; Rojas-Perez, *Mourning Remains*.
46. Francisco Ferrándiz and Antonius C. G. M. Robben, *Necropolitics*, p. 11.
47. *Halil Yavuzel and others v. Turkey* and two other applications (numbers 5317/16, 5628/16 and 39419/16).
48. Crystal Parikh, *Writing Human Rights*, p. 120.
49. Allen Feldman, *Archive of the Insensible*; Brian Ferguson, 'Full Spectrum: The Military Invasion of Anthropology'.
50. *Halil Yavuzel and others v. Turkey* and two other applications, p. 30.
51. Ibid.
52. 'Cenazeler zorla mı gömülecek?', *Agos*, 8 January 2016.
53. 'Sokağa çıkma yasağı olan yerlerde tartışmalı defin uygulaması', *BBC*, 12 January 2016.
54. 'Cizre'de öldürülen Duymak'ın eşi: 5 kilo kemik vererek, "Al bu senin eşin" dediler', *Evrensel*, 26 February 2016.
55. Özsoy, 'The Missing Grave of Sheikh Said'; Antonius C. G. M. Robben, 'Exhumations, Territoriality, and Necropolitics in Chile and Argentina'.
56. *Halil Yavuzel and others v. Turkey* and two other applications.
57. 'Erdoğan, "askere yargı zırhı" yasasını onayladı', *Evrensel*, 13 July 2016.

Bibliography

'16 Ağustos 2015 – 21 Ocak 2016 Tarihleri Arasında Sokağa Çıkma Yasakları ve Sivillere Yönelik Yaşam Hakkı İhlalleri', TIHV, 23 January 2016, <https://tihv.org.tr/16-agustos-2015-21-ocak-2016-tarihleri-arasinda-sokaga-cikma-yasaklari-ve-sivillere-yonelik-yasam-hakki-ihlalleri/> (last accessed 16 November 2018).

Academics for Peace, <https://barisicinakademisyenler.net/English> (last accessed 14 November 2018).

Amar, Paul, *The Security Archipelago: Human-Security States, Sexuality Politics, and the End of Neoliberalism* (Durham, NC: Duke University Press, 2013).

'Aydın ve sanatçılardan Cizre çağrısı: Siz kurtarmazsanız biz kurtarmaya hazırız', *Diken*, 2 January 2016, <http://www.diken.com.tr/aydin-ve-sanatcilardan-cizre-cagrisi-siz-kurtarmazsaniz-biz-kurtarmaya-haziriz/> (last accessed 16 November 2018).

Azoulay, Areilla, 'When a Demolished House Becomes a Public Square', in Laura Ann Stoler (ed.), *Imperial Debris* (Durham, NC: Duke University Press, 2013), pp. 194–227.

'Bakan Ala'nın "algı yönetimi": Cizre'deki yaralılara giden ambulanslara ateş açıldı', *Diken*, 2 February 2016, <http://www.diken.com.tr/bakan-alanin-algi-yonetimi-cizredeki-yaralilara-giden-ambulanslara-ates-acildi/> (last accessed 14 November 2018).

Bargu, Banu, *Starve and Immolate: The Politics of Human Weapons* (New York: Columbia University Press, 2014).

'Başbakan: Cizre'de bodrum katında muhtemelen hiç yaralı yok, getirilen yaralı olmadı', *T24*, 3 February 2016, <http://t24.com.tr/haber/davutoglu-genisletilmis-il-baskanlari-toplantisinda-konusuyor,326678> (last accessed 16 November 2018).

'Basın Duyurusu', Türkiye Cumhuriyeti Şırnak Valiliği, 14 December 2015, <http://www.sirnak.gov.tr/basin-duyurusu-14122015≥ (last accessed 16 November 2018).

Baysal, Nurcan, 'Avrupa Parlamentosu'na açık mektup', *T24*, 9 February 2018, <http://t24.com.tr/yazarlar/nurcan-baysal/avrupa-parlamentosuna-acik-mektup,13848> (last accessed 16 November 2018).

Biner, Zerrin Ö., 'Documenting "Truth" in the Margins of the Turkish State', in Julia Eckert, Brian Donahoe, Christian Strümpell and Zerrin Ö. Biner (eds), *Law Against the State: Ethnographic Forays into Law's Transformations* (Cambridge: Cambridge University Press, 2012), pp. 228–45.

'Briefing: End abusive operations under indefinite curfews in Turkey', Amnesty International, 21 January 2016, <https://www.amnesty.nl/actueel/briefing-end-abusive-operations-indefinite-curfews-turkey≥ (last accessed 16 November 2016).

Butler, Judith, 'Endangered/Endangering', in Robert Gooding-Williams (ed.), *Reading Rodney King* (New York: Routledge, 1993), pp. 15–23.

Butler, Judith, *Frames of War: When Is Life Grievable?* (London: Verso, 2009).

'Cenazeler zorla mı gömülecek?', *Agos*, 8 January 2016, <http://www.agos.com.tr/tr/yazi/13944/cenazeler-zorla-mi-gomulecek≥ (last accessed 16 November 2018).

'Cizre'de öldürülen Duymak'ın eşi: 5 kilo kemik vererek, "Al bu senin eşin" dediler', *Evrensel*, 26 February 2016, <https://www.evrensel.net/haber/273580/cizrede-oldurulen-duymakin-esi-5-kilo-kemik-vererek-al-bu-senin-esin-dediler> (last accessed 16 November 2018).

Crisis Group in Turkey, <http://www.crisisgroup.be/interactives/turkey/> (last accessed 15 November 2018).

'Curfew measures in south-eastern Turkey: Court decides to give priority treatment to a number of complaints', ECtHR, 5 February 2016, <file:///Users/serrahakyemez/Downloads/Curfew%20measures%20in%20south-eastern%20Turkey%20-%20priority%20treatment%20of%20complaints.pdf> (last accessed 16 November 2018).

Darıcı, Haydar, '"Adults See Politics as a Game": Politics of Kurdish Children in Urban Turkey', *International Journal of Middle East Studies* 45, no. 4 (2013): 775–90.

'Davutoğlu: O ilçeler gerekirse ev ev temizlenecek', *Evrensel*, 14 December 2015, <https://www.evrensel.net/haber/267570/davutoglu-o-ilceler-gerekirse-ev-ev-temizlenecek> (last acsessed 16 November 2018).

Eckert, Julia M., *The Social Life of Anti-Terrorism Laws: The War on Terror and the Classifications of the 'Dangerous Other'* (London: Transcript Verlag, 2008).

'Erdoğan, "askere yargı zırhı" yasasını onayladı', *Evrensel*, 13 July 2016, <https://www.evrensel.net/haber/284969/erdogan-askere-yargi-zirhi-yasasini-onayladi> (last accessed 16 November 2018).

'Erdoğan: Sokağa çıkma yasağı ilan edildi; belli saatler arasında sokağa çıkılmaz, çıkan teröristtir', *T24*, 16 September 2015, <http://t24.com.tr/haber/erdogan-bunlar-lafa-geldigi-zaman-saz-lafa-geldigi-zaman-caz,309896> (last accessed 16 November 2018).

'European Court of Human Rights looks into complaints about curfew measures in Turkey', ECtHR, 15 December 2016, <https://www.hdp.org.tr/en/news/from-hdp/our-application-to-the-committee-of-ministers-of-the-council-of-europe/8898> (last accessed 16 November 2018).

Fassin, Didier, *Humanitarian Reason: A Moral History of the Present* (Berkeley: University of California Press, 2012).

Feldman, Allen, *Archive of the Insensible: Of War, Photopolitics, and Dead Memory* (Chicago: University of Chicago Press, 2015).

Ferguson, Brian, 'Full Spectrum: The Military Invasion of Anthropology', in Neil L. Whitehead and Sverker Finnström (eds), *Virtual War and Magical Death Technologies and Imaginaries for Terror and Killing* (Durham, NC: Duke University Press, 2013), pp. 85–111.

Ferrándiz, Francisco, and Antonius C. G. M. Robben, 'Introduction: The Ethnography of Exumations', in F. Ferrándiz and Antonius C. G. M. Robben (eds), *Necropolitics: Mass Graves and Exhumations in the Age of Human Rights* (Philadelphia: University of Pennsylvania Press, 2015), pp. 1–41.

Foucault, Michel, *'Society Must Be Defended': Lectures at Collège de France 1975–1976*, ed. Mauro Bentani and Alessandro Fontana, trans. David Macey (New York: Picador, 2003).

'HDP milletvekilleri İçişleri Bakanlığı'nda açlık grevine başladı', *T24*, 27 January 2016, <http://t24.com.tr/haber/hdpli-vekiller-icisleri-bakanliginda-aclik-grevine-basladi,325820> (last accessed 15 November 2018).

'HDP'li vekiller Davutoğlu ile Cizre'yi konuştu', *Ihlas Haber Ajansı*, 26 January 2016, <http://www.iha.com.tr/haber-hdpli-vekiller-davutoglu-ile-cizreyi-konustu-530761/> (last accessed 14 November 2018).

Göral, Özgür S., Ayhan Işık and Özlem Kaya, *Unspoken Truth: Enforced Disappearances* (Istanbul: Truth, Justice and Memory Center, 2013).

Gregory, Derek, *The Colonial Present: Afghanistan, Palestine, Iraq* (Oxford: Blackwell Publishing, 2003).

Kurt, Mehmet, *Kurdish Hizbullah in Turkey: Islamism, Violence and the State* (London: Pluto Press, 2017).

Mahmood, Cynthia Keppley, 'Terrorism, Myth, and the Power of Ethnographic Praxis', *Journal of Contemporary Ethnography* 30, no. 5 (2001): 520–45.

Malkki, Liisa, 'Children, Humanity and the Infantilization of Peace', in Ilana Feldman and Miriam Ticktin (eds), *In the Name of Humanity: The Government of Threat and Care* (Durham, NC: Duke University Press, 2010), pp. 58–72.

Mbembe, Achile, 'Necropolitics', *Public Culture* 15, no. 1 (Winter 2003): 11–40.

Monk, Daniel Bertand, *An Aesthetic Occupation: The Immediacy of Architecture and the Palestine Conflict* (Durham, NC: Duke University Press, 2002).

Öcalan, Abdullah, *Democratic Confederalism* (London: Transmedia Publishing, 2011).
'Our Application to the Committee of Ministers of the Council of Europe', HDP, 20 January 2016, <https://www.hdp.org.tr/en/news/from-hdp/our-application-to-the-committee-of-ministers-of-the-council-of-europe/8898> (last accessed 16 November 2018).
Özcan, Ömer, *Waiting as a Way of Life in a Kurdish Border Town in Turkey*, unpublished PhD dissertation, University of Texas Austin, 2017.
Özsoy, Hişyar, 'Between Gift and Taboo: Death and the Negotiation of National Identity and Sovereignty in the Kurdish Conflict in Turkey', unpublished PhD dissertation, University of Texas at Austin, May 2010.
Özsoy, Hişyar, 'The Missing Grave of Sheikh Said: Kurdish Formations of Memory, Place, and Sovereignty in Turkey', in Kamala Visweswaran (ed.), *Everyday Occupations: Experiencing Militarism in South Asia and the Middle East* (Philadelphia: University of Pennsylvania Press, 2013).
Parikh, Crystal, *Writing Human Rights: The Political Imaginaries of Writers of Color* (Minneapolis: University of Minnesota Press, 2017).
Robben, Antonius C. G. M., 'Exhumations, Territoriality, and Necropolitics in Chile and Argentina', in Francisco Ferrándiz and Antonius C. G. M. Robben (eds), *Necropolitics: Mass Graves and Exhumations in the Age of Human Rights* (Philadelphia: University of Pennsylvania Press, 2015), pp. 53–76.
Rojas-Perez, Isaias, *Mourning Remains: State Atrocity, Exhumations, and Governing the Disappeared in Peru's Postwar Andes* (Stanford, CA: Stanford University Press, 2017).
Şendağ, Duygu, *State Violence and Human Rights: The European Human Rights Court Cases Submitted against Turkey on Detention*, master's thesis, Sabancı University, 2010.
'Sokağa çıkma yasağı olan yerlerde tartışmalı defin uygulaması', *BBC*, 12 January 2016, <https://www.bbc.com/turkce/haberler/2016/01/160111_hatice_kamer_cenazeler> (last accessed 16 November 2018).
Stein, Rebecca, *Digital Militarism: Israel's Occupation in the Social Media Age* (Stanford, CA: Stanford University Press, 2015).
Taylor, Diana, *Disappearing Acts: Spectacles of Gender and Nationalism in Argentina's 'Dirty War'* (Durham, NC: Duke University Press, 1997).
'The Anatomy of Brutality: Comprehensive and Updated Report on Turkey's Blockade on Cizre District', Democratic Peoples' Party, 5 March 2018, <https://www.scribd.com/document/373008068/Cizre-Report-in-English-5th March2018#from_embed> (last accessed 16 November 2018).
Valentine, Gill, 'Angels and Devils', *Society and Space* 14, no. 5 (1996): 581–99.
Weizman, Eyal, *Hollow Land: Israel's Architecture of Occupation* (London: Verso, 2007).
Weizman, Eyal, *The Least of All Possible Evils: Humanitarian Violence from Arendt to Gaza* (London: Verso, 2012).

Wilson, R. A., *Human Rights in the 'War on Terror'* (Cambridge: Cambridge University Press, 2005).

Yeğen, Mesut, *Müstakbel Türk'ten Sözde Vatandaşa: Cumhuriyet ve Kürtler* (Istanbul: İletişim Yayınları, 2014).

Yönücü, Deniz, 'The Absent Present Law', *Social &Legal Studies* 27, no. 6 (2018): 716–33.

Zengin, Aslı, 'Cemile Çağırga: A Girl is Freezing under State Fire', *Jadaliyya*, 17 September 2015, <http://www.jadaliyya.com/Details/32470> (last accessed 16 November 2018).

Part Two

Negotiating Life: Resistance and Democracy

FIVE

The Necropolitics of Documents and the Slow Death of Prisoners in Turkey

Başak Can

There is a health crisis in Turkey's prisons. Ill prisoners cannot access proper medical treatment as they wait for documents for their transfer to a medical institution or their discharge, and they die prematurely as a result, turning prisons into spaces of death.[1] Since the mid-2000s, human rights groups, leftist and Kurdish political organisations have been campaigning for the release of ill prisoners, drawing upon two humanitarian laws regulating how to deal with ill prisoners: the first is the presidential pardon, which allows the president to intervene 'to alleviate penalties or suspend them for a person with chronic illness, disability or for the reason of ageing'[2] and the second is the article related to the suspension of the execution of a penalty due to illness (Article 399 in Law 1412 before 2004, Article 16 in Law 5275 after 2004) – to support their cause. The decision of postponement can be made by the Chief Public Prosecutor's Office 'upon a report issued by the Council of Forensic Medicine or issued by the health committee of a fully equipped hospital designated by the Ministry of Justice and approved by the Council of Forensic Medicine', which is the premier official expert authority on issues concerning forensic medicine and forensic sciences, including the investigation and documentation of prisoner illnesses. Despite calls for the decentralisation of document-making processes, the dependence on Council of Forensic Medicine (CFM) reports for making legal decisions continues. This dependence is the source of a heavy workload for CFM experts, causing long waiting periods for ill prisoners.

The problem of long waiting periods for the preparation, circulation and verification of medical reports has been central to the struggles for the rights of ill prisoners. It can take up to ten months for reports to be prepared after the medical examination of the prisoner at the Council[3] and ill prisoners become further vulnerable to bodily injury and death as they wait for these documents to be processed in prison. The families of prisoners, human rights activists working on their behalf and lawyers representing them aim to undo the violence of slow documents by forming counter-publics that also draw upon these reports. In other words, these medical documents can be both instruments of necropolitical violence and the grounds for making biopolitical arguments centred on the preservation of life.

To understand the relationship between life and death in contemporary power regimes, scholars, following Achille Mbembe and Michel Foucault, have elaborated upon the notion of necropolitics as the underside of biopower[4] and have shown the centrality of the reproduction of death and its representations for the modern state.[5] The analytics of necropolitics explores how lives are exposed, expended or violated under biopolitical regimes, how 'vast populations are subjected to conditions of life conferring upon them the status of living dead'.[6] The spatial seclusion and dividing of populations are critical mechanisms for the reproduction of necropolitical violence. This is especially so in prisons where 'the biopolitical project of disciplining and controlling bodies to create a healthier, more productive citizenship'[7] often co-exists with necropolitical practices, which incapacitate and debilitate already vulnerable populations.

The trajectories of official medical reports produced about the health condition of ill prisoners reveal the intersecting histories of necropolitics and biopolitics in Turkey's prisons. Starting off with a discussion of hunger strikes in Turkish prisons in 2000 and the social mobilisation for the discharge of Güler Zere, an ill political prisoner, in 2009, this chapter examines the role of official medical reports in mediating the relationship between politicised bodies, the bureaucracy and the wider public. As expert documents central to legal institutions and processes, these medical reports are not simply the reflections of the bad faith of official authorities towards political prisoners or instruments for the truthful representations of political prisoners' illnesses. In other words, these medical reports are not transparent elements of bureaucratic functioning; rather, they reframe the meaning of illness, health and the body as well as the relationships between the state and the citizen because they are 'produced, used, and experienced through procedures, techniques, aesthetics, ideologies, cooperation, negotiation, and contestation'.[8] The material and aesthetic qualities of medical reports are not separable from their meaning and efficacy. More specifically, what differentiates medical expert reports from other bureaucratic documents is their deployment of scientific medical knowledge to analyse the health situation of ill prisoners in order to answer questions raised by legal authorities.

The unique amalgamation of scientific and legal languages in these medical documents provides them with authority, which is difficult to challenge. The making of these medical reports at the CFM is also dependent on a series of other documents issued by other institutions which sometimes work at odds with each other. This chapter traces the associations afforded by the production and circulation of medical reports about the health situation of ill political prisoners within and outside the offices of the state[9] respectively. These associations challenge a monolithic conception of the state and ask us to envision something more fluid and strategic, but also one that is less consistent with having an overarching purpose.

Within state offices, these medical reports are the necessary but not entirely sufficient condition for the discharge of ill prisoners for two reasons. First of all, these documents might not be processed in time. There might be intentional and unintentional factors behind these delays, which potentially inflict necropolitical violence on ill prisoners irrespective of the content of the documents. Second, these reports can be declared null by other types of documents such as police reports concerning the security risk posited by the ill political prisoner. This is what I call a 'necropolitical hierarchy' of documents, which highlights the dynamic interactions between social and political actors that coalesce around such documents. As an index of official expert knowledge produced through the ailing bodies of ill prisoners, these medical reports also circulate outside these bureaucratic offices and become the object of anger and the evidence of suffering used by the advocates of prisoners' rights. Appropriating these documents for their own ends, advocates strive to show the worth of prisoners' lives and save them from being the objects of necropolitical violence. Overall, focusing on the associations afforded by medical reports reveals the contingency of these documents' articulations within the state's field of operation as well as the dynamics between the state and the oppositional forces in civil society.

The Limits of the Biopolitical Regime in Turkey: Ill Bodies in Prison

In Turkey, ill prisoners are frequently exposed to neglect, bodily injury, abuse and thus premature death. Despite the lack of comparative statistics on death rates in prisons, the number of people who have died in prison has regularly increased in the last two decades.[10] A prisoner's access to healthcare involves multiple stages that require the collective work of state officials including security forces, doctors, prison administrators, guardians, prosecutors and the gendarme. It also requires written petitions, approval documents, the availability of prison transfer vehicles, ambulances and personnel. Ill prisoners go through difficult and time-consuming bureaucratic processes only to access, if they can, low-quality health care service in either a prison ward or hospital ward.[11]

Against such necropolitical practices of the state, prisoners as well as prisoners' rights advocates appeal to the state's protection by mobilising national and international laws concerning the state's biopolitical responsibilities towards populations under its care. For example, they resort to the European Prison Rules prepared by the Committee of Ministers of the Council of Europe in 2006 for member states and the candidates for membership, including Turkey. According to Article 102.2 in these Rules, 'imprisonment is by the deprivation of liberty a punishment in itself and therefore the regime for sentenced prisoners shall not aggravate the suffering inherent in imprisonment'. In a similar vein, Article 39 states that 'prison authorities shall safeguard the health of all prisoners in their care'. The activists also refer to the Standard Minimum Rules for the Treatment of Prisoners, which were first adopted by the United Nations in 1955 and which describe health-related measures that prison administrations and medical officers are required to undertake. At the national level, according to Article 71 of Law 5275 on the Execution of Penalties and Security Measures, 'the convict shall have the right to benefit from examination and treatment possibilities and medical means for protection of his bodily and mental health and the diagnosis of his diseases'. The prisoner's health is also protected by Article 56 of the Constitution, which states that 'everyone has the right to live in a healthy and balanced environment. [...] The State shall regulate central planning and functioning of the health services to ensure that everyone leads a healthy life physically and mentally, and provide cooperation by saving and increasing productivity in human and material resources.' These legal frameworks require the state to ensure the health and wellbeing of prisoners.[12]

Biopolitical and necropolitical practices in this sense are not at odds with each other in Turkish prisons. They co-exist on a continuum between life-affirming and death-making mechanisms. That the experiences of ill prisoners often oscillate between biopolitical and necropolitical ends of state power can be best understood against the backdrop of the contentions between the state and political prisoners in Turkey. Historically, the Turkish state has intensive experience in dealing with the crisis of deteriorating health conditions amongst prisoners, since political prisoners frequently resort to hunger strikes.[13] By 'weaponising' their bodies through hunger, prisoners have not only resisted repressive and violent policies but have also challenged the state's biopolitical hegemony over their bodies in prisons.[14] Various governments have often responded to hunger strikes by softening or withdrawing their repressive practices or projects. According to the state's logic, the prolongation of hunger strikes would imply more dead bodies in prison, which would challenge the government's biopolitical sovereignty. However, the state policy towards the value of prisoners' lives and the importance of keeping them alive for maintaining biopolitical legitimacy have changed significantly due to one of the most recent hunger strikes in Turkey.

In the year 2000, political prisoners from the three radical organisations on the Turkish Left[15] began a hunger strike to protest the state's decision to transfer all political prisoners to high-security prisons. The hunger strike was transformed into a 'death fast' to show the prisoners' determination to continue fasting until death unless the high-security prison project was suspended. The representatives of civil society institutions, intellectuals and scholars got involved to mediate negotiations between the representatives of hunger strikers and the government. However, the state ended negotiations abruptly and carried out a military operation called 'Return to Life' to put an end to the death fast in prisons. Hunger strikers were transferred to hospitals, forcibly fed and then sent to the newly built high-security prisons. As a response to the state's violent intervention, other radical leftist organisations also decided to carry out hunger strikes in solidarity with prisoners already on the fast unto death. However, the government refused to negotiate with the prisoners and did not concede its original plan to open the high-security prisons. Consequently, the government was faced with the problem of numerous rapidly ailing bodies as hundreds of hunger strikers moved closer to the brink of death each day.

The sick, wounded and dying bodies of prisoners pose a danger to the biopolitical workings of the modern state, for which the reproduction of living subjects in its care is an important source of justification. If the government were to let hundreds of prisoners die in prison cells, prisons could turn into sites of collective anger and grief due to such politicised deaths.[16] When the death fast started to affect the health of hundreds of prisoners towards mid-2001, the government responded to this full-blown biopolitical crisis by resorting to Article 399 in Law 1412, an illness clause in Turkish criminal law, and the presidential pardon regulated in Article 104 of the Constitution. These humanitarian articles were implemented for hunger strikers, and hundreds of them were discharged[17] based on their medical reports. The Council of Forensic Medicine prepared the reports on the health condition of hunger strikers, which showed that they suffered from a form of irreversible brain damage known as Wernicke-Korsakoff, a condition caused by lack of vitamin B1 and, that, as such, they could not take care of themselves in prison.[18] In other words, the government preferred to solve the political crisis precipitated by the pending deaths in the mass hunger strike by resorting to technical and medical processes that would discharge ill and dying prisoners from prison.

The government's policy started to change in mid-2003, especially due to increased pressure from right-wing and conservative media outlets concerned with the discharge of numerous leftist political prisoners on the grounds of illness and through the presidential pardons. However, the repercussions of the extensive use of medical reports for discharge constituted a critical event that enabled new modes of action among social actors around questions of prisoner health and the use of medico-legal documentation of illness. As more ill prisoners started to resort to this article for their discharge, the power of medical reports, as well as the institutions issuing them, was augmented. Medical reports have a tendency to operate as invisible mediators of state bureaucracies. In order to restore the visibility of documents, Hull invites us to 'look at rather than through them'.[19] The manner in which medical reports are produced and circulated shapes not only governmental practice but also alternative publics and coalitions concerning ill political prisoners. The following will explore the ways in which the circulation of these documents between diverse state institutions over time contributes to their (in)efficacy to inflict premature death and to promote biopolitical protections for ill political prisoners.

The Necropolitical Violence of Documents

The illness article was not frequently discussed in the public sphere before the 2000s. Research into newspaper achieves and parliamentary debates yields very limited results, suggesting that the visibility of ill prisoners before the 2000s was quite restricted. Even though Article 399 regulating the suspension of execution of a penalty in case of a serious illness was in effect since the early twentieth century, it had rarely been invoked. The most comprehensive research concerning the health situation of prisoners was conducted by the Turkish Medical Association in 1999.[20] Their report mostly emphasises the bodily consequences of torture, ill-treatment and hunger strikes for prisoners. According to the self-reporting of prisoners examined in preparation for the Medical Association's report, there were 498 ill prisoners who did not have proper access to medical treatment in 1997. What is crucial here is that the question of ill prisoners was not on the agenda of the Turkish Left or Kurdish parties and human rights organisations as a systematic problem that warranted significant political attention at the time.

Towards the end of the first decade of the 2000s, the demands for a more humanitarian interpretation of the illness article became a pivotal agenda for different political groups and these demands were voiced more frequently in Turkey's public sphere. The first public campaign concerning ill prisoners sought the discharge of Güler Zere. Although Zere had been convicted of being a member of an illegal Marxist organisation, the campaign demanding her release was publicised with humanitarian and human rights slogans. The Zere campaign was initiated by those affiliated with one of the three radical organisations on the Turkish left that started the death fast in 2000 and thus familiar with the legal process concerning the release of ill prisoners. Despite continuing to make radical political arguments against the state's prison policy, they also actively invoked humanitarian and human rights articles related to the ill prisoners. This rights-oriented discourse echoed across other groups as well. The members of Human Rights Associations organised a sit-in protest every Saturday in Istanbul in 2011. Their goal was to publicise the plight of ill prisoners and ask for their quick discharge. The Kurdish political movement made the discharge of ill Kurdish prisoners their top demand during the peace process between 2013 and 2015.

The events surrounding the Zere campaign vividly highlight the central role that medical documents played in the service of the necropolitical practices of the state, and, concurrently, how they contributed to prisoners' rights struggles. Zere fell ill with cancer in the Elbistan Prison in the south-eastern province of Kahramanmaraş in the last months of 2008, after having served fourteen years of her sentence. The slowness of the document preparation processes and the inconsistencies evident among different medical reports were at the centre of the activist campaign demanding her release. For example, when her condition worsened after an operation she had in early 2009, she was transferred to the prisoner ward of Çukurova University Hospital. The medical report prepared by the hospital doctors reads: 'She is a heavily disabled person whose life is under serious risk. She is in need of care and supervision by another person as well as intense and severe treatment including radiotherapy, which cannot be provided under prison conditions. Therefore, it is advisable to postpone her sentence until she recovers.'[21] Despite this university hospital report, the public prosecutor was required by law to demand the certification of this report by the Council of Forensic Medicine in Istanbul. The Third Specialisation Board, which is responsible for preparing reports concerning the suspension of the execution of penalty among others,[22] could have just certified the report without seeing the patient in person due to the fact that it was a medical emergency, but the Board insisted on examining Zere in person, thus delaying a final decision in her case.[23]

Public prosecutors avoid using medical reports prepared by university hospitals, which they regard as less 'official' than medical reports prepared by the Council of Forensic Medicine because the former eventually need to be certified by the CFM according to Article 16. As a result, prosecutors often order ill prisoners across Turkey to be transferred to Istanbul CFM headquarters in unventilated, dirty and windowless prisoner transport vehicles to receive official expert reports. The ill prisoners refer to this transfer process to get reports from the CFM as 'report torture'. This torturous transfer process is presented by state officials as the only way for the bureaucratic process to move forward. Yet, only a small per cent of ill prisoners receive reports from the CFM that affirm their illness. According to an investigative report prepared on the health care services provided to inmates in penal institutions by the Grand National Assembly of Turkey Human Rights Investigation Commission in 2015, out of 3,663 applicants for the implementation of Article 16, 343 received affirmative reports from the CFM while 1,832 received negative reports and 1,043 were waiting for documents to be processed.[24] Most prisoners simply end up exhausted by the trip, which dashes their hopes for discharge and blocks their access to proper medical care. Subsequently, their lawyers may file an appeal against the reports issued by the CFM, starting the bureaucratic process all over again.

Zere was also transferred to Istanbul via a fourteen-hour trip on 6 July 2009. However, the final CFM report did not certify the conclusion in the report issued by the university hospital. It concluded instead with a contrary assessment: 'her treatment can continue in the prisoner ward of the Çukurova Hospital'.[25] Zere's lawyers objected to this report, pointing out the contradiction between the two expert reports. The CFM agreed to discuss this contradiction at its General Assembly's next meeting. However, Zere's case could not be discussed for months due to the fact that there were some medical reports missing in her file. Zere spent this time waiting in a prisoner ward in an Istanbul hospital. These ad hoc rooms converted into prisoner wards are located in the basement of hospitals and are often dark, dirty and unhygienic spaces. Guards often used handcuffs to tie her to hospital beds during her treatment. Two soldiers continuously watched over her. Because contact with families and attendants are kept at a minimum, she was not allowed to have a family attendant stay with her in the hospital room.

Towards the end of the summer of 2009, many state officials from the Ministry of Justice to the President's Office began to face questions about the fate of Güler Zere. The circulation of a picture of Zere lying in the fetal position on a bed in the prison ward, with a policeman standing next to her, contributed to the publicity of her case. Human rights activists and different political groups organised campaigns, marches and press statements demanding 'Freedom for Güler Zere'. Even the columnists of rightwing newspapers wrote articles supporting the discharge of Zere and her right to access medical care. Political groups and organisations affiliated with the People's Front (*Halk Cephesi*), of which Güler Zere was a member, were drawn towards the place where these expert documents are produced. They organised a month-long sit-in in front of the Council of Forensic Medicine in August 2009 in order to protest the delays in the Council's reporting process.

The Council of Forensic Medicine was in need of further documents from the hospital regarding Zere's latest condition to prepare its final assessment. Her lawyers were trying to submit medical reports stamped with a date that preceded the meeting by only a few days in order to not compromise the validity of the reports. If the reports were considered not to be up-to-date, the Council could have postponed the meeting. Given the fact that Zere's health condition was continuously deteriorating, her latest medical assessment deemed her condition unstable. It took a lot of time and energy on part of her lawyers and family to make sure that they had her latest medical reports ready right before the general meeting of the Council. Her father describes their experiences concerning these reports as follows:

> We've sent a pack of reports. We are embarrassed to ask for further reports from doctors here (Çukurova University Hospital). They (CFM) keep saying that 'a file is missing'. The process got stuck at the Council of Forensic Medicine. They do not want to discharge her, they want to kill her. This is the truth behind it. Our lawyers are trying hard, we are working hard. Most recently, they asked for another medical report. We sent it. She just had another operation, so we had to send a new report. Then they found some missing documents in her file again. Then a friend of us sent it to them, but all this to no avail.[26]

On 4 November 2009, approximately four months after Zere's first examination at the CFM, the Third Specialisation Board finally gathered to prepare its ultimate report on Zere. The report testified that her illness was permanent and that there was no prospect of recovery, recommending that she should be released. The then President Abdullah Gül intervened and pardoned Güler Zere amidst the public outcry for her release.[27] She passed away only seven months later.[28]

After her release, Zere said: 'When I was released from prison, it was too late. They brought me next to death and left me there. My right to life was usurped. I was given the right to die outside the prison. I will never forget this.'[29] Like Zere, most prisoners are discharged only when their illness reaches a terminal stage. As the ill prisoners are transferred between institutions, waiting for the necessary documents to be prepared, verified and circulated amongst institutions, they are reduced to the 'status of living dead' in prison wards of hospitals or prisons. As human rights lawyer Gülizar, who deals with numerous cases of ill prisoners as part of the Human Rights Association, says, 'they are delivered to their families half-dead'.[30] The prisoners' right to life is conditional upon the documentation of their near-death condition. The criterion of the 'absolute danger to life' in the illness clause turns into an absolute expectation of death because legal authorities are reluctant to discharge any political prisoner who can even partially recover from their illness after such a discharge. The CFM doctors write their reports according to this unstated criterion and declare their opinions at the end of their reports as to whether the prisoner is fit to live in prison on their own. Most of the prisoners who receive reports affirming their terminal condition are often in the final stages of their illness. In many cases, they are either effectively unconscious or extremely ill, necessitating their immediate transfer to intensive care units for better treatment. Many of them survive only for a couple of months after their discharge. If not, they die before their discharge decision.[31] This is what I call the 'necropolitical violence of documents'.

If an ill prisoner dies outside the prison, it is as if the state and penal system have had nothing to do with this death. Instead, the discharge of ill prisoners at the point of death lowers the mortality rate in prisons. In other words, the necropolitical violence of documents saves the biopolitical face of the state by reducing the number of prisoners who die under state care. The ill prisoners and the documents concerning their rights, health status and medical treatment are continuously bounced amongst the prison, the court house, the hospital and the Council of Forensic Medicine. This mundane state practice of circulating prisoners and official documents amongst different agencies reveals the extent to which a bureaucracy operates in relation to ill prisoners, inflicting necropolitical violence that often contributes to their premature death. The prison administration and guardians, who are affiliated with the Ministry of Justice, are the ones who have the authority to accept or deny the prisoner's petition to see a doctor. The doctors who took care of Zere in prison or the hospital are affiliated with the Ministry of Health. Yet the ultimate decision about the prisoner's situation is taken by the prosecutors and judges who are affiliated with the Ministry of Justice. The transfer of ill prisoners between the hospital, the prison and the Council of Forensic Medicine is organised by the gendarme of the Ministry of Interior

Affairs. As a result, there are cracks, inconsistencies and intentional and unintentional delays during these transfers between different parts of the state bureaucracy. In other words, despite the systematic delays in issuing, verifying and circulating these documents, these temporal gaps are not always necessarily intentional, but rather due to the fragmented nature of the state bureaucracies. The following section deals with two elements in this process: First, different parts of the state bureaucracy might be at odds with each other in ways that reinforce or diminish the efficacy of medical reports, and thus function either to reproduce or to challenge the necropolitical violence of documents. Second, these medical documents afford new social relations amongst ill prisoners, their families and supporters, and the doctors who are issuing these reports.

The Necropolitical Hierarchy of Documents

The government's response to the rising visibility of prisoner illness cases was inconsistent. It first expanded the scope of Article 16, but then introduced a new security criterion which would further complicate the discharge of ill prisoners. In the earlier version of the law, ill prisoners could resort to this article only if the execution of their sentence presented 'an absolute danger to the life of the convict'. The recent amendment made it possible for those who could not take care of themselves in prison to request a reprieve of the execution of their sentence. However, both criteria, that is, 'an absolute danger to life' and 'not being able to take care of oneself in prison', focus only on the life-threatening consequences of remaining in prison for the duration of the prisoners' sentence. The doctors in the Council and hospitals are thus asked to examine patients and their medical records to answer whether the ill prisoners meet these criteria. This narrow legal focus adopted by doctors in the reports inevitably renders invisible the complex health context of ill prisoners and the debilitating effects that prison conditions have upon them. Moreover, even if the medico-legal report concludes that the ill prisoner should not stay in prison, the deferral of the sentence is made conditional upon a further assessment by security forces that must declare that the prisoner 'constitutes no danger in terms of social security'.[32]

One high-profile case was that of Ramazan Özalp, who was paralysed due to a brain tumor. The medical reports from both the hospital and the CFM advised postponing his sentence. The prosecutor requested the written opinion of the anti-terrorism unit and law enforcement officials in his village to ascertain whether or not Özalp would pose a security threat to society. After evaluating the opinion of the gendarmerie along with the forensic medicine report, the prosecutor denied the release request with the following statement:

> He himself does not pose a threat to the security of society, but in the case of his arrival at the village of Dirsekli in the Idil province, he might be used as a propaganda tool by some political people and citizens, and this might give rise to various political actions and cause tension and conflict between citizens with different political views and security forces, and this situation might be reflected in the press and cause unrest.[33]

In order to protect the social body, he was thereby expended. He was kept in prison for another eight months before his condition worsened and then he was transferred to a hospital. He was discharged only to live another four months in a private clinic in his hometown. There are more than 800 prisoners like Ramazan Özalp who, despite having received reports from the CFM affirming the need for their release, are not being discharged for security reasons.[34] This 'danger to social security' amendment has thus expanded the discretionary powers of security forces, as well as of political and legal authorities for whom the bodies and lives of political prisoners are almost always considered dangerous to the social body.

The centrality of the notion of 'danger' in this article is telling. The 'danger to the life of the convict' can be prevented if the prison sentence is suspended, but this can only occur if the prisoner is not deemed a 'danger' to society. This article very neatly summarises the contradiction between the protection of the individual body and the social body. This biopolitical contradiction is resolved through a necropolitical logic, which divides society and declares certain people a 'danger' to the rest of society. Lawmakers want to reassure the public that political prisoners, who are regarded as potential terrorists, do not constitute a danger to society. The article requires the prosecutor to make sure that such danger does not exist. Even after an illness is documented by the Council of Forensic Medicine, the prosecutor has to ask security forces to determine if the prisoner would pose a security threat to society if they were to be released. With this regulation, the practice of not discharging prisoners becomes legalised, even when they have reports affirming that their condition necessitates release. The arbitrary decision-making process concerning ill political prisoners is included in the law in a way that further empowers state officials, specifically the security forces.

With the legalisation of arbitrariness in the illness clause, medical expertise and documentation concerning ill prisoners have diminished in importance. However, documents including medical reports are mobile and context-bound entities and their meaning and import change as they circulate. Human rights activists and relatives of political prisoners rely on reports obtained from university hospitals and the CFM in order to make biopolitical claims in favour of ill prisoners. They create alternative public spaces where these documents circulate and reach a wider audience in order to make the suffering of ill prisoners visible. These practices aim to rescue medico-legal documents from being solely an instrument of necropolitical violence. For example, human rights activists and families of ill prisoners organise campaigns around the biological basis of prisoner illness using these documents. This is most visible in the weekly F-Type protests organised by the Prison Commission of the Human Rights Association (*İnsan Hakları Derneği Hapishane Komisyonu*). During these protests, people sit in the form of a capital F with reference to high-security prisons, also known as the F-types. There are two prominent banners in these protests, which read: 'The isolation policy kills. Close down F-type prisons!' and 'We do not want any more deaths in prison. Discharge seriously ill prisoners!' Protest participants stand behind these banners and hold them aloft. They also carry the pictures of ill prisoners and A3 size posters with the names of ill prisoners and their illnesses, such as the following: 'Özgür Uygun: paralyzed', 'Siraç Toğluk: severe cardiac patient', 'Fesih Aslan: 80% mental retardation', 'Fatih Gül: advanced tuberculosis', 'Fırat Özçelik: brain overgrowth'. This is an uncanny form of protest where the onlooker is invited to witness the slow death of ill prisoners. The medical diagnoses of the prisoners' illnesses are turned into slogans to make demands for the suspension of the execution of a penalty.

These biologically based rights claims are central to prisoners' rights movements, which draw heavily upon the medico-legal reports prepared by general hospitals or the Council of Forensic Medicine. Protestors read these medical documents alongside the letters from ill prisoners to put pressure on relevant political and bureaucratic authorities. These letters often describe the progression of the illness, the kind of medical treatment the ill prisoner has received or was denied, how the prisoner currently feels, who takes care of the prisoner behind bars or what kind of diet is needed. If the relatives or lawyers of the prisoner are at the protest, they narrate the most recent information available on the prisoner's health and the bureaucratic obstacles they have encountered in order to see a doctor, to access medical treatment or to obtain medico-legal reports from the Council of Forensic Medicine. Drawing on the principles of medical ethics and national and international conventions, they challenge the legal practices that reproduce the marginality of political prisoners by substantiating medico-legal reports with prisoners' personal illness stories.

At a broader level, this is a very effective way of mobilising humanitarian sentiments amongst the wider population, considering the government's insistence on classifying ill political prisoners as a 'dangerous population'. Resorting to the state's claim of biopolitical protection only becomes effective if the prisoner is classified as a human being whose life is valuable. These struggles and complaints against the arbitrary implementation of the illness article have prompted the government to respond by amending the article a third time, almost a year and a half after it had already been revised. The adjectives of 'severe or substantial' (*ağır ve somut*) were added in front of the clause 'danger in terms of social security' to curtail, at least partially, the arbitrariness embedded in the law.

The F-type protests demonstrate that the necropolitical power of documents can be challenged by human rights activists and families who insist on the humanity of the ill prisoners over and against state practices that tend to label them as terrorists, criminals or enemies of the state. Such protests draw attention away from the acts committed by these prisoners that landed them in prison in the first place and instead track the progression of their illnesses and the difficulties they endure in securing access to proper medical care. As the critical literature on biological citizenship has shown, there are limits to the use of biology as the basis for demanding political or social citizenship rights. More specifically, the emphasis on bodily suffering might obstruct a person's political agency or the broader political-economic dynamics that cause illness in the first place.[35] This framework fails to account for the complex repercussions of ill political prisoners and their supporters using bodily illness to make biopolitical demands. Given the fact that state officials, prison administrators, guardians, security forces and even some doctors tend to see the body of the political prisoner first and foremost as a political body that poses a danger to the social body, one can argue that there is a resistance on their part to focus solely on the bodily suffering of the ill political prisoner. For example, it is a very common practice for prison administrators to add little notes on the medical files of political prisoners, notes that indicate their political affiliation or their 'terror-related crimes' before transferring them to a health centre outside the prison. This breach of confidentiality placed on court records aims to dehumanise the political prisoner as a patient in the eyes of the doctor and places the prisoners at greater risk of receiving substandard treatment when they are transferred. In other words, making biopolitical demands in this context does not necessarily indicate a politics that is reduced to bodily suffering. It rather suggests a radical political position against the historically informed pejorative attitudes of some state officials against political prisoners.

The state apparatuses' conflicting biopolitical priorities vis-à-vis ill political prisoners creates a necropolitical hierarchy between different types of documents. Which type of document is more likely to contribute to the making-of-death for the ill prisoner depends on the political conjuncture, the current version of the law and the power struggles between diverse political groups and state institutions. In other words, a document might well become both an instrument of necropolitics and one of biopolitics at different times, depending on the context in which it is used. Most of the time, a report confirming illness is not sufficient in and of itself to guarantee the discharge of the prisoner. This report must also be issued, verified and transferred to the related authorities on time. Moreover, a report issued by a university hospital might be overruled by a report prepared by the CFM. The CFM report might be overruled by a document prepared by the police to keep the ill prisoner behind bars, unless the prisoner's lawyers and advocates push to start the legal process all over again. Finally, while medico-legal documents frequently emerge as the death-making mechanism for some prisoners, these same documents can later be appropriated by human rights activists to make biopolitical claims for others.

The necropolitical hierarchy of documents is always in the making and reflects the social and political contentions between diverse actors. This is reflected in the contradictory classifications of ill prisoners, which characterise them as criminals, enemies of the state or patients, depending on the institutional context in which these documents are embedded. State officials do not publicly engage in debates that could enable working through these differences. Rather, it is through the circulation of different documents within the bureaucratic machinery that the contradictory approaches of state officials towards ill prisoners are negotiated. In this sense, the necropolitical power of documents is not absolute. It is constantly calibrated through the daily struggles between the biopolitical and necropolitical priorities of actors both within and outside of the institutions of the state bureaucracy. These negotiations are almost always mediated and finalised through a set of official documents, which provide the legal or medical evidential basis for diverse claims concerning the bodies of ill prisoners and the worth of their lives.

Conclusion: Documents as Necropolitical Technologies

Throughout the first decade of the 2000s, we have witnessed the increasing visibility of the question of ill prisoners and a heightened awareness regarding the illness clause that regulates their rights. The prisoners' rights advocates have aimed to capitalise on the wave of 'democratisation' that came along with the EU integration process and the relatively optimistic atmosphere of the peace process regarding the Kurdish problem in order to address the situation of ill prisoners. However, their overall achievements were minimal. The situation reversed in early 2015, when the peace process was aborted and relations with the EU deteriorated. The situation of ill prisoners has worsened after the coup attempt in 2016, which has not only swelled the prison population to an all-time high but also curtailed many prisoners' rights with the declaration of emergency rule. Against the backdrop of increasingly intolerant and authoritarian practices perpetrated by the state apparatus towards ill political prisoners in the last decade, this chapter has traced medical reports about ill political prisoners and situated them as emblems of the rational logics of medicine and law, as well as instruments of necropolitical violence.

Documents tell us a complex story about the intermingling of disciplinary, humanitarian and violent state practices vis-à-vis ill political prisoners. Rather than being transparent and neutral instruments of bureaucratic organisations, documents act as mediators and material vehicles that transform the meaning of what they are documenting.[36] This makes them context-dependent. Documents also endure over time,[37] travel across space and connect diverse state institutions and political movements. Documents concerning ill prisoners gain their necropolitical power only vis-à-vis other documents, and over time. The socially consequential roles of these documents can be analysed within the totality of the bureaucratic and non-bureaucratic life-worlds in which they are produced and circulated. By tracing documents, this chapter has analysed the interaction of the medical, legal and administrative operations of legal and bureaucratic technologies concerning the value of a prisoner's life.

Criminal law in Turkey is ostensibly designed to provide health care to ill prisoners in line with international conventions. However, the more we scrutinise the daily workings of the article concerning the 'suspension of execution of penalty', the more we observe the proliferation of death rather than life, of illness rather than health. The biopolitical protections afforded to prisoners that should work to ensure their health easily slip into necropolitical violence that hastens their death. Necropolitical violence or the making-of-death in the case of ill prisoners requires more than 'letting die' or 'disallowing life to the point of death' in the Foucauldian sense. It requires the involvement of multiple legal and administrative institutions that manage the bureaucratic process by controlling the circulation of documents and, by extension, the fate of ill prisoners.

Analysing the workings of necropolitics through medical documents opens up a new analytics for thinking about the relationship between the body, the state and death-making processes. Documents are not inherently violent, but they are important analytical vehicles to trace how necropolitical violence takes effect through the daily workings of the state's bureaucratic machinery. Tracing the work of documents in relation to ostensibly 'humanitarian' laws that should protect prisoners' rights allows us to see the ramifications of the exceptional violence conducted underneath their purview. Analysing these documents reveals the quotidian, unstable and intricate workings of necropolitics vis-à-vis ill prisoners. Documents thus work as complex technologies of violence that might confer ill prisoners to the status of 'living death'. However, documents can also be taken up and recirculated by human rights activists and political parties to make biopolitical claims in favour of ill prisoners. Their endurance as material artefacts gives documents unexpected powers as potential evidence of ill-treatment and torture, especially as they are put to an alternative use in challenging the limits of necropolitical violence exercised by the state.

Notes

1. According to the report of the Human Rights Association released on 22 June 2017, there are 1,025 ill prisoners in Turkey's prisons. See 'Hasta Mahpuslar Ölüme Sürükleniyor', *Gazete Duvar*, 26 October 2017.
2. This right was granted to the president in Article 104 of the Constitution.
3. TBMM İnsan Haklarını İnceleme Komisyonu, *Ceza İnfaz Kurumlarında Hükümlü ve Tutuklulara Sunulan Sağlık Hizmetleri Hakkında İnceleme Raporu*, 2015, p. 42.
4. Inda, 'Analytics of the Modern: An Introduction'.
5. Melissa W. Wright, 'Necropolitics, Narcopolitics, and Femicide'; Banu Bargu, *Starve and Immolate*; Banu Bargu, 'Another Necropolitics'; John Round and Irina Kuznetsova, 'Necropolitics and the Migrant as a Political Subject of Disgust'.
6. Achille Mbembe, 'Necropolitics', p. 40.
7. Jessi Lee Jackson, 'Sexual Necropolitics and Prison Rape Elimination', p. 199.
8. Matthew S. Hull, *Government of Paper*, p. 25.
9. Nayanika Mathur, *Paper Tiger*.
10. Berivan Korkut, 'Hapiste Sağlık Proje Kitabı', p. 20.
11. See the following web page devoted to the health-related problems of prisoners across Turkey: 'Hapiste Sağlık: Hapishanelerdeki hastaların durumları, hakları, ihtiyaçları', <https://hapistesaglik.com/> (last accessed 17 October 2018).
12. See the following report for a comprehensive discussion of these legal protections: TBMM İnsan Haklarını İnceleme Komisyonu, *Ceza İnfaz Kurumlarında Hükümlü ve Tutuklulara Sunulan Sağlık Hizmetleri Hakkında İnceleme Raporu*, 2015.
13. See the following page for a brief history of hunger strikes in Turkey: 'Türkiye'deki cezaevlerinde yapılmış açlık grevleri', *Wikipedia* (2014).
14. Bargu, *Starve and Immolate*.
15. The Revolutionary People's Liberation Party-Front (DHKP-C) and Communist Party of Turkey (Marxist Leninist)–Workers' Peasants' Liberation Army of Turkey (TKP(ML)–TİKKO) and Communist Workers' Party of Turkey (TKİP).

16. Noam Leshem, '"Over Our Dead Bodies"'; Bargu, 'Another Necropolitics'.
17. Ahmet Necdet Sezer, the then president of the Republic, pardoned more than 181 political prisoners, who suffer from Wernicke-Korsakoff syndrome, between 2001 and 2006. See the parliamentary question no 7/13337, 12/05/20106.
18. According to doctoral thesis research conducted in the Council of Forensic Medicine in 2003, 325 out of 344 hunger strikes, who were transferred to the Council for receiving medico-legal reports, were diagnosed with Wernicke-Korsakoff syndrome. See Küçükçallı, 'Uzun Süreli Açlıkların Adli Tıptaki Yeri ve Önemi'. Between May 2011 and March 2002, the sentences of 234 convicts were suspended in accordance with Article 399 based on the reports prepared by the Council. See the parliamentary question no 7/5719, 12/3/2002.
19. Hull, *Government of Paper*, p. 13.
20. Ata Soyer, *Cezaevi ve Sağlık*.
21. This report was quoted in a parliamentary question submitted by Durdu Özbolat.
22. For more information on the specialisation boards of the Council of Forensic Medicine, see 'İdari Yapı: İhtisas Kurulları'.
23. Tolga Korkut, 'Adli Tıp Gecikiyor, Güler Zere İçin Hala Karar Veremiyor', *Bianet*, 11 September 2009.
24. TBMM İnsan Haklarını İnceleme Komisyonu, *Ceza İnfaz Kurumlarında Hükümlü ve Tutuklulara Sunulan Sağlık Hizmetleri Hakkında İnceleme Raporu*, 2015.
25. 'Güler Zere Cezasını Hastanede Çekebilir', *Habertürk*, 23 July 2009.
26. 'Güler Zere Yaşayan Ölü Gibi', *Milliyet*, 3 November 2009.
27. 'Cumhurbaşkanı Gül Zere'yi affetti', *Hürriyet*, 7 November 2009.
28. 'Güler Zere Öldü', *Radikal*, 7 May 2009.
29. Güler Zere, 'Güler Zere'nin Mektubu Bu Kez Dışarıdan', *Bianet*, 16 November 2009.
30. Gülizar Tuncer, 'Türkiye'de haftada 5 hasta mahpus yaşamını yitiriyor', *YouTube*, 5 June 2018.
31. See the following news report for further examples: 'Ramazan Özalp geciken tahliyesinden sonra ancak 4 ay yaşadı: "Adalet"in ömür törpüsü', *Hapiste Sağlık*, 2014.
32. According to the new version, 'The execution of the penalty of a convict who cannot continue his life in prison conditions due to a severe illness or disability or who are evaluated to constitute danger in terms of social security may be deferred until his/her recovery according to the procedures determined in the third paragraph' (Turkish Criminal Law Article 5275 Addendum: 24/1/2013-6411/3).
33. Bakırköy Public Prosecutor's decision to decline the postponement of execution of sentence, dated 19 August 2013.
34. According to data released by the Ministry of Justice in February 2017, 841 ill prisoners are waiting to be released despite having positive reports from the Council of Forensic Medicine. This number was sixty-three in 2013. In other words, in the space of five years, there was a 1,235 per cent increase in the

number of prisoners who are waiting to be discharged. See '451 hasta mahpus hayatını kaybetti, 1086'sı ölümü bekliyor', *Evrensel*, 8 May 2017.
35. Adriana Petryna, *Life Exposed*; Miriam Ticktin, *Casualties of Care*.
36. Hull, 'Documents and Bureaucracy'.
37. Annelise Riles, *Documents*; Hull, 'Documents and Bureaucracy'; Ian Hodder, 'The Interpretation of Documents and Material Culture'.

Bibliography

'451 hasta mahpus hayatını kaybetti, 1086'sı ölümü bekliyor', *Evrensel*, 8 May 2017, <https://www.evrensel.net/haber/318866/451-hasta-mahpus-hayatini-kaybetti-1086si-olumu-bekliyor≥ (last accessed 1 September 2018).

Bargu, Banu, 'Another Necropolitics', *Theory & Event* 19, no. 1, February 2016.

Bargu, Banu, *Starve and Immolate: The Politics of Human Weapons* (New York: Columbia University Press, 2014).

'Cumhurbaşkanı Gül Zere'yi affetti', *Hürriyet*, 7 November 2009, <http://www.hurriyet.com.tr/gundem/cumhurbaskani-gul-zereyi-affetti-12879606>_(last accessed 10 October 2018).

'Güler Zere Cezasını Hastanede Çekebilir', *Habertürk*, 23 July 2009, <https://www.haberturk.com/yasam/haber/160625-guler-zere-cezasini-hastanede-cekebilir≥ (last accessed 25 January 2019).

'Güler Zere Öldü', *Radikal*, 7 May 2009, <http://www.radikal.com.tr/turkiye/guler-zere-oldu-995584/> (last accessed 10 October 2018).

'Güler Zere Yaşayan Ölü Gibi', *Milliyet*, 3 November 2009, <http://www.milliyet.com.tr/guler-zere-yasayan-olu-gibi-gundem-1157734/> (last accessed 10 October 2018).

'Hapiste Sağlık: Hapishanelerdeki hastaların durumları, hakları, ihtiyaçları', <https://hapistesaglik.com/> (last accessed 17 October 2018).

'Hasta Mahpuslar Ölüme Sürükleniyor', *Gazete Duvar*, 26 October 2017, <https://www.gazeteduvar.com.tr/gundem/2017/10/26/ihdden-adli-tip-tepkisi/≥ (last accessed 1 September 2018).

Hodder, Ian, 'The Interpretation of Documents and Material Culture', in *Handbook of Qualitative Research* (Thousand Oaks, CA: Sage Publications Inc, 1994), pp. 393–402.

Hull, Matthew S., 'Documents and Bureaucracy', *Annual Review of Anthropology* 41, no. 1 (2012): 251–67.

Hull, Matthew S., *Government of Paper: The Materiality of Bureaucracy in Urban Pakistan* (Berkeley: University of California Press, 2012).

'İdari Yapı: İhtisas Kurulları', n.d., <http://www.atk.gov.tr/adli-tip-ihtisas-kurulu.html> (last accessed 10 October 2018).

Inda, Jonathan Xavier, 'Analytics of the Modern: An Introduction', in Jonathan Xavier Inda (ed.), *Anthropologies of Modernity: Foucault, Governmentality, and Life Politics* (Malden, MA: Blackwell Publishing, 2005), pp. 1–22.

Jackson, Jessi Lee, 'Sexual Necropolitics and Prison Rape Elimination', *Signs* 39, no. 1 (2013): 197–220.

Korkut, Berivan, 'Hapiste Sağlık Proje Kitabı', TCPS Kitaplığı (Istanbul: Ceza İnfaz Sisteminde Sivil Toplum Derneği, 2017).

Korkut, Tolga, 'Adli Tıp Gecikiyor, Güler Zere İçin Hala Karar Veremiyor', *Bianet*, 11 September 2009, <https://m.bianet.org/bianet/insan-haklari/117002-adli-tip-gecikiyor-guler-zere-icin-hala-karar-veremiyor> (last accessed 1 September 2018).

Küçükçallı, Nevin, 'Uzun Süreli Açlıkların Adli Tıptaki Yeri ve Önemi', *Adli Tıp Uzmanlık Tezi* (2003), <https://www.ttb.org.tr/eweb/aclik_grevleri/tez_nevin_k.pdf≥ (last accessed 1 September 2018).

Leshem, Noam, '"Over Our Dead Bodies": Placing Necropolitical Activism', *Political Geography* 45 (March 2015): 34–44.

Mathur, Nayanika, *Paper Tiger: Law, Bureaucracy and the Developmental State in Himalayan India* (Cambridge University Press, 2015).

Mbembe, Achille, 'Necropolitics', trans. Libby Meintjes, *Public Culture* 15, no. 1 (Winter 2013): 11–40.

Özbolat, Durdu, 'Parliamentary Question', 4 August 2009, <http://www2.tbmm.gov.tr/d23/7/7-9276s.pdf≥ (last accessed 1 September 2018).

Petryna, Adriana, *Life Exposed: Biological Citizens after Chernobyl* (Princeton: Princeton University Press, 2002).

'Ramazan Özalp geciken tahliyesinden sonra ancak 4 ay yaşadı: "Adalet"in ömür törpüsü', *Hapiste Sağlık*, (2014), <https://hapistesaglik.com/2014/11/05/ramazan-ozalp-geciken-tahliyesinden-sonra-ancak-4-ay-yasadi-adaletin-omur-torpusu/≥ (last accessed 1 September 2018).

Riles, Annelise, *Documents: Artifacts of Modern Knowledge* (Ann Arbor: University of Michigan Press, 2006).

Round, John, and Irina Kuznetsova, 'Necropolitics and the Migrant as a Political Subject of Disgust: The Precarious Everyday of Russia's Labour Migrants', *Critical Sociology* 42, no. 7–8 (2016): 1017–34.

Soyer, Ata, *Cezaevi ve Sağlık: Cezaevi, Ezaevi, Sayrıevi, Ölümevi* (Yenişehir, Ankara: Türk Tabibleri Birliği Merkez Konseyi, 1999).

TBMM İnsan Haklarını İnceleme Komisyonu, *Ceza İnfaz Kurumlarında Hükümlü ve Tutuklulara Sunulan Sağlık Hizmetleri Hakkında İnceleme Raporu*, (2015), <https://www.tbmm.gov.tr/komisyon/insanhaklari/docs/2015/saglik_hizmetleri_hakkinda.pdf≥ (last accessed 17 October 2018).

Ticktin, Miriam, *Casualties of Care: Immigration and the Politics of Humanitarianism in France* (Berkeley: University of California Press, 2011).

Tuncer, Gülizar, 'Türkiye'de Haftada 5 Mahpus Yaşamını Yitiriyor', *YouTube*, 5 June 2018, <https://www.youtube.com/watch?v=K0_MM_5PYhk≥ (last accessed 1 September 2018).

'Türkiye'deki cezaevlerinde yapılmış açlık grevleri', *Wikipedia*, 2014, <http://ob.nubati.net/wiki/T%C3%BCrkiye%27deki_cezaevlerinde_yap%C4%B1lm%

C4%B1%C5%9F_a%C3%A7l%C4%B1k_grevleri#.22Hayata_D.C3.B6n.C3.BC. C5.9F.22_Operasyonu> (last accessed 1 September 2018).

Wright, Melissa W., 'Necropolitics, Narcopolitics, and Femicide: Gendered Violence on the Mexico–US Border', *Signs* 36, no. 3 (2011): 707–31.

Zere, Güler, 'Güler Zere'nin Mektubu Bu Kez Dışarıdan', *Bianet*, 16 November 2009, <https://bianet.org/bianet/siyaset/118278-guler-zere-nin-mektubu-bu-kez-disaridan> (last accessed 10 October 2018).

SIX

Proper Subjects of Gendered Necropolitics: A Case of Constructed Virginities in Turkey

Elif Savaş

In Turkey the disruptive force of misogyny kills women twice; both literally and metaphorically, through the recalcitrant appropriation and glorification of virginity by a gendered necropolitical regime. Virginity, with its (assumed) presence, functions as the signifier of a proper female subject. Put differently, its (supposed) absence implies a threat to the idealised construction of Turkish and Sunni Muslim morality and to the body politic of masculine sovereignty. Hence, this threat, the sexually autonomous female body, must be subjugated.

In this chapter, I examine hymen reconstruction operations in Turkey as an example of a medico-political assemblage that portrays the necropolitical vectors of Turkey's 'gender regime'. In applying the term gender 'regime', I follow Judith Butler's use of the term regime to delineate gender as a 'regulatory practice'.[1] Gender regime is a 'power matrix' and a 'regulatory economy of sexual desire'[2] that aims at a certain knowledge production which renders gender identities 'intelligible'.[3] Butler claims that 'intelligible genders are those which in some sense institute and maintain relations of coherence and continuity among sex, gender, and sexual practice and desire'.[4] In our times, these identities are largely heteronormative and hegemonic.

A gender regime functions by enforcing norms of gender and sexual desire over a terrain of unequal distribution of power. It is, at least in Turkey, intrinsically 'phallogocentric'[5] in that it aims to build a masculine hegemony in which there is a patriarchal male as power-holder and norm-giver whose objective is to consolidate itself as the sovereign and a female subject as its 'Other'. The masculine centre of the regime is constituted by the creation of its Other and his sovereignty is reinstituted in each instance where any deviation from the prescribed roles of the submissive feminine is diagnosed and disciplined. The production of a sovereign-male figure, his relations to the Other and the Other's resistance to his power lead us to the point where the gender regime meets necropolitics, understood as the capability to rule by exposing the subjects to the logic of death.

The gender regime co-exists and is even partly co-centric with other systems of hegemony that are cultural, institutional and medical. The Turkish gender regime has cultural specifications related to the marriage bond in addition to the general matrix of gender and desire. An intelligible female, i.e., an identity with proper attributes of the feminine, is not only a cis woman with heterosexual desires but also a woman whose enjoyment of sexuality is chronologically ordered in relation to the marital bond. As premarital sex is prohibited, virginity becomes a definitive aspect (for the intelligible or prescribed gender identity) that later enables the 'necropolitical' treatment of the non-virgin as well as the medical opportunities to bring her back into the fold of the dominant norm – rendering the woman 'virgin' again with an artificially made hymen.

The medico-political assemblage that enables the reproduction of virginity is the surgery known as hymenoplasty, and its basic function is either to bring the remnants of a hymen membrane together through sewing them together, or to form a new hymen by assembling neighbouring tissue that can imitate the original structure of the hymen. These medical approaches seek to resurrect a woman's virginal state and thus allow for the shedding of blood upon sexual intercourse. I appeal to the term 'medico-political assemblage' because it carries us beyond the simple depiction of a medical site or act and instead illuminates the aggregate economic, biopolitical, necropolitical and gendered forces that undergird the procedure of hymenoplasty. I argue that hymenoplasty can be envisioned as an assemblage that interweaves various acts, actors and notions that are facilitated by technological advancements and the idolatry of virginity. The components of this assemblage include: doctors, medical techniques and technologies, the hymen as physiological tissue, the female body as a political topography, the female patients who want to erase their sexual history and conform to the norms of marriage, and a medical market that moves with the supply and demand logic that channels and enhances the traffic amongst all of these components. When the hymenoplasty operation is completed, the assemblage dissolves, leaving behind constituent elements that no longer look or function as they did before. The whole process is enabled by the use of cutting-edge medical technology that reconstructs a hymen so that it becomes intact; it is designed and constructed in order to produce a brand-new virgin who will bleed again. Virginity thus turns out to be a concept that does not signify what patriarchal interpretations of sexuality expect from it because the presence of blood does not at all guarantee the absence of premarital sex. As Fatima Mernissi indicates, prospective husbands are at the mercy of the silence of their wives concerning their sexual history.[6]

In my reading of hymenoplasty cases, I make several claims. First, virginity is the disciplinary whip of Turkey's gender regime. This regime is deeply intertwined with necropolitics, particularly as it is manifested in honour killings related to premarital sex where the non-virgin woman is punished by the husband, male relatives or in-laws. However, symbolic interpretations of death lead to a wider set of necropolitical interventions in women's lives. Even if women are not threatened and ruled by the actual punishment of death, they have to endure various forms of intimidation and humiliation throughout their marriages once they are deemed to be non-virgins by their husbands and in-laws. Inflicted emotional pain intensifies with 'neighbourhood pressure'[7] while the ostracisation of these women within their own social circles might become a form of 'social death'.[8] Second, hymenoplasty operations also excise a crucial aspect of one's personhood, thereby highlighting the social pressures to conform, by virtue of eradicating a woman's autonomy over her own sexual desire and gratification. Coupled with this loss is the fact that hymenoplasty gynaecologists attempt to undo the bodily impact of a sexually active past by imitating the expected performance of an unbroken and ready to bleed hymen. The metaphorical implications of the death of personhood and sexual autonomy are intertwined with a multifaceted unfolding of gendered necropolitics in Turkey. However, and this is the third claim, as 'where there is power there is also resistance',[9] through hymenoplasty women can also create zones of resilience and survival by circumventing what was asked of them; namely, staying away from sexual experience and intercourse until marriage, or else bearing the (at times, fatal) consequences of the failure to conform. To the contrary, hymenoplasty enables some women to have intercourse and yet not surrender to the necropolitical gender regime, which attempts to enforce their symbolic death through a loss of personhood, sexual autonomy and exclusion from conventional society. Their resistance is enabled because they can meet the requirements of the gender regime through another symbolic death – that of virginity itself. Through the repetitive reproduction of the hymen within a large percentage of the female population, virginity effectively exists *no more*.

Virginity and Necropolitics

In Turkey virginity functions as the backbone of a disciplinary gender regime: although some families/social circles adopt allegedly more 'decorous' or less traumatic methods to keep young women away from premarital sex through their moral education, creating a docile female sexual figure also goes hand in hand with more oppressive and even fatal methods. Such is the case when a woman is forced to go through virginity examinations and/or is rendered the target of honour killings when the woman is found to be a 'non-virgin' either through such an examination or, at times, simply based on rumors that she allegedly had intercourse. The institutionalised presence of virginity examinations – secured by the legal code,[10] demanded by a wide array of institutions ranging from families to boarding schools, military schools,[11] hospitals and asylums,[12] and practised with the medical expertise of a doctor – routinises the centrality of virginity.

When virginity is instrumentalised as a part of the socialisation process used to habituate generations of young women to prescribed forms of sexuality, it resurfaces as part of cultural and aesthetic practices. For instance, feminist circles in Turkey have long fought to erase the euphemistic application of the title *miss* from colloquial language. Instead of addressing an adult third person simply as 'woman', to call her 'miss' works in favour of a strategic blindness to the presence of sex and the absence of virginity. The slogan 'not miss, but woman' responds to the silent ban upon a woman's active sexuality or the mature feminine gender roles inscribed in language and reclaims this invisible zone through a counter-discursive practice.[13] Marriage ceremonies provide an example of a suggestive and prescriptive appeal to virginity through aesthetics. The most well-known example is the display of a blood stain on bed linens on the morning after a wedding ceremony. The blood stain is proudly displayed and proves many things all at once before a curious collective neighbourhood gaze: the potency of the groom, the biological presence of the hymen, the physical presence of virginity embodied by the bride and the bride's modest and honourable upbringing into the proper female gender role are all showcased by this act. And, even though this sort of a display is limited to certain areas in Turkey and its practice is not widespread, the red belt tied around the bride's waist during the wedding ceremony is quite ubiquitous and symbolises a bride's virginity and soon to be bled hymen. Through such practices and performances, a new generation of young girls are taught the venerated icons of femininity; the modest daughter, the honourable bride and, at a mature stage of life, the proud mother. So, in one way or another, growing up in Turkey means going through a certain pedagogy of sexually acceptable roles, which instils the belief that there is something very precious down there, and that it should be protected until it is broken and properly bled by the 'right one' – for girls – or it should be regarded as the desirable criterion to choose the proper future wife – for boys. To what capacity one can undo the effects and lessons of this pedagogy depends on the status of the person embedded within the gender regime, for there are different kinds of social behaviour, ranging from the more prescriptive to the violently punitive. Women who have to endure forced virginity examinations and survive honour killings are certainly in the least advantageous position, for they are facing the most strongly necropolitical facets of the gender regime.

The notion of virginity swiftly travels from the disciplinary domain to the necropolitical end of power. With necropolitics, death enters the scene as a major theme and modality of power. According to Achille Mbembe,

> the ultimate expression of sovereignty resides, to a large degree, in the power and capacity to dictate who may live and who must die. Hence, to kill or to allow to live constitute the limits of sovereignty, its fundamental attributes. To exercise sovereignty is to exercise control over mortality and to define life as the deployment and manifestation of power.[14]

Parting from the struggle for autonomy as a normative account of sovereignty, Mbembe is rather interested in defining sovereignty as 'the generalised instrumentalisation of human existence and the material destruction of human bodies and populations'.[15] The sovereign claims, establishes and asserts itself by creating 'death-worlds'[16] in which the sovereign shows itself by creating subjects to be killed or by exposing them to the logic of death.[17] This involves 'new and unique forms of social existence in which vast populations are subjected to conditions of life conferring upon them the status of *living dead*'.[18] Here, the Foucauldian notion of biopower – make live, let die – is flipped upside down.

In the context of virginity, this sovereign is the patriarchal male who is enhanced by the despotic gender regime in Turkey. The hegemonic gender regime in Turkey sets as its central objective the needs of a heteronormative and non-pluralistic masculinity and functions through the phallic expansion of this masculinity. However, the singularity of the idealised male figure and the material, social and discursive privileges he enjoys would not go beyond some idiosyncrasies of a 'phallogocentric'[19] modality of a gift economy, unless it can apply necropolitical tools and tactics to ground the male sovereign on his terrain and to institutionalise these advantages.

These necropolitical tools are exercised especially around the question of virginity. A woman's virginity or its assumed absence is easily subject to punitive inflictions of intimidation, ostracisation, pain or even death. Looking at Turkey's gender regime, therefore, it is possible to observe different levels of necropolitical intervention: whenever there is a deviation from the intelligible gender roles and the corresponding forms of sexual behaviour, those deviant women are either punished directly with death or exposed to the logic of death at different instances and with multiple aims. Whereas honour killing[20] is the necropolitical instance of the gender regime per se, other punitive practices augment the necropolitical force of Turkey's gender regime by disciplining women into the prescribed, i.e., intelligible, gender roles without the force of death. Forms of necropolitical intervention aim to prevent the rest of the female community from committing such acts by inflicting the fear of death upon them and function to re-embed them in the gender regime, thereby establishing a male sovereign and sustaining the gender regime in the long run. When the subjugation of the woman does not involve actual killing, it works through her stigmatisation, deprivation from the social and economic help she needs, and the denial of the societal respect she deserves from her family and community, thereby rendering her 'socially dead'.[21] At a third level, necropolitics functions through meaning-making; namely, as the imposition of proper or intelligible gender roles and economy of sexual desires in which honour is lost with the improper loss of virginity. In all these instances, the sovereign creates a death-world, targeting the deviant woman as an enemy, and 'killing' her literally or metaphorically. Finally, as a fourth instance, it is possible to detect an attempt of resistance that is interestingly necropolitical again – this is the case in which women manage to survive even though they have contradicted the dictates of the gender regime by rendering the concept of virginity, the valuable currency of the gender regime, dysfunctional with the help of hymen reconstruction operations.

Considered through this lens, honour killing is an instance where the non-virgin's body, a threat to the family's honour and the gender regime's integrity, is allocated to the position of an enemy; thus, her life must be annihilated. In this instance of murder, the male sovereign surfaces as a predator after his female enemy. With the help of an honour code in kinship his ends are favoured and his deeds are justified. The polarisation between these two figures as the male sovereign and the female Other also represents a moment of saturation where gender practices mature into a gender regime. Female subjects who are stripped of the protections that their community might provide them are in turn transformed into 'ungrievable lives'.[22] Women who are inimical to the gender regime are killed insofar as their very presence presents a challenge to the male power-holder and to the inner dynamics of gender regime by showing the possibility of another life outside of dictated gender norms. Each act of killing – literal or metaphorical – is an attempt to reinstitute an endangered sovereignty and the vulnerable power of its central figure, a heterosexual male, in need of a virgin's body for a marital bond. Thus, sovereignty equates itself with killing while the rationale of its politics becomes the work of death. The necropolitics of the gender regime depends on those who will be pushed to that state of exception – of being killable – based on where they fall within that spectrum of enmity.[23]

Between the easily disposable life[24] of a female body as enemy and the male perpetrator of an honour killing there lies a large spectrum of disciplined female subjects – proper virgins, for instance – or outcast/ostracised lives suffering social deaths – women who were forgiven and let live, but who remain stigmatised and punished in different ways. Hence, side by side with the necropolitical attempts to kill and establish sovereignty over women, we can also observe more subtle and symbolic actions.[25] Necropolitics is implemented through a strategic topographic division into zones of life and death. The sovereign creates 'death-worlds'[26] to allocate those to be killed or those to be let live. The logic of a death-world can be applied to the social insofar as it resembles a physical topography; it includes the community of women and their larger families with the inclusion of relatives, their neighbourhood, friends and workplace. Within this topography, it becomes possible to observe the slow pace of social death, in the concrete form of ostracisation.[27] Here, social death could be understood in the broad sense of 'weaving death to the fabric of every day politics',[28] from political institutions to the discursive norms through various tools and tactics, including corporeal/physical violence, economic and social abandonment and verbal intimidation. Combined with Orlando Patterson's notion of social death as the basis of master and slave relations, it names the process of depersonalisation that relies on 'the suspension of personhood and belonging' through the slave's 'exclusion from the community or slave's internal exile'.[29] I take Patterson's account as a model to highlight a similar depersonalisation in the case of women who find themselves as outsiders to an 'accepted' community of women or who withdraw from such a community as a result of being shamed. Over a continuum of necropolitical intensity, zones of social death are produced through the loss of reputation and prestige once the woman loses her social status of the 'proper virgin' when her premarital sexual activity becomes known to the community. Although these women are not directly threatened by other women, they are no longer included among those women who are considered 'proper' based on their conformity to accepted sexual experience, which limits sexual intercourse to the purpose of procreating or else remaining a virgin. Zones of exclusion are marked by the presence of women who are intimidated by their husbands or relatives (including relatives-in-law), after not having been found valuable in the marriage market once they were labelled non-virgins, as well as those women who have internalised such intimidations and recoiled into a self-imposed exile from any emotional or sexual bond.

Insofar as marriage rituals symbolise and extol virginity as the absence of prior sexual and emotional bonds, one should ask whether the women who are outcast for their 'improper' actions are victims of premarital sex or, rather, their incapacity to hide their premarital sex from a tightly knit neighbourhood gaze. What is interesting with the virginity cases in Turkey is that they provide instances where biological/vaginal and physical/social aspects of virginity[30] are separated from each other. In most cases, from medical examinations of virginity to the display of bed sheets after the marriage is consummated, virginity appears solely in its vaginal/biological aspect. It is closely tied to the hymen that may (or may not) bleed and produce visible proof of virginity or cast doubt about its presence. Far from the pre-modern implications of virginity as celibacy and being stripped of emotional and sexual engagements, virginity in contemporary and hypermasculine gender regimes such as the one in Turkey indicates and functions on the basis of a single act of desire with one simple vector, which is the penetration of a vagina by a penis. This gender regime has multiple blind spots, of course. For example, would non-penetrative sex between two adults, either in a same-sex or a heterosexual setting, count as the presence of sex and hence the absence of virginity? Or what happens if that which should remain intact, i.e., the hymen, could be brought together again after penetration? Can the repair of the tissue imply that virginity itself has also been repaired? The intriguing nature of hymenoplasty cases becomes most vivid in this context. While the gender regime in Turkey deifies virginity, turning the hymen into an idol, the hymen remains an elusive matter to grasp and pinpoint. Its vibrant vitality, combined with the proper technology, provides an opportunity to be repaired and hence, to reenact virginity.

Hymenoplasty: Vulnerable Masculinities and Matters of Sabotage

The hymen is, according to the mainstream medical definition, a membrane that partially closes the opening of a vagina and whose presence is traditionally taken to be a mark of virginity. According to the more critical-feminist voice of *Our Bodies, Our Selves*, it is 'the stuff of legend and lore in many cultures, the treasured prize a woman gives her husband on their wedding night'.[31] Hymen is the core of many rituals and taboos. It occupies an important place in both public and private life in Turkey. It increases its power over women's lives by entering into the discursive and ceremonial practices of virginity.

However, Turkey is also an interesting context in which technological advancements in medicine render the hymen a whirlpool of new strategies for women to cope with a male-dominant gender regime. Medical technology combined with the vitality of the hymen as matter opens a resistance zone for most women who want to 'perform' virginity through the repair of their hymen or by creating a fake one altogether.

Hymen is simply a membrane that could easily be observed enjoining various bodily structures. It is a mucosal fabric, the same as the texture that covers the interior surface of one's mouth and throat. It comes in different shapes, colours, textures and elasticity levels. Sometimes it does not even exist. There might be some nerves or veins enjoined to its texture, but not necessarily; this is why some hymens do not bleed when they are ruptured – for there are no veins present to begin with. The potential power of the matter also resides in the elasticity and reversibility of hymen's fabric. Hymen is not a bone, muscle, flesh or skin. It is a mucosal structure that can be easily ruptured but can also be easily restored.

Colloquial usage refers to the hymen as the *girlhood membrane*. This signifies a functional reasoning to remind what the presence of this membrane underscores – girlhood. For the very same reason, hymenoplasty is known in the public as the 'repair' of the 'girlhood' membrane. Another usage is the 'sewing of girlhood membrane', which has more graphic connotations. This colloquial reference literally describes the procedure in which the doctor brings together the remnants of the hymen and attaches them together with the help of a micro needle and thread or with laser technology, depending on how expensive the procedure is. This method cannot bring every woman back to their 'girlhood', however. The hymen structure should be sewable; that is, it should not have been ruptured long ago. The second drawback is more serious when one considers the aim of the women who think about undergoing surgery: if they wait too long after the operation there will be no show of blood during the first intercourse. The bride should have the operation ideally ten days before the marriage night. As the time gap between the operation and the wedding night expands, the chances of bleeding decrease.

The hymen to be brought back with hymenoplasty represents a norm, an ideal. This ideal is also reflected in the hymen drawings designed to depict the difference between the before and after of surgery. In reality, however, the hymen comes in many shapes and textures, requiring medical creativity to make it conform to the ideal. Such creativity is also needed when the wedding schedule is not in line with the appointment book of the doctor or when the hymen was ruptured long ago with little remaining tissue that could be stitched together. The solution is to make a brand-new hymen with flap technology. Flaps are thin units of tissue that are transferred from one site (donor site) to another one (recipient site) while maintaining its own blood supply. Hymens are perfectly imitable structures and materialities, while the flaps are organic materials that are thinner than skin and that can also provide blood. The donor site is the vagina.[32] From a part close to the vaginal opening, the doctor lifts a thin texture of flaps and attaches the open ending of these flaps to the ring where the hymen used to be located. This method is offered as an alternative to the traditional stitching and its advantage is that it has no expiration date. Therefore, it is introduced as a 'permanent repair' and it is still a sub-category of one procedure: girlhood membrane repair. By that intrinsic capacity to be repaired or to be constructed from scratch, hymens create possibilities for women who are otherwise destined to be murdered or ostracised by their gender regimes to manoeuvre within these regimes and survive.

Hymenoplasty is an important example of a medico-political assemblage. I apply the term assemblage in the sense Deleuze and Guattari would substantiate it, as a 'rhizomatic network'[33] of material, structural and semiotic conflations. A constellation of actors, both living and non-living, is embodied in the effects it produces through the coming together of these elements.[34] This assemblage is characterised by its medical aspects (bodily parts and textures entering the assemblage and applied medical technology in particular), and it gains the capacity to produce political outcomes as a result of the necropolitical threads of power and resistance that run through the assemblage.

In an assemblage there are various elements, ranging from medical techniques to the location of the doctor's clinic, from nonliving or nonhuman actors to human elements, which come together and help produce its overall effect. Not all of these elements are conscious human beings, let alone political agents with willpower. Jane Bennett calls the elements of an assemblage *actants* or, borrowing the term from Spinoza, conative bodies. Assemblages are swarm-like emergings, in which material vitalities and vibrant matter act, interact and counteract in the production of an overall impact. 'Thing-power', which is the active vibrant matter, has a potential capacity to resist, absorb, change direction and exacerbate its effects. In the case of hymenoplasty, while the medical site provides the general contour of the assemblage, the hymen is that matter which contributes to the creation of new political phenomena.

Anne Phillips in her timely and interesting book *Our Bodies, Whose Property?* discusses the risks tied to understanding the female body as property and how that might leverage the biopoliticisation of life through the objectification of the body and the financialisation of its parts.[35] The critical turning point is the division of the body into parts as minuscule as blood, body tissues and cells, or even DNA.[36] By dividing the body into parts with a utilitarian logic, each separate part becomes an entity in and of itself. The body no longer looks like the corporeal quality of an individual, an automated aggregation which is bigger than the sum of its parts; on the contrary, we are looking at walking and singular *Guernica*, a cluster of alienated bodily organs.[37] Neoliberal logic has lurked into medicine and is palpable in all instances in which resolving health problems is conceptualised as a 'service' that can be bought and sold, instead of a need that should be met or a right to claim. The arbitrariness and the fluctuations in the price of hymenoplasty operations, the convenient locations of clinics (opened in neighbourhoods close to airports), the offering of hotline assistance during weekends – through extra work hours of clinic assistants – all show how neoliberalism has permeated the site of medicine.[38]

In this conceptualisation of medicine, health and the body, it is not surprising that the hymen is separated from a bodily totality of the patient. This move makes the woman even more vulnerable to 'the medical disciplinary gaze' as well as to the hegemonic demands of gender regime. As a result of the narrowed-down, heteronormative and blood-fetishist interpretations of virginity in Turkey, which all equate virginity to a bleeding hymen, the hymen becomes the focus of medical intervention. Yet, still, there is another interesting outcome of the separate reification of bodily parts in medicine: the potentials hidden in their material vitality surfaces more easily, making them equipped with agential powers. In this case, the hymen becomes the 'thing power' or 'active matter' of hymenoplasty operations. On its own, it is an elastic layer with an easily imitable texture. As part of the assemblage, it becomes something which can be sewn and made to bleed again.

Second, being part of an assemblage elevates the matter above the divide between agentic intentionality and structural rigidity. From an agentic perspective, one would attribute cases of hymenoplasty to individuals' full-fledged authority in decision-making. From a structuralist perspective, one would locate the decision-making process within the structural dynamics of a system and depict the subject as destined or determined to act in a certain way. From the perspective of an assemblage, hymenoplasty cases emerge and function in the space between the structural determinism of gender regime and the actions of a (putatively) fully autonomous female subject. This new topology no longer entails a flat or horizontal surface comprised of clearly positioned actors; it is rather a 'fibrious, thread-like, wiry, capillary' net in which the connections and interactions between actors can be combined in infinitely different ways. Within a rhizome, nodes from the uppermost corners are easily connected to each other. Distance – in the literal and verbal sense – can no longer be an issue.[39] So the network is both the form and the flow. In that sense, too, hymenoplasty is an assemblage: the unit of analysis can no longer be confined to the top-down prerogatives of hegemonic masculinity as the structuring gender regime, nor the overarching volitional acts of female subjects. It is the flaps cut and attached with novel laser technology that draw women who had their first sexual intercourse long ago into the domain of medicine; it is the location of the clinics that helps women have the operation in a shorter span of time without attracting the neighbours' curious gaze. The assemblage thus puts structure and human volition on equal footing.

During its medical remaking, the hymen ironically sheds the metaphors bestowed on it, such as the sexual illiteracy of an untouched and intact feminine body. A remade hymen cunningly hides away the female subject's past experiences and it becomes 'untouched' in this artificial construction. As such, the hymen is embedded in the medico-political assemblage as merely a material part. This shift in perspective provides considerable analytical leverage. First, imagining hymen reconstruction cases as an assemblage widens the scope of analysis by inviting non-living elements, medical technologies or bodily textures onto an equal footing with the living actors, volitional acts and ideologies. Second, it creates a concomitant environment of structural imperatives with a volitional account of agency.[40] Matter, technology and bodily fabric surround the wilful actors and dictating structures; by filling the gaps they provide a buffer zone and initiate an act of translation between the two. Bruno Latour warns his readers that 'there are no compulsory paths' or 'no strategically positioned' nodes. I depart from his approach, claiming that there should be crucial intersections within the assemblage, which might even be strategically positioned. Following Bennett's idea that 'the assemblages are uneven topographies, because some of the points at which the various affects and bodies cross paths are more heavily trafficked than others, and so power is not equally distributed across its surface',[41] I also claim that there should be a centre of gravity where these various actors and acts fall upon. I take the hymen, and the virginity it represents, to constitute these prominent elements.

A third reason to appeal to the assemblage model is related to its ability to help frame the strategic ability of women to navigate the gender regime and the unintended consequences that emerge from this ability. Just as the hymen is the most strategically positioned element in the assemblage both as matter and as semiotics, the necropolitical intervention of the gender regime constitutes the pulse of the swarm, which makes it move. This intervention aims to create disciplined virgins by hindering female sexuality and the resilience of women not to become the victims of gender regime. All the other diverse elements of the assemblage must be directly or indirectly connected to the hymen/virginity (or hymen-virginity) and channelled by the force of power and resistance.

However, the posthuman interpretations of the assemblage that build on the work of Latour and Bennett often fall short in highlighting how the assemblage relates to power and resistance in political terms. This is why I appeal to Banu Bargu's concept of a 'biosovereign assemblage' in order to delineate the ways in which this particular medical assemblage is subject to power relations and has the capacity to produce resistance. In this framework, both violent and invisible interventions of power and resistance are two sides of the same coin: they are the forces that disrupt and then reorder the medico-political assemblage while also reshaping each other. Moments of rupture and stages of continuity together are the rhythm and the source of the dynamism of the effects produced by the assemblage and they are grounded in that 'paradoxical co-existence as *biosovereignty*'.[42] Bargu argues that the *biosovereign assemblage* allows the reading of a multidimensional nexus of 'contradictory logics of sovereign power and biopower' and, even more importantly, of the differential logics of resistance, which will probably be 'non-totalising, local and dispersed'. In her reading, forms of resistance that are embedded in the 'valorisation and politicisation of life' are juxtaposed against forms of *necroresistance*, which are the 'self-destructive practices of disobedience' stemming from 'the weaponisation and politicisation of death'.[43]

The main ideological weapon of the hegemonic gender regime in Turkey is a paradoxical notion of virginity and honour. This weapon is launched to claim the feminine body as a territory to dominate and to force women towards certain performances of femininity through necropolitical means: either women should become proper subjects as decent wives or honourable mothers, or they are enemies to be outcast or killed in the most severe instances – transformed into ungrievable femininities or lives. In between these two positions based on the presence or absence of virginity, however, there lies the *performance* of virginity, an act of sabotage that is realised by *pretending that one is a virgin*, a performance that is enabled by hymenoplasty. Those who resort to the operation could be literally rescuing themselves from honour killings and from a death that might find them in the hands of their male relatives. In that sense, these women can be considered the survivors of a gendered necropolitics.

In the imposition of virginity as the source of a proper femininity and through ostracisation of the non-virgin, the feminine identity and its social bonds are threatened with the logic of death. Women who attempt to reverse the social death that they are threatened with through hymenoplasty operations display a very interesting revenge. They kill the biological aspect of virginity, which happens to be the hymen. Their prospective husbands who have idolised virginity in the form of a hymen and fetishised blood will never know if the goddess they pray to *truly* exists. Women answer the death of their identity – which was deemed to be improper by the regime – with the death of virginity.

Virginity dies on the discursive level, for the hymen, which was artificially reconstructed after being broken during intercourse, does not mean anything anymore. It becomes an empty signifier. The hymen is there, as is the blood, but does that mean the absence of previous sexual intercourse? As Fatima Mernissi indicates, in a society where the hymenoplasty operation is so widespread that it creates its own market, every man is aware of the high probability of 'breaking' a 'fake' one. So, 'they are at the mercy of the silence of their wives' on a wedding night.[44] This moment, I believe, provides a gendered form of the weaponisation of virginity, or its metaphorical death, as a response to the necropolitical modalities of the gender regime. The women who resort to hymenoplasty become social survivors in that they can re-enter the marriage market by going back to the socially accredited zone of being a virgin. They can also climb up in the kinship structure since they can claim back what was always narrated as the most honourable position for a woman in the gender regime – they can become honourable mothers in the very system they tricked by having successful marriages as 'virgin' brides.

The Revenge of the Female Saboteur

Framing hymenoplasty as a medico-political assemblage allows us to depict the potential resilience and resistance channels in hymenoplasty operations as a response to necropolitical deployments of virginity. This is because such operations open a space of manoeuvre within the bounds of the gender regime. By rendering the very credentials of the gender regime meaningless, women can engage in acts of sabotage that are intrinsic to the gender regime itself. However, I am also cautious to call hymenoplasty an organised form of resistance that can overthrow the gender regime altogether or a 'social movement' per se. One of the aims of this chapter is to remind readers that social movements that are led by ideological motives and organised towards concrete political objectives are not the only way to resist, though they could, arguably, be the most powerful and most effective way. Instead of blaming women who go through these operations as having 'false consciousness' and thus partaking in an organised system of oppressive gender relations, I prefer to view them as saboteurs whose positionality and socio-economic conditions may only enable them to confront the system in such cunning ways. Their attempt not to surrender and continue to survive is worth a mention.

I truly believe that women, more than merely surviving, can live freely only with the legal and institutional advancements provided by organised feminist solidarity and the complete and utter rejection of a gendered hegemony. In that sense, constructed virginities and hymenoplasty operations provide temporary solutions and end up perpetuating the hegemonic gender regime. However, not every woman can confront this regime openly or directly. Women who are undergoing these operations – especially with the help of the widening scope of the hymenoplasty market and its supply–demand logic – perhaps reveal more about the difficulty of participating in a feminist fight than about their overall complicity. Dilek Cindoğlu's research shows that the women who resort to hymenoplasty operations are usually working at secondary/auxiliary level service sector jobs, such as an assistant manager at an office, a retail shop assistant or a pharmacy clerk.[45] Even though they have achieved some financial detachment from their families, their incomes do not enable them to plan an independent future. Their work allows them an urban experience and a chance to have their own social life instead of being confined to a few neighbouring households that surround their parents' home. This experience not only increases the chances of having dates and sexual partners, it also provides a shelter from the tight-knit surveillance of their local neighbourhood. Yet, despite their access to monetary sources and relief from neighbourhood pressure, these women are often not able to marry men who are culturally and ideologically detached from this hegemonic sex regime. Such a marital match would require these women to have greater social and economic capital, often necessitating generations of upward social mobility. From a political economy vantage point, then, the increasing demand for the medical expertise of hymenoplasty can also be interpreted as showing the limits of female autonomy. At the centre of this assemblage there are female figures caught in the uneven development of a neoliberal economy: they come to the city and work, but their class background does not allow them to fully belong and to leverage urban life to find a marital match that is different from their own social background. The same background also prevents them from refusing a marital bond altogether, eliminating the possibility of enjoying their life freely as single women or with partners outside of marriage. While these women have some access to sexual experience, only a small number can liberate themselves from the traditional wedding market. Fatima Mernissi suggests that wherever inequality dwells, the oppressed will – consciously or unconsciously – develop feelings of revenge.[46] From this perspective, hymenoplasty can be seen as a site of necropolitical sabotage. While hymenoplasty does not organise a large-scale feminist movement to change the gender regime altogether, and while it is questionable that it can even alter the established norms around virginity, it does allow individuals to navigate the gender regime and turn themselves from victims into survivors, and even saboteurs.

From the perspective of women undergoing surgery, doctors become their accomplices insofar as they aid these women in 'tricking' their prospective husbands into believing they are virgins at the time of marriage. As men can no longer differentiate the 'fake' hymens/virginities from the 'real' *untouched history*,[47] do these women not also kill virginity altogether by rendering the concept meaningless? Hymenoplasty can thus be read as a site of resistance, one that not only subverts virginity but also leaves husbands at the mercy of their wives' silence about their sexual past. Men can only doubt whether their partners may have gone through the operation.

If the operation was rendered possible by a fractured corporeality and the disjuncture between the bodily elements and corresponding societal meanings, it is ironically the same fracture that rescues individual histories of sexual desire. The reversal of hymenoplasty into a site of resistance implies a challenge to both the oppressive economy of sexual desire and the forged female subjectivities of the hegemonic gender regime, which depends on keeping the hymen intact until marriage. From the view that women undergoing hymenoplasty are docile subjects, it is possible to move to a conception of empowerment where their resort to hymenoplasty is the result of a strategised anger that consciously sabotages virginity and intends to deceive their male partners. Between these two extremes, there is a portion of cases that resort to hymenoplasty as part of a survival strategy rather than as a form of sabotage or disruptive protest. Nonetheless, we can still find traces of an emergent female subject who is resilient, who did not simply accept surrendering to the punitively coded gender regime – whether the punishment was a literal death at the hands of her male relatives or being rendered an outcast, being considered unfit for marriage and humiliated. This is a female subject who persists and navigates the dominant gender norms imposed on her by society as well as the economy of sexual desire by resorting to an operation that disguises her history of sexuality. Not only do these female subjects reject death and survive, but they can also surpass social death by refashioning themselves as 'proper' candidates of marriage in the societal gaze. If virginity is one goddess of Turkish society and its gender regime, there is also a competing one – motherhood. These women who resort to hymenoplasty may even become mothers after successfully escaping social death. In each case of hymenoplasty there is a political story of refusing the deployments of a gendered necropolitics, from the literal to the metaphorical.

According to Bargu, 'necropolitical resistance transforms the body from a site of subjection to a site of insurgency, which by self-destruction presents death as a counter conduct to the administration of life'.[48] While hymenoplasty is not comparable to political insurgents' necropolitical resistance who 'sacrifice their biological existence' and claim their 'political existence' back by demolishing the bare life to which they have been reduced,[49] it is nonetheless a disruptive instance of necropolitical sabotage. The very moment the hymen is objectified as the ultimate emblem of virginity, these two notions are in fact disentangled: while the hymen's equivalence to virginity endangers female social vitality by the logic of death, it also presents a disruptive opportunity for necropolitical sabotage. Women, by 're-enacting' medical technology, 'interact'[50] with their past, their sexual desires and their future; they recuperate the hymen with the help of the needle, the thread or the lasered flaps. As a result, they drop a dead virginity – a concept that is rendered meaningless without its content – into the hands of their *Humen* worshipping husbands.[51] They thus rescue themselves by weaponising their *now* dead virginities. Hymenoplasty, then, may embody a large variety of agential intra-activity, which can be clustered under the unfolding of a recalcitrant female psyche aimed at sabotage or survival.

Notes

1. Judith Butler, *Gender Trouble*, pp. 22–34.
2. Ibid. p. 25.
3. Ibid. pp. 22–3.
4. Ibid. p. 23.
5. Ibid. p. 17.
6. Fatima Mernissi, 'Bekaret ve Ataerki', p. 103.
7. Şerif Mardin, *Turkiye'de Din ve Siyaset, Makaleler 3*.
8. Orlando Patterson, *Slavery and Social Death: A Comparative Study*.
9. Michel Foucault, *History of Sexuality*, pp. 94–6.
10. Turkish Criminal Code (TCK) Article 287 protects doctors who performed 'genital' examinations following a court decision or any concern for the public health while rendering illegal any case not performed by a medical doctor or arbitrary applications of the 'genital' examination. Verbatim translation of the legal code does not include any specification as virginity examinations; however, virginity examinations are practically considered part of genital examinations.
11. Leyla Şimşek-Rathke, *Dünden Kalanlar, Türkiye'de Hemşirelik ve GATA TSK Sağlık Meslek Lisesi Örneği*.

12. In this lead, sociologist Dilek Cindoğlu refers to the speeches of Yıldırım Aktuna. As Minister of Health back in 1992, Yıldırım Aktuna admitted that in the past he had ordered all female patients to go through virginity examinations on a regular basis when he was the chief physician of Bakirkoy Psychiatric Hospital, Istanbul. He defended his actions on the grounds that it was a preventative measure aimed at protecting female patients from a possible sexual assault by the other male patients or the health personnel. See Dilek Cindoğlu, 'Modern Turk Tibbinda Bekaret Testleri ve Suni Bekaret', pp. 115–32.
13. 'Asıl Bayan Sizsiniz, Biz Kadınız!', *Bianet*, 2010.
14. Achille Mbembe, 'Necropolitics', pp. 161–92.
15. Ibid. p. 163.
16. Ibid. p. 186.
17. Ibid. p. 161.
18. Ibid. pp. 184–6.
19. Butler, *Gender Trouble*.
20. Filiz Kardam, *The Dynamics of Honor Killings in Turkey*. In most honour killing cases a female victim is condemned with having crossed the borders of imposed gender roles, dishonouring the family's name and legacy, and she is murdered by male perpetrators – again, most (if not all) of whom happen to be her male relatives. To have a general idea of the dynamics of honour killing UNDP report dating to 2007 can be helpful, although a brief media research will show most recent incidents: <https://www.unfpa.org/sites/default/files/pub-pdf/honourkillings.pdf> (last accessed 22 January 2019).
21. Patterson, *Slavery and Social Death.*
22. Judith Butler, *When is Life Grievable?*, pp. 13–15, 31, 41–2.
23. Mbembe, 'Necropolitics', pp. 173–4, 186.
24. I employ the term 'disposable' in an attempt to grasp Butler's conceptualisation of the 'ungrievable' life; that is, a life that will not be grieved if it is lost.
25. See Banu Bargu's analysis as the embeddedness of the sovereign imperative and disciplinary tools in *Starve and Immolate*.
26. Mbembe, 'Necropolitics', p. 186.
27. Lauren Berlant, 'Slow Death', pp. 754–80.
28. Jin Haritaworn, Adi Kuntsman and Silvia Posocco, pp. 4–6.
29. Patterson, *Slavery and Social Death*, pp. 38–9.
30. Lama Abu-Odeh, 'Arap Toplumlarinda Namus Cinayetleri ve Toplumsal Cinsiyetin Inşası', p. 257.
31. Available at <https://www.ourbodiesourselves.org/book-excerpts/health-article/what-exactly-is-a-hymen/> (last accessed 22 January 2019).
32. In colloquial usage, the term 'vagina' may refer to most parts of the female genitalia; here, I am referring to the usage of the term in anatomy. The vagina is an inner structure of the female genitalia that connects the vaginal opening to the womb, and is also known as the birth canal.

33. Gilles Deleuze and Félix Guattari, *A Thousand Plateaus: Capitalism and Schizophrenia*, pp. 4, 7–9.
34. Bruno Latour, 'On Actor-Network Theory', pp. 372–5.
35. Anne Phillips, *Our Bodies Whose Property?*, pp. 18–41.
36. Ibid. pp. 97–101.
37. A comprehensive and intriguing discussion can be found in Nikolas Rose, *The Politics of Life Itself*.
38. My preliminary field research indicates that Istanbul is the pulsing heart of this emerging health tourism/market. Related online forums are full of comments by women from close geographies such as Iran, Iraq or Morocco. Apparently, doctors in Turkey – mostly in urban areas of Turkey, led by Istanbul as the most populous city – have discovered how 'profitable' the 'business' is for them: the cost of the operation varies in an arbitrary fashion. Depending on the popularity of the doctor, the city where the doctor's clinic is located and what techniques s/he uses, costs may range from TRY 1,500 to TRY 5,000. To make sense of what this amount means, we may compare it to the monthly minimum wage in Turkey, which is TRY 1,603. Doctors usually do not declare the price of hymen restoration on their websites. Instead, they suggest an initial examination to decide on the suitable procedure and provide a phone number for a brief price consultation. Some gynaecologists who specialise in and heavily rely on these operations have two clinics where they work interchangeably; ideally, one of these is at a strategic location such as a neighbourhood close to the international airports, to make it easier for a patient to come from another city/abroad, access the clinic easily and travel back on the same day.
39. Latour, 'On Actor-Network Theory', p. 372.
40. On this note, I differ from Bruno Latour to a large extent: Latour's interpretation of agential actors is the denial of both the volitional and structural explanations. I prefer on the other hand to bring these two perspectives on agency and change into conversation. In dialogue, I believe, we can have a better picture of emerging effects and/or decision-making procedures in a political setting. This is another aspect, of course, where I differ from Latour: I still believe in decision-making subjects. To what extent these subjects take deliberate actions forged by their fully determined free will, or to what extent they can create impact, are different questions.
41. Jane Bennett, *Vibrant Matter*, p. 24.
42. Bargu, *Starve and Immolate*, p. 60.
43. Ibid. pp. 62–3, 126, 216–20, 245.
44. Fatima Mernissi, 'Bekaret ve Ataerki', p. 103.
45. Dilek Cindoğlu, p. 122.
46. Mernissi, p. 107.
47. Hanne Blank, *Bekaretin El Değmemiş Tarihi*.
48. Bargu, *Starve and Immolate*, p. 85.
49. Ibid. pp. 82–5.

50. I borrowed the strategic word choice from Karen Barad, 'Posthumanist Performativity', pp. 826–7.
51. Etymologically, the word 'hymen' is believed to originate from the Greek word which stands for both the thin skin that that binds, joins or sews and the Humen, the god of marriage, who is a 'joiner', i.e., the one who 'sews' the parties to be wed. See <https://www.etymonline.com/word/hymen> (last accessed 22 January 2019).

Bibliography

Abu-Odeh, Lama, 'Arap Toplumlarında Namus Cinayetleri ve Toplumsal Cinsiyetin İnşası', in Pınar Ilkkaracan (ed.), *Müslüman Toplumlarda Kadın ve Cinsellik* (Istanbul: Iletişim Yayınları, 2015), pp. 243–64.

'Asıl Bayan Sizsiniz, Biz Kadınız!', *Bianet*, 2010, <https://bianet.org/cocuk/medya/120518-asil-bayan-sizsiniz-biz-kadiniz> (last accessed 22 January 2019).

Barad, Karen, 'Posthumanist Performativity: Toward an Understanding of How Matter Comes to Matter', *Signs* (Spring 2003): 801–30.

Bargu, Banu, *Starve and Immolate: The Politics of Human Weapons* (New York: Columbia University Press, 2014).

Bennett, Jane, *Vibrant Matter: A Political Ecology of Things* (Durham, NC: Duke University Press, 2010).

Berlant, Lauren, 'Slow Death (Sovereignty, Obesity, Lateral Agency)', *Critical Inquiry* (Summer 2007): 754–80.

Blank, Hanne, *Bekaretin El Değmemiş Tarihi* (Istanbul: İletişim Yayınları, 2014).

Butler, Judith, *Gender Trouble* (New York: Routledge, 1990).

Butler, Judith, *Frames of War: When is Life Grievable?* (New York: Verso, 2016).

Cindoğlu, Dilek, 'Modern Türk Tıbbında Bekaret Testleri ve Suni Bekaret', in Pınar Ilkkaracan (ed.), *Müslüman Toplumlarda Kadın ve Cinsellik* (Istanbul: Iletişim Yayınları, 2015), pp. 115–32.

Deleuze, Gilles, and Félix Guattari, *A Thousand Plateaus: Capitalism and Schizophrenia* (London: Continuum, 2003).

Ergün, Emek, 'Reconfiguring Translation as Intellectual Activism: The Turkish Feminist Remaking of Virgin: The Untouched History', *Trans-Scripts* (2013): 264–89.

Foucault, Michel, *History of Sexuality, Volume 1: An Introduction* (New York: Vintage Books, 1990).

Haritaworn, Jin, Adi Kuntsman and Silvia Posocco (eds), *Queer Necropolitics* (New York: Routledge, 2014).

Ilkkaracan, Pınar, 'Türkiye'nin Doğu Bölgelerinde Kadın Cinselliği Bağlamının Incelenmesi', in *Müslüman Toplumlarda Kadın ve Cinsellik* (Istanbul: Iletişim Yayınları, 2015), pp. 133–50.

Kardam, Filiz, *The Dynamics of Honor Killings in Turkey*, United Nations Population Fund 2005, <https://www.unfpa.org/sites/default/files/pub-pdf/honourkillings.pdf> (last accessed 22 January 2019).

Latour, Bruno, 'On Actor-Network Theory. A Few Clarifications Plus More Than a Few Complications', *Soziale Welt* 47 (1996): 369–81.

Latour, Bruno, *Reassembling the Social: An Introduction to Actor-Network Theory* (New York: Oxford University Press, 2005).

Mardin, Şerif, *Türkiye'de Din ve Siyaset, Makaleler 3* (Istanbul: Iletişim Yayınları, 1993).

Mbembe, Achille, 'Necropolitics', in *Biopolitics: A Reader* (Durham, NC: Duke University Press, 2013), pp. 161–92.

Mernissi, Fatima, 'Bekaret ve Ataerki', in Pınar Ilkkaracan (ed.), *Müslüman Toplumlarda Kadın ve Cinsellik* (Istanbul: Iletişim Yayınları, 2015).

Parla, Ayşe, 'The "Honor" of the State: Virginity Examinations in Turkey', *Feminist Studies* 27 (Spring 2001): 65–88.

Patterson, Orlando, *Slavery and Social Death: A Comparative Study* (Cambridge, MA: Harvard University Press, 1982).

Phillips, Anne, *Our Bodies Whose Property?* (Princeton, NJ: Princeton University Press, 2013).

Rose, Nikolas, *The Politics of Life Itself: Biomedicine, Power and Subjectivity in the Twenty-First Century* (Princeton, NJ: Princeton University Press, 2006).

Roye, Carol, 'What Exactly is a Hymen', *Our Bodies Ourselves*, 2018, <https://www.ourbodiesourselves.org/book-excerpts/health-article/what-exactly-is-a-hymen/> (last accessed 22 January 2019).

Shalhoub-Kevorkian, Nadera, 'Tecavüzün Kültürel Bir Tanımına Doğru: Filistin Toplumunda Tecavüz Mağdurlarıyla Çalışırken Karşılaşılan Ikilemler', in Pınar Ilkkaracan (ed.), *Müslüman Toplumlarda Kadın ve Cinsellik* (Istanbul: Iletişim Yayınları, 2015).

Şimşek-Rathke, Leyla, *Dünden Kalanlar, Türkiye'de Hemşirelik ve GATA TSK Sağlık Meslek Lisesi Örneği* (İstanbul: İletişim Yayınları, 2011).

SEVEN

Necropolitics, Martyrdom and Muslim Conscientious Objection

Pınar Kemerli

Since the mid-1980s Turkey has been at war with the Kurdistan Workers' Party (*Partiya Karkerên Kurdistanê,* PKK) – a war that has oscillated between acute combat and low-intensity confrontations involving security operations, states of emergency, curfews and intimidations targeting Turkey's Kurdish south-east.[1] This protracted war has been the site of multiple forms of necropolitical violence including terrorist attacks, the brutal killing of declared enemies and civilian populations on both sides, the torture of captured insurgents, the exposure of large segments of the Kurdish population to indiscriminate state violence and, more recently, the desecration and humiliation of their dead and the prevention of customary burial practices.[2] In this chapter, I focus on the role played by militaristic invocations of theological concepts such as jihad and martyrdom in relation to the Turkish conscript army in order to legitimise and perpetuate the war and its necropolitical violence. I analyse these phenomena from the perspective of those who refuse this necropoliticisation: a group of Muslim Conscientious Objectors (COs) who reject the draft and peacefully accept the consequences of this criminalised disobedience.

Established in 1927 as a constitutionally protected right and duty of citizenship, compulsory male conscription is one of the most esteemed institutions of Turkish nationalism. Promoted in conjunction with a militarist imagining of Turkish national identity,[3] male conscription is codified as a rite of passage to manhood, ensures a level of prestige unattainable by women[4] and enjoys wide popularity amongst large segments of the Turkish population – despite the significant burdens it places on individuals and families.[5] And most importantly for my purposes, a pervasive discourse of sacred duty and religious martyrdom inflects this institution, providing ample opportunities for the state to imbue its biosovereign goals with theological significance and to promote religious enthusiasm for militarist policies.[6]

This theologisation of Turkish militarism and its necropolitical undercurrent constitutes the primary targets of Muslim COs' antiwar activism and political critique.[7] In what follows I examine this critique by drawing upon ethnographic research and interviews conducted with Muslim COs and antiwar activists. My argument will unfold in several steps. I will begin with an overview of Turkish conscription policies and the role played by theologically supported martyrdom narratives in legitimating military service and state violence. I emphasise the republican state's systematic involvement in generating this theological valuation, especially in the aftermath of the 1980 coup d'état. I will then move to an analysis of conscientious objection and the Muslim COs' antiwar critique. I focus on Muslim conscientious objection both for the important shifts its emergence signals in terms of the mutually supportive relationship that has been established between 'Turkish Islam' and militarism, and for this critique's ability to target and deconstruct the specific theological claims raised to advance state violence.[8]

Muslim COs offer a sustained and religiously inspired condemnation of Turkish military aggression and necropolitics. This critique is raised in two steps. Muslim COs first protest Turkish conscription policies and how these policies bear upon their understanding of sovereign power and just governance. They invoke multiple claims, including that of divine sovereignty, to support their critique of conscription, but the primary political point they make is a diagnosis of the necropolitical nature of the violence and oppression that the Turkish army unleashes against the Kurds. Against this background, Muslim COs theorise their objection as a refusal to become agents of what they consider to be a necropolitical and an unjust oppression.

Particularly offensive for them in this context is the invocation of theological values of jihad and martyrdom in reference to the Turkish army and its actions. Building upon the first part of their critique, Muslim COs proceed to offer rival reinterpretations of these theological concepts that transform them into a basis for antiwar activism. I focus in particular on their reinterpretation of conscientious objection as a potential venue to achieve martyrdom and to resist necropolitics – a reinterpretation that complicates conventional understandings of both martyrdom and conscientious objection, imbuing them with new symbolic and political significance. The concluding part of the chapter underscores how essentialist assumptions about 'what Islam is' and 'how it may inspire politics' are complicated in light of Muslim COs' dissenting vernacular imaginaries and actions.

Conscription and Martyrdom

The modern Turkish republic upholds restrictive conscription policies in a contemporary global context where professional armies are becoming increasingly the norm.[9] According to the Turkish Military Service Act, all able-bodied male subjects are obligated to perform twelve months of military service.[10] Conscientious objection is not recognised within the republic, despite the fact that Turkey is a member of several international institutions including the United Nations and a signatory of the European Convention on Human Rights, which consider conscientious objection to be a legitimate exercise of the right to freedom of thought, conscience, religion and belief.[11] In the absence of laws regulating their act, those who refuse to serve for conscientious reasons are imprisoned for crimes that do not correspond to their civil dissent, including desertion, persistent disobedience and alienating the public from the institution of military service. When found 'guilty' of any of these charges, they are imprisoned for periods ranging from three months to up to two years. COs are condemned to a life of illegality even after their release. The European Court of Human Rights defines their subsequent living conditions as 'civil death', resulting in 'an inability to vote, marry, legally register a child, work, or get a passport'.[12]

This uncompromising attitude regarding military service is reinforced through a civic republican ethos and security discourses concerned with Turkey's domestic and geostrategic vulnerabilities. The civic republican perspective promotes a state-centred approach to citizenship, prioritising the duties arising from political membership. In this context the right to serve is identified as a privileged duty reserved for men as 'first-class' citizens, reflecting the gendered economy of Turkish citizenship. The national security discourses mobilised in defense of compulsory conscription, on the other hand, focus on the threats facing Turkey. While the nation's perceived 'external enemies' evolve with changing historical conditions and foreign policies, the Kurdish minority and their nationalist aspirations remain the primary reference point in terms of 'internal enemies', fuelling militarism both on an institutional and social level, especially since the rise of the PKK. The onset of internal armed conflict has also transformed the actual risks involved in military service. With an estimated 44,000 dead since the onset of armed conflict in mid-1980s, death during service has become a very real possibility for conscripted men in Turkey.[13] Nonetheless, existing alongside these civic republican and national security discourses, and enhancing their affective reach and potency, there is also a strong martyrdom narrative that significantly helps the Turkish state generate legitimacy and enthusiasm for military service.

As Benedict Anderson has taught us, discourses of martyrdom are immensely effective in (re)generating and legitimising national identities and aspirations, thereby providing people with the emotional resources required to endure sacrifices for the nation.[14] A large body of interdisciplinary literature explores the characteristics and functions of martyrdom discourses across the globe. Focusing on Israeli nationalism, for example, Yael Tamir shows how the glorification of fallen soldiers as martyrs is closely intertwined with reassertions of state power and legitimacy. 'The fact that exemplary individuals willingly give up their lives for the state', she writes, 'is purported to prove that the state is worthy of such an offering, while the merits of the state make the sacrifice of the fallen worthwhile.'[15] In his study of Kurdish commemorative practices, Hişyar Özsoy emphasises martyrdom's regenerative power even in the absence of a unified state: 'Kurds resurrect their dead through a moral and symbolic economy of martyrdom as highly affective forces that powerfully shape public, political and daily life, promoting Kurdish national identity and struggle as a sacred communion of the dead and the living.'[16] Studying the historical evolution of Palestinian narratives of martyrdom, Laleh Khalili further reminds us that martyrdom narratives may sometimes work to 'depoliticise the act of dying for a cause', with exclusive emphasis on the innocence of the fallen – often at the expense of the complex situations encountered in combat.[17] Most martyrdom discourses involve similar kinds of depoliticisation by way of the selective narration of events and/or their simplification, which could silence or underplay the distasteful inverse of heroic death: participation in violence and the act of killing. For this reason in particular, the realm of the dead and the meaning of their death become intense sites of contestation amongst peoples at war, producing uneven, disproportionate and mutually exclusive narratives of innocence, sacrifice and justice/injustice.

All of these qualities are discernible to different extents in Turkish nationalist narratives of martyrdom, and they significantly enhance the state's ability to generate societal support and enthusiasm for militarism. The commemoration of fallen soldiers through martyr funerals and local and official ceremonies, as well as public celebrations organised by institutionalised networks and civil society organisations, such as the Martyr Families Aid and Solidarity Association (*Şehit Aileleri Yardımlaşma ve Dayanışma Derneği*), helps reaffirm the Turkish nation's unity and resolve, and strengthens the legitimacy of conscription. Turkish martyrdom narratives are also distinctly uneven, granting an exclusive space to the stories and suffering of the soldiers (and their families) and the righteousness of the Turkish sovereign within the country's contested geographies, while strictly excluding Kurdish deaths. This uneven presentation works to disregard and dehumanise Kurdish suffering, further strengthening support for military solutions to the conflict. In addition to providing vital psychological relief to the communities affected by military loss – the families of the fallen soldiers most immediately, but also the whole population whose sons, husbands and brothers may well suffer a similar fate given the mandatory nature of conscription and the ongoing war – Turkish martyrdom narratives thus contribute to the (re)militarisation of society and hinder the search for a peaceful resolution.

But there is another and perhaps even more powerful component of Turkish martyrdom narratives that undergirds and bolsters all of these other qualities: their militarist invocations of Islamic traditions of warfare and martyrdom. What I have in mind here is not simply the longstanding and well-known religiously inflected cultural valuation of military service in Turkey, manifesting in the popular referencing of conscription as the Hearth of the Prophet (*Peygamber Ocağı*), affectionate addressing of conscripts as little Muhammed (*Mehmetçik*), and the use of the word *şehit* (religious martyr) to denote those who die while on active duty.[18] But alongside these invocations, and more systematically managed than them, there is an institutionalised Islamic legitimisation of conscription and martyrdom, mobilised to advance Turkish state violence and its biosovereign goals.

This Islamic legitimisation has deep roots in Turkish statecraft and institutions. Since the introduction of compulsory military service in 1927 – a mere four years after the founding of the republic – Turkey has systematically trained conscripted civilians in a militarist understanding of Islam and Islamic warfare. The primary tenets of this training are presented in the book *Askere Din Kitabı* (The Religion Book for the Soldier), originally prepared in 1925 for use in military education and since reprinted in seven further editions, the last being in 2002. This training manual emphasises the Islamic mandate of the Turkish conscript army as 'God's sword', presents military disobedience and desertion as sacrilegious, considers death in the military as religious martyrdom and portrays Turkish military aggression as righteous, thereby contributing to the valuation of military service not just as a nationalist but also as a religious duty.[19]

Importantly, the religious content of military education was carried into the civilian sphere after the 1980 coup, the third intervention of the Turkish Armed Forces into civilian politics. Alongside the devastating crackdown on the Turkish left, the three years of junta government (1980–3) also saw a new alliance between the state and the sponsors of an ideological movement known as the 'Turkish-Islamic Synthesis' – a cultural programme promoting the systematic transformation of national education, public culture and the public sphere through the integration of Sunni Islamic values with

Turkish nationalism.[20] This alliance generated a new national education curriculum, which incorporated the Islamic tenets of Turkish militarism into mainstream education.[21] This pedagogical transformation has become one of the most consequential policies of the junta government, effectively initiating a new citizenship ethos. The ensuing Kurdish insurgency reinforced this religious inflection further with widespread popular references to the Turkish army as an Islamic force fighting godless (communist) Kurds. All in all, the post-1980s transformations in republican statecraft and its embrace of a distinct 'Turkish-Islamic' undercurrent have widened and strengthened Turkish militarism's extant religious tenets, making military service an essential part of the new religious-militarist socio-political consensus and a further emblem of pious patriotism.

War-resistance and Conscientious Objection in Turkey

The concatenation of a state-imposed duty to serve, strong nationalist traditions of militarism, and the religiously inflected narratives of martyrdom makes critiques of military service difficult to articulate and dangerous to endorse in Turkey. The socio-political marginalisation confronting the COs and antiwar activists was the most common complaint I heard during my fieldwork in Turkey while researching war-resistance. But despite this marginalisation and the legal prosecution they face, these activists continue to refuse service and critique militarism, generating an important antiwar discourse.

Conscientious objection emerged in Turkey during one of the most intense periods of the war between the army and the Kurdish guerrilla in the 1990s. This phase of the conflict is known as the 'dirty war' in reference to the pervasive involvement of paramilitary forces and 'death squads' in the Kurdish region, terrorising the population, kidnapping and 'disappearing' Kurdish leaders and politicians and 'assassinating moderate Turkish military commanders'.[22] Turkey's first CO rights activists were predominantly anarchists, and they founded War Resisters' Associations in Izmir and Istanbul. They sought to raise awareness about conscientious objection by organising public conscientious objection declarations and panels focusing on the history and achievements of conscientious objection struggles elsewhere, and by forming ties with COs in other countries. In the summer of 1993, for instance, an International Conscientious Objection Meeting was organised in a small town near Izmir, bringing together around a hundred activists from many different countries. Activists like Osman Murat Ülke – who later became the first CO imprisoned for his refusal to serve in Turkey – publicly burned their draft calls and called for both the Turkish soldiers and Kurdish guerilla to refuse partaking in the war.[23] They also engaged in literary productions, seeking to disseminate information about antimilitarism and conscientious objection through journals and websites. While both War Resisters' Associations were eventually closed by the year 2000, the antiwar activism of the 1990s was nonetheless successful in drawing attention to conscientious objection, especially amongst the youth. By the mid-2000s conscientious objection had come to be 'known' and began to be demanded by individuals from diverse ideological orientations including feminists, socialists and Kurdish and LGBTQ rights activists.

The emergence of Muslim COs in the mid-2000s was part of this evolution of antiwar activism, reflecting also the increasing diversification of the Turkish dissident public sphere. This was a period of vibrant change and civil society activism. A relatively free socio-political context was still maintained by the ruling Justice and Development Party (*Adalet ve Kalkınma Partisi*, AKP), which nominally pursued European Union membership as it continued to consolidate its power. Practicing Muslims had become active participants in many socio-political movements, transforming the shape and scope of both religio-political activism and Turkish democracy. As Muslims' presence and involvement in civil society grew and diversified, so did the possible political positions and imaginaries endorsed by them. The rise of a religiously grounded critique of the war and conscription from within a cultural context wherein 'Islam' and 'militarism' have historically reinforced each other was thus an important indication of transformations occurring amongst Turkey's Muslim publics. And, most importantly for my purposes, Muslim conscientious objection strongly targeted the above noted martyrdom narratives, which had been securely linked to militarist goals, and reclaimed them in order to advance a rival, religiously grounded antiwar critique. I turn to the analysis of this critique below.

Muslim Conscientious Objection

On the question of violence, Muslim COs diverge from the Gandhian and Christian frames that serve as a basis for much of the existing literature on religiously motivated conscientious objection.[24] But neither a pacifist orientation nor an ethical commitment to nonviolence constitutes the primary ground of Muslim COs' refusal. While most of them are critical of organised violence, especially in the form of a standing army, this is not because of a principled opposition to violence as such. On the contrary, they consider the use of violence to be not only sometimes necessary but also a vital part of Muslims' responsibility to defend the oppressed and redeem their suffering – a responsibility they associate with the Islamic ideal of jihad. İhsan

Eliaçık, a Turkish theologian whose teaching emphasises anti-acquisitive and social justice oriented strains of the Qur'an and wields a strong influence on Muslim COs and antiwar activists, explains that Muslims' critique of militarism should be separated from a categorical opposition to warfare. Both the Qur'an and the Prophet Muhammed, Eliaçık argues, condemn belligerent wars waged for conquest, land appropriation and the forceful submission of people:

> But what we Muslims call jihad entails the struggle/war to eliminate the conditions of oppression (*zulüm*) and slavery. This is the highest responsibility. A world free of wars is surely the ideal but at our current moment in history this is also a utopia. Muslims cannot abandon their highest responsibility when *zulüm* persists in the world for the sake of ethical qualms about fighting. Sometimes you need to fight to end violence and warfare.[25]

A scepticism of principled pacifism is endorsed by all the Muslim COs and antiwar activists I talked to. Enver Aydemir, Turkey's first Muslim CO, who is not affiliated with Eliaçık's movement, similarly distinguishes his refusal to serve from pacifism: 'Violence is not a method of resistance I endorse and support,' he argued, 'but as Muslims I believe we have the responsibility to defend the innocents who are under threat.'[26] Other Muslim COs who integrate Muslim ideals and practices with other intellectual traditions such as anti-colonial and socialist thought carry this position even further and point out historical instances of violent resistance such as the Paris Commune and the Spanish Civil War as legitimate attempts to transform the world for the better – a political act they refer to as 'creating heaven on earth'. This qualified stance with respect to violence suggests that what is at stake in Muslim COs' refusal is neither an idiosyncratic Islamist pacifism nor a principled ethical opposition to war. Their refusal instead derives from a more complex and religiously inspired political critique, involving two interrelated axes: a) a critique of conscription and the actions of the Turkish army, and b) a condemnation, and discursive reversal, of militarised interpretations of Islamic martyrdom that the state mobilises in the service of war and death-making.

Muslim objectors consider compulsory conscription to be the most transparent expression of the secular state's 'usurpation' of an essential attribute of sovereignty that they consider to belong to God only: making decisions regarding life and death.[27] This stance is consistent with broader twentieth-century Islamist critiques of sovereignty developed by thinkers such as Sayyid Qutb, who became popular in Turkey's Islamist public sphere in the aftermath of the Iranian revolution.[28] However, the Muslim

COs' position is different from most other principled Islamist oppositions to popular sovereignty in Turkey, represented more typically by radical strains of political Islam that advocate the replacement of the secular state with Islamist governance. None of the Muslim COs are members of such radical groups, nor do they advocate a form of Islamist governance. Therefore, while they consider the act of serving an institution (the army/the state) that claims authority over matters reserved for God only (life/death) to be problematic, this is not the primary basis of their political critique. Much more troubling for these COs is the fact that military service operates as the institutional mechanism of the forceful imposition of Turkish sovereignty over an unwilling Kurdish people and as part of an attempt to subdue and assimilate them. This violent compelling of an unwilling people into submission does not sit well with Muslim COs' understanding of just conduct either on an individual or popular level. 'The Prophet never forced anyone to follow or obey him,' a CO pointed out, and 'condemned those who pursue such violent submission'.[29] Their conscientious objection thus expresses the refusal to become agents of what they consider to be an oppressive sovereign imposition, which also goes against their convictions concerning who holds power over life and death.[30]

In a 2010 court hearing, Enver Aydemir voiced this dual critique powerfully. After identifying conscription as an expression of the state's undue challenge to God's authority, he proceeded to criticise Kurdish repression in Turkey through a powerful analogy. He invoked then Prime Minister Recep Tayyip Erdoğan's highly publicised rebuke of the Israeli President Shimon Peres in a panel on Gaza during the 2009 World Economic Forum in Davos where Peres sought to justify Israel's Operation Cast Lead, which caused devastating damage in Gaza, including a high number of civilian deaths.[31] Drawing a parallel between the Israeli oppression of the Palestinians and the Turkish suppression of the Kurds, Aydemir accused the Turkish government of hypocritically speaking up for oppressed peoples internationally while prosecuting the Kurds who struggle for similar rights at home. As an example, he further referred to the routine confrontations between the soldiers and Kurdish children in Turkey's Kurdish region, and the criminalisation of these children for throwing stones at soldiers – paralleling Israel's treatment of stone-throwing children in Palestine.[32] On this basis, Aydemir reiterated his opposition to serving in the army, which he thought acted as an agent of injustice, harming rather than protecting innocent people entrusted to its care (Kurdish children and Kurdish citizens at large).

Central to Muslim COs' critique of the Turkish–Kurdish conflict's injustices is the manner in which religion is mobilised to sustain and advance the necropolitical policies of military submission. Grounded in Michel

Foucault's work on sovereignty, necropolitical violence denotes the kinds of 'death-making', involving the rendering of certain populations disposable and permanently exposed to vulnerability through multiple structural mechanisms including their class position, race and ethnicity.[33] Achille Mbembe elaborated Foucault's insights and offered a more developed theory of necropower as the destructive mechanism that generates concrete spaces of exception, traps that decimate populations within them, and/or reduces the conditions of their life to a 'death in life'.[34] Banu Bargu further highlighted the existence of a more 'spectacular and morbid form of necropolitics' existing within and beyond these other kinds, which targets 'the bodies of those killed in armed conflict, by way of their mutilation, dismemberment, denuding, desecration, dragging, and public display', while also prohibiting commemorative rites and practices concerning the newly dead.[35] All of these forms of necropolitical violence occurring in Turkey's Kurdish region are the targets of the COs' critique. But the latter form of morbid and degrading necroviolence that Bargu highlights especially troubled the COs and their religious convictions.

The place and role of necropower was a theme of discussion in an interview with Sedat, a self-identified Kurdish anarchist, who organises the Kurdish youth there to advance local antimilitarist agendas.[36] Sedat came to the interview with a co-editor of the journal that they then published, and they shared the story of their participation in the excavation of a mass grave in the Kurdish region.[37] The excavation unearthed the bodies of forty-one suspected guerrillas and among the dead was a young German woman, a socialist who joined the Kurdish cause and fought with the PKK. The village guards who helped the excavation team in locating the place of the grave reported that this woman was killed and then raped by Turkish soldiers – as a 'punishment' for the crime of being a terrorist and a non-Muslim. This story, Sedat argued, tragically depicts the pathological intermingling of masculinity and religiosity within Turkish militarism, which he believed should be the fundamental focus of an antiwar critique.[38] Another example of this pathological logic, he added, is the widespread portrayal of the captured PKK guerrillas as 'Armenians' by ultra-nationalist politicians and the media. In a 1994 military operation in Van's Çaldıran province (where Sedat is from), the army reportedly killed nine militants and displayed them naked on a farm for two days, inviting the local population to view the uncircumcised dead bodies of the guerrillas as proof of their status as 'infidel Armenians'. While reflecting the fact that the workings of necropower in Turkey's geographies of exception are informed by historically grounded enmities – such as the legacy of the Armenian genocide – such reported actions of the army and paramilitary forces in the region further reinforce the Turkish army's self-promoted image as the armed force of a Muslim nation.

Turkish militarism's inflection with this kind of necropower was brought up frequently in my conversations with Muslim COs. A CO stated that for him such morbid violence is the ultimate sign of the Turkish army's 'moral degeneracy' and was sufficient on its own to make the refusal to serve an essential Islamic responsibility. In line with the denigrating symbolic reference to 'the Armenian roots of Kurdish terrorism' noted above, another Muslim objector pointed out that the logic of necropolitical violence has deep roots in Turkish statecraft. This necropolitical logic, he suggested, is premised upon the strategy of forcing people to fight against their own kin ('other Muslims' and 'other Kurds') and it first emerged in the Ottoman empire, whose elite fighting force, the Janissaries, comprised of converted Christian subjects who were then made to fight against the 'infidel' enemies of the empire, 'their own blood and kin'. In this sense, he argued, compulsory conscription is a 'modern Janissary imposition', inherited by the republic, and works to brutalise and dehumanise the people who continue to live in these lands.[39]

Muslim COs' discomfort with this necropolitical undercurrent of Turkish militarism deeply informs the other axis of their civil dissent as well: their opposition to martyrdom narratives advanced to generate legitimacy and enthusiasm for the Turkish regime. This critique is developed in two steps, the first involving an attack on the state's mobilisation of a militarised understanding of Islamic martyrdom in the service of war and death-making, and a following rival reinterpretation, which reverses the operating logic of Turkish martyrdom narratives and portrays conscientious objection as a potential venue by which to pursue martyrdom. In the first instance, Muslim COs criticise the invocation of this theological idiom by an army engaged in the systematic oppression of another Muslim community, the Kurds. Drawing upon injunctions against killing other Muslims in the Qur'an and the distinctions Muslim jurists have historically made between Darul Islam – 'realms of Muslim authority, where one could practice faith freely under the protection of a Muslim ruler' – and Darul Harb – 'hostile places, where a Muslim lacked legal protection and safety'[40] – a Muslim CO claims that martyrdom is not a 'blessing' achievable in the Turkish army:

> The Kurd in the Southeast is a Muslim, and so am I. He shouts at me the battle cry, 'Allah, Allah'; and I shout the same. It is forbidden (*haram*) to shed the blood of another Muslim in the Qur'an. How could one talk about martyrdom when committing *haram* acts?[41]

The perceived 'forbidden' nature of the acts that conscripted civilians are expected to perform during their military service is a concern shared by other Muslim COs, too. This sentiment is particularly acute with regard to the degrading necropolitical violence unleashed by the Turkish military in the Kurdish region. Indeed, I frequently observed that Muslim activists were affectively offended by the association of a sacred ideal like martyrdom with death occurring within an institution whose political justice and moral aptitude they seriously questioned.

Muslim COs further support the claim that Islamic martyrdom cannot be achieved in the Turkish army by invoking scepticism about the nation-state system at large.[42] Drawing attention to the theological origins of the concept of martyrdom in the claim to 'bear witness' to God's sovereignty and greatness, Muslim COs problematise the usage of this idiom in reference to the military force of a Turkish sovereign and within the context of a compulsory imposition to kill and die for it. For them, Turkish martyrdom narratives wrongly use this concept to advance a nationalist cause that lacks religious credibility. As one CO put it, 'it is a pity if people genuinely believe that fallen soldiers die as martyrs; their death "bears witness" not to the greatness of God, but to the power of the national sovereign', who 'sacrifices' them for a cause that Muslim COs consider unjust.[43] Coupled with their earlier critique of necropolitical violence, this argument portrays soldiers who lose their lives during their military service not as heroic martyrs (as claimed in nationalist narratives) but victims of state violence in a broad sense, powerfully complicating the religio-moral claims of Turkish militarism.

However, Muslim COs' critique goes beyond discussions about what kind of death would 'truly' qualify as martyrdom. After disputing the legitimacy of the biosovereign mobilisations of this idiom by the Turkish state, they proceed to offer a rival reinterpretation that seeks to secure this theological concept as the basis of resistance against war and death-making. Criticising the limitation of martyrdom to sacrificial death (which is prevalent not just in Turkism militarism but arguably in most post-9/11 global security discourses), Muslim COs advance a more capacious understanding of martyrdom – one that is grounded in their earlier critique of conscription as an undue rivalry of the state with divine sovereignty, but remobilising this claim to support antiwar activism, not theocratic governance. A CO puts this idea forth as follows:

> What I understand from martyrdom is not dying in battle. It means bearing witness (*shahada*) to God and God's sovereignty in all your actions, especially in matters of life and death. By refusing to serve in the military, I refuse to obey authorities that rival God – in so doing, I bear witness to God's sovereignty. As such, I consider myself as always already a martyr.[44]

The striking feature of this argument is its interpretation of conscientious objection as a potential venue for achieving martyrdom. If martyrdom means 'bearing witness' to the greatness and sovereignty of God, this perspective asks, what better way to pursue it than by refusing to serve the Turkish sovereign whose power is wielded, as Muslim COs insist, to oppress other people (especially other Muslims) and to advance unjust ends? Reinforcing their earlier critiques of conscription and the nation state, this rival reinterpretation of martyrdom as something that Muslims could pursue through refusing to provide manpower to Turkish militarism reclaims conscientious objection from its pejorative signification as unpatriotic and sacrilegious. In Muslim COs' alternative reading – and when set against their broader critique of the necropolitical characteristics of Turkish militarism – conscientious objection becomes an essential virtue and a powerful political medium through which dissenting Muslims, as 'living martyrs', could express their opposition to the war.

Importantly, this reconceptualisation further brings forth an unexpected potentiality of martyrdom: that of life preservation. In addition to expressing a rejection of necropolitics, martyrdom as conscientious objection further entails a normative and strategic embrace of life and its dignity. In becoming 'living martyrs' through their refusal to serve in the Turkish army, Muslim COs actively protect not only their own lives but most importantly the Kurdish lives that are routinely targeted by that army's violence.[45] Their approach to martyrdom thus releases this idiom from the necropolitical embrace not only of state power but also of Islamic martyrdom narratives that promote violence. In Muslim COs' reinterpretation, martyrdom is empowered with new life-preserving and peace-making functions that do not serve the sovereign end of obedience (in the Hobbesian sense) but that express a principled commitment not to harm and kill the innocents even when such a commitment may put the freedoms and wellbeing of the COs themselves at risk.

Conclusion

Muslim COs' critique offers a sustained, religiously inspired condemnation of Turkish military aggression and its necropolitical undercurrent while also demonstrating the flourishing of diverse vernacular Muslim imaginaries and practices in Turkey's dissident public sphere.[46] Muslim COs' criticism of military conscription and the religiously inflected discourses of martyrdom mobilised to justify this institution and its role in perpetuating state violence involves both a contestation of the theological claims advanced in support of Turkish militarism and an insurgent reinterpretation of them. Their rethinking of martyrdom transforms this theological idiom into a basis for antiwar resistance in their critique.

Conventional interpretations of both martyrdom and conscientious objection are complicated as a result of Muslim COs' interventions, gaining new symbolic and political significance. With respect to conscientious objection, their refusal diverges from conventional theorisations of this disobedience as a form of apolitical ethics or individual withdrawal that is primarily concerned with the purity of individual consciences. By contrast, Muslim COs' civil dissent is an antiwar critique and resistance, which is often at pains to dissociate itself from both a liberal politics of conscience and an ethics of nonviolence. In addition to confronting the state publicly, Muslim COs identify state violence against the Kurds and the military's necropolitical conduct as the main targets of their critique – rather than seeking accommodation on account of their religious convictions. They portray their conscientious objection as an integral expression of their opposition to what they perceive to be an unjust war and a violent political regime – an opposition they portray as part of their faith's sociopolitical demands on them (*'Islamlık'*). For all these reasons, Muslim conscientious objection provides us with important resources to rethink our conventional approaches to conscientious forms of dissent and their role in contentious politics.

Muslim COs' provocative association of martyrdom with their refusal further complicates the association of the Muslim ideal of martyrdom with violent sacrificial death, not just in Turkish militarism and some other strains of Muslim thought, but more broadly in the post-9/11 global securitisation discourses. Their approach to martyrdom instead renders this theological concept a this-worldly pursuit that could be achieved through resisting the form of sovereign power that forcibly and unjustly decimates people and condemns them to permanent states of war, deprivation and suffering. Martyrdom here becomes part of a broader repertoire of civil resistance against unjust political systems – and one that does not operate through, or idealise, violent tactics. In this sense, their portrayal of conscientious objection as a potential venue to achieve martyrdom and resist necropolitics constitutes a powerful example of how martyrdom could be differently imagined by dissenting Muslims confronted with diverse historical circumstances. Demonstrating the shifting, contested and historical nature of what Islam and Islamic ideals such as martyrdom may mean to actual Muslims in their lived experience, Muslim COs' critique thus invites us to further consider how our understanding of religious actors' contributions to, and contestation of, political concepts such as sovereignty, necropolitics and resistance could be enriched if we take into account vernacular religious imaginaries and practices, instead of essentialist notions about 'what Islam is' and 'how it influences radical politics'.

Bringing vernacular critiques such as Muslim conscientious objection to bear upon our debates on 'Islam' and 'Muslims' political agency' not only complicates conventional misconceptions and essentialisms, but, perhaps more importantly, it further compels us to inquire how these (mis)conceptions emerged and with what consequences. Scholars such as Cemil Aydın and Elizabeth Shakman-Hurd have recently drawn attention to the ways in which essentialisms of this kind have complicated and contingent histories and concrete political consequences in domestic and international politics. Referencing the Trump administration's recent immigration ban, for instance, Shakman-Hurd underscores the democratic dangers involved in rebranding certain countries as 'Muslim' and equating religious affiliation with potential belligerence: 'To posit extremism as an organic expression of Islam renders us incapable of apprehending the broader political and social contexts in which discrimination and violence occur and empowers those who benefit from the notion that Islam is at war with the West.'[47] In his recent book *The Idea of the Muslim World*, Aydın similarly argues that 'it is not enough to demonstrate that presumptions such as "Muslim unity" are recent and contingent constructs produced by complex historical conditions including imperial racism'.[48] We must also engage with contemporary historical realities and political manoeuvres that continue to bring the consequences of these essentialisms to bear upon the lives and wellbeing of Muslims living near and far. Critical thinking today requires moving beyond historical corrections and the debunking of such theories and assumptions and acting towards preventing and overcoming the harms they do. The Muslim COs whose critique I have shared in this chapter would call such a critical attitude and political intervention a form of martyrdom: the act of 'bearing witness' to the everyday struggles of those who are routinely subjected to the concrete consequences of discriminatory and punitive essentialisation, and joining the struggle to end such injustices. Perhaps there is much we can learn from them.

Notes

1. Perhaps the most important interregnum in this protracted war is the historic peace agreement that the Turkish government and PKK sought to reach between 2013 and 2015. As Serra Hakyemez notes, during this unprecedented process, 'top-tier bureaucrats from the Turkish Intelligence Agency and the National Security Council sat at the negotiation table with the PKK's long-imprisoned leader, Abdullah Öcalan, to strike a deal, and the Turkish Army and PKK guerrillas subsequently declared a mutually recognized cease-fire that held for twenty-seven months, opening a space for deliberation on the political and collective rights that the Kurds would enjoy in post-conflict Turkey. The peace process

collapsed quite decisively and dramatically with the Turkish state's strong military offensive beginning in July 2015, claiming over 2,000 lives, displacing about half a million and resulting in devastating destruction in the region.' Serra Hakyemez, 'Turkey's Failed Peace Process with the Kurds: A Different Explanation', pp. 1–2.
2. Banu Bargu, 'Another Necropolitics', pp. 1–21.
3. Ayşe Gül Altınay, *The Myth of the Military-Nation: Militarism, Gender, and Education in Turkey*.
4. Emma Sinclair-Webb, '"Our Bülent Is Now a Commando": Military Service and Manhood in Turkey'; Pınar Selek, *Sürüne Sürüne Erkek*; Serdar Şen, *Silahlı Kuvvetler ve Modernizm*.
5. Zeki Sarigil, 'Deconstructing the Turkish Military's Popularity'; Yaprak Gürsoy, 'Turkish Public Attitudes toward the Military and Ergenekon'.
6. Sinem Gürbey, 'Islam, Nation-State, and the Military'; Şen, *Silahlı Kuvvetler ve Modernizm*.
7. I borrow the reference 'necropolitical undercurrent' from Banu Bargu's introduction to this volume.
8. Şerif Mardin uses the term 'Turkish Islam'. See his 'Ideology and Religion in the Turkish Revolution' and 'Turkish Islamic Exceptionalism Yesterday and Today'.
9. However, and especially after the failed coup attempt of 15 July 2016, Turkey began to seriously discuss a gradual transition to a professional army. The Turkish government under Recep Tayyip Erdoğan's AKP blamed the coup attempt on the Gülen movement – an influential transnational socio-religious movement also known as *Hizmet* (Service) under the leadership of the US-based cleric Fethullah Gülen, which has now been declared a 'terrorist organisation' and is referred to as FETÖ (for *Fethullahçı Terör Örgütü*). The failed coup attempt resulted in extensive purges in the military and saw a rejuvenated effort on the part of the AKP to recreate a securely controlled armed force. In July 2018, President Erdoğan confirmed that the Ministry of National Defense had begun discussing the possibility of reforming conscription and transitioning to a professional army. However, it has also been stressed that given the sacred position of military service in Turkey, the government favours a form of mixed system in which citizens will continue to receive military education while the Turkish Armed Forces will become fully professional.
10. The length of military service was reduced from fifteen months to twelve months in 2013. University graduates are offered the option to perform six months of military service. See <http://www.mevzuat.gov.tr/MevzuatMetin/1.3.1111-20141210.pdf> (last accessed 28 May 2019).
11 The relevant clauses are Article 18 of the International Covenant on Civil and Political Rights, <http://www.ohchr.org/en/professionalinterest/pages/ccpr.aspx>, and Article 18 of the Universal Declaration of Human Rights, <http://www.un.org/en/documents/udhr/> (last accessed 28 May 2019).
12. Hülya Üçpınar, 'The Criminality of Conscientious Objection in Turkey and Its Consequences'.

13. Human Rights Watch reports that 'according to official estimates, by 2008 the armed struggle between the military and the PKK had resulted in an estimated 44,000 deaths of military personnel, PKK members, and civilians'. Human Rights Watch, 'Time for Justice: Ending Impunity for Killings and Disappearances in 1990s Turkey'.
14. Benedict Anderson, *Imagined Communities*.
15. Yael Tamir, 'Pro Patria Mori! Death and the State', p. 227.
16. Hişyar Özsoy, 'Between Gift and Taboo', p. 1.
17. Laleh Khalili, *Heroes and Martyrs of Palestine*, p. 141.
18. Gareth H. Jenkins, *Context and Circumstance*, p. 13.
19. For a more detailed analysis of the book, see Pınar Kemerli, 'Religious Militarism and Islamist Conscientious Objection in Turkey'.
20. Bozkurt Güvenç and Şaylan Tekeli, *Türk-İslam Sentezi*; Sam Kaplan, *The Pedagogical State*.
21. Kaplan, *The Pedagogical State*.
22. Hakyemez, 'Turkey's Failed Peace Process with the Kurds: A Different Explanation', p. 3; Human Rights Watch, 'Time for Justice: Ending Impunity for Killings and Disappearances in 1990s Turkey'.
23. Osman Murat Ülke spent 701 days in prison as a result of eight separate convictions between 1996 and 1999. In 2006, he appealed to the European Court of Human Rights. In *Affaire Ülke c. Turquie* (Ülke v. Turkey), the court found Turkey guilty of violating the prohibition against degrading treatment under Article 3 of the European Convention. Turkey was sentenced to pay monetary compensation to Ülke, and was also asked to implement a legal framework 'providing an appropriate means of dealing with situations arising from the refusal to perform military service on account of one's beliefs'. While Turkey paid the said compensation to Ülke, it has still not reformed its legal system. Cf. 'European Court of Human Rights affirms the right to conscientious objection to military service', War Resisters' International, 7 July 2011, <http://www.wri-irg.org/de/node/13272> (last accessed 5 June 2014).
24. William Smith and Kimberley Brownlee, 'Civil Disobedience and Conscientious Objection'; Michael Walzer, *Obligations*; Hannah Arendt, 'Civil Disobedience'; Alexander Livingston, 'Fidelity to Truth: Gandhi and the Genealogy of Civil Disobedience'.
25. Author's interview with Ihsan Eliaçık, August 2017.
26. Author's interview with Enver Aydemir, 3 July 2011. Further quotations from Aydemir are from this interview unless otherwise indicated. All translations into English belong to the author.
27. The imposition of compulsory conscription is indeed a powerful expression of the two interrelated sides of sovereignty, highlighted by Foucault and Mbembe respectively: the biopolitical managing of life and necropolitical administration of death. Michel Foucault, *History of Sexuality*; Michel Foucault, *'Society Must Be Defended'*; Achille Mbembe, 'Necropolitics'.
28. Ruşen Çakır, *Ayet ve Slogan*.

29. Author's interview with Mehmet Lütfü Özdemir, 27 December 2011.
30. I want to highlight a further point concerning Muslim COs' invocation of divine sovereignty. As indicated earlier, this approach is part of a broader repertoire of resistance in twentieth-century Islamic political thought. Juridical debates about sovereignty and constitutionalism and attendant concerns about how the state should be restructured in accordance with God's will are typically central to political assertions of this approach by Islamist groups around the world. But I suggest that in Muslim COs' appropriation this view takes a different articulation. More than constitutional dilemmas, their primary concern here is the conditions of armed conflict in Turkey, which they consider to endanger not just the possibilities of peace and justice here on earth but also their spiritual and ethical state of being and conduct as Muslims – a condition they refer to as their 'Islamism'. Understood as part of their Islamism, conscientious objection is in this instance associated with a broader struggle that Muslim COs pursue – one that involves all dimensions of their lives. So the invocation of divine sovereignty here serves as an ethico-political injunction that Muslim COs take heed of while managing their daily conduct and political activism, rather than an institutional proposal to overthrow popular governance. While certainly not devoid of its own contentions and ambiguities, Muslim COs' position is nonetheless more flexible and accommodates a wider variety of engagement with institutions and mediums of popular governance and activism.
31. For more on this point see Human Rights Watch, 'White Flag Deaths Killings of Palestinian Civilians during Operation Cast Lead'.
32. Aydemir here refers to the hundreds of Kurdish children who had been prosecuted by Turkish authorities in late 2000s under terrorism charges for participating in protests and confronting the security forces. Referred to as 'stone-throwing children', some of these kids were sentenced to extended jail time (up to eight years), drawing criticism from the European Union and domestic and international human rights organisations. In 2010, the Turkish parliament passed new laws reducing the penalties for these children, and juvenile courts (rather than adult courts) were authorised to deal with their cases. Despite the softening of the law, however, the mistreatment and prosecution of the children continued. 'Turkey Softens Law That Jailed Young Kurds', *New York Times*; Jonathan Head, 'Young, Kurdish, and Jailed in Turkey'.
33. Foucault, *History of Sexuality*; Foucault, *'Society Must Be Defended'*.
34. Mbembe, 'Necropolitics'; Bargu, 'Another Necropolitics', p. 20.
35. Bargu, 'Another Necropolitics', p. 21.
36. Sedat is a pseudonym I use to protect this activist's anonymity. I first got to know him at an antiwar activists' meeting in Istanbul, where he was visiting, and later met with him for a private interview.
37. While the Turkish state's involvement in political associations and illegal activities in the Kurdish region remained a taboo in Turkey, there were signs of change in 2009 when 'a remarkable trial began in the southeastern city of Diyarbakır of a gendarmerie officer, retired colonel Cemal Temizöz, three former PKK members turned informers, and three members of the "village

guard" (local paramilitary forces armed and directed by the gendarmerie)'. As Human Rights Watch reports, 'the prosecution accused the defendants of working as a criminal gang involved in the killing and disappearance of twenty people in and around the Cizre district of Şırnak province between 1993 and 1995'. This momentum 'to pursue accountability for past abuses' also resulted in excavations of mass graves in south-east and eastern Turkey. The activism by the families of the victims of these human rights abuses, most prominently the weekly protests in Istanbul by the Saturday Mothers, 'relatives of victims who campaign for justice for disappearances and killings by suspected state perpetrators', was crucial in triggering this change. Another important factor was the efforts of the AKP government at the time 'to curtail military power in Turkey and to pursue criminal proceedings in the Ergenekon and similar trials against state, military, and criminal networks for alleged collaboration in coup plots'. The mass grave excavations that Sedat refers to here took place in this period of relative change and accountability. See Human Rights Watch, 'Time for Justice: Ending Impunity for Killings and Disappearances in 1990s Turkey'.
38. Such a critique was essential, Sedat's friend added, as it would also problematise the gendered economy of Kurdish militarism, which has sought to avoid the religious moralism of Turkish militarism but has generated its own myths of masculinity, especially around the sacred image of the PKK's currently imprisoned founder and leader, Abdullah Öcalan.
39. Author's interview with Enver Aydemir, 3 July 2011.
40. Cemil Aydın, *The Idea of the Muslim World*, p. 18.
41. The Muslim CO Muhammed Serdar Delice cited relevant Qur'anic references extensively in our conversation while making this argument.
42. I want to point out here that Muslim objectors' critique on this point is not derivative of essentialist notions of *ummah* or an imagined Muslim unity. In other words, their critique of the nation-state system does not idealise ahistorical notions of a unified 'Muslim world', 'Islamic civilisation' or 'caliphate', and instead addresses concrete instances of nation-state making and its violence. In this sense, though not directly invoked in this particular example, what Roxanne Euben has noted as the essentially colonial nature of the imposition of the nation-state system in the broader Middle East and its association with 'domination' rather than 'self-determination' is also relevant to their critique. Roxanne L. Euben, 'Spectacles of Sovereignty in Digital Time', 1007–33; Aydın, *The Idea of the Muslim World*.
43. Author's interview with Inan Mayis Aru, 5 July 2011.
44. Ibid.
45. I thank Francesca Romeo and Banu Bargu for encouraging me to develop this point.
46. For more on the significance of taking such vernacular practices into theoretical account, see Aydın, *The Idea of the Muslim World*, p. 9.
47. Elizabeth Shakman-Hurd, 'The Myth of the Muslim Country'.
48. Aydın, *The Idea of the Muslim World*, p. 229.

Bibliography

Altınay, Ayşe Gül, *The Myth of the Military-Nation: Militarism, Gender, and Education in Turkey* (New York: Palgrave Macmillan, 2004).

Anderson, Benedict, *Imagined Communities* (London: Verso, 1983).

Arendt, Hannah, 'Civil Disobedience', in *Crises of the Republic: Lying in Politics; Civil Disobedience; On Violence; Thoughts on Politics and Revolution* (New York: Harcourt Brace Jovanovich, 1972).

Aydın, Cemil, *The Idea of the Muslim World* (Cambridge: Harvard University Press, 2017).

Bargu, Banu, 'Another Necropolitics', *Theory & Event* 19, no. 1 (January 2016).

Bilefsky, Dan, 'Turkey Softens Law That Jailed Young Kurds', *New York Times*, 29 July 2010, <https://www.nytimes.com/2010/07/30/world/asia/30kurds.html> (last accessed 15 November 2018).

Çakır, Ruşen, *Ayet ve Slogan* (Istanbul: Metis Yayinlari, 1990).

Euben, Roxanne L., 'Spectacles of Sovereignty in Digital Time: ISIS Executions, Visual Rhetoric and Sovereign Power', *Perspectives on Politics* 15, no. 4 (2017): 1007–33.

Foucault, Michel, *'Society Must Be Defended': Lectures at Collège de France 1975–1976*, ed. Mauro Bentani and Alessandro Fontana, trans. David Macey (New York: Picador, 2003).

Foucault, Michel, *History of Sexuality, Volume 1: An Introduction* (New York: Vintage Books, 1990).

Gürbey, Sinem, 'Islam, Nation-State, and the Military: A Discussion of Secularism in Turkey', *Comparative Studies of South Asia, Africa and the Middle East* 29, no. 3 (2009): 371–80.

Gürsoy, Yaprak, 'Turkish Public Attitudes toward the Military and Ergenekon: Consequences for the Consolidation of Democracy', 2014, <http://eu.bilgi.edu.tr/images/pictures/working_paper_5.pdf> (last accessed 10 June 2019).

Güvenç, Bozkurt, and Şaylan Tekeli, *Türk-İslam Sentezi* (Istanbul: Sarmal Yayinevi, 1991).

Hakyemez, Serra, 'Turkey's Failed Peace Process with the Kurds: A Different Explanation', *Middle East Brief*, no. 111 (2017).

Head, Jonathan, 'Young, Kurdish, and Jailed in Turkey', *BBC World*, 24 May 2010, <https://www.bbc.com/news/10146284> (last accessed 15 November 2018).

Human Rights Watch, 'White Flag Deaths Killings of Palestinian Civilians during Operation Cast Lead', 2009, <https://www.hrw.org/report/2009/08/13/white-flag-deaths/killings-palestinian-civilians-during-operation-cast-lead> (last accessed 15 November 2018).

Human Rights Watch, 'Time for Justice: Ending Impunity for Killings and Disappearances in 1990s Turkey', 2012, <https://www.hrw.org/report/2012/09/03/time-justice/ending-impunity-killings-and-disappearances-1990s-turkey> (last accessed 15 November 2018).

Jenkins, Gareth H., *Context and Circumstance: The Turkish Military and Politics* (London: Routledge, 2005).

Kaplan, Sam, *The Pedagogical State: Education and the Politics of National Culture in Post-1980 Turkey* (Stanford, CA: Stanford University Press, 2006).
Kemerli, Pınar, 'Religious Militarism and Islamist Conscientious Objection in Turkey', *International Journal of Middle East Studies* 47, no. 2 (2015): 281–301.
Khalili, Laleh, *Heroes and Martyrs of Palestine: The Politics of National Commemoration* (Cambridge: Cambridge University Press, 2009).
Livingston, Alexander, 'Fidelity to Truth: Gandhi and the Genealogy of Civil Disobedience', *Political Theory* 46, no. 4 (2017): 511–36.
Mardin, Şerif, 'Ideology and Religion in the Turkish Revolution', *International Journal of Middle East Studies* 2 (1971): 197–211.
Mardin, Şerif, 'Turkish Islamic Exceptionalism Yesterday and Today: Continuity, Rupture and Reconstruction in Operational Codes', *Turkish Studies* 6 (2005): 145–65.
Mbembe, Achille, 'Necropolitics', trans. Libby Meintjes, *Public Culture* 15, no. 1 (Winter 2013): 11–40.
Özsoy, Hişyar, 'Between Gift and Taboo: Death and the Negotiation of National Identity and Sovereignty in the Kurdish Conflict in Turkey', unpublished PhD dissertation, University of Texas at Austin, May 2010.
Sarigil, Zeki, 'Deconstructing the Turkish Military's Popularity', *Armed Forces & Society* 35, no. 4 (2008): 709–27.
Selek, Pınar, *Sürüne Sürüne Erkek Olmak* (Istanbul: Iletişim Yayınları, 2011).
Şen, Serdar, *Silahli Kuvvetler ve Modernizm* (Istanbul: Sarmal Yayınevi, 1996).
Shakman-Hurd, Elizabeth, 'The Myth of the Muslim Country', *Boston Review*, January 2017.
Sinclair-Webb, Emma, '"Our Bülent Is Now a Commando": Military Service and Manhood in Turkey', in Mai Ghoussoub and Emma Sinclair-Webb (eds), *Imagined Masculinities: Male Identity and Culture in the Modern Middle East* (London: Saqi, 2000), pp. 65–91.
Smith, William, and Kimberley Brownlee, 'Civil Disobedience and Conscientious Objection', *Oxford Research Encyclopedia of Politics*, 2017.
Tamir, Yael, 'Pro Patria Mori! Death and the State', in Robert McKim and Jeff McMahan (eds), *Morality of Nationalism* (Oxford: Oxford University Press, 1997).
Üçpınar, Hülya, 'The Criminality of Conscientious Objection in Turkey and Its Consequences', in Özgür Heval Çınar and Coşkun Üsterci (eds), *Conscientious Objection: Resisting Militarized Society* (New York: Zed Books, 2009).
Walzer, Michael, *Obligations: Essays on Disobedience, War and Citizenship* (Cambridge: Harvard University Press, 1970).

EIGHT

The Use of Blood Money in the Establishment of Non-Justice: Necrodomination and Resistance

Cem Özatalay, Gözde Aytemur Nüfusçu and Gülistan Zeren

Workplace homicides, state homicide crimes justified by the 'war on terrorism' discourse and diverse homicide crimes (gun homicide, traffic homicide and so on) committed by powerful people in the ordinary course of life have significantly increased in Turkey. More importantly, these incidents are mediatised more than ever before, as evidenced by the last three decades. The mediatisation of homicides has been accompanied by a rise in the role of blood money bargaining during the justice establishment process. The institutionalisation of blood money has become increasingly commonplace within the current neoliberal judicial system, though the custom itself bears roots in ancient practices that sought to rectify social ills through such exchanges. An analysis of how and to what extent blood money comes into play during the management of deadly crimes in contemporary Turkey can illuminate the conditions that perpetuate its use today, even in an era where a court-based judiciary system is more dominant than ever before. This chapter aims to interrogate this fact in terms of its relationship to the debate on the transformation of governmentality. This debate exposes how power operates in the twenty-first century and how the use of necropolitics, based on the subjugation of life to the power of death,[1] increasingly substitutes for biopolitics. Can the contemporary use of blood money be correlated to the emergence of necropolitics, and if so, is it an explicit management tool used to enable killing and death?

In addressing these questions, we will rely on a sample of five cases from Turkey, of which four have entailed blood money bargaining and all of which concluded in favour of the perpetrators. Our main interest with these cases will be to focus on the different strategies deployed by both the perpetrator and the victim during the blood money bargaining process. We will examine the consequences of such strategies and their effects upon the establishment of justice. In this manner, we proceed from an analysis of the 'domination relationship' between the parties within a blood money negotiation, while distinguishing certain traits of these 'power relations' with respect to the necropolitics of contemporary Turkey. Integral to our discussion of necropolitics in Turkey is the distinction between the Bourdieusian concept of a 'domination relationship' (*rapports de domination*) and the Foucauldian concept of 'power relations' (*relations de pouvoir*). We are in agreement with Christian Laval, who has underlined that there is an exigent conceptual distance between a Foucauldian genealogy of the power dispositive and a Bourdieusian sociology of dispositions determined by social structures.[2] However, these conceptual frameworks do not entirely exclude each other. We consider it fruitful to pair them in an analysis that, on the one hand, aims to understand how and to what extent the strategies of the perpetrators' and that of the victims' relatives differ due to their positions in social space relative to each other; and on the other hand, seeks to identify the material and symbolic extensions of these strategies within the power dispositive. The following briefly elucidates the link between current blood money bargaining cases and the prevalent governmentality while exposing the parameters of this dispositive.

The Emergence of Necropolitics or the Expansion of Necrodomination

Achille Mbembe has developed the concept of necropolitics as the subjugation of life to the power of death, and emphasised that the resource of sovereignty resides in a necropolitics that functions neither in the capacity or will to kill, nor in that of making live. Instead, Mbembe locates this discretionary authority in the 'power and capacity to dictate who may live and who must die'.[3] In this inversion of Foucault's dictum, Mbembe both refers to and criticises Foucault's distinction between sovereign power and biopower. As one can recall, Foucault used two famous epigraphs to distinguish biopower from sovereign power. While sovereign power is principally understood as the ability to 'make die and let live' (*'faire mourir et laisser vivre'*), biopower has relied on the principle of 'make live and let die' (*'faire vivre et laisser mourir'*).[4] Many thinkers (Mbembe perhaps most prominent amongst them) have interpreted this change of emphasis upon living and dying as a governmentality of biopolitics, which focuses on making live while excluding killing and death from its purview. In fact, for Foucault, the relationship between sovereign power and biopower was not a rupture or a wholesale substitution of the latter for the former but, rather, an improvement and transformation in governmentality.[5]

Furthermore, the theoretical results that Foucault had deduced from his genealogical analysis of racism were quite obvious: 'racism is the emergence at the end of the nineteenth century of a particular form of biopolitical government'[6] and 'it describes the return of a (decentred) sovereign right to kill at the heart of biopolitics'.[7] Unlike the war relationship, which is proper to all human societies, Foucault asserted that racism is 'a hybrid form of power that combines the "right to kill" of sovereignty [. . .] with elements of the disciplinary and normalising strategies of biopolitical power'.[8] Even if Foucault analysed the Nazi and Soviet states as exemplary forms of a racist state, as Banu Bargu points out, the Foucauldian approach sees all modern states as 'the "demonic combinations" of these modalities of power'.[9] That is to say, it can be inferred that, according to Foucault, biopower has never ignored the relationship between sovereignty and killing; it was merely positioned as a latent discourse within sovereignty, even during the period in which racism arose and modern wars were fought. In other words, as Elizabeth Dauphenee and Cristina Masters emphasise, 'death needs to be made invisible because death . . . undermines the sovereign claim that its primary activity is to "make live"'.[10]

If it is true that biopolitics has never located the action of killing completely outside the concept of sovereignty, why has Mbembe needed to define a new form of governmentality characterised by necropolitics? Before answering this question, we turn to Judith Butler's discourse on mourning, which was developed at the same time that Mbembe was working on the concept of necropolitics. Butler takes post-9/11 discourse as a source of revelation in which certain populations were deemed disposable and thus 'ungrievable', exposing a hierarchy of grief contingent upon social and racial classifications. This instinct to classify whose life is worthy of being mourned can be interpreted as one of the manifestations of sovereign violence imbedded within Mbembe's theory of necropolitics. In other words, sovereignty does not solely exercise its power in making a decision about who shall live and who must die, but also determines which lives are deemed visible and grieved within a public forum.

The correlation between Butler and Mbembe's respective theories in a post-9/11 context can be compared to the context in which Foucault developed his own concept of biopolitics. In Foucault's era, the state sought to reshape itself in order to meet the need for reconstruction and reparation after World War II, an event considered to be a global crisis. During this period the state in France had been defined as a Providential State (*l'État Providence*), which described its primary function as that of guarding and protecting its citizens. However, in the post-9/11 context, in which the concept of necropolitics has been elaborated, the state had already abandoned its 'providential' functions. As Mark Neocleous emphasises, security has become 'the central category of liberal order-building' in the twenty-first century[11] and the providential state has been replaced by the security state. Within this shift, social security expenses have decreased and civil security expenses have increased. And, in parallel with the needs of a growing security-state nexus, the security industry has adopted a position that emphasises the struggle to annihilate elements assumed to threaten state security. The post-9/11 period is linked to the 'war on terrorism' discourse that has sought to justify an increase in personal armament as a reflection of the state's security concerns. These radical security measures actually lead to the proliferation of weapons within society and consequently an increase in homicides across the population in the name of individual justice or collective security. The function of 'making die' has thereby become prominent in the new governmentality.

This shift has also corroded the 'old' instruments of biopolitics, especially those designated to its 'making live' function. For example, occupational security was one of the main social functions of biopower's capacity to make live, whereas 'asocial' neoliberal securitisation has degraded life by relegating it to a mere factor within increasing production costs. The current dramatic increase in workplace homicides was an inevitable outcome of reducing occupational security expenses, and it should be thought of as one of the expressions of change in governmentality from the 'making live' perspective to the 'letting die' one.

At this stage of the analysis, we may underline that both the 'making die' and 'letting die' perspectives, as two strategies of *necrodomination*, are combined and foregrounded under the new governmentality, and that death – and the management of death – has become its major preoccupation. In other words, in a neoliberal context, 'letting live' consequently means 'letting die' for the majority of the population that suffers in the wake of class domination. Thus 'making live' under neoliberalism requires the sovereign to produce a co-equal amount of 'making die' according to the dictates of identity/race domination (see Table 8.1).

In this sense, unlike Mbembe, we believe that the 'management of death' has grown in prominence as a technique of governmentality that targets not only the periphery or the colonies, but also the very centre of capitalism. Of course, there is a difference in the intensity and the manner in which necropolitics is being used, and this varies according to the position of each party in a given relationship of domination, which is shaped by a racial

Table 8.1 The Effects of Neoliberal Governmentality on Relations of Domination

		Identity/Race Domination	
		Sovereign (+)	Subaltern (−)
Class Domination	Dominant (+)	Letting Live (which practically means Making Live)	Letting Live (which in a crisis of domination might transform into Letting Die and sporadically into Making Die)
	Dominated (−)	Letting Live (which practically means Letting Die and, in a crisis of domination, might sporadically transform into Making Die)	Letting Die (which regularly alternates with Making Die)

and/or identity-based hierarchy as well as class inequalities. This relationality and variability led us to use the notion of necrodomination instead of necropower, which has already been identified as a technique of power essentially rooted in the racial and colonial order of things. Through this concept of necrodomination, we are able to note the similarities between a 'workplace homicide' and a 'state homicide crime' in terms of the 'management of death' in the twenty-first century.

This shift in which diverse forms of death are subsumed under the neoliberal state showcases how the state seeks to reshape citizens as responsible individuals and death as a set of navigable risk factors. In accordance with this, the neoliberal state also redefines individual security as a series of major risks in which each and every dead person will be responsible for their own proper death, regardless of where this occurs and why it happens. It is in this context that blood money is foregrounded, for though it was used to prevent a bloodied revenge on the part of families, clans and tribes in ancient laws, it has now become a tool to manage death and mitigate the true perpetrator's accountability. This tool is utilised on the basis of a specific relationship of domination – necrodomination – revealing the asymmetrical relation between a powerful perpetrator and the victims' relatives, whose antagonism is veiled by the implementation of neoliberal logic.

This chapter examines the way in which the relationship between homicides and blood money compensations reflect this radical change in governmentality, providing us with meaningful data about how sovereignty has been restructured in Turkey according to new forms of neoliberal logic that reframe homicides as 'accidents' within a securitised state discourse. We specifically select cases that emphasise blood money payments as a way of circumventing criminal prosecution and examine a wide range of divergent instances in which this strategy was deployed in order to highlight that the very nature of homicide has been transformed by a neoliberal state logic. The dramatic increase in deaths due to personal armament, traffic accidents, workplace homicides and the war on terrorism in Turkey have all contributed to the veiling of this logic. The common trait of all these cases is that they have been described as 'accidents' by the dominant discourse: operation accident, stray bullet accident, workplace accident and traffic accident. However, it is not a secret that the workplace and traffic 'accidents' are related to a global security discourse, which reduces the function of 'making live' to a cost element. This shift emphasises the fact that necropolitics has developed to the detriment of biopolitics.

Powerful Criminal Defendants within the Relations of Necrodomination

Deaths due to an unnatural cause create perpetrators and victims, placing them within a relationship in the criminal justice system. The title of perpetrator is transformed into that of a 'defendant' within a court context. The defendant who caused the death is thus 'indebted' to the life of the slain. The main issue for justice then is how this debt shall be paid back, or if it shall be paid at all. Public conscience[12] that has been hurt recklessly or purposefully because of this unexpected death needs to be recovered in order to ensure social continuity. At the same time, there must also be a form of recompense demanded for 'the offense [. . .] committed against the sovereign, the state, the law'.[13] At the end of legal proceedings, which start with the intervention of the police and public prosecutor, the legal system promises to provide justice within the scope of an 'illusion of autonomy' and the 'rhetoric of objectivity'.[14] As a reflex against the legal system's promise to reveal the truth and rectify an acknowledged social asymmetry, the perpetrators seek innovative ways to escape judicial power.

We can categorise the perpetrators into three groups: a) law enforcement forces representing the state, which is the organised political power that holds a legal monopoly over violence; b) corporate representatives on behalf of big capital; and c) powerful individuals who commit homicides as a result of their tendencies and preferences. All such perpetrators adopt both legal and illegal tactics in order to develop their defence arguments in criminal cases.

Besides pecuniary and non-pecuniary forms of compensation and/or payments dispersed by insurance companies, one of the most common forms of financial compensation that rests outside traditional legal procedures, but that influences them nonetheless, is the blood money payment. Such payments convey the conflict outside the scope of the legal authority of the sovereign. Thus, the parties bargain with each other to determine a compensatory amount for the death and this amount is paid by the perpetrator to the relatives of the injured party 'in cash'[15] in order to ensure that they drop their charges within the criminal proceedings.

The use of blood money thus subverts the judicial norms of law and justice and transforms them into an instrument of economic power based upon hierarchical advantages that privilege powerful defendants. In this process, the perpetrators attempt to bypass[16] the penal sphere, in which the sovereignty of legal power appears in its most explicit form.

Judicial Reasoning of Death: By Accident

In January 2016, Rüzgar Çetin, the son of a famous Turkish film director, crashed his car into a police vehicle while drunk. This was not his first offence; he had already received twenty-eight traffic tickets and five citations for driving under the influence. As a result of this accident, one police officer was injured and another died. A criminal lawsuit was filed against Rüzgar Çetin citing that he was liable for 'causing [the] death of one person and injury of one person due to conscious negligence'.[17]

In cases of accidental death, it is expected that the circumstances of the death will be examined in detail, and that from these findings a perpetrator will be identified and charged with a crime. In this study's samples, it does not matter if the death arises because of the intentional will of a public officer or the indiscretions of a young drunk driver. The defendants in these cases all emphasise the 'negligence' factor, which means that fault is determined by citing the 'carelessness, unwariness, professional inexperience, or breach of the regulations, orders and rules that the defendant neglected'.[18] The defense strategy based on the argument of 'negligence' aims to minimise the defendant's responsibility for the death that occurred and to imply that their actions did not harbour homicidal intent.

In Çetin's case, the perpetrator initiated negotiations to compensate for the accident with blood money and the injured police officer initially dropped his charge. The wife of the deceased police officer İsmet Fatih Alagöz criticised this by stating that 'the only religion of people is money', and she also declared that she would not participate in any compensation negotiations related to the criminal lawsuit.[19] Aiming to dismiss Alagöz's declaration, the perpetrator exploited his personal relationships (forged because of his economic superiority) in order to reorient the legal sphere for his own gain. Sinan Çetin, the defendant's father who is known to have ties to the media, started declaring that he had in fact paid out blood money. Ultimately, Özlem Alagöz was pressured by the national press to reveal if she had accepted the blood money or not, and she dropped a hint by stating that the family of her deceased husband might have acted independently from her and accepted it. Throughout this process, Alagöz stated that she suffered oppression at the hands of bureaucrats who impugned her for accepting the payment.

Several other facets of this case were also 'tried' in the media. In his column, tabloid journalist Cengiz Semercioğlu addressed the fact that the police officer was not wearing a seatbelt, but he made no reference to Rüzgar Çetin's drinking, or the fact that he drove the car that killed and injured the officers. Semercioğlu wrote that Rüzgar Çetin would have been judged solely for injuring the police officer, had he put on his seatbelt.[20] His article uses an argument similar to the one deployed by the defendant and he presents this case as a conspiracy targeting Rüzgar Çetin's father, who is widely recognised as a popular public figure. On the other hand, Islamist columnist and activist Hakan Albayrak's article devoted to the case attempted to explain the blood money negotiations with the 'qisas' principle in Islam.[21] According to him, neither the payer nor the receiver of blood money for a death should be judged. He even stated that, in a Muslim society, accepting blood money is an 'extraordinarily gentle way' of avoiding conflict.

In this scenario, Özlem Alagöz was at a great disadvantage, for she had no capital to manage the bureaucratic and media networks that the perpetrator exploited. The press reported that she was convinced that Rüzgar Çetin's mother's sadness was sincere and found their offer to construct a school or a mosque in the name of her late husband to be a valid gesture. Özlem Alagöz also concluded that the event was in fact an 'accident' and that she could not handle the high-profile status of the case, as she was a woman with two children, living outside of Istanbul. Hence she dropped the charges a couple of days before the end of the trial. By making the blood money negotiations into a media spectacle, the defendant's desire to avoid prosecution was achieved by means of an extensive intimidation campaign that exploited both the media sphere and the legal bureaucracy. The injured parties' withdrawal of complaints and the evidence framing the death as an 'accident' worked favourably for the perpetrator in the eyes of court.

Yet even though there was no formal complainant after the families of the deceased withdrew their complaints, the criminal lawsuit continued on and resulted in Rüzgar Çetin being sentenced to six years and three months for the crime of 'causing the death of one person and injury of one person with conscious negligence' despite the contrary vote of the chief judge. Though he was eventually indicted, Çetin was quickly discharged, for the court considered the time that he had already spent in jail as 'time served'.

While the judicial perspective on blood money is not homogeneous, it is still practised as an extra-legal method by the court in 'asking for one's blessing as a religious ritual of forgiveness' (*helalleşme*). While this mainly originates from the social asymmetry between the perpetrator and the relatives of victim and has little to do with spiritual forgiveness, it has nonetheless become an informal, yet integral part of Turkey's legal system.

Monetisation of Justice: Blood Money and Judicial Fines

In September 2014, ten workers lost their lives in a lift accident that occurred in a construction zone located in Mecidiyeköy, Istanbul, which belonged to the Torunlar Construction Company. By means of a lawyer, the Torunlar Company contacted the relatives of the victims in order to offer them blood money. At the end of these communications, the relatives of eight of the ten victims accepted the blood money and withdrew their complaints. However, the relatives of the remaining two victims did not accept the blood money at first. In our interview with the lawyer for the Sarıtaş family, which initially refused the blood money, we understood that they eventually had to accept this compensation because of their extenuating financial problems. As stated by the lawyer, at the first session, the company offered 200,000 TL, which was the maximum amount that they could receive at the end of lawsuit for mental anguish. However, the lawyer found this amount insufficient and continued negotiating until the blood money compensation reached a total amount of 850,000 TL.

How can the difference between these amounts be interpreted from the perspective of the perpetrator? The perpetrator in this case (as the other powerful perpetrators we examine) aimed to resolve their problem through the strategy of avoiding a criminal lawsuit by dispensing blood money. The lawyer for the Sarıtaş family was called directly by Mehmet Torun, one of the shareholders of company. During the communications between the two parties, the lawyer stated that they would not withdraw the criminal lawsuit and Torun stated that they had no criminal liability because they did their best to professionally manage the construction project. Within the scope of this professionalism, the money spent to rectify the death is an intrinsic part of the overall cost calculation, and thus is of no importance when weighed against the profitability of the completed project that rests upon one of the most valuable plots of land in İstanbul. The construction company projected that the deaths would damage the company's image if the case was tried in the media and was willing to pay out large sums in blood money in order to insure discretion.

Besides the use of blood money as a method of 'asking for one's blessing as a religious ritual of forgiveness', there was also another factor influencing the opinion of the court, according to the lawyer. Even though the shareholders of the Torunlar Construction Company have not been judged, the court has silenced every statement made by the lawyers of the victims' relatives who have pointed out the responsibility of company owners. This suggests that the company benefited from its hierarchical relationship of power with the court. The lawyer stated that 'Torunlar has power in place' and emphasised that 'they have effects on the opinion of judges'. This becomes evident when we consider the fact that the CEO of the company, Aziz Torun, is a high school friend of Recep Tayyip Erdoğan, the President of Turkey. This relationship, combined with the Torunlar Group's privileged position due to the privatisation policies of the AKP,[22] expose how the results of the criminal lawsuit were an effect of these power relations. While each of the nine perpetrators was sentenced to eight years and three months in prison for 'causing multiple deaths due to conscious negligence', these sentences were eventually commuted into individual penal fines of 60.800 TL.

This decision can be construed as prejudicial, confirming that workplace homicides were essentially negated and purchased through the penal fine due to the company's financial might and networked power relations. The court, situated within this network of relationships, shaped the penal fine in accordance with the capital power of the perpetrator. This result showed us that financial compensation for a death would be legally accepted under certain circumstances.

Hush Money as a Political Form of Blood Money

In January 2015, Nihat Kazanhan, a twelve-year-old boy, was shot and killed in Cizre, a district of Kurdish province, by a police officer. The Office of the Attorney General ordered confidentiality only two days after Kazanhan's lawsuit, which was closely followed by the lawyer of the family. Thus, the family's access to the file was restricted. We learned from the lawyer of the Kazanhan family that the local bureaucrats offered money and employment to the family, who refused these offers.

In lawsuits in which public officials are the perpetrator, blood money gains a political character differing from the payment made in cash between the parties. In these cases, in which the relationships of legal power and political power are interlaced, there is evidence that the justice that the relatives of victims aimed to obtain is governmentalised by making use of authoritarian methods within the scope of enemy criminal law.[23]

In the Kazanhan case, it was suspected that the police created various forms of false evidence. The police officer arrested in the first court case confessed to the prosecutor that he did not use the firearm assigned to his name, which was used to shoot Kazanhan, and that he collected the empty shell casings together with his colleagues after the event, attempted to delete the video records, and held a secret meeting with the chief of police at the police station in order to cover up the event.[24] Thus the legal procedures were also masked by the dominant party's strategic desire to obscure the rights violation that had occurred.

The dichotomy of today's criminal justice system consists of a 'citizen criminal justice' model that seeks to re-accept criminal citizens into the public order and an 'enemy criminal justice' model, which neutralises enemies understood to be dangerous as a result of their conflict with sovereign power.[25] In the case stated above, we can see that these criminal justice models were turned upside down by both legal and political institutional powers. This fact is made evident by the letter sent to the Communication Center of the Presidency (responsible for management of public relations and for receiving complaints from citizens) that was redirected by the Prime Ministry to the file of the police officer who killed Nihat Kazanhan. This letter included such illuminating statements as follows: 'We need such heroes since there are so many traitors in our country and when our country is under attack from inside and outside we should protect these heroes.'[26] Such letters work to ensure that the police officer's actions are framed in positive terms in order to grant them leniency. The court then applied 'unjust provocation' and 'good conduct abatement' articles of criminal law to the officer's resulting sentence of thirteen years and four months' imprisonment. The protective attitude of the Ministry of Interior and Ministry of Justice was evident in the statement of one of its police officers, who said: 'we believed that no one would be arrested in this case'.[27]

The lawyer for the family also stated that it was unjust and foolish that the claim for damages filed by the family nine months after the end of criminal lawsuit resulted in a mere 50,000 TL of compensation. In similar cases, where the model of citizen criminal justice was applied to the perpetrator and the model of enemy criminal justice was applied to the relatives of victims, the government reinforces its sovereignty by making reference to the 'war on terrorism'.

The Roboski incident of 2011 in which thirty-four persons, eighteen of whom were children, doing frontier trade lost their lives as a result of the bombing by Turkish Armed Forces is also a good example, since it reveals how some of these relationship networks are kept hidden while others are made visible because of political conflicts. First of all, the investigation was referred to Diyarbakır because the Military Prosecutor's Office of the Turkish Armed Forces decided to reject the initial venue. This procedure, which resulted in a decision of non-prosecution, was conveyed to the Constitutional Court, but the lawsuit was rejected because the lawyer had not submitted the power of attorney documents on time.

Since the Roboski case did not reach the phase of prosecution, 4,182,000 TL of blood money was sent by the Prime Ministry to the Şırnak Governorate without the knowledge or approval of the families of the deceased victims.[28] The fact that Erdoğan, then Prime Minister, recognised Roboski as a massacre committed by the state and showed his regret in the name of the Turkish Armed Forces in his speech at the opening of the parliament,[29] reveals that he accepted responsibility for this transfer. This statement is very important when considered from the perspective of that period's anti-militarist politics. The Roboski incident, which has been politically acknowledged but never prosecuted, was nevertheless used as a political trump card by the government. Considering this political context, the families refused the payment and thus the money was transferred back to the account of the Prime Ministry. Ferhat Encü, speaking on behalf of the families, described this money as 'hush money'[30] because, contrary to the government, they emphasised the malfunction of legal procedures as human rights and democratisation issues. The fact that these families attempted to invert the economic compensation of death and transform it into a form of political recognition made them the target of 'enemy criminal justice', in which sovereignty continuously reconstructs itself.

Finally, the legal and extra-legal strategies that the perpetrators adopted in cases of homicide constitute the policy of managing the deaths/killings in cooperation with different agents within the judicial field. In this death management policy, 'the government is not represented by a sovereign equipped with legal qualifications anymore'[31] but is shared by the powerful parties using their legal and extra-legal strategies in parallel with their power based on class and ethnicity. The border between these strategies is sometimes very porous, which renders the institutional nature and homogeneous structure of legal power questionable. When blood money negotiations put the parties against each other over the economic and social relationships that they effect, it was revealed that 'the government is everywhere' – 'not because it involved everything but because it comes from everywhere'.[32]

Blood Money Offers and Necrodomination

The strategies adopted by the relatives to manage the legal and social procedures ensuing from these homicides differ from each other. These strategies range from 'submission' to the necrodomination established by the 'powerful' assuming the sovereign right to kill to 'resistance' to such forms of necrodomination. These diverse strategies are shaped in accordance with the various positions that each member occupies in social space.

For the cases discussed in this section, it can be stated that the complainant or the representative of a complainant can be classified into three categories based on their reciprocal positions in social space, which are in turn formed historically by the dynamics of both racial/ethnic domination and class domination. The first category of complainant/procurator consists of those who have been most exposed to systematic forms of necrodomination because of their disadvantageous social position with regard to their racial identity (Kurd) as well as their social class ('disorganised' working class). A bourgeois family whose son was killed by a 'stray' bullet while at his schoolmate's home represents the second category of complainant in our sample. This family's struggle for truth will allow us to discuss why occupying an advantageous position in the class hierarchy is not always sufficient to overcome necrodomination, and how it may force such a complainant, regardless of their class position, to conduct a determined and tenacious struggle against necropower. And finally, our third category is represented by the modest family of a police officer who was the victim of a car 'accident' in which the perpetrator was the son of a famous film director (as mentioned in the previous section). In this case, we will be able to observe the powerlessness that arises even while fulfilling an official duty as a police officer in the face of a potent public personality. Furthermore, we will also be able to see the submissive effect that is induced by taking part in a case that challenges the majoritarian identity group when the prosecuting party only possesses modest means.

Powerless Truth versus Truthless Power

In the lawsuit of Nihat Kazanhan, a twelve-year-old boy from Cizre targeted and killed by a police officer, the lawyer made a significant effort to collect evidence on the same day as the event, and he interviewed the other children that witnessed it. However, the public prosecutor ordered confidentiality only two days after the killing. According to the defendant party's statement, the public prosecutor's office did not provide the lawyers of the parties with any information about the course of the case. In other words, the public prosecutor restricted access to the file. Most of the lawyers interested in the case believed that nothing would be achieved throughout the prosecution. Nonetheless, the opinion that the perpetrator would not be sentenced did not prevent the lawyer of the victim's relatives from struggling to reveal the truth. In order to prevent the perpetrator's impunity, the lawyer made a special effort to convey the case to the media and to have NGOs' support for the case. Although the family did not believe that justice would be served, because they knew that none of the lawsuits of any child killed in the province had yielded any results,[33] the lawyer made a special effort to keep their hopes alive. Amidst all these legal challenges, public authorities sought to discredit the family, trying to pressure them into withdrawing their complaint through repeated phone calls. Within this context, the father of the slain victim was even offered a job, but the family refused the money and employment offers and followed through on their criminal lawsuit. Their motivation was not their belief in the idea that the law would make a decision in their favour, as the lawyer of the family pointed out: 'In fact, we made use of the legal mechanisms in Turkey as steps to be taken so that the case would go to the European Court of Human Rights (ECtHR). Not to achieve a result per se but to exhaust the domestic remedies.'[34]

The slain boy's grandfather's statement reveals why the family did not accept the blood money offer and chose to seek justice in court, even if the ultimate court of appeal was a European court and not a domestic one. He narrated the family's story as follows:

> We are originally from Siirt. We were living in a village called Bash Aval (Tünekpınar) of the Eruh district. One day, they came to us and offered us to become a village guard.[35] We didn't accept it. We were expelled from our own village. Nobody has lived in the village for over twenty years. Maybe a hundred of the neighbouring villagers had to migrate like us just because they didn't agree to become a village guard. I dare say that, in our village, there was no man who hadn't been taken into custody and tortured by soldiers. This happened because I am a Kurd. Due to the seizure of Kurds' rights by the state, many of our relatives and neighbours went to the mountains.[36]

Clearly, this family's background in civil disobedience played a role in their current stance to pursue charges. Even though the father of the slain boy is a truck driver with a modest position in the social hierarchy, in light of the support of the politically engaged lawyers, human rights organisations and the Kurdish political movement, the family was able to resist the offers of blood money and thus oppose necrodomination as a manifestation of truthless power.

However, a certain weakness of resisting victim families in terms of capital (economic, cultural and social) may sometimes cause unpredictably negative outcomes despite their determination to resist. A good example of this is the case of Roboski. As we mentioned in the previous section, thirty-four persons lost their lives as a result of aerial bombing while they were engaged in frontier trade. The Roboski families were similar to the Kazanhan family with respect to their will for resistance. Actually, some of the Roboski families had accepted the state's offer for employment as village guards in the 1990s, and thus had not been forced to leave their village. Even though this decision allowed them to remain in their own village, it did not immunise them from state oppression. After this deplorable incident, the Roboski families followed the same line of action as that of the Kazanhan family.

When the incident triggered a big reaction in public opinion, the government offered the Roboski families blood money, but without bringing those responsible to justice. According to the decision of the Şırnak Governorate's Commission of Damage Determination, a total amount of 4,182,000 TL (123,000 TL for each victim of the bombing) was wired to each of the families in February 2012. But the families did not withdraw the money and it was eventually returned to the account of the Prime Ministry. In 2012, Ferhat Encü, who lost eleven relatives in the massacre, became the spokesperson for the victims' families, pressing the government for answers in court. This led to Encü's election to parliament from Şırnak on June 2015.

Families and human rights lawyers have called for the case to be investigated to determine who ordered the airstrike and what the source of the faulty intelligence was. However, an investigation was not conducted because both the Parliament and the Military deemed this bombardment to be unintentional. As for the judicial authority, in June 2013, the Diyarbakır prosecutor's office adjudicated that the military was negligent but did not intentionally bomb the victims. Hereupon, Ferhat Encü stated in 2016, 'Years have passed since the massacre. Primarily, our goal was to bring the perpetrators to justice and to punish them within the national judicial system but this was not possible.'[37] But as human rights lawyer Benan Molu has said, 'The Roboski application, which was rejected by the Constitutional Court on the ground that applicant lawyers did not send the missing documents in time, has been rejected by the ECtHR on the same grounds.'[38]

Since the families were lacking in both the language and the knowledge of the bureaucratic and judicial fields, they had to delegate the management of legal procedures to their lawyers. The procedural deficiencies caused by Nuşirevan Elçi, the lawyer and the president of the Şırnak Bar, caused the judiciary process to be stuck. The families were abandoned in this process. They stated: 'The summary of the present point is that the Case of Roboski is awarded with impunity because of the irresponsibility of the President of the Bar and the close contact of the Court of Cassation and the ECHR with the government.'[39] For these families who were conscious about the existing relationships of domination due to their historically subaltern position within the identity/racial order, the main goal was to reveal the truth, to identify the responsible people, and to attribute their 'loss' to a cause. But this does not mean that they do not care about the pecuniary compensation they might obtain at the end of the legal procedure. This was one of the reasons why they tried to bring their case in front of the EHCR as soon as possible. However, their weakness in terms of capital possessions rendered them powerless within the relationship of necrodomination, both in terms of seeking the truth and pecuniary compensation.

Memorial NGOs: A Tool of Resistance against Necrodomination

Umut Önal, the seventeen-year-old grandson and successor of the Dedeman family, which is one of the very first industrialist families of Turkey, was murdered by his friend, İdris Melih Turgut, in 1993. Nazire Dedeman, the mother of the victim, claimed that the well-known mafia leader Ahmet Turgut, the father of the perpetrator, obfuscated the evidence through his deep connections with law enforcement and relevant legal and bureaucratic institutions. The theory posited by the mother has been proven accurate because it was later revealed that the two police officers who investigated the case had in fact received bribes from the Söylemez Gang on a regular basis, compelling them to whitewash the events.[40] In this case, the blood money did not come into question because it was improbable that the industrialist family would accept this offer. However, because of irregularities in the case and the fact that their rights were violated, the Dedeman family nonetheless experienced necrodomination over the course of the legal proceedings. During these procedures, the connections between the perpetrator's family and the judiciary did not remain confined to the court room. The sentences mandated for 'unwary and negligent homicide' and for 'possession of an unregistered firearm' by the local court and the Court of Cassation were commuted to penal fines.

Nazire Dedeman's book titled 'Hopeless Justice' (*Umutsuz Adalet*) clearly shows that 're-establishing the truth' in this case has been a long and difficult process. In the book, the mother expressed her awareness about the impossibility of attaining the truth through legal procedures, but, even so, she has continued to struggle to fulfil her obligation to her son. Unlike the victim families mentioned above, however, given her stature as the vice-chairman of Dedeman Holding, she was able to keep tabs on the legal procedures. In a short span of time, she noticed that the evolution of the lawsuit was in favour of the perpetrator and that the lawyers of the victim's family were content to watch this unfold. She also remarks that the forensic report had been delayed for a year, and that the lawyers of the family did not pay attention to the lawsuit during this period. These prompted her to change lawyers and get personally involved in the legal struggle for truth and justice. Nazire Dedeman defines her psychological state during this period as defenseless and confused. At first the new lawyers requested that the court-appointed judge be recused on the grounds that the judge in question and the father of the perpetrator were friends, having had their photo taken together at a recent wedding. However, this request was rejected. Regardless, the judge left the lawsuit of his own accord. Nazire Dedeman defines this situation as 'the justice mechanism beginning to work for the first time'.[41] On the other hand, Nazire Dedeman tells how she received threatening calls in which she was told that a decision detrimental to the perpetrator would end up costing her life. After the decision of the Court of Cassation, Nazire Dedeman stated:

> Before society, I complain about the state, public prosecutor, law enforcement, judges and prosecutors of the Court of Cassation, and I file a complaint against them. The individuals who have not backed my complaints and denunciations have established a chain of benefits and relationships. As a citizen, I don't know to whom I can apply for recourse . . .[42]

The fact that Umut's ex-girlfriend was married to the perpetrator in the September of the year in which Umut was murdered augmented suspicions, as Nazire Dedeman had testified that the murder occurred because of this girl. She and her lawyers presented this development as evidence to the court, but it was not accepted.

Even though the Dedeman family lawsuit resulted in the perpetrator's impunity, similar to the other lawsuits we examined, their process was unlike that of the Kazanhan and Roboski families who had to delegate almost all of the management of their legal process to their lawyer. In contrast, the Dedeman family was able to direct their own case for they had broad access to government representatives, individuals, institutions and networks for negotiation, a form of power that was absent in the other families' cases. But the Dedeman family's efforts to communicate with state representatives were thwarted, especially after the mother of the deceased announced in protest that corrupt mafia relationships undergirded the process. The perpetrator's father's relationship to the bureaucrats and elected individuals from every level of the state overwhelmed the relationships of the industrialist family, who had never before defied the state.

Another distinguishing factor is related to the agents who supported the victims' families. Kazanhan's family and the Roboski families took action together with NGOs, political parties and associations after the murder of their relatives. The presence of human rights defenders rendered the Kazanhan and Roboski lawsuits symbolic from a political perspective. The Dedeman family's social capital also played an effective role during their lawsuit on behalf of Umut Önal, for they received support from the media. However, they never enjoyed the political support of relevant parties in the judicial or governmental spheres.

From the perspective of resistance, all the deaths that occurred in these cases exceeded their individual circumstances and became collective deaths within broader social memory. Regardless of their identities, the victims' relatives did not give up on life, peace and hope during their legal struggles. As noted amongst the variety of cases that we presented, a family either possessed a culture of political resistance against the state while being short on capital possessions, or was in an advantageous position in terms of capital possessions, but lacked a background in political resistance. In either scenario, these two groups of victims' families eventually found themselves trying to transform the relationship of domination in order to prevent the subjugation of life to the power of death.

In an effort to promote such resistance, Nazire Dedeman established the Hope (*Umut*) Foundation in order to champion individual disarmament and further develop relevant legislation. The Roboski families established the Association of Justice for Roboski and Peace for Earth in order to memorialise the massacre of their relatives and promote a peaceful solution for the Kurdish problem while disclosing the injustice they faced during their legal procedures.

However, class differences ultimately determine not only how a person's existence is handled while they are alive, but also how their death is remembered (as a 'unique' or 'collective' loss). For instance, Umut was a well-educated child, who had a 'priceless life', raised in a family that enjoyed an advantageous position within the social hierarchy. Thus this family perceived their son's murder by a bullet as contrary to the order of things. The family, especially the mother, noticed over the course of time that in Turkey there are a lot of families who lose relatives to either a stray or targeted bullet as a result of increased individual armament. Unlike Umut, Nihat, who was killed by a police officer, was a member of a modest Kurdish family with nine children. As the son of a truck driver whose family, as we learned from his grandfather, had been expelled from their own village more than two decades earlier by the army on grounds of refusing the state's offer to become village guards, Nihat lacked Umut's social capital. Thus Nihat's murder (like the Roboski incident) is considered in light of a larger social collective in which the Kurdish people alongside other political agents (engaged lawyers, political parties and human rights defenders) believe that the victims died precisely because they are Kurds or namely, 'bad citizens' in the eyes of the state. It is evident that a relatively privileged family's 'unique' loss is not socially equal to the thousands of losses endured by an oppressed community. It is especially the case when the victim's family occupies a modest place within the class hierarchy. The results of this inequality directly affect the permanence and the efficiency of memorial associations established on behalf of such losses. In essence, class is an important factor in the resistance against the subjugation of life to the power of death.

The Submissives

Özlem Alagöz is the wife of İsmail Alagöz, the police officer who was killed by the drunk driving accident that occurred because of the famous film director's son mentioned earlier. Having neither the culture of resistance embedded in her familial history, nor the financial and moral conditions of managing a legal case against the powerful killer, Alagöz's withdrawal of her complaint is an example of the submission before necrodomination frequently observed in such cases. Here, we can remember Özlem Alagöz's reason for withdrawing from the lawsuit. Alagöz's first reaction to the case was to declare that 'the only religion of people is money'[43] and that she would not participate in any compensation negotiations related to the criminal lawsuit. But, after a period during which the killer's family launched an efficient media campaign, she asserted that her deceased husband's family was inclined to forgive the murderer after the promise that they would build a mosque or school dedicated to her late husband. With this overture on the part of the perpetrator's family she acquiesced and declared that she accepted the murderer's family's sincere regret. Right at the moment in which she relented and tacitly absolved the perpetrator's family of the crime, news appeared in the media announcing that Alagöz had accepted the blood money offer.

The Torunlar Construction Company case echoes the preceding case. After the lift accident in which ten workers lost their lives, eight of the victims' families directly accepted the blood money offer presented by the company's lawyer, and seven of them dropped their charges in the criminal case launched against the company. When we asked the lawyer of the family of the deceased construction worker İsmail Sarıtaş the reasons for the withdrawal, she emphasised two factors: lack of a culture of resistance, and the weakness of her clients in terms of financial power.[44]

Overall we have seen that weakness in terms of financial power is not the only obstacle to putting up a fight against necrodomination. In Turkey, the proactive lawyers and human rights activists are always ready to support the legal struggles of victims against the might of powerful offenders. However, the families who attempt to confront them are well aware of the high social cost of doing so: degradation within the identity/racial hierarchy. This cost causes many to abstain from pursuing legal actions. Having capital possessions might help counter the potential of social degradation, as we saw in the case of the Dedeman family. Conversely, having nothing to lose but their chains to identity/race domination might also encourage confronting a powerful offender. However, if one feels oneself integrated within a majority identity/racial community but powerless in terms of capital possessions, one would be more inclined to accept a blood money offer and be subjected to necrodomination.

Conclusion

Blood money offered by powerful perpetrators to victims' relatives has assumed a relatively new function in an increasingly neoliberalised judiciary system. This function, which consists of speeding up the establishment of 'non-justice', is vital for the new governmentality, for which the management of the death increasingly takes precedence over the management of life. Because of the decline of the welfare state, which was the most developed form of biopolitics, and the transformation of security into the central component of the neoliberal order, 'making die' and 'letting die' have become deeply entwined in the governmentality of force. Those in power tend to legitimise the impulse to 'make die' by referencing security concerns and especially the war on terrorism, and they support the effort to 'let die' by reference to a neoliberal discourse that deems individuals responsible for their own lives against the risk of death. Thus, the dominant mode of governmentality now focuses on managing deaths rather than decreasing the number of factors causing death. Hence the number of 'accidental' deaths has increased, while the methods of managing death have diversified. The use of blood money has thus been updated in order to meet the needs of this new governmentality.

The cases discussed in this chapter indicate that the blood money offers were made by powerful perpetrators in order to minimise the potential penalties that they could incur within penal courts. These offers were used to persuade the victim's relatives to accept blood money payments so that they would not actively participate in criminal lawsuits against perpetrators, and if they did, their acceptance of blood money prompted the courts to reduce the perpetrator's penalty in light of this financial compromise.

The secondary function of the use of blood money is the perpetuation of the social hierarchy. Blood money enables the powerful, who have become indebted in the eyes of victims' relatives and society because of the death that they have caused, to purchase the 'right to kill'. Paying this debt back reasserts the dominant status of the powerful. In other words, blood money becomes a tool of necrodomination to the extent that it reaffirms the social status of the powerful by ensuring that they do not experience any loss of freedom.

Meanwhile, the course of blood money negotiations indicates the patterns of resistance to necrodomination – and finally to power as a whole. These resistance patterns allow us also to draw some conclusions about the determinants of social structure in Turkey, which may also provide insights about other neoliberal states and their respective social structures. The variation of attitudes vis-à-vis blood money due to the positions that victim's families occupy in the social structure can be illustrated as follows (see Table 8.2).

The course of the encounter between the victim's family and the perpetrators is determined by their respective positions in the class and identity/race hierarchies. Those at higher levels in the identitary/racial and class hierarchies, and/or those that play a more important role in the re-establishment

Table 8.2 Uses of Blood Money in the Context of Necrodomination

		Identity Domination	
		Sovereign (+)	Subaltern (−)
Class Domination	Dominant (+)	To offer blood money to purchase the right to kill and to guarantee the continuance of sovereignty.	Not to accept blood money in order to be able to resist necrodomination. To use the death recompense determined by the Court to honour the memory of the loved ones who have been lost.
	Dominated (−)	To accept blood money as a sign of subjugation to the necrodomination of the powerful and the sovereign majority. To use it as a pecuniary resource to survive.	Not to accept blood money for as long as possible in order to be able to resist necrodomination. To use the death recompense determined by the Court as a pecuniary resource to survive.

of the state's sovereignty, are much stronger and advantageous against the individuals and institutions in lower positions. Individuals and institutions having a stronger position in terms of identity and class have resorted to means, such as paying them blood money in exchange for the death they have caused or the murder they have committed, leading the relatives of victims to show a passive attitude in the criminal lawsuit procedures. In cases where they succeeded in convincing the opponent party, the court tended to determine the minimum possible sentence considering that the perpetrator already paid blood money.

On the other hand, the victims' relatives or individuals having an 'identity/race advantage' (as a member of the majority) but also a disadvantage in terms of class show less resistance to accepting the blood money paid by the powerful. These families have accepted blood money generally before filing a criminal lawsuit or right after filing it, and thus did not follow through with legal procedures.

By contrast, the families at a disadvantage against the perpetrator in terms of identity (that is, those who were not members of the majority or dominant identity group) and who maintained a relative disadvantage in terms of class, show greater resistance. The families have chosen to act together especially when they could gather together around an identitary relationship. However, these underprivileged families have frequently been dependent on politically engaged volunteer attorneys in their legal struggle and had financial problems that in many cases rendered them vulnerable to necrodomination. The state has especially targeted those families that did not accept blood money for their relatives who were killed in operations carried out in the name of the war on terrorism. Thus, families that were politically engaged have continued the legal battle in order to memorialise their lost ones, whereas those without strong political commitments gave up struggling earlier.

Meanwhile, the victims' relatives who were at a partial disadvantage in terms of identity but with a significant advantage in terms of class have been able to conduct long-range struggles against the perpetrators regardless of their positions within the social hierarchy or the state. These families with the power to refuse blood money insisted on seeing their lawsuits through to the end in order to ensure the maximum level of penalty for the perpetrators. The compensation for monetary damages that these families received after the court decision was generally transferred to an NGO that would keep the memory of their loved ones alive.

All these cases indicate that the confrontations over blood money are an important representation of how necrodomination operates, whether it be through the actions of powerful perpetrators that seek to manage death or through the resistance of victims' families to 'selling' their loved ones' 'right to live'. This field of necrodomination, which combines both race/identity war and class war dynamics, is also one of the fields of struggle between life and death, peace and war, and resistance and subjugation. Blood money functions as an intermediary of necrodomination. If accepted, consent is given to the power of death and its subjugation of life. However, if rejected, the practice of resisting necrodomination in defense of life yields to varied forms of disobedience that may proliferate and potentially restructure necropolitical power relations in their entirety.

Notes

1. Achille Mbembe, 'Necropolitics'.
2. Christian Laval, *Foucault, Bourdieu et la question néolibérale*, p. 10.
3. Mbembe, 'Necropolitics', p. 11.
4. Michel Foucault, *'Society Must Be Defended'*.
5. For example, see Michel Foucault, *History of Sexuality*, pp. 138–49.
6. Kim su Rasmussen, 'Foucault's Genealogy of Racism', p. 41.
7. Matthew Coleman and Kevin Grove, 'Biopolitics, biopower, and the return of sovereignty', p. 493.
8. Couze Venn, 'Neoliberal Political Economy, Biopolitics and Colonialism', p. 214.
9. Banu Bargu, *Starve and Immolate*, p. 50.
10. Cristina Masters and Elizabeth Dauphinee, *The Logics of Biopower and the War on Terror*, p. xii.
11. Mark Neocleous, *Critique of Security*.
12. Emile Durkheim, *Les règles de la méthode sociologique*, p. 68.
13. Foucault, 'Truth and Juridical Forms', p. 43.
14. Pierre Bourdieu, 'La force du droit', pp. 4–5.
15. Tom Baker, 'Blood Money, New Money, and the Moral Economy of Tort Law in Action', p. 276.
16. Bourdieu, 'Droit et passe-droit', p. 88.
17. Article 85 of Turkish Criminal Code (Law 5237 of 26 September 2004).
18. Turkish Language Association, 'Taksir', available at <http://www.tdk.gov.tr/index.php?option=com_gts&kelime=TAKS%C4%B0R> (last accessed 4 November 2018).
19. 'Bir polisin ölümüne yol açan Rüzgar tahliye edildi', *Diken*, 4 October 2016.
20. Cengiz Semercioğlu, 'Rüzgar, Sinan Çetin'in oğlu olmasaydı . . .', *Hürriyet*, 14 September 2016.
21. Hakan Albayrak, 'Rüzgar Çetin Meselesi', *Karar*, 3 October 2016.
22. 'İnşaatın Sahibi Erdoğan'ın Okul ve Dava Arkadaşı', *Birgün*, 8 September 2014.
23. Günther Jakobs, 'Yurttaş Ceza Hukuku ve Düşman Ceza Hukuku', p. 490.
24. 'Nihat Davasının Sanığı Polis H.V.: Amirlerimizin Talimatıyla Delilleri Gizledik', *Evrensel*, 8 May 2015.

25. Jakobs, 'Yurttaş Ceza Hukuku ve Düşman Ceza Hukuku', pp. 490–1.
26. 'Başbakanlıktan Kazanhan'ı Öldüren Polis İçin İkinci Mektup', *Evrensel*, 9 March 2017.
27. 'Kimse Tutuklanmaz Diye Düşünüyorduk', *Bianet*, 25 February 2015.
28. 'Roboski'nin "Kan Parası" Başbakanlığa İade Edildi', *Cumhuriyet*, 23 January 2015.
29. 'Tayyip Erdoğan Uludere Katliamı Özür Konuşması,' *YouTube*, 30 March 2012.
30. Ferit Aslan, 'Uludere Tazminatları Başbakanlığın Hesabına İade Edilmiş', *Hürriyet*, 23 January 2015.
31. Foucault, 'Entretien avec Michel Foucault', p. 150.
32. Foucault, *Histoire de la sexualité*, p. 122.
33. '3,936 Children's Right to Life Violated in 7 Years', *Bianet*, 23 April 2018.
34. Filiz Ölmez, interview by Gülistan Zeren.
35. The village guard system, established in 1985, recruited villagers – mostly Kurdish themselves – to act as a paramilitary force, both to protect their villages and to aid the Turkish military. The Turkish state has kept the system in place since then, despite opposition both from human rights groups and from within the Turkish parliament.
36. Halil Savda, 'Nihat Kazanhan, Kendi Katilini Haksızca Tahrik Etmiş', *Bianet*, 25 November 2016.
37. 'Roboski Massacre Brought Before ECTHR With 281 Claimants', *Bianet*, 23 August 2016.
38. 'ECTHR Rejects Application About Roboski Massacre', *Bianet*, 17 May 2018.
39. 'Roboskili aileler: Bu dava, bu mezarlıktan yeniden başlamak zorunda', *Gazete Duvar* 24 May 2018.
40. Nazire Dedeman, *Umut'suz Adalet*, p. 107.
41. Ibid. p. 86.
42. Ibid. p. 104.
43. 'Rüzgar Çetin'in çarparak öldürdüğü polisin eşi: İnsanların dini para olmuş', *Diken*, 26 May 2016.
44. Gülsüm Karacan, interview by Cem Özatalay.

Bibliography

'3,936 Children's Right to Life Violated in 7 Years', *Bianet*, 23 April 2018, <https://bianet.org/english/human-rights/196419-3-936-children-s-rights-to-life-violated-in-7-years> (last accessed 6 November 2018).

Albayrak, Hakan, 'Rüzgar Çetin Meselesi', *Karar*, 3 October 2016, <http://www.karar.com/yazarlar/hakan-albayrak/ruzgar-cetin-meselesi-2262> (last accessed 21 October 2018).

Aslan, Ferit, 'Uludere Tazminatları Başbakanlığın Hesabına İade Edilmiş', *Hürriyet*, 23 January 2015, <http://www.hurriyet.com.tr/gundem/uludere-tazminatlari-basbakanligin-hesabina-iade-edilmis-28031076> (last accessed 4 November 2018).

Baker, Tom, 'Blood Money, New Money, and the Moral Economy of Tort Law in Action', *Law & Society Review* 35, no. 2 (2001): 275–319.
Bargu, Banu, *Starve and Immolate: The Politics of Human Weapons* (New York: Columbia University Press, 2014).
'Başbakanlıktan Kazanhan'ı Öldüren Polis İçin İkinci Mektup', *Evrensel*, 9 March 2017, <https://www.evrensel.net/haber/311467/basbakanliktan-kazanhani-olduren-polis-icin-ikinci-mektup> (last accessed 30 September 2018).
'Bir polisin ölümüne yol açan Rüzgar tahliye edildi', *Diken*, 4 October 2016, <http://www.diken.com.tr/bir-polisin-olumune-yol-acan-ruzgar-cetin-tahliye-edildi/> (last accessed 20 October 2018).
Bourdieu, Pierre, 'La force du droit', *Actes de la recherche en sciences sociales* 64, no. 1 (1986): 3–19.
Bourdieu, Pierre, 'Droit et passe-droit', *Actes de la recherche en sciences sociales*, no. 81–2, (1990): 86–96.
Bourdieu, Pierre, 'Stratégies de reproduction et modes de domination', *Actes de la recherche en sciences sociales*, no. 105 (1994), 3–12.
Coleman, Mathew, and Kevin Grove, 'Biopolitics, biopower, and the return of sovereignty', *Environment and Planning D: Society and Space* 27, no. 3 (2009): 489–507.
Commaille, Jacques, *À quoi nous sert le droit?* (Paris: Gallimard, 2015).
Dedeman, Nadire, *Umut'suz Adalet. 'Hukuk Devleti' Türkiye'de Bir Hukuk Mücadelesi* (Istanbul: Destek Yayınları, 2016).
Durkheim, Emile, *Les règles de la méthode sociologique* (Paris : PUF, 1993).
'ECTHR Rejects Application about Roboski Massacre', *Bianet*, 17 May 2018, <https://bianet.org/english/human-rights/197265-ecthr-rejects-application-about-roboski-massacre> (last accessed 6 November 2018).
Fish, Morris J., 'An eye for an eye: Proportionality as a moral principle of punishment', *Oxford Journal of Legal Studies* 28, no. 1 (2008): 57–71.
Foucault, Michel, *Histoire de la sexualité. La volonté de savoir* (Paris: Gallimard, 1976).
Foucault, Michel, *The History of Sexuality, Volume I: An Introduction* (New York: Pantheon Books, 1978).
Foucault, Michel, 'Entretien avec Michel Foucault', in *Dits et écrits 1976–1979*, ed. Daniel Defert and François Ewald (Paris : Gallimard, 1994), pp. 140–160.
Foucault, Michel, 'Truth and Juridical Forms', in *Foucault, Power*, ed. James D. Faubion (New York: New Press, 2000), 1–89.
Foucault, Michel, *'Society Must Be Defended': Lectures at Collège de France 1975–1976*, ed. Mauro Bentani and Alessandro Fontana, trans. David Macey (New York: Picador, 2003).
'İnşaatın Sahibi Erdoğan'ın Okul ve Dava Arkadaşı', *Birgün*, 8 September 2014, <https://www.birgun.net/haber-detay/insaatin-sahibi-erdogan-in-okul-ve-dava-arkadasi-68248.html> (last accessed 12 October 2018).
Jakobs, Günther, 'Yurttaş Ceza Hukuku ve Düşman Ceza Hukuku', in Kayıhan İçel and Yener Ünver (eds), *Terör ve Düşman Ceza Hukuku* (Ankara: Seçkin Yayınları, 2008), pp. 489–507.
Karacan, Gülsüm, interview by Cem Özatalay, tape recording, Istanbul, 9 July 2018.

'Kimse Tutuklanmaz Diye Düşünüyorduk', *Bianet*, 25 February 2015, <http://bianet.org/bianet/insan-haklari/162607-kimse-tutuklanmaz-diye-dusunuyorduk> (last accessed 21 September 2018).

Laval, Christian, *Foucault, Bourdieu et la question néolibérale* (Paris: La Découverte, 2018).

Lindgren, James, 'Measuring the Value of Slaves and Free Persons in Ancient Law', *Chicago-Kent Law Review* 71, no. 1 (1995): 149–217.

Masters, Cristina, and Elizabeth Dauphinee (eds), *The Logics of Biopower and the War on Terror: Living, Dying, Surviving* (New York: Palgrave MacMillan, 2007).

Mbembe, Achille, 'Necropolitics', trans. Libby Meintjes, *Public Culture* 15, no. 1 (Winter 2013): 11–40.

Neocleous, Mark, *Critique of Security* (Edinburgh: Edinburgh University Press, 2008).

'Nihat Davasının Sanığı Polis H.V.: Amirlerimizin Talimatıyla Delilleri Gizledik', *Evrensel*, 8 May 2015, <https://www.evrensel.net/haber/112228/nihat-davas-inin-sanigi-polis-h-v-amirlerimizin-talimatiyla-delilleri-gizledik> (last accessed 23 October 2018).

Ölmez, Filiz, interview by Gülistan Zeren, tape recording, Cizre, 5 July 2018.

Rasmussen, Kim-Su, 'Foucault's Genealogy of Racism', *Theory, Culture & Society* 28, no. 5 (2011): 34–51.

'Roboskili aileler: Bu dava, bu mezarlıktan yeniden başlamak zorunda', *Gazete Duvar*, 24 May 2018, <https://www.gazeteduvar.com.tr/gundem/2018/05/24/roboskili-aileler-bu-dava-bu-mezarliktan-yeniden-baslamak-zorunda/> (last accessed 04 November 2018).

'Roboski Massacre Brought before ECTHR with 281 Claimants', *Bianet*, 23 August 2016, <http://m.bianet.org/bianet/human-rights/178084-roboski-massacre-brought-before-ecthr-with-281-claimants> (last accessed 04 November 2018).

'Roboski'nin "Kan Parası" Başbakanlığa İade Edildi', *Cumhuriyet*, 23 January 2015, <http://www.cumhuriyet.com.tr/haber/turkiye/194939/Roboski_nin__kan_parasi__basbakanliga_iade_edildi.html#> (last accessed 21 September 2018).

Rosenbaum, Thane, *Payback: The Case for Revenge* (Chicago and London: The University of Chicago Press, 2013).

'Rüzgar Çetin'in çarparak öldürdüğü polisin eşi: İnsanların dini para olmuş', *Diken*, 26 May 2016, <http://www.diken.com.tr/ruzgar-cetinin-carptigi-aracta-hayat-ini-kaybeden-polisin-esi-insanlarin-dini-para-olmus/> (last accessed 20 October 2018).

Savda, Halil, 'Nihat Kazanhan, Kendi Katilini Haksızca Tahrik Etmiş', *Bianet*, 25 November 2016, <https://m.bianet.org/bianet/insan-haklari/181125-nihat-kazan-han-kendi-katilini-haksizca-tahrik-etmis> (last accessed 4 November 2018).

Semercioğlu, Cengiz, 'Rüzgar, Sinan Çetin'in oğlu olmasaydı . . .' *Hürriyet*, 14 September 2016, <http://www.hurriyet.com.tr/yazarlar/cengiz-semercioglu/ruzgar-sinan-cetinin-oglu-olmasaydi-40223698> (last accessed 15 October 2018).

'Tayyip Erdoğan Uludere Katliamı Özür Konuşması', *YouTube*, 30 March 2012, <https://www.youtube.com/watch?v=z79ShpbHXMo> (last accessed 11 October 2018).

Turkish Criminal Code, Law 5237, adopted 26 September 2004.
Turkish Language Association, 'Taksir', <http://www.tdk.gov.tr/index.php?option=com_gts&kelime=TAKS%C4%B0R> (last accessed 4 November 2018).
Venn, Couze, 'Neoliberal Political Economy, Biopolitics and Colonialism: A Transcolonial Genealogy of Inequality', *Theory, Culture & Society* 26, no. 6 (2009): 206–33.

NINE

Money for Life: Border Killings, Compensation Claims and Life-Money Conversions in Turkey's Kurdish Borderlands

Fırat Bozçalı

On 28 December 2011, Turkish warplanes bombed a group of Kurdish smugglers entering Turkey from Iraq, near the village of Roboski. Thirty-four smugglers were killed. Public indignation exploded in the media, the parliament and on the streets of Turkey. To mitigate this reaction, the Turkish government stated that the smugglers were mistaken for members of the PKK (*Partiya Karkarên Kurdistanê* [Kurdistan Workers' Party]), a pro-Kurdish armed organisation that Turkish authorities legally designate as terrorist. Based on Law 5233 – a law that aimed to compensate for the 'damages arising from terror and combatting terror'– state authorities unilaterally offered monetary compensation (*tazminat*) to the families of the killed smugglers and according to this law, if the families accepted the compensation, they would automatically give up their right to go to court for any further compensations claims. The compensation offers, however, caused the public reaction to flare up. Although the authorities directly deposited the compensation payments to bank accounts under the names of certain family members of the killed, the families refused the compensation awards and demanded that state authorities bring those responsible for the killings to justice: 'We would not be relieved until the perpetrators are found and prosecuted . . . we would not sell our sons for the money,' said a father who lost his son in the bombardment to a news agency.[1]

In May 2006, Zeki[2] and a few other smugglers came across Turkish border patrols on their way back from Iran. The commander of the Turkish soldiers asked the smugglers to stop and surrender, and in response, Zeki and the other smugglers started running. The commander asked the soldiers to shoot up into the air as a warning. Following the third round of shooting, the commander ordered the soldiers to shoot at the ground, in front of the smugglers. In that shooting, Zeki was killed. In the criminal case that reviewed this event, the court determined which soldier had killed Zeki but did not convict the soldier due to the fact that he was following his commander's order to shoot. Yet the court did not acquit the soldier either, because it determined that the order was unlawful. Based on this decision, Zeki's relatives held the National Defense Ministry responsible for the unlawful order and filed a compensation claim in a civilian court. They received the compensation award despite the fact that a compensation decision did not result in a criminal sentence for the perpetrator, and thus allowed the killing to occur with impunity.

In the Roboksi incident, state authorities directly and unilaterally offered compensation outside of the court proceedings, but the families rejected this offer for the sake of pursuing criminal proceedings that could also lead to compensation claims being filed in civilian courts. Zeki's family opted to first pursue the criminal case. As the court confirmed and recorded the unlawful act of killing, the family claimed and obtained compensation only through a very long and difficult set of court processes. How can one understand different accounts of pursuing or rejecting compensation for border killings, or more explicitly, the killing of smugglers by border patrols? Since court-processed compensation claims can only be pursued following, and in addition to, criminal cases that officially confirm the unlawful act of killing by state authorities, what political, moral and economic significance did Kurdish claimants and their lawyers attribute to these claims? When and how did Kurdish claimants justify or dismiss compensation claims that were pursued outside of court proceedings? I pursue these questions in this chapter in which I unpack the political, moral, legal and economic challenges that Kurdish claimants must navigate in making compensation claims. I specifically examine how Kurdish claimants and their lawyers attributed political significance to court-processed compensation claims and framed them as a way to make state authorities recognise and act upon their responsibility in the killings. I further discuss how Kurdish claimants also pursued compensation claims in addition to the court-processed compensations, due to the limited scope of the latter, and show how these alternative compensation claims provided Kurdish claimants with an opportunity to reveal and criticise the ways in which lives and livelihoods have been subjugated within Kurdish borderlands.

Using Achille Mbembe's conceptualisation of necropolitics and necropower, I depict the Kurdish borderlands as a necropolitical site in which state authorities constantly claim and arbitrarily exercise a 'right to live, or allow to live, or expose to death'.[3] My analysis of compensation claims that

Kurdish claimants pursued or rejected further modifies this depiction by showing how political and economic subjugation in the Kurdish borderlands are inherently linked. Necropower within these borderlands bestows the 'status of living dead' upon its communities. However, this occurs not only through political subjugation in which freedom of movement and the right to life are constantly restricted, but also through economic subjugation by which the right to a livelihood has been restrained. The latter restraint compels borderland inhabitants to earn their livelihood through smuggling, thus exposing them to the constant risk of death.[4]

This chapter is based on ethnographic fieldwork that I conducted in the Van city centre and four border districts – Çaldıran, Saray, Özalp and Başkale – of Van Province between September 2012 and June 2014. This area is a predominantly Kurdish-populated Turkish province located near the Iranian border. During this period I also conducted ethnographic fieldwork in Van's central courthouse and four district courthouses. As a researcher, I have joined the Human Rights Commission of the Van Bar Association and participated in a research project on border killings and the legal status of investigations opened regarding these killings.

Smuggling, Border Killings and Compensation Claims

Sınır ölümleri (border deaths/killings) is the Turkish term that local human rights activists, lawyers, journalists and borderland communities have used to refer to the killings of smugglers by border patrols. Although this term can be translated as border deaths, I translate the term as border killings due to the fact that the locals with whom I consulted used the verb killing (*öldürmek* or *öldürülmek* in Turkish, *kuştin* or *hatin kuştin* in Kurdish) in referring to individual incidents. I use the term border killings to refer to the smugglers who were killed while crossing the border. Yet, it must be noted that the term might also refer to other forms of borderland killings and deaths, such as the deaths/killings that occur by stepping on a landmine or due to unattended and unexpected ammunition being activated. My use of the phrase border killings in this chapter thus exclusively refers to Kurdish smugglers who were killed by border patrols. This reference to Kurdish smugglers and smuggling economies is not arbitrary, because specific patterns of pursuing or rejecting compensation claims for border killings are construed and justified in regard to the larger political legitimacy of Kurdish smuggling economies established across many Kurdish borderland communities.

Kurdish smuggling economies have mostly been seen as a legitimate means of earning subsistence within borderland communities. Both sides of the Turkish–Iranian border have been populated predominantly by Kurds and the familial, social and economic relations across Kurdish communities have long predated the national border that divided these communities. With the imposition of the national border, however, both Turkish and Iranian state authorities have attempted to regulate and restrict the social and economic exchanges that occur across borders. Despite the fact that state authorities have deemed some of these cross-border social and economic exchanges illegal, Kurdish communities have continued to maintain these exchanges. In this sense, Kurdish borderland communities have mostly viewed the cross-border trade activities that state authorities have criminalised and called smuggling as socially legitimate economic activities. The social legitimacy of smuggling has expanded alongside the increasing militarisation of Kurdish borderlands by state authorities. As the clashes between the PKK and the Turkish military increased in the 1990s, the state authorities started forcibly evacuating mountain villages and prohibiting civilian entry to agricultural lands and pastures.[5] The ongoing clashes and the militarisation of borderlands have led to the destruction of local economies such as agriculture and animal husbandry and have consequently turned smuggling, especially the smuggling of mass consumption items such as oil, cigarettes, tea, sugar, etc., into one of the main means of subsistence for borderland communities.[6] While smuggling economies have gained social legitimacy as a means of survival, this has not attenuated the risk of getting caught and/or shot by border patrols, for borderland zones and passages are heavily militarised and monitored. As Kurdish smugglers have faced the constant risk of death in earning their livelihoods, their smuggling has been viewed as not only a socially legitimate illegal activity, but also a form of living that marks the political as well as economic subjugation of Kurdish subjects and the necropower that dominates Kurdish borderlands. This particular understanding of smuggling among Kurdish borderland communities has enabled Kurdish claimants to frame compensation claims for border killings in such a way that enables them to expose the political and economic subjugation of Kurdish borderlands.

With the increase of militarisation in the area, border killings have become frequent incidents in Turkey's Kurdish borderlands.[7] The aforementioned Roboski incident directed both national and international public attention to these killings when thirty-four Kurdish smugglers were killed at once in an air bombardment. Yet other border killings, namely the killing of individual smugglers by border patrols, have mostly been reported in local newspapers and only to a lesser extent in national newspapers and online news portals. Thus, such killings have not normally attracted much attention at either the national or international level. The actual number of border killings and the status of the legal investigations of these killings are not commonly known. In December 2012, as a response to a question posed in parliament, the Ministry of Interior reported that forty-eight smugglers were killed on the Van border in the last ten years.[8] As part of its research project, the Van Bar Association's Human Rights Commission asked the Van governorate if there are any official statistics on the border killings. In March 2013, the governorate reported that forty people had been killed, and that fifty-two people had been wounded in Van Province in the last ten years. Although the governorate is technically the highest office in the Interior Ministry's provincial organisation, the lack of consistency between these official figures might be due to the fact that state authorities did not have a centralised database on the border killings, even within the same ministry. Different incidents could be reported to different state authorities, explaining why one state institution would be familiar with a particular case, while another institution did not have a record of the same incident. That being said, once a killing incident has been reported to the state authorities, the incident becomes official and requires an investigation by prosecutors and law enforcement agencies.

The investigations of border killings have generally led to two possible results. The first and most common result of a border killing investigation in Van was that neither the prosecutor nor the court could find a perpetrator for the killing due to the lack of sufficient legal evidence.[9] This kind of result would turn the killing into an unresolved incident, and no other legal steps could be taken within the Turkish legal system.[10] The other possible result was that a perpetrator – a security officer – is found during the course of the investigation, allowing the court to confirm the fact that the perpetrator actually committed the killing. Depending on the criminal courts' verdict, the relatives of the killed person would be able to go to civilian courts and claim compensation for the killing from the perpetrators and/or administrative authority if the latter's involvement could also be demonstrated. The compensation claims processed throughout the judicial system became stronger cases if the criminal courts did not acquit the perpetrator. Even if the court could confirm an identifiable perpetrator, however, it could still acquit this perpetrator if the act of killing was deemed an act of self-defense in reference to Article 25 of the 2004 Turkish Criminal Law. Even if the killing was determined to be a disproportionate use of force, going beyond the scope of physical force that is necessary for self-defense, the courts could still acquit the perpetrator(s) by reference to Article 27 of the Turkish Criminal Law, which legitimises the use of excessive force in the case of excitement, fear or agitation. In cases where criminal courts ended up acquitting perpetrators, civilian courts have mostly rejected the compensation claims against them. The strongest cases for border-killing-related compensation claims have relied on criminal court decisions in which the perpetrators received criminal sentences.

As the perpetrators were state security officers in these cases, the act of killing often happened while on duty and as a result of following an order given by the officer's superiors, requiring criminal courts to examine the legality of the given order. According to Article 137 of the 1982 Turkish Constitution,[11] a state officer is obliged not to execute an order that involves a criminal act. However, in the case of an order that might seem to be unlawful (instead of involving a criminal act) the state officer could resist the order, but might still need to execute the order if it was reissued. Based on this article of the constitution, the courts have to examine if the given order involves a criminal act or if the order is in breach of the law in some other way. Although at first glance, an order that involves a criminal act (*konusu suç teşkil eden emir*) and an unlawful order (*hukuka aykırı emir*) appear to be similar, they are actually understood as two different situations leading to different legal consequences. While the former type of order involves an act that is openly addressed and defined as a crime (such as killing) in Turkish Criminal Law dating from 2004, the latter involves an act that is not necessarily defined as a crime (such as shooting), but that can be deemed unlawful under certain conditions.

If a border killing happens as a result of an order that involves a criminal act (such as an order to shoot to kill an unarmed person), then the perpetrator is supposed to receive a criminal sentence because he or she is obliged not to execute an order that involves a criminal act. If the courts establish that the order that the perpetrator followed was merely unlawful (such as an order to shoot where shooting is an unnecessary and disproportionate use of force), then, referring to Article 223/3b of the Turkish Criminal Procedural Law dating from 2004, the courts would decide that there was 'no need for conviction (*ceza verilmesine yer yoktur*)'. According to this article, while the perpetrator, or security officer in the case of border killings, should not receive a criminal sentence, he or she should not be acquitted either. Moreover, since the perpetrator is a state security officer, the state authority to which the perpetrating officer belongs can indeed be held responsible for the damage that the unlawful order has caused. In other words, based on these specific Article 223/3b decisions, relatives of a killed smuggler would be able to pursue compensation claims against state authorities deemed responsible for the killing in civilian courts, even if the perpetrators did not receive any criminal sentence themselves. As the Van borderlands are patrolled by either Turkish gendarmerie or the Turkish military, the state authorities that could be deemed responsible for killings would be either the Interior Ministry (if the perpetrator is a member of the gendarmerie) or the National Defense Ministry (if the perpetrator is a member of the military). In this way, while the 223/3b decisions have enabled the perpetrators to evade responsibility by virtue of not being convicted, they have also allowed for the state authorities to become financially responsible for the border killings. Thus, while individuals could be absolved of criminal responsibility in such killings, state authorities could still be held liable as members of a governing entity. In the next section, I discuss how claimants reframed such cases as a means of justice-seeking not only by holding state authorities financially responsible, but also by revealing their criminal responsibility.

Court-Processed Compensation Claims and the State's Financial Responsibility

During my fieldwork and throughout the research project that the Van Bar's Human Rights Commission conducted, I did not come across a single case in which a state officer received a criminal sentence for a border killing incident. Although killings by state officers as perpetrators were confirmed by courts in a number of cases, the courts acquitted the accused officers by referring to the Turkish Criminal Law (specifically Articles 25 and 27). Zeki's case was one of the first cases in which a civilian court processed and accepted a compensation claim based on a criminal court's 'no need for conviction' decision regarding a border killing incident in Van. This decision created the very possibility of holding state authorities responsible financially, even though impunity for the crime was still maintained. How was that possible? How could impunity be conferred upon individual perpetrators while the state was found to be financially responsible for border killings?

To answer these questions, I closely examine Zeki's case. When I met Metin, the lawyer who handled Zeki's case, he explained to me how their efforts to open an additional criminal case against the commander who gave the unlawful order failed, but that they still succeeded in their compensation case.

> We tried all possible legal ways to get the soldier who shot Zeki or the commander who ordered the shooting to receive a criminal sentence, but we failed. With the civilian case, however, we still managed to make the state recognise its responsibility at least. It was not that easy, either. We needed to

process an inheritance case first to be able to proceed with the civilian case. The civilian case itself took years and it was not that much money, but still the fact that we made the state pay for Zeki's killing was important. It meant that the state had accepted its responsibility.[12]

Metin's statement shows how both himself and Zeki's relatives viewed the compensation claim as a means of justice-seeking, for it recorded the state's responsibility in an unlawful killing and forced the state authorities to take the additional measure of issuing financial compensation for this act. After the criminal prosecution ended in impunity for the perpetrator as well as the commander who had given the unlawful order, Zeki's relatives, and Metin as their lawyer, turned to the only remaining court procedure that they could continue to pursue, which was to file a compensation claim in civilian court for the act of unlawful killing. Filing the compensation claim in a civilian court allowed Zeki's relatives to initiate another (final) court process in which they could prove the state's responsibility for the unlawful act of killing, even though this responsibility was deemed 'purely financial' in the eyes of the court. Nonetheless, the compensation payment issued by state authorities ensured a modicum of justice for the victim and his relatives.

The importance of the varying court processes resided in the fact that through them, Kurdish claimants and their lawyers could make state authorities recognise their responsibility, which would not necessarily be admitted otherwise. Even though the perpetrators did not receive criminal sentences, Kurdish claimants and their lawyers were still able to make state authorities both recognise and act upon their responsibility in borderland killings. The court-processed compensation claims, in this sense, granted a particular form of legal agency to Kurdish claimants to refute the state authorities' constant claim to, and arbitrary exercise of, a 'right' to kill. To the extent that these proceedings enabled Kurdish claimants and their lawyers to make state authorities compensate for the arbitrary exercise of the 'right' to kill, the court-processed compensations that were secured in civilian courts came to be seen as an extension and a means of justice-seeking among Kurdish claimants and their lawyers. In this way, the court-processed compensation claims gained political and social significance irrespective of their monetary value.

In the context of Moroccan reparations offered to compensate human rights violations, Susan Slyomovics has shown how some claimants dismissed the reparations offered by the state authorities for the sake of political and social concerns.[13] These reparations were offered outside of the court processes and did not lead to any judicial consequences. To criticise the overall reparations system and make the state's crimes publicly visible, some claimants asked for one dirham (Moroccan currency) even though they were entitled to much larger compensation payments. Underlining the already symbolic nature of money in reference to George Simmel's work, Slyomovics shows how 'the symbolic penny as reparation is an extreme example of endowing money with social as opposed to financial significance'.[14] Kurdish claimants have also associated the court-processed compensation claims for border killings with a particular form of political significance independent of their monetary values, as these claims have allowed claimants to extend their justice-seeking in the sense of recording the unlawful character of the act of killing, holding state authorities responsible and making state authorities both recognise and act upon their responsibility.

For Kurdish claimants, the political value of court-processed compensation claims became more salient than their monetary value, but this does not mean that the monetary value of compensations did not matter at all. Due to the necropolitical setting in which Kurdish borderland communities were subjugated both politically and economically, loss of a smuggler's life often meant loss of livelihood for all of the family members whose subsistence depended on the killed smuggler. The fact that court-processed compensation payments did not often correspond to the actual livelihood that was lost with the killing heightened the need to make this particular form of political violence visible within the court system. At the same time, the discrepancy between the court-calculated compensation and the lost livelihood gave rise to additional, alternative compensation claims often pursued in the form of social assistance payments requested from district governorates (*kaymakamlık*) and municipalities (*belediye*). In the rest of the chapter, I unpack how these claims enabled Kurdish claimants to expose and criticise the economic subjugation of communities within the Kurdish borderlands.

Courts' Conversion of Life to Money

In this section, I turn to the ways in which the compensation claims for border killings were processed and calculated in Turkish civilian courts, in other words, how courts converted life to money and expressed the monetary value of a lost life. I specifically examine the compensation claim that the relatives of Zeki filed in an administrative court.

A week after Zeki's dead body was found, his relatives hired Metin as their lawyer. Zeki was single and his nuclear family consisted of three brothers and a mother. A month after the incident, Metin asked the Interior Ministry and National Defense Ministry to compensate Zeki's mother and brothers for the damages they incurred due to the killing. Both ministries rejected the compensation claim, and Metin filed a compensation case in an administrative court, but the court decided to wait for the result of the criminal case filed by the public prosecutor. Even if the criminal court might eventually determine a perpetrator and impose a criminal sentence, these initial compensation demands needed to be made within a particular timeframe, in order for Zeki's family to be able to proceed with compensation claims in civilian courts. Following four years of criminal prosecution, referring to Article 223/3b of the 2004 Turkish Criminal Procedural Law, the criminal court recognised that the act of killing in Zeki's case had resulted from an unlawful order. Relying on that decision, Metin proceeded with the compensation claim that he had filed in the administrative court. In the meantime, Metin also filed an inheritance case in a civil court to determine the legal inheritors of the killed smuggler, as well as the legal share of each inheritor. While the criminal court's decisions were taken as the main reference point for confirming the compensation award, the distribution of the actual award among the claimants was supposed to be determined by the inheritance case. As compensation awards through courts could only be paid to legal inheritors, the inheritance case also functioned to identify the rightful heirs of the killed smuggler. The compensation case thus could not be processed without a court decision on the inheritance case as well.

As a technical category, legal inheritors only referred to close relatives, namely, the victim's spouse, children, parents and siblings (according to the 2001 Turkish Civil Code). In doing so, the inheritance cases excluded other relatives from making claims to compensation awards and ruled out their possible subsistence upon the killed smuggler's income. Their needs and expenditures were not taken into consideration when calculating the actual compensation amount. As a result, neither the calculation nor the distribution of the awards necessarily intersected with the local patterns of revenue allocation and subsistence calculation, which often included members of the extended family, such as second and third cousins. In that sense, the courts' calculation of the monetary value of lost lives ended up undervaluing the victim's livelihood and disregarding its multiple beneficiaries.

After a few months, lawyer Metin managed to get a court decision on Zeki's inheritance. The decision identified his three brothers and their mother as the legal inheritors (and therefore the rightful claimants for the compensation claim) and allocated half of the inheritance to the mother, while equally dividing the other half among the three siblings. Meanwhile, following the criminal court's initial verdict, as well as the settling of Zeki's legal inheritors through the court, the compensation claim was finally processed in administrative court. The judge evaluated and calculated two kinds of compensation: pecuniary (*maddi*) and non-pecuniary (*manevi*). For the non-pecuniary compensation, claimants had demanded 5,000 Turkish Lira for each of the claimants.[15] Recognising the symbolic character of non-pecuniary compensation in the court decision, the judge mentioned that there is 'not any other mechanism of mitigating sadness and pain, and the lack of such a mechanism necessitates calculating the monetary value of the non-pecuniary compensation'.[16] By saying this, the judge did not engage in a detailed calculation and only noted that, as a general principle, the non-pecuniary compensation must not result in the enrichment of the claimants. In this sense, non-pecuniary compensation was treated as a symbolic recognition of the claimants' suffering due to the loss of a loved one. The judge decided on a 5,000 Turkish lira non-pecuniary compensation award for the mother, and 3,000 Turkish lira for each brother, without explaining why each brother received less than the mother's share.[17]

To decide on the pecuniary compensation, the judge appointed a court expert who provided a detailed calculation of Zeki's counterfactual income and expenditure. The expert first looked at the life/mortality tables and calculated 'the residual life period (*bakiye yaşam*)' for Zeki.[18] When he was killed, Zeki was twenty-two years old. The expert witness projected forty-four years of residual life for him. Then, the expert calculated the aggregate income, had Zeki not been killed and had he actually lived his projected residual life. In doing this, the expert did not calculate Zeki's aggregate income by taking into consideration his actual revenue as a smuggler, given the informal and illegal character of smuggling. Instead, the expert looked at Zeki's education level and presumed the victim would have worked as a blue-collar, unskilled worker, who would have earned a monthly minimum wage. In other words, the life of the killed smuggler was first reframed in the form of abstract labour, and the total amount of income that he could earn throughout his life was projected based on this frame.

Additionally, the expert also projected and calculated the aggregate expenditure that Zeki would have made, had he not been killed. While the very calculation of the aggregate income can be seen to rely on both plausible and implausible assumptions about Zeki's work conditions, namely the assumption that he would have had a stable job that paid him a monthly minimum wage, the aggregate expenditure was mostly calculated with counterfactual assumptions and projections. The expert counterfactually assumed that Zeki would have married and had three children. After calculating the expenses for his counterfactual wife and children, and subtracting their expenses from the counterfactual income, the expert concluded that if the victim had survived, he would only have had the financial capacity to contribute to his mother but not to his brothers. Such a contribution would also have been limited to the mother's residual life period, which was calculated as twelve years. Relying on these counterfactual assumptions and calculations, compensation payments were calculated.

In Zeki's case, the court expert recommended a mere 9,000 Turkish lira pecuniary compensation for the mother. The court adhered to this expert recommendation and issued this exact sum to the mother only. Zeki's mother and brothers did eventually receive a separate compensation payment for his unlawful killing, though it took three different court cases – a criminal case, an inheritance case and a compensation case processed in administrative court– and seven years of lawyering for this to come to fruition. As compensation for Zeki's killing, which was achieved cumulatively via all three cases, his mother received approximately 7,000 US dollars and each of his brothers received approximately 1,500 US dollars.

This calculation of a counterfactual compensation payment (or a counterfactual livelihood) was specific neither to the cases of extrajudicial killings of smugglers nor to the cases in Van courts. For a life insurance award dispute or a case of workplace injury or death, a civilian court would appoint a court expert who would also make similar assumptions, calculations and projections. Yet, for border killing cases, the projected and calculated amounts for livelihood do not often correspond to the actual income earned by smugglers. This lack of correspondence forces claimants to engage in alternative ways of claiming compensation. These ways are important in that they also expose how the economic subjugation of Kurdish borderlands is inherent to their political subjugation, and that both forms of subjugation collectively create a necropolitical setting in the Kurdish borderlands. In the next section, I examine how Kurdish claimants framed the economic subjugation that they experience in the borderlands. I focus on a specific compensation claim made by the wife of a killed smuggler, who employed both creative and unusual tactics in order to navigate the Turkish court system.

Claimants' Conversion of Money to Life

In December 2011, Asiye, a twenty-four-year-old woman with two daughters, gave testimony on the killing of her husband. She recounted this testimony to the prosecutor who was investigating the death of her husband, whose lifeless body was found near the Turkish–Iranian border. In her testimony, Asiye said that her husband had been killed during a smuggling operation in which he had initially crossed the border alongside official Turkish border patrols:

Other villagers who had gone smuggling with my husband told me that Turkish soldiers shot at my husband . . . The perpetrators are still free and here I am reporting the killing of my husband and demanding justice . . . Our financial situation is not good. Since my husband's death, we have been trying to survive with the help of villagers . . . Due to my husband's death, we fell into a great deal of suffering both financially and emotionally [hem madden, hem de manen] . . . We want to see the state side with us and heal our wounds . . . Moreover, my husband used to work and was registered with a pension plan, [so] I think we must be entitled to a [survivor's pension] payment but I am not educated enough to follow up on this issue, so I want authorities to process our request.[19]

The prosecutor later forwarded this testimony to the local governorate and asked about the possibility of providing economic aid to the family. The prosecutor also filed a request with the Turkish Social Insurance Institution's Van headquarters to see if Asiye's husband was registered with a pension plan. Ultimately, however, the aid was not provided. The Social Insurance Institution confirmed that her husband had worked in Istanbul's Province and that 343 days of pension contributions had been deposited. Yet in order to collect a survivor's pension, the employed must have been registered with a pension plan for at least five years and have made at least 900 days of pension contributions.

I came across Asiye's testimony when I was reviewing the court files of different cases of border killings in Metin's law office. A few weeks later, I visited Asiye's village with a friend from this area to update her about the criminal case concerning her husband's killing. I knew this friend through the pro-Kurdish BDP's (Barış ve Demokrasi Partisi) town branch. On our way to the village, my friend told me how he had visited Asiye's house to express his condolences shortly after her husband was killed and about the financial difficulties that she was suffering through because of his death. He also mentioned that the husband's only brother had joined the PKK ranks a few years earlier.

When we arrived, Asiye recognised my friend and started complaining about the fact that everyone had abandoned her. I updated her regarding the ongoing criminal case, which was still in its initial stage. The prosecutor was waiting for detailed ballistic tests to see if he could determine a perpetrator and proceed with the prosecution. Yet she was more interested in talking to my friend, and asked him whether he could address her situation with some party supporters to enquire whether they could provide her with financial support. 'I lost my husband in the mountains and his brother already left us for the mountains. I need to look after my father-in-law, mother-in-law and daughters. I cannot carry this burden anymore. And now our people would leave me all alone?' she charged.[20] I asked her about the status of her request for financial aid from the district governorate, and learned that she had not received a response. She then turned to the party branch representative and asked him if there was anyone who could volunteer to go to court and help her claim a survivor's pension (*ölüm aylığı*). I did not understand for which case she was asking for a volunteer, or why Asiye would need another person to claim a survivor's pension through her deceased husband. I later realised that what Asiye wanted to pursue was an alternative way of claiming compensation.

As the Turkish Social Insurance Institution's Van branch confirmed, Asiye's husband had worked for a company for a few years. During this time, 343 days of pension contributions had been made. Turkish law allows for payment of a survivor's pension in case of death, if at least 900 days of pension contributions were paid for the employed person. After consulting with another lawyer, Asiye came up with a plan that relied on a creative use of the legal system. She was contemplating going to court to claim that her husband had worked for an additional 557 days, but that his employment had not been reported. After proving that her husband had worked for the additional days through court testimony provided by the company owner and the retroactive payment of 557 counterfactual days of pension contributions, she could claim and obtain a survivor's pension.

Asiye's plan for collecting a survivor's pension might be perceived as an act of abusing the legal system. But I consider it a creative use of the courts, because it emerges and operates through a set of assumptions and calculations that are similar to the ones that the courts use in calculating compensation payments for border killings. Although the additional 557 days of work were counterfactual, Asiye's husband had already been registered with the pension system and a portion of pension contributions was paid, so he could have worked for these additional days had he not been killed. In this sense, Asiye's claim to a survivor's pension also relied on a 'what if' assumption common to counterfactual calculations that the court relied on in Zeki's case, for a future that could never be realised. In that future, Asiye's husband could have found a job and have paid additional pension contributions to secure a survivor's pension. That opportunity was lost by virtue of the killing. Yet neither the courts nor the court experts considered a survivor's pension as a lost opportunity that warranted compensation. Asiye's creative use of the courts and her deft legal manoeuvring presented an alternative calculation of the monetary value of lost life/livelihood and was aimed at recognising this lost opportunity (of paying additional pension contributions) in order to justify her compensation.

For this creative use of the legal system to be successful, however, Asiye still needed to find a volunteer who had a registered company. This volunteer also had to agree to make a false statement in court and to receive an administrative fine that would be documented in his company's record for 'failing' to pay the additional pension contributions. And the fine needed to be paid, too. I told Asiye that it might be very difficult to find a volunteer, with which she agreed. But she also stated that even if she won a compensation award for her husband's killing through the court, it would be a small amount of money relative to her needs and not sufficient to live on. She needed to find a sustainable way to afford her family's expenses, which was what prompted her to seek out a survivor's pension. From her point of view, this was the only viable route to a long-term source of income that could provide the financial stability that both she and her family needed.

> If my husband had not been killed, he would have still smuggled. There is no work, no factory, we only have military posts [here] . . . My husband was working in Istanbul, we were separated, but we accepted it because there was no job here. But even that did not work. The company that he was working for went bankrupt. He stayed for a few months in Istanbul to find another job but he could not find one. He did not have much money left and then he returned to our village and started smuggling.[21]

In her statement, Asiye underlined the economic conditions under which she lived and how border villagers are an economically subjugated community, leaving them with no choice but to smuggle. In heavily militarised borderlands, the dependence on smuggling for daily subsistence also means facing the constant risk of death while earning a living. This unavoidable risk translates the Kurdish borderlands into a necropolitical site where political and economic subjugation co-exist and co-constitute each other. Asiye's claim to a survivor's pension, in this sense, can be considered a way of marking the status and economic subjugation of those living in the Kurdish borderlands. This economic subjugation is cast against a backdrop of political subjugation, which circumscribes these borderlands through both permanent and temporary no-civilian-entry zones, arbitrary military patrols and contingent military operations. The infrastructure of this domination is evidenced through road checkpoints, military bases, watchtowers and the use of military aircraft such as helicopters and drones. This collective assault on the freedom of Kurdish borderland inhabitants has resulted in an increasing restriction of movement within and across borders, as well as a constant claim to and arbitrary execution of a 'right' to kill by governmental forces. This political subjugation has both created and reproduced an economic subjugation in which the local economies of agriculture and husbandry have been destroyed and smuggling has become a main means of livelihood in the absence of alternative forms of work.

Under the conditions of political and economic subjugation, pursuing a claim for a survivor's pension or other forms of financial compensation after a border killing has come to be seen as key to maintaining a daily subsistence for the relatives left behind. During my fieldwork, I met other claimants who often pursued alternative claims of financial compensation for border killings. These alternative claims took the form of social assistance payments, from both the central state authorities and municipalities that were run by the pro-Kurdish political party, alongside the criminal cases and compensation cases that were filed in courts. These claimants continued to pursue such alternative claims because even when their cases were resolved with financial compensation in courts and even if the perpetrators received sentences, they still faced the challenge of earning a substantial livelihood in these borderlands. The economic marginalisation and subjugation, which made their relatives turn to smuggling and risk their lives for economic gain, persisted. The salience and frequency of these alternative claims, in this sense, signified the economic subjugation of the Kurdish borderlands as a whole, exposing how necropower is both invested and entrenched in this frontier.

Conclusion

In looking at compensation claims that Kurdish claimants pursued or rejected for border killings, I have unpacked how the Kurdish borderlands have turned into a necropolitical site in which whole communities have been both politically and economically subjugated. I have shown how Kurdish claimants and their lawyers have viewed the compensation claims that they pursue through civilian courts as a way to make state authorities both recognise and act upon their responsibility in these killings. The court-processed compensation claims have also allowed these claimants to expose and criticise the state authorities' constant claim to and arbitrary exercise of a 'right' to kill in Kurdish borderlands. Hence, these claims have come to be seen as an effective means of justice-seeking among Kurdish claimants.

In addition to the articulation of court-processed compensation claims as a way of seeking justice for border killings, I have also identified alternative compensation claims that Kurdish claimants pursue to seek daily subsistence on the one hand, and to reveal the economic subjugation that they were compelled to live under, on the other hand. While these alternative claims often relied on social assistance payments filed in district governorates as well as municipalities run by the pro-Kurdish party, I have focused on the unusual case of claiming a survivor's pension through legal manoeuvring and the creative use of the courts. This case was striking for its ability to show how just as the civilian courts' calculation of lost life relied on counterfactual assumptions, the claimants could resort to a similar set of counterfactual assumptions to support their own compensation claims.

The alternative compensation claims, I have argued, mark how the political and economic subjugation of lives and livelihoods have been co-constituted and co-exercised in the necropolitical order established in Turkey's Kurdish borderlands. Based on the increasing militarisation of these borderlands, the state authorities constantly resort to the arbitrary exercise of a 'right' to kill, thereby perpetuating the political subjugation of the population. Meanwhile, economic subjugation is perpetuated by the destruction of local economies such as agriculture and animal husbandry, compelling borderland communities to engage in smuggling at the risk of death.

Notes

1. The full statement goes as follows: 'We would not get relief until the perpetrators are found and prosecuted. The Prime Minister should not mislead the facts. It was not true that we did not accept the compensation because we were scared of the PKK. I call out to the Prime Minister! They should not be unfair to our sons. We would not sell our sons for the money.' The statement was provided after the prime minister and other state officials claimed that families of the killed smugglers did not accept the compensation because they were threatened by the PKK. See 'Roboski Köylüleri: Satılık Çocuğumuz Yoktur', *Emek Dünyası*, n.d.
2. All names used in this chapter are pseudonyms. In order to maintain the anonymity and confidentiality of research subjects, I have also changed personal information such as the location and dates of incidents, found in court files.
3. Achille Mbembe, 'Necropolitics', p. 11.
4. Ibid. p. 40.
5. Joost Jongerden, *The Settlement Issue in Turkey and the Kurds*.
6. It is difficult to record the exact scope of Kurdish smuggling economies due to the informality and illegality of smuggling activities. The Turkish Police Department of Anti-Smuggling and Organized Crime's annual reports, for example, show Van Province with higher rates of smuggling incidents, especially in the case of cigarette smuggling, for the time period between 2005 and 2016. Yet it must also be noted that these statistics only show the frequency of the smuggling incidents that

were caught by state authorities, and thus do not show the actual scope of smuggling. Additionally, these statistics are vulnerable to various political biases, since they have been collected and published by state authorities without transparent collection and selection processes. The annual reports are available at <http://www.kom.pol.tr/Sayfalar/Raporlar.aspx> (last accessed 30 October 2018).
7. Numerous border killings targeting Kurdish smugglers (*kulbaran* in Kurdish) have also been reported across the Iraq–Iran border. The United Nations Special Rapporteurs on the situation of human rights in the Islamic Republic of Iran reported the killings of at least thirty-six smugglers in 2015 and fifty-one smugglers in 2016, and blamed the Iranian authorities for these killings. For the report see <https://www.ohchr.org/EN/Countries/AsiaRegion/Pages/IRIndex.aspx> (last accessed 17 October 2018).
8. The parliamentary question (No. A.01.1.KKB.0.10.00.00-86735) was submitted by Van MP (Member of Parliament) Nazmi Gür on 2 October 2012; and the answer was submitted by the Minister of Interior Affairs on 12 December 2012.
9. In some cases, prosecutors might be able to detect a suspect (*şüpheli*) and indict that person during the prosecution, but courts can still decide that there is not sufficient evidence to prove beyond reasonable doubt that the accused (*sanık*) person committed the killing.
10. The relatives of the killed person could still bring the case to the European Court of Human Rights and blame Turkish authorities for not conducting an effective investigation.
11. Article 137 (as amended on 16 April 2017; Act No. 6771) reads as follows: 'If a person employed in any position or status in public services finds an order given by his/her superior to be contrary to the provisions of by-laws, presidential decree, laws, or the Constitution, he/she shall not carry it out, and shall inform the person giving the order of this inconsistency. However, if his/her superior insists on the order and renews it in writing, his/her order shall be executed; in this case the person executing the order shall not be held responsible. An order which in itself constitutes an offence shall under no circumstances be executed; the person who executes such an order shall not evade responsibility.' The English translation of the article is taken from the Turkish Parliament's website: <https://global.tbmm.gov.tr/docs/constitution_en.pdf> (last accessed 30 October 2018).
12. Interview with Metin (a pseudonym that I chose for him to conceal his identity), Van, 5 February 2014.
13. Susan Slyomovics, 'Reparations in Morocco: The Symbolic Dirham'. Also see Susan Slyomovics, 'Financial Reparations, Blood Money, and Human Rights Witness Testimony: Morocco and Algeria'.
14. Slyomovics, 'Reparations in Morocco', p. 110.
15. At the date of the court decision, 1 US dollar was exchanged for 1.9 Turkish lira. The minimum wage was around 1,000 Turkish lira before tax, and 800 Turkish lira after tax.

16. A court decision published by Van First Administrative Court (*Van Birinci İdare Mahkemesi*). The exact file number and date of decision are not provided for the sake of anonymity and confidentiality of the research subjects.
17. Ibid.
18. Ibid.
19. Taken from the court file and translated from Turkish by the author. The exact date and number of the file are not cited in order to maintain the anonymity and confidentiality of research subjects.
20. Interview with Asiye (a pseudonym that I chose for her to conceal her identity), Van, 13 April 2013.
21. Ibid.

Bibliography

Constitution of the Republic of Turkey (Türkiye Cumhuriyeti Anayasası), Law 2709, 11 November 1982, <https://www.tbmm.gov.tr/anayasa/anayasa_2018.pdf> (last accessed 31 October 2018).

Jogerden, Joost, *The Settlement Issue in Turkey and the Kurds: An Analysis of Spatial Policies, Modernity and War* (Leiden: Brill, 2007).

'Law on Compensation for Damage Arising from Terror and Combating Terror' (*Terör ve Terörle Mücadeleden Doğan Zararların Karşılanması Hakkında Kanun*), Law 5233, Official Gazette, No. 25535, 27 July 2004.

Mbembe, Achille, 'Necropolitics', trans. Libby Meintjes, *Public Culture* 15, no. 1 (Winter 2013): 11–40.

'Roboski Köylüleri: Satılık Çocuğumuz Yoktur', Emek Dünyası, n.d., <http://www.emekdunyasi.net/ed/toplum-yasam/15799-roboski-koyluleri-satilik-cocugumuzyoktur.> (last accessed 30 October 2018).

Slyomovics, Susan, 'Financial Reparations, Blood Money, and Human Rights Witness Testimony: Morocco and Algeria', in Richard Ashby Wilson and Richard D. Brown (eds), *Humanitarianism and Suffering: The Mobilization of Empathy* (Cambridge: Cambridge University Press, 2009).

Slyomovics, Susan, 'Reparations in Morocco: The Symbolic Dirham', in Barbara Rose Johnston and Susan Slyomovics (eds), *Waging War, Making Peace: Reparations and Human Rights* (Walnut Creek, CA: Left Coast Press, 2009).

Turkish Civilian Code (*Türk Medeni Kanunu*), Law 4721, Official Gazette, No. 24607, 8 December 2001.

Turkish Criminal Law (*Türk Ceza Kanunu*), Law 5237, Official Gazette, No. 25611, 26 September 2004.

Turkish Criminal Procedural Law (*Ceza Muhakemeleri Kanunu*), Law 5271, Official Gazette, No. 25673, 17 December 2004.

Part Three

Political Afterlives: Governing the Living and the Dead

TEN

Another Necropolitics

Banu Bargu

The election of 7 June was a watershed moment in Turkey because the success of the Peoples' Democratic Party (HDP) practically eliminated an antidemocratic electoral threshold of 10 per cent – one of the highest around the world – that was put into place under military rule after the 1980 coup d'état. This threshold meant not only that political parties unable to gather at least 10 per cent of the national vote lost the right of representation in parliament but also that the votes they were able to gather would be proportionately distributed among the other parties that succeeded in passing the threshold, thereby enabling successful parties to gain a higher number of seats in the parliament. HDP's electoral success, which corresponded to eighty seats in parliament, was therefore momentous both as a symbolic conquest for the coalition of forces that came together within it and as a big blow to the Justice and Development Party (AKP), which suffered not only the loss of its parliamentary majority but also the benefit of overrepresentation that the electoral threshold bestowed upon it as the majority party since 2002. Lost, or at least suspended, with the election results, of course, was President Recep Tayyip Erdoğan's ambition to transform Turkey's parliamentary system into a presidential one, an ambition that required a super-majority of AKP, without which such a constitutional change would necessitate resorting to a popular referendum whose results would be either unfavourable to Erdoğan's plans or unpredictable at best. Tarnished in the election, therefore, was also Erdoğan's personal political reputation, having forcefully campaigned for the move towards presidentialism despite the existing constitutional ban on the active partisanship of the republic's president.

That HDP's victory was temporary, however, became painfully apparent in the renewed elections that were held on 1 November, elections called by President Erdoğan due to a hung parliament unable and unwilling to establish a ruling coalition. In this second election, while HDP still managed to pass the electoral threshold, thereby retaining its symbolic victory, it suffered a significant loss in votes (losing a quarter of its seats and maintaining only fifty-nine). By contrast, AKP, considered by most commentators as firmly moving on a declining curve of popularity prior to the elections, managed to make a surprising comeback, both regaining its majority in parliament and increasing its support by 4.5 million votes, or almost nine points, thereby reaching an all-time high of 49.47 per cent. The social democratic CHP neither lost, nor gained much ground (two additional seats were gained in parliament, bringing their number to 134), whereas the ultranationalist MHP, like HDP, suffered the most, losing half its seats in parliament (declining to forty).[1] The new election gave AKP 317 seats in a parliament of 550, which, while falling short of the super-majority necessary to change the constitution singlehandedly, was sufficient to revive the proposal of a new presidentialism, along with the hitherto failed efforts for writing a new, civilian constitution to replace the current one drafted in the aftermath of the 1980 military coup d'état.

How should we read this surprising reversal that took place within the span of a few months? What happened in the summer of 2015 that led many voters to rally to AKP's support? While many commentators expressed worries that the election might be rigged, these allegations have largely been unfounded.[2] The most important reason for this reversal was the conjuncture of escalating violence between the two elections, coming from different quarters at once. Most importantly, Turkey became the target of deadly suicide attacks carried out by Islamic State militants, first in Suruç, killing thirty-three young socialists, and more recently, in Ankara, killing 102 demonstrators participating in a peace rally. With the execution-style murder of two police officers in their sleep in Ceylanpınar, the peace process that was already stagnant prior to the June election broke down completely, marking a speedy devolution into armed conflict between the army and PKK (Kurdistan Workers' Party) within Turkey's borders. PKK's attack on Dağlıca, which killed sixteen soldiers, was another momentous development that escalated the conflict.[3] This was complemented by Turkish military airstrikes over northern Iraq and Syria, nominally as part of the coalition against the Islamic State led by the United States but also in tension with it (insofar as the target has been the Kurdish forces in the region).[4] Armed conflict claimed a significant death toll of soldiers, policemen, PKK militants and civilians, including children, a toll that quickly climbed to several hundreds.⁵ Meanwhile, a more diffuse and largely civilian violence was also on the rise, inflicting significant physical damage on HDP headquarters and offices around the country by acts of arson and vandalism and targeting Kurdish citizens with multiple hate crimes.⁶ The police took little action to prevent the mobs roaming the streets and authorities conspicuously refrained from prosecuting those who participated in these collective acts of *discriminate* violence.

With the escalation of armed conflict inside Turkey, compounded by the memory of the protracted war that has claimed forty thousand lives, the transborder position of the Kurdish population, and the volatility of politics upon the collapse of former states in the region, both the securitisation of public discourse and the militaristic polarisation among the civilian population have also escalated and with great speed.⁷ Meanwhile, the declaration of self-government in Kurdish towns,⁸ the emergence of urban militia, composed especially by members of youth organisations affiliated with PKK, such as YDG-H (Patriotic Revolutionary Youth Movement), in the name of defending neighbourhoods from state intrusion, and the diffusion of armed conflict into cities in the form of trench warfare have further precipitated the widespread security operations in those towns, now declared by the government to be curfew zones.⁹ Hence, entire cities have been put under lockdown, special operations forces and snipers have surfaced, targeting any violators of the curfew regardless of their civilian status, and casualties have escalated, reviving the spectre of the 'state of emergency' rule that remained in force for two decades in the southeastern provinces, even after military rule had formally ended in 1983.

In the public sphere, the interim government was subjected to fierce criticism for instrumentalising conflict as a way to buttress AKP's electoral base on nationalistic grounds rather than working towards reactivating the peace process, as well as for being negligent in taking the necessary precautions against Islamic State militants and affiliates, some of whom operating and organising in Turkey were allegedly known to intelligence agencies and local security personnel of the Turkish state.¹⁰ Concomitantly, HDP also bore the brunt of criticism for not taking a stronger stance against PKK's war tactics on the one hand, and for not taking a stronger stance in favour of growing Kurdish radicalism on the other, thus finding itself in the swiftly shrinking ground of democratic politics. This shrinkage manifested itself in the even swifter contraction of the public sphere as some of the vocal critics of the government in the media lost their jobs or were intimidated into silence while the arrests and persecution of journalists continued apace.¹¹

However, the depiction of this bleak interregnum between the two elections of 2015 would remain incomplete if we were to overlook the necropolitical violence perpetrated by the security forces of the state. By *necropolitical violence*, I mean not the sovereign violence of the state that 'take[s] life', nor the biopolitical violence of governmental power that 'let[s] die', or 'disallow[s life] to the point of death', according to Michel Foucault's famous categorisation of the modalities of power.[12] Foucault has taught us that the right to punish by death is not only the sovereign act par excellence but also reflective of a primary form of necropolitics. Even though he does not use the term necropolitics, Foucault's famous analysis of the brutal execution of Damiens the regicide offers a reading that discusses the intimate link between the brutal display of this killing and the restorative performance of sovereignty. By contrast, Foucault suggests, biopolitical violence is not extractive, but it is exercised indirectly, through a selective affirmation and encouragement of life, often by way of the functioning of racism. Following Foucault, Henry Giroux affirms the logic of biopolitical exposure and neglect when he points us to how structurally subaltern and marginalised populations situated at the intersection of race and class are rendered disposable, a development exacerbated by neoliberal governmentality.[13] In contrast with the sovereign right to kill, the biopolitical form of exposure is a more diffuse or circuitous form of necropolitics.[14] However, neither of these forms is the necropolitics I want to call attention to. Nor do I have in mind the violence that Achille Mbembe famously refers to when he characterises the 'subjugation of life to the power of death'.[15] Mbembe's conception of necropolitics skilfully points us to a modality of power operative in concrete spaces of exception, a power whose operational logic is one of destruction. Necropower, in his formulation, either decimates populations through massacres or else commits populations to unliveable conditions in which they are continually exposed to violence and deprived of a properly human life, where they are destined to a 'death-in-life'.[16]

To be sure, all these forms of death-making are amply present in the myriad of ways that violence is performed in Turkey's geographies of exception where the state takes the life of those who rebel and resort to arms, where populations are differentially exposed to violence and rendered disposable. On the other hand, PKK's resort to violent struggle by way of rural and urban guerrilla warfare and its history of terror tactics constitute the means to assert its proto-sovereignty to further the Kurdish cause, exhibiting its own forms of necropolitical struggle.[17] Notwithstanding these forms of violence, and side by side with them, however, there is a more spectacular and morbid form of violence that is often disregarded. This is the violence that takes as its object the realm of the dead – the corpse, the act of burial, funerary rituals, the graves and cemeteries as sites of burial and commemoration, and forms of mourning and reverence. In distinction from other forms of death-making, I use 'necropolitical violence' to denote those acts that target the dead bodies of those killed in armed conflict, by way of their mutilation, dismemberment, denuding, desecration, dragging and public display, the destruction of local cemeteries and other sacred spaces that are designated for communication with and commemoration of the dead, the delay, interruption or suspension of the conduct of funerary rituals, the imposition of mass or anonymous internment, the pressure for clandestine internment and the repression and dispersion of funeral processions for the newly dead. At issue is not the reduction of the living to 'the status of *living dead*',[18] but something else altogether: *the dishonouring, disciplining and punishment of the living through the utilisation of the dead as postmortem objects and sites of violence.*[19] Necropolitical violence, then, refers to an entire ensemble of diverse practices that target the dead as a surrogate for, and means of, targeting the living.[20]

In the interregnum of 2015, the state security forces' resort to necropolitical violence revitalised the legacy of the 'dirty war' of the 1990s during which it had become an important facet of the conflict. However, the practices of necropolitical violence systematically pursued during the war, ranging from the mutilation of dead bodies and their staged photography to enforced disappearances, condemned only as 'unavoidable excesses' of war, had largely been discontinued with the ending of the regional state of emergency.[21] The revival of necropolitical violence, while not a sui generis cause of the irruption of the new political conjuncture in Turkey, can nonetheless be read as the symptom of its advent, signalling the hold of insecurity over the masses as a factor that fans the desire for militant securitisation and the assurance of political stability on the one hand, and the radicalisation of insurgent violence and the separatist desire on the other. As such, necropolitical violence has wide-reaching implications, both in the way it hyperbolically announces the pervasive state of fear and enmity and by way of its role in the reproduction of this state of insecurity, now generalised to include not only the living but also the dead. Necropolitical violence is also important in what it implies for the possibility of reconciliation between the Turkish and Kurdish peoples in the occasion of the cessation of violent conflict and the establishment of social and political peace. Finally, on a more theoretical register, the close analysis of necropolitical violence is crucial in order to critique unitary and limited conceptions of necropolitics so that we can develop a more accurate understanding of the heterogeneity of its manifestations and their political ramifications.

Dead Once, Dead Twice

On 15 August 2015, the image of the naked and bloody corpse of a woman was leaked to the press. The body lay face down on the street next to a piece of cardboard covered with plastic – a makeshift stretcher with which she was likely (to be) carried – before the feet of three men, all wearing civilian clothes. They were photographed below the shoulders, as standing casually around the body, and one had a pair of blue vinyl gloves, suggesting that he had inspected or handled the body.

As the images of the woman's naked dead body went viral on social media, it incited a river of derogatory and vitriolic ultranationalist commentary, celebrating her death and the exposure of her body. This was soon followed by furious reactions and fierce condemnations by human rights and women's organisations. The body in the images belonged to Kevser Eltürk, also known as Ekin Wan, a PKK militant and guerrilla, who had allegedly died some days earlier on 10 August in a confrontation with the security forces in the rural district of Varto (tied to the city of Muş).[22] Upon the uproar caused by the leak, the Governor of Muş issued a statement:

> It has been established that some images of a female member of the PKK terror organisation, who was rendered ineffective as a result of the clash with our security forces in a rural area of the Varto district of our province on 10 August 2015, are being published on some social media sites. Criminal and administrative investigations have been launched against the person or persons who have photographed, published or served to social media those images that are unacceptable to the public or the governor's office.[23]

As is clear from this statement, what was unacceptable to the governor's office and what became the cause of the public investigation was not the circumstances of the Kurdish woman's death, nor its postmortem denuding, but its photography for public display and the distribution of these images to social media and their ensuing digital circulation.

In response to this violent display of the dead body, armed clashes took place in Varto between the security forces and PKK militants, with four casualties.[24] Kurdish women took to the streets in various different provinces on 16 August and after, with posters that read: 'Ekin Wan is the naked form of our resistance', 'Ekin Wan is our honour' and 'It is dishonourable to play with a people's honour through its body.'[25] Another evocative slogan read: 'When the state undresses itself for torture, women dress on the resistance.'[26] Prominent Kurdish women's organisations condemned the violence in stark terms.[27] On 23 August, a Kurdish woman carried out a naked protest in front of the parliamentary building in Stockholm, lying facedown on the ground with red paint over her body, reenacting the scene that was disseminated in the image.[28] Peace activists and feminists in Ankara and Istanbul also staged demonstrations. Members of parliament from HDP filed a parliamentary motion that asked for a written explanation from the Minister of Interior about what happened, posing questions regarding the circumstances of the woman's death, whether she was killed in a clash or captured alive and killed under torture. Asking for official clarification, their motion underscored the observation that the ligature marks on the body evinced torture and suggested that Eltürk was also dragged around in the streets tied by a rope around her neck.

Outrageous as it was, the dissemination of the image of the postmortem naked display of Eltürk's body was not exactly exceptional. On the one hand, while still infrequent, such violence to the dead body is not unique to this case – in October 2015, for example, there surfaced the video of another lifeless body, belonging to a male militant called Hacı Lokman Birlik, as he was being dragged on the streets of Şırnak behind a military truck to which he was tied with a rope.[29] On the other hand, the Eltürk incident invokes other acts of violence with which it shares significant commonalities, acts directed at the dead body, its remains, burial and commemoration in variegated ways. For example, what are we to make of the fact that between 25 July and 5 August, some two dozen citizens of Turkey who crossed into Syria to fight against Islamic State and who lost their lives in Kobane were held at the border in trucks until their corpses almost decomposed in the scorching heat of the summer?[30] Is the policy to delay the entry of dead bodies back into Turkey for burial by their families not another modality of necropolitical violence that both enables and supplies context to the Eltürk incident? Similarly, how else can we interpret the development of civilian resistance aiming to stop the bombing and demolition of cemeteries and shrines dedicated to fighters who are revered as martyrs? In an especially poignant move, Kurdish activists mobilised their lives as human shields to protect graves from physical destruction by the security forces, who in turn argued that the graves were being used to shield ammunition.[31] Is the profanation of values held sacred by the local population not another form of necropolitical violence whose deployment imbues the Eltürk incident with a different significance? Overall, the sheer variety of these tactics and their repetition should at least be taken as an alarming sign that the denuding and display of Eltürk's dead body is not so exceptional. It should also prompt us to reconsider our conception of a homogeneous necropolitics that is often oblivious to the violence deployed on the dead, and through them, on the living.

The Eltürk incident thus offers itself as an exemplary case that sheds light on the multiple significations of necropolitical violence in contemporary Turkey. Most obviously, this violent targeting of the dead body points us to a remarkable dehumanisation concretised in the body of the Kurdish guerrilla.[32] Beyond the construction of the enemy as existentially 'alien' and 'other' in fundamentally antagonistic terms, which might still recognise her humanity, such postmortem violence reveals an absolutisation of enmity.[33] Both the undignified treatment of the insurgent's body and the intensity of popular reactions on social media in the wake of the release of the image, reeking of personalised hatred and disgust, suggest not only that the reduction of the enemy to something less than human is at work here, but that this reduction overlaps with the racialisation and alterisation of Kurdish identity. As a result, the desecration of the dead becomes a new site of articulating identity, of producing the ethnic, spiritual supremacy of the Turkish nation. The sovereign anxiety concerning ethnic separatism seeks to affirm the unity of the nation by designating some bodies as the threats that should be eliminated in order to produce a 'pure' Turkish body by contrast. The production of some bodies as violable after death renders necropolitical violence as a means of the exclusionary construction of citizenship and its 'others', a construction articulated through the divide between loyal subjects and treacherous subjects.[34] Hence, the politics over the dead becomes a means of 'the production and contestation of sovereign limits of national politics and subjectivity'.[35]

At the same time, the dehumanisation of the enemy merges with its sexualisation and transformation into a vehicle of moralistic reprobation. In reading the necropolitical violence perpetrated upon Eltürk's body, it is impossible to overlook the patriarchy that has thoroughly infused it. At stake is the interweaving of feminisation and denigration, not just racialisation and alterisation. According to Nazan Üstündağ, such war over the dead reveals the 'desire to punish beyond death as well as the state's inscription of itself into the most intimate relationships'.[36] The projected effects of targeting a woman's body, its denuding, the staging of the scene in the form of a duality between the naked dead woman lying on the street at the feet of the fully clothed men standing around her, the photographic recording of the scene, and its dissemination to the public are calculated on the basis of this sexualisation, without further necessitating the allegations of rape, which were nonetheless made. Regardless of the truth of these claims, the general economy of such a staging, it seems to me, is predicated on transforming Eltürk's nakedness into nudity, equating her subjugation to submission and reinscribing her failed insurgency as a sexually and morally transgressive act, a promiscuity that is therefore considered deserving of the fate she suffers. The desired effect of the scene is that it will take away her 'chastity' and not just her dignity, with the wager that this abjection will fall well beyond what is acceptable to dominant norms of being a woman.[37]

While the sexualised character of this instance of necropolitical violence has rightly provoked many feminists to condemn the attack as 'femicide', the key point, in my opinion, is not that she is killed as a female Kurdish guerrilla but that her body is considered to be a pliable instrument for the punishment of the Kurdish people as a whole.[38] There is an instrumentalisation of the body as a woman's body, to be sure, since at issue is its denuding and dishonouring, as the means by which the humiliation of an entire people is aimed for and put into practice. This rests on a prior and implicit equivalence of the chastity and modesty of a woman with the honour and chastity of a nation.[39] Thus, once that chastity is violated, the expectation is that the people embodied in that chastity will be dishonoured. What this implies is that, in tandem with this sexualisation but not crucially dependent on it, there is also a more general logic of *surrogation* in such practices of necropolitical violence.[40] This is because the effectiveness of such violence is crucially dependent on the synecdoche between the part and the whole, the particular and the general: not only between the woman's honour and the nation's honour, but also between the guerrilla's body and the Kurdish body politic, the local insurgency and the transborder nation. Such substitutions cannot work if the guerrilla's body were not taken as the embodiment of the struggle for liberation, if the dead body – man or woman – signified as a martyr of the struggle were not imagined as the generative source of the Kurdish nation in the first place.

As the 'internal enemy' is punished with utmost visibility, undoubtedly emboldened by the voyeurism incited by the sexualisation of the body and its violation, the spectacular and mediatised form of necropolitical violence does more than exacerbate the dehumanisation of the enemy. Enabling the announcement of the forceful restoration of the state's sovereignty otherwise wounded by the insurgency, it also reproduces the effects of that sovereignty viscerally and visually, through the dissemination and circulation of the images of desecration. This (en)forced visibility that displays how an insurgent body is punished thus dictates the parameters of how the proper body must be constituted by way of contrast. Thus, in the same instrumentalisation of the body what is being affirmed and reproduced is precisely the *how* of the proper female citizen, defined through those patriarchal norms of chastity, honour, obedience, submissiveness, as well as the more general political norms of citizenship, such as being a dutiful subject of the law and the duty not to endanger the unity of the country and its future, against Eltürk's defiance of those norms (though, of course, she can be considered as compliant with another series of norms practiced by her insurgent ideology and its attendant imaginary).

Finally, there are serious psychic implications of necropolitical violence, embedded as this act is within a practice of counterinsurgency warfare. Within the context of this struggle, the dead have tremendous power, Hişyar Özsoy tells us: 'the Kurds resurrect their dead through a moral and symbolic economy of martyrdom as highly affective forces that powerfully shape public, political and daily life, promoting Kurdish national identity and struggle as a sacred communion of the dead and the living'.[41] Insofar as these deaths are inscribed within the imaginary of nationalist liberation and are endowed with a (re)generative power through their martyrdom, they have come to constitute a site of political contestation between the state and the Kurds. On the one hand, dead bodies are transformed into the symbolic vehicles of subduing the insurgent population. 'Despite this diversity of its forms and contingency of its applications,' Özsoy argues, 'this politics constitutes a systematic technique of sovereign rule whose objective is to obstruct the politico-symbolic construction of death, to clearly dissociate the dead from the living, and to prevent the dead from being regenerated into the Kurdish national-symbolic.'[42] On the other hand, dead bodies also become the objects of resignification and reappropriation, giving rise to mobilisations and uprisings. In response to different forms of necropolitical violence, Özsoy draws attention to how 'funeral ceremonies are transformed into massive protests, wherein the dead are immortalised through the institution of martyrdom, and the spectral power of the martyr is exchanged or processed into the core of national struggle and identity'.[43] As a result, the dead body and, relatedly, different sites of death become deeply politicised as a new battleground upon which the ongoing conflict continues to be waged.

Beyond the Politics of Mourning

State violence in Turkey is not new. The Eltürk incident should be considered as part of a longue durée of the state's deployment of extralegal violence on its citizens: without even going back to the deep wounds left by atrocities of the early twentieth century on Armenians, non-Muslim minorities, the Kurds, Alevis and the leftist political opposition, it is sufficient to consider the last few decades: the rampant torture within military prisons during the early 1980s, enforced disappearances, extrajudicial killings, enforced population displacements, and the 'dirty war' of the 1990s, Operation 'Return to Life' of the year 2000, that is, the security operation into some twenty prisons in order to quash the hunger strike of political prisoners and transfer them into super-maximum security prisons, as well as, more recently, the police violence unleashed upon unarmed crowds during the occupation of Gezi Park and the ensuing mass mobilisations around the country. Being mindful of this history does not mean we should underestimate the importance of the present moment, but it does caution us against attributing an absolute primacy and exceptionality to it. While the necropolitical violence we witness today has gained a different visibility with the broad reach afforded by social media, it is embedded within a deep-seated tradition of statecraft not unique to Turkey, a tradition that has to be further studied, theorised and critiqued. The Turkish variant of this tradition has never shied away from deploying violent means in order to protect its sovereignty and unity against the forces it designates as threats to its security. Furthermore, in the Turkish case, it is necessary to note that this tradition has commanded a longevity that, despite some ebbs and flows, has resisted a neat distinction between periods of democratic politics and military rule. It might be helpful to recall that while the first elections after the 1980 coup d'état were held in November 1983 and that elections have been regularly held since then, martial law was only gradually phased out by 1987 and was replaced in the eastern and southeastern provinces with a regional 'state of emergency' lifted only at the end of 2002. The low-intensity warfare waged against the armed struggle of Kurdish separatism spanned these decades of civilian rule, continuing into the present, with certain periods of ceasefire but without resolution.

In light of this continuity between the present and the past and across different regimes, where must we turn in our striving towards the resolution of Turkey's internal conflict and our hope for a peaceful, democratic, egalitarian future? Commentators who have written on the death of Eltürk have frequently drawn upon Judith Butler's powerful work on mourning as a potential recourse to our contemporary predicament.[44] When Butler asks what lives are grievable, she is really launching an investigation into our assumptions about what lives are deemed worthy as lives, as liveable and therefore grievable lives.[45] Mourning a lost life not only asserts our relationality in a deep, constitutive sense, but also exposes the power of that relationality to de-constitute and undo us, laying bare our vulnerability to one another. For Butler, the acknowledgement of this sociality entails the acceptance of the vulnerability of others as well as our own. However, some lives are politically disqualified and prohibited from being publicly grieved; 'they cannot be mourned because they are always already lost or, rather, never "were", and they must be killed, since they seem to live on, stubbornly, in this state of deadness'.[46] Situated within a field of power relations and norms of recognition that condition its differential distribution, vulnerability can be denied and transformed into grounds of further violence – this is precisely what sovereignty does, according to Butler – or it can be affirmed as a mutual condition that constitutes the normative ground of a new politics, a politics that might enable us to oppose the conditions that render some more vulnerable than others.[47]

Butler's work is deeply insightful in showing us how the denuding and display of dead bodies is precisely the kind of sovereign boundary-making that separates who is grievable from who is not, who is loyal from who is not, who belongs to the nation from who does not, and who is deemed worthy to live and who is not. Whatever the justifications put forth for these distinctions, and regardless of whether those justifications are simply expedient or really legitimate, what is clear is that selective mourning for the dead is reflective of a deeply polarised country where the affective boundaries of the nation are violently policed, where grievability not only is differentially distributed but gains meaning only by way of being inscribed within one or the other of the antagonistic and increasingly mutually exclusive nationalist imaginaries wherein deaths are resignified as martyrdom. While the politics of mourning can easily affirm the already existing proclivities for war, Butler notes, it may also lead to new political relations that build collective resistances instead: 'And whereas some forms of public mourning are protracted and ritualised, stoking nationalist fervor, reiterating the conditions of loss and victimisation that come to justify a more or less permanent war, not all forms of mourning lead to that conclusion.'[48] However, the question remains: given these conditions of differential and antagonistic grievability, continually deepening the rift among the peoples of Turkey, does the recognition of our common corporeal vulnerability hold the promise of the path that could lead out of the current impasse? Can the politics of mourning, one that insistently questions the permissible boundaries of mourning, and perhaps insists on publicly mourning those deemed ungrievable, enable us to transcend the already existing identifications and psychic attachments to create the mutual ground of solidarity and the will to live together?

Butler's humanism seems less compelling in a political context whose contours are delineated by the politicisation of death, where mourning is already deeply implicated within the lines of demarcation already drawn by necropolitics.[49] If the denuding and exposure of Eltürk functions as a surrogate for the disciplining and punishment of the living, thus transforming the dead body, its burial, funeral rituals, and the practices of public grieving into sites of contention and violence, does the adoption of a counter-politics of mourning not still enclose us within the same political framework? Despite its suggestive potentiality to make us recall our fundamental sociality and mutual vulnerability, thereby helping forge new solidarities that cut across the binary of who is and is not grievable, does it not lock us into a reactive position vis-à-vis power, even while it gives us the ability to refuse the division between lives, to critique the conditions that lead to the differential distribution of vulnerability, to refuse to participate in the drive towards securitisation in denial of the unchangeable fact of our vulnerability? Perhaps the ability to mourn together is already a tremendous accomplishment, one that can be thought of as the fragile flower of the desire for peace that should be protected and cultivated at all costs. Nonetheless, it still seems to be a far cry from the active, creative, constituent power of collective imaginings that can move us beyond the very norms already delineated by dominant power relations, since the very foundations of modern state sovereignty, at least as they have been articulated in the Hobbesian paradigm that remains hegemonic, are based precisely on our corporeal vulnerability, which therefore necessitates (or, at the very least, permits) the security provided by sovereignty. How, then, can we expect the same foundational principles to lead to a substantially different outcome, to transcend the imaginary of the state? Perhaps we need to rely on a more affirmative ontology of ourselves based on 'transindividuality', which challenges the common binary between the individual and society and suggests a conception of subjectivity in which relationality is not predicated on mutual vulnerability.[50] However difficult this re-orientation might prove to be, it is especially in this moment of political urgency that we need the critical-theoretical space to think and imagine otherwise, to invent novel practices of common life and subjectivities, from the ground up, insisting on a new imaginary that is independent from the politics of life and death signified by sovereignty itself.[51]

None of this is to replace the very concrete and absolutely urgent political imperative to further the struggle for peace, to seek the immediate cessation of hostilities, and to hold the politicians and officials accountable for civilian harm and for the multifarious modalities of necropolitical violence whose infliction continually undermines and disables the possibility of peace. Neither does it mean that we should shy away from the critique of the violent tactics of the Kurdish movement, whose destruction of lives cannot be condoned or explained away simply by reference to the asymmetric relations of power and the oppressive conditions out of which it emerges. Might does not make right, no doubt, but it is rarely the case that a wrong can be made right by might. It is important to insist on the question that Étienne Balibar has thoughtfully raised: '[U]nder what conditions can we think a politics that is neither an *abstraction* from violence ("nonviolence") nor an *inversion* of it ("counterviolence" – especially in its repressive forms, state forms, but also in its revolutionary forms, which assume that they must reduplicate it if they are to "monopolise" it) but an internal response to, or displacement of, it?'[52] Insofar as violent conflict remains the primary determinant of politics, it seems to me, the aspiration to build a common life on the basis of an affirmative conviviality and the search for a new political imaginary beyond sovereignty are bound to remain tethered to the hegemonic model of statehood and harried with the continuous threat of securitisation.

In the electoral interregnum of 2015, and even more pronouncedly since then, the prospects of peace in Turkey have come to look bleak indeed. In a political conjuncture marked by forms of death-making, it is difficult to speak of alternatives that move us beyond the predicaments of the present. These predicaments are exacerbated with the resort to necropolitical violence, which is not only symptomatic of the existing state of insecurity, but also one of its determining forces, contributing further to the radicalisation of conflict. Necropolitical violence does more than designate which bodies are violable after death, thereby constituting the injunction to redraw the affective boundaries of the nation through the absolutisation of enmity. Its ambition to discipline and subdue the living through the surrogation of the dead points us to the limits of culture and erodes the bonds of sociality altogether. This is precisely why we must insist on peace. Can we create a politics of solidarity, conviviality and collective action beyond the common ground we discover in the simple humanity of mourning the loss of lives or the violence encountered after death? Can we look beyond the politics of mourning, beyond the politics of life and death that provides its conditions of possibility, to create an alternative where the 'common weal' is really held, shared, experienced, produced and consumed in common, where this commonality leads us to reconfigure our modes of political engagement and togetherness? Necropolitics reminds us that already there are forms of death beyond death. It is incumbent on us to find and advance forms of common life beyond the life we are made to live.

Notes

The author would like to express her sincere thanks to Başak Ertür and James Martel for their insightful comments and invaluable suggestions. An earlier version of this paper has benefited from a roundtable discussion with Andrew Arato and Ertuğ Tombuş organised by Public Seminar at the New School for Social Research. All translations from Turkish are mine.

1. For the composition of the Grand National Assembly of Turkey, see 'Türkiye Büyük Millet Meclisi Milletvekilleri Dağılımı'.
2. Bertil Videt, 'Turkey: Nationalism and War Mongering Won the Election'.

3. *BBC News*, 'PKK Attack Kills Soldiers in South-Eastern Turkey'.
4. See for example Max Zirngast, 'Erdoğan's Bloody Gambit'.
5. For a tally of civilian deaths and human rights violations, see Türkiye İnsan Hakları Vakfı, *Curfews in Turkey between 16 August 2015 – 12 December 2015*, Fact Sheet.
6. Alp Kayserilioglu, Güney Işıkara and Max Zirngast, 'Turkey in Times of War'. Also see Peoples' Democratic Party Foreign Affairs Commission, 'Information File on Violence in Turkey'.
7. For a succinct background on the Kurdish question see Doğu Ergil, 'The Kurdish Question in Turkey'; M. Hakan Yavuz, 'Five Stages of the Construction of Kurdish Nationalism in Turkey'; and Henri J. Barkey and Graham E. Fuller, 'Turkey's Kurdish Question: Critical Turning Points and Missed Opportunities'. For more sustained analyses see Cengiz Güneş, *The Kurdish National Movement in Turkey*, and Fevzi Bilgin and Ali Sarihan (eds), *Understanding Turkey's Kurdish Question*.
8. On the meaning of self-government and its relation to federalism and radical democracy, see for example Cengiz Güneş, 'Accommodating Kurdish National Demands in Turkey', pp. 71–84, and Ahmet Hamdi Akkaya and Joost Jongerden, 'Confederalism and Autonomy in Turkey', pp. 186–204. For recent first-hand accounts of self-government, see for example Haydar Darıcı, 'The Kurdish Self-Governance Movement in Turkey's South East'.
9. For a tally of recent curfews and casualties, see Türkiye İnsan Hakları Vakfı, *Fact Sheet on Declared Curfews between 11–25 December 2015 and Violations of Right to Life against Civilians*. Also see Peoples' Democratic Party, 'Urgent Call for Solidarity and Action'.
10. See for example the commentary by journalist Ezgi Başaran, '15 Yıldır Takip Edilen Adam Nasıl Diyarbakır-Suruç-Ankara'yı Planladı?'.
11. Journalists have not only been censored by the imposition of legal restrictions on what can be reported, but they have also been subjected to verbal and physical attacks and death threats, in addition to layoffs. See Freedom House, 'Turkey: Five Year Decline in Press Freedom'. According to the Committee to Protect Journalists, Turkey is the 'leading jailer of journalists' in the region of Europe and Central Asia. See CPJ, 'Turkey Press Crackdown Continues with Arrests of Three Pro-Kurdish Journalists'. For a detailed list, see CPJ, '2015 Prison Census'.
12. Michel Foucault, *History of Sexuality*, p. 136, and *'Society Must Be Defended'*, pp. 240–1.
13. Henry A. Giroux, 'Reading Hurricane Katrina', p. 175.
14. For the discussion of how biopolitical abandonment and violence plays out within the domain of racialised queer politics, see Jasbir Puar, *Terrorist Assemblages*, pp. 33–6.
15. Achille Mbembe, 'Necropolitics', p. 39.
16. Mbembe, 'Necropolitics', p. 21. Following Mbembe, Lamble argues that the prison, along with the colony and the territories under occupation, should also

be considered as a site of necropower insofar as it destines bodies to a living death through 'mass warehousing'. Sarah Lamble, 'Queer Necropolitics and the Expanding Carceral State: Interrogating Sexual Investments in Punishment', pp. 229–53. Also see Stuart J. Murray, 'Thanatopolitics', pp. 191–215.
17. For still other forms of the politicisation of death, especially as part of resistance movements and prison struggles, see Banu Bargu, *Starve and Immolate*.
18. Mbembe, 'Necropolitics', p. 40.
19. Instead of what Agamben calls 'bare life', as life that is produced as sacred by the operation of sovereignty, perhaps what we are faced with is 'bare death' – one that is defined by its vulnerability to the operation of sovereign violence but also one that becomes the vehicle of disciplining other bodies and rendering them targets of further violence. See Giorgio Agamben, *Homo Sacer: Sovereign Power and Bare Life*.
20. For a similar necropolitics in different contexts, see Emily Jane O'Dell, 'Waging War on the Dead', pp. 506–25; Katherine Verdery, *The Political Lives of Dead Bodies*; Joost Fontein, 'The Politics of the Dead', pp. 1–27; Thomas Gregory, 'Dismembering the Dead', pp. 1–22; Lyman L. Johnson (ed.), *Death, Dismemberment, and Memory: Body Politics in Latin America*; James J. Weingartner, 'Trophies of War', pp. 53–67.
21. On enforced disappearances, see Banu Bargu, 'Sovereignty as Erasure', pp. 35–75; Özgür Sevgi Göral, Ayhan Işık and Özlem Kaya, *The Unspoken Truth*; and Gökçen Alpkaya, 'Kayıp'lar Sorunu ve Türkiye', pp. 31–63. On the symbolism of the white Toros-brand automobiles heavily utilised in disappearances, see Adnan Çelik, 'Savaş ve Bellek', pp. 41–58.
22. See for example Eren Keskin, Leman Yurtsever and Rumet Agit Özer, 'Kader Kevser Eltürk (Ekin Van) Olayına Dair İnceleme Raporu'.
23. *Diken*, 'Muş Valiliği, Çıplak PKK'lı Kadın Cesedi Fotoğrafının Gerçek Olduğunu Duyurdu'. For an analysis of the euphemisms used by the state, see Tanıl Bora, 'Ölü Ele Geçirme'.
24. Sevim Salihoğlu et al., 'Muş İli Varto İlçesinde Meydana Gelen Olayları Araştırma Ve İnceleme Raporu'.
25. *Evrensel*, 'Nusaybinli Kadınlar: Ekin Wan Direnişimizin Çıplak Halidir'.
26. Gamzegül Kızılcık, 'İktidarın Özel Harekatından Kadın Bedenine İşkence: "Ekin Van'a Barış Sözü Verdik"'.
27. The declaration included the following signatories: Kurdish Women's Movement in Europe (TJK-E), International Representation of Kurdish Women's Movement (IRKWM), Office of Kurdish Women for Peace (CENI), Woman's Center (UTAMARA), International Free Woman's Foundation (IFWF), Roj Women, Helin Foundation and local women's councils. See 'Joint Appeal from Kurdish Women's Movement calls for signatures'.
28. *Evrensel*, 'Ekin Wan İçin Çıplak Protesto'.
29. *Evrensel*, 'İnsanlık Hala Sürükleniyor'.
30. İlhan Taşcı, 'Sınırda YPG'li Cenaze Krizi'.
31. Mahmut Bozarslan, 'Why Have PKK Cemeteries Become a Target?'

32. K. Murat Güney, 'The Body and Politics: The Power of Death over Life'.
33. On the role of enmity in the constitution of the political, see Carl Schmitt, *The Concept of the Political*. On the absolutisation of enmity with the development of partisan warfare, see Carl Schmitt, *Theory of the Partisan: Intermediate Commentary on the Concept of the Political*, which is a sequel to his *Concept of the Political*.
34. Güney, 'The Body and Politics', pp. 17–18.
35. Hişyar Özsoy, 'Between Gift and Taboo: Death and the Negotiation of National Identity and Sovereignty in the Kurdish Conflict in Turkey'.
36. Nazan Üstündağ, 'Ekin Wan Bedeninde İfşa Olan Devlet ya da Kadınlar Sıra Bizde'.
37. On the importance of the virtue of chastity in the construction of the 'modern' Turkish woman, see Deniz Kandiyoti, 'Slave Girls, Temptresses, and Comrades', pp. 35–50; Yeşim Arat, 'The Project of Modernity and Women in Turkey', pp. 95–112; and Ayşe Parla, 'The "Honor" of the State: Virginity Examinations in Turkey', pp. 65–88.
38. Melissa W. Wright, 'Necropolitics, Narcopolitics, and Femicide', pp. 707–31.
39. On the relationship between female purity and state formation, see Sherry B. Ortner, 'The Virgin and the State', pp. 19–35; Nira Yuval-Davis and Floya Anthias (eds), *Woman-Nation-State*; and Diane King, 'The Personal is Patrilineal: Namus as Sovereignty', pp. 317–42.
40. According to Michelle R. Martin-Baron, surrogation is 'the drive to replace that which is inevitably lost with a copy that will always fail to be that which it replaces'. While military funerals bring out the surrogation between the soldier and the nation, however, they also render bodies 'ultimately interchangeable and perpetually replaceable'. See Martin-Baron, '(Hyper/in)visibility and the military corps(e)', p. 52.
41. Özsoy, 'Between Gift and Taboo', p. 1.
42. Ibid. p. 29.
43. Ibid. p. 58. Also see p. 204.
44. See for example Hakan Sandal, 'Kürt Savaşçılarının Cenazeleri ve Devletin Sınırları'; Nicholas Glastonbury, '"What Does the State Want from Dead Bodies?" Suruç and the History of Unmournability'; Derya Aydın, 'Yası Tutulmaya Değer Görülmeyen Bedenlerin Süreklileşmiş Yası: Devlet Mezarlıkları Neden Bombalıyor?'
45. Judith Butler, *Precarious Life*, p. 20.
46. Ibid. p. 33.
47. Ibid. p. 30.
48. Ibid. p. xix.
49. It is not just that certain bodies have been rendered ungrievable; mourning itself has become a tool of government. Let us recall that a day of national mourning was officially declared after the passing of King Abdullah of Saudi Arabia, but not after the Suruç bombing in which thirty-three citizens were killed.
50. Étienne Balibar, *Spinoza: From Individuality to Transindividuality*, and Jason Read, 'The Production of Subjectivity', pp. 113–31.

51. Does the Kurdish turn towards a federative politics of 'democratic autonomy' within the existing borders of Turkey, in place of the hitherto dominant goal of establishing a separate nation-state, hold such a promise? Might it transcend the horizon of sovereignty and cut across the antagonistic positionality of both nationalist imaginaries? I will not be able to pursue these questions in depth within the limits of this essay. However, for a recent theoretical assessment, see Bülent Küçük and Ceren Özselçuk, 'The Rojava Experience: Possibilities and Challenges of Building a Democratic Life', pp. 184–96. According to Küçük and Özselçuk, 'democratic autonomy, in its critique of the nation-state, places itself in a relation of *deconstructing*, rather than *destroying* the state and, thus, does not rule out the possibility of coexistence with a state form, even a Kurdish state form' (194). The authors thus suggest that neither the critique of the nation-state nor that of the centralised, bureaucratic state should be construed as equivalent to the critique of the state-form or of sovereignty as such. In a more enthusiastic assessment of the way this politics is being played out in Rojava, Nazan Üstündağ argues that 'the state is being unmade', even though she recognises that, through the mechanism of internal and external representation and the performance of certain functions, there is also the ongoing possibility of the state being remade. See Nazan Üstündağ, 'Self-Defense as a Revolutionary Practice in Rojava, or How to Unmake the State', p. 208.
52. Étienne Balibar, *Violence and Civility*, p. 22.

Bibliography

Agamben, Giorgio, *Homo Sacer: Sovereign Power and Bare Life*, trans. Daniel Heller-Roazen (Stanford, CA: Stanford University Press, 1998).

Akkaya, Ahmet Hamdi, and Joost Jongerden, 'Confederalism and Autonomy in Turkey: The Kurdistan Workers' Party and the Reinvention of Democracy', in Cengiz Güneş and Welat Zeydanlıoğlu (eds), *The Kurdish Question in Turkey: New Perspectives on Violence, Representation and Reconciliation* (Oxon: Routledge, 2013), pp. 186–204.

Alpkaya, Gökçen, '"Kayıp'lar Sorunu ve Türkiye"', *Ankara Üniversitesi SBF Dergisi* 50, nos. 3–4 (1995): 31–63.

Arat, Yeşim, 'The Project of Modernity and Women in Turkey', in Sibel Bozdoğan and Reşat Kasaba (eds), *Rethinking Modernity and National Identity in Turkey* (Seattle: University of Washington Press, 1997), pp. 95–112.

Aydın, Derya, 'Yası Tutulmaya Değer Görülmeyen Bedenlerin Süreklileşmiş Yası: Devlet Mezarlıkları Neden Bombalıyor?' *Zan*, <http://zanenstitu.org/yasi-tutulmaya-deger-gorulmeyen-bedenlerin-sureklilesmis-yasi-devlet-mezarliklari-neden-bombaliyor-derya-aydin/#footnote_0_2321> (last accessed 3 January 2016).

Balibar, Étienne, *Spinoza: From Individuality to Transindividuality* (Rijnsburg: Eburon, 1997).

Balibar, Étienne, *Violence and Civility: On the Limits of Political Philosophy*, trans. G. M. Goshgarian (New York: Columbia University Press, 2015).

Bargu, Banu, 'Sovereignty as Erasure: Rethinking Enforced Disappearances', *Qui Parle: Critical Humanities and Social Sciences* 23, no. 1 (2014): 35–75.

Bargu, Banu, *Starve and Immolate: The Politics of Human Weapons* (New York: Columbia University Press, 2014).

Barkey, Henri J., and Graham E. Fuller, 'Turkey's Kurdish Question: Critical Turning Points and Missed Opportunities', *Middle East Journal* 51, no. 1 (1997), 59–79.

Başaran, Ezgi, '15 Yıldır Takip Edilen Adam Nasıl Diyarbakır-Suruç-Ankara'yı Planladı?', *Radikal*, 14 December 2015, <http://www.radikal.com.tr/yazarlar/ezgi-basaran/15-yildir-takip-edilen-adam-nasil-diyarbakir-suruc-ankarayi-planladi-1491958/> (last accessed 3 January 2016).

BBC News, 'PKK Attack Kills Soldiers in South-Eastern Turkey', 7 September 2015, <http://www.bbc.com/news/world-europe-34169988> (last accessed 4 January 2016).

Bilgin, Fevzi, and Ali Sarihan (eds), *Understanding Turkey's Kurdish Question*, reprint ed. (Lanham, MD: Lexington Books, 2015).

Bora, Tanıl, 'Ölü Ele Geçirme', *Birikim Haftalık Yazılar*, 14 October 2015, <http://www.birikimdergisi.com/haftalik/7250/olu-ele-gecirme#.VphjMOmKjZt> (last accessed 5 January 2016).

Bozarslan, Mahmut, 'Why Have PKK Cemeteries Become a Target?' *Al-Monitor*, 30 September 2015, <http://www.al-monitor.com/pulse/originals/2015/09/turkey-kurdish-rebels-accused-of-using-cemeteries-as-bases.html> (last accessed 7 January 2016).

Butler, Judith, *Precarious Life: The Powers of Mourning and Violence* (New York and London: Verso, 2004).

Çelik, Adnan, 'Savaş ve Bellek: Doksanların Zorla Kaybetme Fenomeni Olarak *Beyaz Toros*', *Toplum ve Kuram*, no. 10 (2015): 41–58.

Committee to Protect Journalists, '2015 Prison Census: 199 Journalists Jailed Worldwide', 14 December 2015, <https://cpj.org/x/6691> (last accessed 3 January 2016).

Committee to Protect Journalists, 'Turkey Press Crackdown Continues with Arrests of Three Pro-Kurdish Journalists', 22 December 2015, <https://cpj.org/2015/12/turkey-press-crackdown-continues-with-arrests-of-t.php> (last accessed 3 January 2016).

Darıcı, Haydar, 'The Kurdish Self-Governance Movement in Turkey's South East: an Interview with Haydar Darıcı', *LeftEast*, 22 December 2015, <http://www.criticatac.ro/lefteast/kurdish-self-governance/> (last accessed 3 January 2016).

Diken, 'Kobani Sınırında Bekletilen Cenaze Sayısı 20'ye Yükseldi, Ailelerin Bekleyişi Altıncı Gününde', 10 August 2015, <http://www.diken.com.tr/kobani-sinirinda-bekletilen-cenaze-sayisi-20ye-yukseldi-ailelerin-bekleyisi-altinci-gununde/> (last accessed 4 January 2016).

Diken, 'Muş Valiliği, Çıplak PKK'lı Kadın Cesedi Fotoğrafının Gerçek Olduğunu Duyurdu', 16 August 2015, <http://www.diken.com.tr/mus-valiligi-ciplak-pkkli-kadin-fotografinin-gercek-oldugunu-duyurdu/> (last accessed 6 January 2016).

Ergil, Doğu, 'The Kurdish Question in Turkey', *Journal of Democracy* 11, no. 3 (2000): 122–35.

Evrensel, 'Ekin Wan İçin Çıplak Protesto', 23 August 2015, <http://www.evrensel.net/haber/258876/ekin-wan-icin-ciplak-protesto> (last accessed 6 January 2016).

Evrensel, 'İnsanlık Hala Sürükleniyor', 4 October 2015, <http://www.evrensel.net/haber/262001/i> (last accessed 7 January 2016).

Evrensel, 'Nusaybinli Kadınlar: Ekin Wan Direnişimizin Çıplak Halidir', 16 August 2015, <http://www.evrensel.net/haber/258484/nusaybinli-kadinlar-ekin-wan-direnisimizin-ciplak-halidir> (last accessed 7 January 2016).

Fontein, Joost, 'The Politics of the Dead: Living Heritage, Bones and Commemoration in Zimbabwe', *ASA Online* 1, no. 2 (2009): 1–27.

Foucault, Michel, *History of Sexuality, Volume 1: An Introduction* (New York: Vintage Books, 1990).

Foucault, Michel, *'Society Must Be Defended': Lectures at Collège de France 1975–1976*, ed. Mauro Bentani and Alessandro Fontana, trans. David Macey (New York: Picador, 2003).

Freedom House, 'Turkey: Five Year Decline in Press Freedom', <https://freedomhouse.org/report/freedom-press/2015/turkey> (last accessed 3 January 2016).

Giroux, Henry A., 'Reading Hurricane Katrina: Race, Class, and the Biopolitics of Disposability', *College Literature* 33, no. 3 (2006).

Glastonbury, Nicholas, '"What Does the State Want from Dead Bodies?" Suruç and the History of Unmournability', *Jadaliyya*, 7 August 2015, <http://www.jadaliyya.com/pages/index/22351/what-does-the-state-want-from-dead-bodies_suruç-an> (last accessed 7 January 2016).

Göral, Özgür Sevgi, Ayhan Işık and Özlem Kaya, *The Unspoken Truth: Enforced Disappearance* (Istanbul: Truth, Justice and Memory Center, 2013).

Gregory, Thomas, 'Dismembering the Dead: Violence, Vulnerability and the Body in War', *European Journal of International Relations* (2015): 1–22.

Güneş, Cengiz, *The Kurdish National Movement in Turkey: From Protest to Resistance* (London and New York: Routledge, 2012).

Güneş, Cengiz, 'Accommodating Kurdish National Demands in Turkey', in Ephraim Nimni, Alexander Osipov and David J. Smith (eds), *The Challenge of Non-Territorial Autonomy: Theory and Practice* (Bern: Peter Lang, 2013), pp. 71–84.

Güney, K. Murat, 'The Body and Politics: The Power of Death over Life', unpublished MA thesis, Department of Anthropology, Columbia University, 2008.

Johnson, Lyman L. (ed.), *Death, Dismemberment, and Memory: Body Politics in Latin America* (Albuquerque: University of New Mexico Press, 2004).

'Joint Appeal from Kurdish Women's Movement calls for signatures', 28 August 2015, <http://peaceinkurdistancampaign.com/2015/08/28/joint-appeal-from-kurdish-womens-movement-calls-for-signatures-for-a-new-appeal/> (last accessed 6 January 2016).

Kandiyoti, Deniz, 'Slave Girls, Temptresses, and Comrades: Images of Women in the Turkish Novel', *Feminist Issues* 8, no. 1 (1988): 35–50.

Kayserilioglu, Alp, Güney Işıkara and Max Zirngast, 'Turkey in Times of War', *Jadaliyya*, 18 September 2015, <http://www.jadaliyya.com/pages/index/22680/turkey-in-times-of-war> (last accessed 10 June 2016).

Keskin, Eren, Leman Yurtsever and Rumet Agit Özer, 'Kader Kevser Eltürk (Ekin Van) Olayına Dair İnceleme Raporu', *İnsan Hakları Derneği Özel Raporu*, 4 September 2015, <http://www.ihd.org.tr/kader-kevser-elturk-ekin-van-olay-ina-dair-inceleme-raporu/> (last accessed 5 January 2016).

King, Diane, 'The Personal is Patrilineal: Namus as Sovereignty', *Identities: Global Studies in Culture and Power* 15, no. 3 (2008): 317–42.

Kızılcık, Gamzegül, 'İktidarın Özel Harekatından Kadın Bedenine İşkence: "Ekin Van'a Barış Sözü Verdik"', *Gaia Dergi*, 19 August 2015, <https://gaiadergi.com/iktidarin-ozel-harekatindan-kadin-bedenine-iskence-ekin-vana-baris-sozu-verdik/> (last accessed 6 January 2016).

Küçük, Bülent, and Ceren Özselçuk, 'The Rojava Experience: Possibilities and Challenges of Building a Democratic Life', *South Atlantic Quarterly* 115, no. 1 (January 2016): 184–96.

Lamble, Sarah, 'Queer Necropolitics and the Expanding Carceral State: Interrogating Sexual Investments in Punishment', *Law & Critique* 24 (2013): 229–53.

Martin-Baron, Michelle R., '(Hyper/in)visibility and the military corps(e)', in Jin Haritaworn, Adi Kuntsman and Silvia Posocco (eds), *Queer Necropolitics* (Oxford: Routledge, 2014).

Mbembe, Achille, 'Necropolitics', trans. Libby Meintjes, *Public Culture* 15, no. 1 (Winter 2013): 11–40.

Murray, Stuart J., 'Thanatopolitics: On the Use of Death for Mobilizing Political Life', *Polygraph* 18 (2006), 191–215.

O'Dell, Emily Jane, 'Waging War on the Dead: The Necropolitics of Sufi Shrine Destruction in Mali', *Archaeologies: Journal of the World Archaeological Congress* 9, no. 3 (December 2013): 506–25.

Ortner, Sherry B., 'The Virgin and the State', *Feminist Studies* 4, no. 3 (1978): 19–35.

Özsoy, Hişyar, 'Between Gift and Taboo: Death and the Negotiation of National Identity and Sovereignty in the Kurdish Conflict in Turkey', unpublished PhD dissertation, University of Texas at Austin, May 2010.

Parla, Ayşe, 'The "Honor" of the State: Virginity Examinations in Turkey', *Feminist Studies* 27, no. 1 (Spring 2001): 65–88.

Peoples' Democratic Party Foreign Affairs Commission, 'Information File on Violence in Turkey', 11 September 2015, <https://hdpenglish.files.wordpress.com/2015/09/information-file-on-crisis-in-turkey-en.pdf> (last accessed 3 January 2016).

Peoples' Democratic Party, 'Urgent Call for Solidarity and Action', press release, 23 December 2015, <https://hdpenglish.wordpress.com/2015/12/23/urgent-call-for-solidarity-and-action/> (last accessed 3 January 2016).

Puar, Jasbir K., *Terrorist Assemblages: Homonationalism in Queer Times* (Durham, NC: Duke University Press, 2007).

Read, Jason, 'The Production of Subjectivity: From Transindividuality to the Commons', *New Formations: A Journal of Culture/Theory/Politics*, no. 70 (2010): 113–31.

Salihoğlu, Sevim, et al., 'Muş İli Varto İlçesinde Meydana Gelen Olayları Araştırma Ve İnceleme Raporu', *İnsan Hakları Derneği Özel Raporu*, 20 August 2015, <http://www.ihd.org.tr/mus-ili-varto-ilcesinde-meydana-gelen-olaylari-arastirma-ve-inceleme-raporu/> (last accessed 3 January 2016).

Sandal, Hakan, 'Kürt Savaşçılarının Cenazeleri ve Devletin Sınırları', *Evrensel*, 4 October 2015, <http://www.evrensel.net/haber/262002/kurt-savascilarin-cenazeleri-ve-devletin-sinirlari> (last accessed 3 January 2016).

Schmitt, Carl, *The Concept of the Political*, trans. George Schwab (Chicago and London: University of Chicago Press, 1996).

Schmitt, Carl, *Theory of the Partisan: Intermediate Commentary on the Concept of the Political*, trans. G. L. Ulmen (New York: Telos Press, 2007).

Taşcı, İlhan, 'Sınırda YPG'li Cenaze Krizi', *BBC Türkçe*, 3 August 2015, <http://www.bbc.com/turkce/haberler/2015/08/150803_ypg_cenaze_sinir> (last accessed 3 January 2016).

'Türkiye Büyük Millet Meclisi Milletvekilleri Dağılımı', <https://www.tbmm.gov.tr/develop/owa/milletvekillerimiz_sd.dagilim> (last accessed 30 December 2015).

Türkiye İnsan Hakları Vakfı, *Curfews in Turkey between 16 August 2015 – 12 December 2015*, fact sheet, <http://en.tihv.org.tr/curfews-in-turkey-between-16-august-2015-12-december-2015/> (last accessed 3 January 2016).

Türkiye İnsan Hakları Vakfı, *Fact Sheet on Declared Curfews between 11–25 December 2015 and Violations of Right to Life Against Civilians*, <http://en.tihv.org.tr/fact-sheet-on-declared-curfews-between-11-25-december-and-violations-of-right-to-life-against-civilians/> (last accessed 3 January 2016).

Üstündağ, Nazan, 'Ekin Wan Bedeninde İfşa Olan Devlet ya da Kadınlar Sıra Bizde', *Evrensel*, 23 August 2015, <http://www.evrensel.net/haber/258899/ekin-wanin-bedeninde-ifsa-olan-devlet-ya-da-kadinlar-sira-bizde> (last accessed 6 January 2016).

Üstündağ, Nazan, 'Self-Defense as a Revolutionary Practice in Rojava, or How to Unmake the State', *South Atlantic Quarterly* 115, no. 1 (January 2016).

Verdery, Katherine, *The Political Lives of Dead Bodies* (New York: Columbia University Press, 1999).

Videt, Bertil, 'Turkey: Nationalism and War Mongering Won the Election', *Jadaliyya*, 4 November 2015, <http://www.jadaliyya.com/pages/index/23097/turkey_nationalism-and-war-mongering-won-the-elect> (last accessed 30 December 2015).

Weingartner, James J., 'Trophies of War: US Troops and the Mutilation of Japanese War Dead, 1941–1945', *Pacific Historical Review* 61, no. 1 (1992): 53–67.

Wright, Melissa W., 'Necropolitics, Narcopolitics, and Femicide: Gendered Violence on the Mexico-US Border', *Signs* 36, no. 3 (March 2011): 707–31.

Yavuz, M. Hakan., 'Five Stages of the Construction of Kurdish Nationalism in Turkey', *Nationalism & Ethnic Politics*, 7, no. 3 (2001): 1–24.

Yuval-Davis, Nira, and Floya Anthias (eds), *Woman-Nation-State* (New York: Palgrave Macmillan, 1989).

Zirngast, Max, 'Erdoğan's Bloody Gambit', *Jacobin*, 3 August 2015, <https://www.jacobinmag.com/2015/08/turkey-nato-isis-hdp-kpp-suruc/> (last accessed 30 December 2015).

ELEVEN

The Cemetery of Traitors

Osman Balkan

The corpse arrived on a balmy summer afternoon. Neither the ambulance driver nor the cemetery workers knew the identity of the deceased, whose unwashed, bloodied body was shrouded in mystery and a simple white cloth. No prayers or religious incantations were uttered as workers lowered the body into an unmarked, anonymous grave. No friends or family members were present to witness the burial. The only onlookers were a pack of stray dogs who languidly roamed the rock-strewn fields of the hastily constructed cemetery. The body, that of thirty-four-year-old military captain Mehmet Karabekir, was not to be mourned.

Karabekir had the dubious honour of being the first inhabitant of the 'Cemetery of Traitors' (*Hainler Mezarlığı*), a burial ground established by Turkish authorities to house the remains of putschists killed during their attempt to overthrow the government of President Recep Tayyip Erdoğan in a failed military coup on 15 July 2016, which led to the imposition of a two-year state of emergency and the arrest and/or dismissal of an unprecedented number of civil servants, teachers, academics and journalists in Turkey. The cemetery was the brainchild of Istanbul's then mayor, Kadir Topbaş, who unveiled his plans at a massive public rally held in the name of safeguarding democracy on 19 July 2016. 'I ordered a place to be reserved and to call it the Cemetery of Traitors,' he told the flag-waving crowd that had gathered in Taksim Square. 'Those who pass by should curse them! They cannot escape hell but we must also make them suffer in their graves!'[1]

Adjacent to an open-air municipal dog shelter on the eastern outskirts of Istanbul, the Cemetery of Traitors is not a typical graveyard. As its name unmistakably asserts, it is intended as a burial ground for the enemies of the Turkish state. To be buried there is a form of posthumous punishment. The cemetery is a striking example of Turkish statecraft that reflects a longstanding strategy of targeting the dead as a means of governing the living. It is part of a morbid set of practices that political theorist Banu Bargu subsumes under the heading of 'necropolitical violence', that is, 'violence that takes as its object the realm of the dead'.[2]

Necropolitical violence includes the disfiguration, desecration, denuding and public display of corpses as well as the destruction of cemeteries and memorials to the dead, the prohibition or violent repression of funerary rituals and processions, and the inhumation of bodies in mass or anonymous graves.[3] Different groups, including Kurds, Alevis, Armenians, leftist political dissidents and LGBTQ communities have all been subjected to such acts of necropolitical violence by the state or parastate organisations at various moments in the tumultuous history of the Turkish Republic.[4] According to Bargu, the point of such violence is not to produce 'bare life' or to reduce the living to the status of 'living dead', but rather to target the dead in order to *dishonour, discipline and punish the living*.[5]

In this chapter I examine the aftermath of the failed military coup in Turkey through the political afterlives of its victims and perpetrators. Building on the work of Bargu and other theorists of necropolitics, I consider the relationship between sovereign power and the dead body in an effort to illustrate how corpses become politicised sites of struggle and resistance. I argue that the determination of where and how dead bodies are buried (or otherwise disposed of) is a critical means through which states and other actors demarcate the contours of national, religious and political communities. Focusing on the Cemetery of Traitors as well as the funerals of soldiers and civilians who died during the coup attempt and in its immediate aftermath, I show how the treatment and commemoration of the dead marks the difference between martyrs and renegades, friends and enemies, Muslims and infidels, and more broadly, serves to delineate the boundary of the nation and its authentic demos.

Necropolitical Statecraft

Max Weber famously observed that the state is 'the form of human community that (successfully) lays claim to the monopoly of the legitimate use of physical force within a particular territory'.[6] States mete out violence and death on a regular basis, though by no means is this violence distributed evenly across the population at large. In an effort to make sense of this variation and to better understand its underlying causes and long-term consequences, recent scholarship has theorised politics as 'the work of death' and has investigated the ways in which sovereign power functions through the division of populations into those who must live and those who must die.[7] Building on the work of Michel Foucault and the proposition that the ultimate expression of sovereignty lies in the ability to exercise control over life and death, Achille Mbembe has developed the concept of necropolitics to describe and interpret 'contemporary forms of subjugation of life to the power of death'.[8]

Drawing on examples such as the slave plantation, the penal colony and territories under military occupation, such as contemporary Palestine where 'new and unique forms of social existence' have appeared, Mbembe sees the emergence of necropolitical regimes whose function is not to foster or optimise life but rather, to create conditions of maximum deprivation. In these 'death-worlds', populations are not killed off en masse in spectacular acts of violence. Rather, they are reduced to conditions of life that confer upon them the status of 'living dead' through wilful neglect. The exercise of sovereign power in these spaces lies in its ability to define which lives matter for the vitality and future strength of the political community. In Mbembe's framework, by marking certain lives as valuable or expendable, necropolitics is thoroughly invested in the uneven allocation and distribution of death among certain populations.

Mbembe's influential account has generated a wealth of scholarship on the politics of death, destruction and precarity that has helped advance our understanding of the modalities of necropolitical statecraft. In focusing on the differential allocation of death, however, many of these studies overlook one of the key sites where necropolitics occurs: the human corpse. Dead bodies are critical sites of statecraft, not least because of their materiality, symbolic power and association with the sacred.[9] As anthropologist Katherine Verdery has argued, a body's materiality can be vital to its symbolic efficacy. Unlike abstract notions like 'patriotism' or 'the nation', dead bodies 'can be moved around, displayed, and strategically located in specific places', but what makes them effective as political symbols is their ambiguity or 'capacity to evoke a variety of understandings' to different actors.[10] Drawing on such examples of what she calls 'dead body politics' during the transitions from socialism in Eastern Europe, Verdery skilfully demonstrates how the corpses of both (in)famous and ordinary people become sites of political contestation in moments of political upheaval or change, as different groups struggle over where they should be (re)buried and what they should signify.[11]

Dead body politics need not involve 'exceptional' or politically charged corpses such as those of public leaders, notable citizens or enemies of the state. The corpses of ordinary citizens also play a role in routinised, banal practices of necropolitical governance. As Finn Stepputat has argued, all states, irrespective of their regime type or level of socioeconomic development, establish a range of institutions, laws and practices to oversee transitions from life to death, including what happens to dead bodies.[12] Even in situations where states delegate certain responsibilities over the dead to non-state actors, such as private firms or religious entities, they usually claim ultimate authority over the definition and governance of the dead within their jurisdiction through legislation and institutionalised procedures. For Stepputat, the death of a person is an occasion for the performance of sovereignty by both states and a range of sub-, trans-, and supranational entities that manage (or aspire to manage) dead bodies in ways that overlap or come into conflict with legally institutionalised state practices.

In light of these examples, it may be useful to expand the notion of necropolitics to try to make sense of the ways that power is exercised and contested *after* the termination of life. By doing so we can better appreciate the multiple registers through which necropolitics operates. At one level, the creation of 'death-worlds' where certain populations are reduced to the status of the 'living dead' by means of deprivation or wilful neglect reflects a biopolitical logic in which sovereign power manifests as the imperative to 'make live and let die'. At another level, murderous practices aimed at certain individuals or groups fall within a paradigm of sovereignty that understands power in terms of its ability to 'let live or make die'. Finally, there are those practices that Bargu subsumes under the heading of 'necropolitical violence', and which Verdery calls 'dead body politics', which take place upon or around the corpse itself. These include both explicit acts of violence directed upon the body (dismemberment, desecration, etc.) or acts of symbolic violence that aim to erase or strip an individual of her identity (anonymous burial or interment in mass graves).

To understand why sovereign power targets posthumous subjects requires engaging with both material and symbolic dimensions of necropolitical statecraft. This means paying attention to how states and other actors treat and handle dead bodies (are they physically harmed, violated, disappeared, displayed, kept in confinement, buried in secret or not buried at all?) and to the symbolic practices, rituals and narratives that different groups employ in their efforts to commemorate, memorialise and ultimately (re)signify the dead (funeral processions, public rallies, obituaries, memorials, prayers, mourning practices, etc. in which the central protagonist is the deceased and the narrative arc concerns their biography, the circumstances behind their death and how they should be remembered). Taking dead bodies as a field of struggle over meaning and signification allows us to identify how the management of the dead helps constitute, consolidate and territorialise national, political and religious communities around the world.

The political stakes of corpse management become clearer when we juxtapose 'problematic' corpses such as those of individuals that have an antagonistic or conflictual relationship with the state, with those that the state relies upon to consolidate and reproduce a particular way of imagining the national community. The most spectacular example of corpse management in Turkey is arguably the mausoleum built to house the remains of Mustafa Kemal Atatürk, founder of the Turkish Republic. The Anıtkabir ('Memorial Tomb') structure in Ankara is a massive, open-air complex that architectural historian Sibel Bozdoğan has described as the 'holiest' site in modern Turkey.[13] Anıtkabir incorporates a range of different architectural styles, including twenty-four Hittite lions, representing the 'strength and power of the Turkish nation', a Greco-Roman mausoleum that resembles the Parthenon, and Soviet realist statues of a soldier, a peasant, a teacher/student and three women holding wheat, one weeping, which honour the ordinary citizens that comprise the body politic and guarantee its reproduction and survival.[14] Groups of soldiers constantly patrol the grounds in complex step formations, while other soldiers stand motionless, guarding key points in the complex.

Anıtkabir hosts millions of visitors annually and serves as a central site for the public commemoration of important milestones in the history of the Republic (including 10 November, the anniversary of Atatürk's death). It is a striking example of monumental political architecture that is as much a homage to Atatürk as it is to the Turkish nation itself. Its symbolic power derives from the materiality of Atatürk's remains, which are buried under a 40-ton sarcophagus in Anıtkabir's 'Hall of Honour'.[15] Etched in a marble slab near the sarcophagus are Atatürk's famous words, 'One day my mortal body will turn into dust, but the Turkish Republic will stand forever.' Visiting dignitaries frequently lay wreaths at this site, which has a quasi-religious aura.

Atatürk is an exceptional figure in the historiography of the Turkish nation-state and plays a central role in the national self-imaginary. As soldier/statesman, his story is one of heroic sacrifice in the service of a higher cause. However, such tropes are quite common in commemorative acts that honour ordinary soldier dead. As Onur Bakıner shows in his contribution to this volume, tropes of sacrifice and martyrdom are central features of Turkey's death-politics nexus, and have helped legitimate acts of state violence in Turkey. The Turkish word for martyr, şehit, has religious connotations, though it is applied to all soldiers killed in combat (most often in reference to those who have perished in the ongoing civil conflict with the Kurdistan Workers' Party, i.e., the PKK). Martyrs are buried in cemeteries that are reserved for them (called Şehitlik) and their funerals are often broadcast by the media, thereby transforming what would otherwise be a private, familial affair into a public one, allowing citizens across the country to participate in collective mourning. Such rituals have been impacted by new media technologies, as evinced by the creation of internet websites and Facebook groups dedicated to Turkish martyrs, which create new potentials for communicative action between the living and the dead and help to extend the memory and presence of those who have departed from this world.[16]

Beyond martyrdom, we can point to the constitutive work that dead bodies perform in the creation and reproduction of national and political communities the world over. Consider the Tomb of the Unknown Soldier. A memorial invented by the Italian, French and British governments during the last years of World War I, the Tomb of the Unknown Soldier has been described by Benedict Anderson as the most 'arresting emblem of the modern culture of nationalism'.[17] The sacred admiration that such monuments command reminds us that the nation is an altar that demands the blood sacrifice of its citizens. The fungibility of the unknown in the tomb (he or she could be any one of us) reflects a democratic ethos. The same logic is at work in the uniformity of tombstones in grand national war cemeteries like Arlington, Tyne Cot or Gallipoli. 'Void as these are of identifiable mortal remains or immortal souls,' writes Anderson, 'they are nonetheless saturated with ghostly *national* imaginings.'[18] These dead are *our* dead. Their veneration, through physical monuments and commemorative rituals, helps consolidate the idea of a national community by linking past sacrifices to present political orders.

What about the bodies of the enemies of a given political community? How are they incorporated into the national imaginary? Like fallen heroes or celebrated public figures, the enemies of the state also serve an important boundary maintenance function. They lay bare the distinction between insider and outsider. As I have already suggested, one important strategy through which states and other political actors make claims about the boundaries of the nation and its authentic demos is through material and symbolic acts that target human remains. In the next two sections I aim to further substantiate this claim by analysing the funerals of the victims and perpetrators of the failed military coup of 15 July 2016, a watershed moment in Turkish political history.

As the self-appointed guardian of the Turkish Republic and its values, the military has been an active and powerful force in Turkish politics, staging three bloody coups in 1960, 1971 and 1980, as well as a bloodless so-called 'post-modern' coup in 1997 during which it removed Islamist prime minister Necmettin Erbakan from power via memorandum rather than by force. In 2016, the military's attempt to violently overthrow the government of Recep Tayyip Erdoğan backfired, in no small part because of the intervention of ordinary citizens who took to the streets to repel putschist soldiers. Many people on both sides were killed in the process.

In the next section I analyse the public ceremonies held in honour of pro-government soldiers and citizens who died in clashes with putschist forces on 15 July 2016. Held up as martyrs, the funerals for these individuals were public spectacles that attracted thousands of onlookers and offered an emotionally charged site for the reaffirmation of political loyalties, communal solidarities and national boundaries. I focus on the pageantry of the funerals, paying particular attention to the speeches and eulogies delivered by high-level state authorities in honour of the dead.

'They may have tanks and guns but we have faith'

The Cemetery of Traitors was established by Turkish authorities after putting down a military coup that left more than 300 dead and several thousand injured. At around 11 p.m. on 15 July 2016, a faction of the Turkish Armed Forces calling themselves the 'Peace at Home Council' launched attacks on key sites in Istanbul and Ankara. Armoured tanks rolled in to block the Fatih Sultan Mehmet and Bosphorus bridges, the two main land routes across the Bosphorus Strait in Istanbul. Armed soldiers occupied Taksim Square in central Istanbul and descended upon the city's major air hub, the Atatürk Airport. Meanwhile, military helicopters and tanks opened fire on the parliament building as well as the headquarters of the special police forces in Ankara.[19] Around midnight, armed soldiers entered the offices of the Turkish Radio and Television Corporation in Ankara (the national public news station) and coerced a news anchor to read a prepared statement asserting that the Turkish military had 'completely taken over the administration of the country to reinstate the constitutional order'. The statement also noted that 'the democratic and secular rule of law has been eroded by the current government' and that the Peace at Home Council would 'preserve the democratic order' and 'ensure the safety of the population'.[20]

The coup itself was short-lived. President Recep Tayyip Erdoğan, who was on holiday at the seaside resort town of Marmaris and barely eluded capture by military forces, took to the airwaves via FaceTime urging the public to pour out onto the streets to defend the nation. Similar messages were broadcast via loudspeakers in mosques across the country. Throngs of people took heed of Erdoğan's message. Hundreds made their way to the Bosphorus Bridge to confront the military. In the clashes that followed, several civilians were killed and a soldier was lynched and beheaded by the angry mob. In a rapid turn of events, the coup plotters were repelled and defeated.

By daybreak, the government could confidently assert that it had regained control over the country. The soldiers on the bridge had surrendered and hundreds of military personnel were arrested. Turkish newspapers hailed the event as a victory for democracy. Prime Minister Binali Yıldırım and other high-ranking members of the Turkish government laid the blame for the coup on Fethullah Gülen, an exiled cleric living in the Pocono Mountains in Pennsylvania. Others saw an American hand behind the coup attempt. A poll published by a pro-government newspaper reported that sixty-nine per cent of Turks believed that the CIA had supported the coup plotters.[21] Still others speculated that it had been an inside job in order to shore up the AKP's power. While investigations are still ongoing, arrests and purges of individuals believed to have links with Gülen and his organisation have taken place at an unprecedented scale.[22]

In the immediate aftermath of the failed coup, Turkish authorities were faced with the question of what to do with all the dead bodies. According to Prime Minister Yıldırım, 240 pro-government forces, including civilians, were killed during the coup attempt, while a further 2,195 were wounded. On the other side, thirty-six putschist soldiers died, while forty-nine others were wounded.[23] Turkish officials bestowed honours upon the pro-government forces, praising them as martyrs. Many received heroic public funerals that were attended by high-ranking members of parliament and thousands of ordinary citizens.

Major Ömer Halisdemir, one of the first pro-government soldiers killed in action, was buried in his hometown of Çukurkuyu in central Anatolia on 17 July 2016. Halisdemir had played a critical role in preventing the success of the coup attempt by assassinating one of its leaders, Brigadier General Semih Terzi, as he and a group of soldiers tried to seize the Special Forces Command building in Ankara. Halisdemir was mortally wounded after shooting Terzi in the head at short range. His body was taken to Çukurkuyu and displayed in a flag-draped coffin in the town's central square, where close to five thousand onlookers gathered to pay their final respects.

According to İleri Koçak, the town's mayor, more than one hundred thousand individuals from across Turkey have since visited his grave. 'If

Ömer hadn't intervened where he did, perhaps thousands of people would have died,' noted Koçak. 'He brought honour to our town and to our nation. We thank our citizens for the respect they have given him. Çukurkuyu now belongs to all of us.'[24] The local university was subsequently renamed Ömer Halisdemir University in his honour, as were several public schools in Ankara, Istanbul and Izmir. In interviews with the press, his father, Hasan Hüseyin Halisdemir, told reporters: 'I'm honoured. I raised him for the nation and I gave him to the nation. I accept the sacrifice he has made. He's a child of the nation now . . . Long live the nation.' Noting that Ömer 'saved our people and our nation', Hasan said that he thanked God for giving him such a son.

Another notable public funeral was that of Erol Olçok, an advertiser with longstanding links to the AKP. Olçok and his sixteen-year-old son, Abdullah Tayyip, were both killed on 15 July 2016 as they confronted soldiers that had taken the Bosphorus Bridge. A close ally of Recep Tayyip Erdoğan, having worked with him during his tenure as Istanbul's mayor, Olçok was the campaign manager of the AKP's 2002 electoral campaign and a close ally of Erdoğan. He designed the party's name and logo and helped formulate its slogans and party platforms. Erol and Abdullah Tayyip Olçok were buried in Istanbul's Karacaahmet Cemetery after a public funeral ceremony held at the Marmara University Faculty of Theology.

The funeral attracted thousands of citizens and was attended by many high-ranking political officials, including President Erdoğan, Speaker of the Grand National Assembly Ismail Kahraman, former President Abdullah Gül, former Prime Minister Ahmet Davutoğlu, Governor of Istanbul Vasip Şahin and a dozen other ministers, cabinet members and members of parliament, all of whom stood within close proximity to the flag-draped coffins.[25] Flanked by a row of imams wearing Ottoman-style taqiyahs and ornamental robes in white and gold, President Erdoğan told the crowd that 'the funeral prayers of our martyrs are being performed after the Asr prayer across various locations in Turkey'. 'Erol was my comrade,' he continued, his voice straining as he began to weep into the microphone. As he wept, the crowd erupted, chanting 'Ya Allah, Bismillah, Allahu Ekber!' 'May God rest his soul!' Erdoğan cried out, his voice cracking as he embraced Olçok's coffin. 'We want the death penalty!' the crowd responded.

Visibly distressed, Erdoğan struggled to contain his sobs. 'I can't continue,' he said, 'my condolences to the nation. But let it be known that we will march with our burial robes towards these assassins, this Fethullah Terrorist Organisation, and we will eradicate them! We will carry this country into the future with solidarity and unity. May God's mercy be upon our martyrs!' Putting down the microphone as he wiped his tears away, Erdoğan moved back into the crowd, which continued its chants. Erol Olçok's name was subsequently given to a football stadium, a hospital and several public schools in Çorum, the city of his birth.

Erdoğan attended other funerals, notably that of Ilhan Varank, brother of Erdoğan's chief consultant Mustafa Varank. Varank died in front of the Istanbul Municipality Building after a group of putschist soldiers opened fire upon the crowd that had gathered there after Erdoğan urged Turkish citizens to take to the streets to defend the nation. He and several other civilians killed during the coup attempt were honoured at a public funeral held at the Fatih Mosque in Istanbul, one of the largest and most important mosques in the city. Many high-ranking political officials were present, including Erdoğan, Abdullah Gül and Ahmet Davutoğlu. As Erdoğan took the microphone to deliver a speech, again flanked by a row of imams in traditional dress, the crowd of several hundred people that had gathered to pay their respects broke into a spontaneous chant, exclaiming, 'Here is our army and our commander!'[26]

'My dear brothers, we are gathered here for a very meaningful funeral ceremony,' began Erdoğan, this time speaking coolly and assuredly. 'Here we have our 15 July martyrs. These martyrs have reached the highest rank after the prophets . . . Those who could not stand our nation's unity, solidarity and brotherhood, turned 15 July into an armed insurrection and attempted to take control of our government!' The crowd hissed, jeered, booed and then began chanting 'Fethullah will come here and pay for what he's done!' Gaining momentum, Erdoğan spoke of the valiant efforts of ordinary citizens who filled the nation's squares and challenged the putschists. 'They may have tanks and guns but we have faith!' he bellowed as the crowd burst into another set of chants, this time 'Allahu Ekber' (God is Great) and 'We want the death penalty!' 'In democracies, you cannot ignore the will of the people!' he continued. 'This is your right!'

Speaking about the ways in which the Gülenists had infiltrated different branches of the Turkish state, Erdoğan outlined the ongoing arrests and purges, promising the frenzied crowd that he would continue to wipe out this 'virus' which has 'spread throughout the state like a cancer'. Noting that he had formally requested the extradition of Gülen from the United States, he called on the crowd to maintain vigilance, urging them to continue to fill the public squares with their bodies and voices. 'This isn't a twelve-hour-operation, we can't slow down now. We must continue with determination!' he said as the crowd roared in approval.

The public ceremonies held in honour of the '15 July martyrs' offered an emotionally charged stage for the performance of sovereign power and necropolitical statecraft. The ritualistic veneration of the dead, their conspicuous display in coffins adorned with the Turkish flag, and the patriotic eulogies delivered by elected officials all served to uphold a triumphalist narrative about the indivisible Turkish nation, which perseveres in the face of threats both foreign and domestic thanks to the sacrifices of its heroic citizens. The very public display of the material remains of individuals killed in the coup attempt offered incontrovertible visual evidence of the truth of sacrifice, while the paeans made by political officials helped discursively and symbolically link the individual to the nation. The (dead) body stood for the body politic.

'They must suffer in their graves'

The funerals of the coup plotters offer a stark contrast. Unlike the heavily orchestrated spectacles surrounding the burial of the victims of the coup attempt, the funerals of the perpetrators were secretive, ad hoc and stigmatised events that, in some cases, took place under considerable duress. In what follows, I offer a few brief vignettes to illustrate how the corpses of coup plotters became politicised sites of conflict.

A few days after the coup attempt, the Turkish Directorate of Religious Affairs (the highest official religious body in the country) issued a formal directive to its imams concerning their religious obligations vis-à-vis the dead coup plotters. 'A funeral prayer is intended as an act of exoneration for the faithful,' it read. 'But these people, with the actions that they undertook, have disregarded not just individuals but also the law of an entire nation and therefore do not deserve exoneration from their faithful brothers and sisters.'[27]

The Directorate prohibited its imams and all other religious functionaries from performing any sort of religious ceremony for individuals involved in the coup attempt. Its public statement read as follows: 'Our office will not provide funerary services (washing, shrouding, prayers) to the coup plotters who revolted against our country's legitimate government and targeted the survival of our state, who dropped bombs on the Turkish Parliament and other public buildings and who mercilessly took up arms against the people and died in the process.'[28]

The Directorate's unprecedented withholding of Islamic funerary rites was intended as a form of posthumous punishment for both the individual in question and their community. It can be read as an act of necropolitical violence targeting the dead in order to discipline and dishonour the living. As a form of necropolitical statecraft, moreover, the official denial of burial rites served to delimit the boundaries of the political community by casting the illegitimate or problematic dead outside of the demos. In a further twist, the coup plotters were excised not only from the imagined community of the Turkish nation, but from the broader community of the faithful Muslim Ummah, a point to which I shall return below.

In light of the Directorate's orders, the funerals of the coup plotters were highly circumscribed. As I mentioned above, the first person buried at the Cemetery of Traitors was thirty-four-year-old Mehmet Karabekir, a military captain killed during the coup attempt.[29] Speaking about his decision to establish the cemetery, Istanbul's then mayor, Kadir Topbaş, told reporters:

> No cemetery will accept these people. We can't bury them in our indigent (pauper's) cemeteries because people of faith are buried there and that's not acceptable. So I ordered a place to be reserved and to call it the Cemetery of Traitors. Those who pass by should curse them. Everyone should curse them and not let them rest in their tombs. They cannot escape hell but we must make them suffer in their graves as well.[30]

Topbaş echoed the order issued by the Directorate of Religious Affairs and went even further, encouraging citizens to curse the dead. 'It's a loaded term,' he admitted, speaking of his decision to label the burial ground the Cemetery of Traitors. 'But they deserve it. They used bullets that ripped people apart. Wouldn't you call these men "traitors"?'[31] Karabekir was buried in an anonymous, unmarked grave with no family or witnesses present. To date, he is the only inhabitant of the rock-strewn, makeshift cemetery located near an open-air municipal dog shelter on the eastern outskirts of Istanbul. Several other graves have been opened up in anticipation of new arrivals, though the site resembles an abandoned worksite more than a burial ground. There is no tombstone or grave marker indicating the location of Karabekir's corpse. A large black-and-white sign that marked the entrance to the Cemetery of Traitors (*Hainler Mezarlığı*) was eventually removed by municipal authorities after gunshots were fired at Karabekir's grave.[32]

In other instances around the country, family members of coup plotters faced many obstacles in their efforts to bury their dead. Municipal authorities in the north-eastern coastal city of Ordu denied requests to bury junior officer Nedim Şahin in the town's cemetery. Şahin died in clashes with pro-government forces at the Police Special Forces Headquarters in Gölbaşı, just outside of Ankara. Speaking at the regional parliament, Ordu's mayor, Enver Yılmaz, asserted that 'We refuse to provide any burial space or funerary services for this individual, who betrayed the Turkish military and the Turkish nation. I informed all of our officials that Ordu is not a city that will harbour traitors in its soil. There will be no compromises with traitors!'[33]

Şahin's family had petitioned the city to bury his body in a public cemetery after holding requisite funeral prayers at a local mosque. All of these requests were denied. Ordu's mufti (a senior Muslim legal expert), Mustafa Kolukısaoğlu, said that 'These are traitors who rebelled against the state and were killed. They will not receive funeral prayers. Their bodies will not be brought into our mosques. No one will pray for them. Our religion commands this.'[34] Kolukısaoğlu added that he would bring legal charges against any religious functionary who performed religious rites for coup plotters or allowed their corpses to be brought into the city's mosques. Having been denied both a burial plot and religious funerary services, Şahin's family interred his body in their own land, in a hazelnut grove adjacent to their house. A similar dynamic unfolded in at least three other cities in Turkey, including Sivas, Samsun and Erzincan. In each case, local authorities denied family requests for public cemetery plots and religious services. Consequently, the families were compelled to bury the bodies themselves on their own properties.[35]

In another instance, local residents prevented the body of a coup plotter from being brought into the town mosque for funeral services. On 18 July 2016, family members of Major Mehmet Akkurt repatriated his corpse to his hometown of Umurlu (near Aydın) in southwestern Turkey in an effort to bury him there.[36] Umurlu residents turned out in droves believing that the body belonged to a pro-government soldier, but upon learning that it was a coup plotter, blocked access to the mosque where they had congregated. Police were brought in to maintain order. 'The funeral prayer will not be held here [at the mosque], because he is not a martyr,' a mosque official explained.[37] While local authorities allowed Akkurt to be buried in the municipal cemetery, the town's imam refused to perform funerary rites and prayers. Instead, this task was undertaken by a local citizen who finished his prayers with the statement: 'May God protect our people and our nation from internal and external enemies.'[38]

Public officials in Turkey were vehemently opposed to the idea that these infamous dead would be buried in their hometowns and, in many cases, they were able to block access to public cemeteries. While Turkish law guarantees citizens the right to burial, the state denied this possibility and went even further to ensure that no religious rites would be extended to its enemies. Through the differential treatment of the dead, the state sought to distinguish between its friends and foes. In denying burial rites to its enemies, it attempted to foreclose any possibility of public mourning. Through sovereign acts targeting the corpse that rendered the dead ungrievable, the Turkish state articulated the boundaries of its political community.

Conclusion: You Only Die Twice

At a press conference held a few weeks after the failed military coup in Turkey, US State Department spokesman Admiral John Kirby was asked whether the denial of religious rites to coup plotters constituted a violation of religious freedom. Kirby acknowledged that the freedom of expression, religion and worship were universal values that 'we obviously hold in very high regard'. Pressing him to clarify with specific reference to the US government's decision to bury Osama Bin Laden at sea in accordance with Islamic traditions, the reporter asked Kirby whether as a general principle he supported the idea that all individuals, irrespective of their crimes, should be granted requisite religious rites during burial. 'Absolutely,' Kirby responded. '[Bin Laden] was a famous example of how we observe that ourselves . . . In keeping with our belief in the freedom of worship, we believe that individuals should be accorded those customs, those traditions, those rites, to be laid to rest in keeping with the same practices by which they worshipped when they were alive.'[39]

While the actual circumstances behind Osama Bin Laden's burial remain uncertain, given the US government's reluctance to publicly release any photographic evidence of the act, Kirby's insistence that even enemies of the state should be accorded proper funerary rites in line with their religious beliefs and traditions is notable for several reasons.[40] First, it mirrors the position taken by other Western governments in the aftermath of acts of violence and terrorism carried out by self-professed jihadists on their territories. To give one recent example, French authorities buried the perpetrators of the *Charlie Hebdo* attacks, all of whom were French citizens, in Islamic cemeteries in their hometowns in France with requisite funerary rites and rituals.[41] Although their graves were unmarked and anonymous, 'to prevent any threat to public order and to preserve the tranquility of the city', according to one of the mayors who oversaw the process, the decision to extend religious funerary rites and privileges to terrorists is important for at least two other reasons.

First, it affirms the state's commitment to human rights, religious freedom and the dignity of all persons in death, thereby implicitly drawing a distinction between those who respect the bodies of their enemies and those who do not. In practice, this distinction may ring hollow given the well-documented abuse and torture of 'enemy combatants' by US soldiers in places like Abu Ghraib and Guantánamo. Yet the rhetorical force of Kirby's argument stems from the proposition that the US government holds the freedom of religious worship and other 'universal' values in 'very high regard', whereas others do not.

Bin Laden's burial at sea becomes legible within a global economy of violence that hinges upon legitimacy, in both form and content. The sanitary, law-abiding violence of the state stands in contrast to the spectacular violence perpetrated by terrorists and other illegitimate actors like ISIS or al-Qaeda, whose beheadings and suicide bombings are understood as archaic and barbaric. The treatment of bodies, both living and dead, serves a boundary maintenance function that helps distinguish the legitimate from the illegitimate, the civilised from the barbaric.

Furthermore, US and French efforts to extend religious burial rites to jihadists are important because these efforts also affirm the jihadists' identity as Muslims, thereby strengthening the link between Islam and violence and conferring a religious valence upon acts that might otherwise be construed as political. Turkey's decision to withhold religious rites for coup plotters while honouring pro-government soldiers and civilians as 'martyrs' is instructive when read alongside the US and French examples. Whereas American and French officials foreground the religious identities of their enemies, Turkish authorities rely on religious language and symbolism to honour their heroes.

For Turkey, a Muslim-majority country where a laïque state structure ensures that public religion is under the control of the state, the denial of Islamic funerary rites can be understood as a form of posthumous punishment. Religious authorities claimed that Islam forbids the extension of funerary rites in such circumstances, a claim that to the best of my knowledge has no religious justification.[42] Through this denial, officials sought not only to expel the putschists from the Turkish nation (as traitors) but also to dispense with their Muslim identity by turning them into infidels. Recall the public statement released by the Directorate of Religious Affairs, which argued that 'a funeral prayer is intended as an act of exoneration for the faithful, but these people, with the actions that they undertook, have disregarded not just individuals but also the law of an entire nation and therefore do not deserve exoneration from their faithful brothers and sisters'. In this formulation, the coup plotters experience two deaths: a physical, biological death that comes with the cessation of life, and a symbolic, figurative death that comes with their expulsion from the Turkish nation and its community of faith. Sovereign power is invested in the material and symbolic governance of the dead in order to shape the conditions of their memorialisation. In the process, dead bodies become a site upon and a means through which a new chapter of Turkish history is written.

Speaking to reporters after the establishment of the Cemetery of Traitors, Eren Keskin, a prominent lawyer and human rights activist in Turkey, argued that burial is a human right. 'We are living in a space where even the right to burial is taken out of people's hands,' she noted. 'I haven't seen anything like this anywhere in the world. It's completely incongruous with the concept of human rights and has no religious justification either.'[43] In March 2018, Keskin was sentenced to seven and a half years in prison for publishing articles that 'degraded the Turkish nation' and 'insulted the Turkish president'. She is not alone.

While the two-year state of emergency imposed after the failed military coup of 15 July 2016 was allowed to expire by Turkish authorities in 2018, the crackdown on political dissidents and opponents continues with alarming intensity. Turkey now holds the dubious honour of being the world's biggest jailer of journalists, surpassing both China and Egypt. In the years following the coup attempt, more than 30,000 people have been imprisoned on terror and coup related charges. Another 150,000 people have lost their jobs. This figure includes 6,021 academics and 4,463 judges and prosecutors. One hundred and eighty-nine media outlets have been shut down and 319 journalists have been arrested. The deans of more than 1,600 universities have been asked to resign and several academic departments have been shut down entirely.[44]

After a snap election held in July 2018, Erdoğan was sworn in for another five-year term as Turkey's president. His Justice and Development Party (AKP) has since proposed new anti-terrorism bills that retain measures from the state of emergency and that allow local governors to impose curfews and ban demonstrations by making some areas off limits to the public. While the politicisation of the dead and the treatment of dead bodies have been instrumental in legitimising the erosion of Turkey's already precarious democracy, the real victims of Turkey's necropolitics are the living, whose freedoms have deteriorated in the name of national unity and security.

Notes

1. 'Darbeciler için "vatan hainleri mezarlığı"'.
2. Banu Bargu, 'Another Necropolitics'.
3. Ibid.
4. See Aslı Zengin, 'Mortal Life of Trans/Feminism: Notes on "Gender Killings" in Turkey', and Nicholas Glastonbury, 'What Does the State Want from Dead Bodies? Suruç and the History of Unmournability'.
5. Bargu, 'Another Necropolitics', p. 3.
6. Max Weber, 'Politics as a Vocation', p. 33.
7. Achille Mbembe, 'Necropolitics'.
8. Ibid. p. 39.

9. Katherine Verdery, *The Political Lives of Dead Bodies: Reburial and Post-socialist Change*.
10. Ibid. p. 27.
11. For another excellent study of 'dead body politics' in Eastern Europe that uses the exhumation and reburial of Bela Bartók to analyze Hungarian state socialism, see Susan Gal, 'Bartók's Funeral: Representations of Europe in Hungarian Political Rhetoric'.
12. Finn Stepputat, *Governing the Dead: Sovereignty and the Politics of Dead Bodies*.
13. Sibel Bozdoğan, *Modernism and Nation Building: Turkish Architectural Culture in the Early Republic*, p. 282.
14. Leda Glyptis, 'Living Up to the Father: The National Identity Prescriptions of Remembering Atatürk; His Homes, His Grave, His Temple'.
15. For more on Anıtkabir and its role in shaping national memory see Christopher Wilson, *Beyond Anıtkabir: The Funerary Architecture of Atatürk and the Construction and Maintenance of National Memory*.
16. For a fascinating analysis of the internet presence of Turkish martyrs, see Julie Alev Dilmaç, 'Martyrs Never Die: Virtual Immortality of Turkish Soldiers'.
17. Benedict Anderson, *Imagined Communities: Reflections on the Origins and Spread of Nationalism*.
18. Ibid. p. 10.
19. For a timeline of the coup attempt as it unfolded, see <http://www.aljazeera.com/news/2016/07/turkey-timeline-coup-attempt-unfolded-160716004455515.html> (last accessed 28 May 2019).
20. A video of the broadcast is available online: <https://www.youtube.com/watch?v=6MW_MakickE> (last accessed 28 May 2019).
21. Tim Arango and Ceylan Yeginsu, 'Turks Can Agree on One Thing: US Was Behind Failed Coup'.
22. In August 2016, the *New York Times* reported that more than 45,000 civil servants from the Ministries of the Interior, Health, Culture and Tourism, National Education, Development, Economy, Forest and Water Management, Transport, Science Industry and Technology, Family and Social Policy, and Environment and Urban planning were dismissed, alongside thousands of military personnel, for their alleged links to Gülen.
23. 'Başbakan açıkladı: Kaç darbeci öldürüldü'.
24. 'Kahraman asker Ömer Halisdemir'in mezarını 100 bin kişi ziyaret etti'.
25. For video footage of the ceremony, see 'Erdoğan, Erol Olçak'ın cenaze töreninde gözyaşlarını tutamadı'.
26. A video of the funeral ceremony is available online: <https://www.youtube.com/watch?v=rAZra62hDfE> (last accessed 28 May 2019).
27. 'Diyanet: Öldürülen darbecilere din hizmeti verilmeyecektir'.
28. Ibid. The Directorate did, however, make an exception for soldiers who were forced to take part in the coup and 'who had no idea what they were doing or what they were involved in', stating that these individuals would not be barred from receiving religious services.

29. Not everyone has been so enthusiastic about the cemetery. Serhun Baturay, a fifty-seven-year-old volunteer at the municipal dog shelter adjacent to the cemetery, told reporters that 'they should have buried them somewhere far from our animals . . . They shouldn't be placed near our dogs. They shouldn't be anywhere in Turkey. They should be cremated and their ashes tossed into the ocean. There shouldn't be a trace of them anywhere in the country. As a Turkish citizen, I don't want such a thing.' Quoted in Associated Press, 'Turkey Builds Traitors' Cemetery for Insurgents Who Died in Failed Coup'
30. 'Darbeci askerler vatan hainleri mezarlığına gömülsün'.
31. 'Kadir Topbaş: Hain lafını hak ediyorlar'.
32. 'Hainler Mezarlığı'ndan kurşun sesleri . . . Ve tabela kaldırılıdı'.
33. 'Darbeci Astsubay'a mezar yeri verilmedi'.
34. Ibid.
35. For Erzincan (Semih Terzi) see 'Erzincan'da "Semih Terzi" Krizi'. For Sivas (Burak Dinler) see 'Darbeci diye öldürülen er Burak'ın ailesi "şehitlik" istedi'. For Samsun (Ercan Sen) see 'Darbeci subay Şen'e mezar yeri verilmedi, cenaze tarlaya gömüldü'.
36. 'Binbaşı Mehmet Akkurt'un Cenazesi Toprağa Verildi'.
37. See the news report, 'Darbeci Binbaşının Cenazesi Camiye Alınmadı'.
38. 'Binbaşı Mehmet Akkurt'un Cenazesi Toprağa Verildi'.
39. US Department of State, 'Daily Press Briefing', 29 July 2016.
40. For an alternative account of what happened to Osama Bin Laden's body, see Seymour Hersch, *The Killing of Osama Bin Laden*.
41. Although it should be noted that they initially attempted to 'repatriate' the corpses to Algeria and Mali, the two countries from which the perpetrators' parents had emigrated to France. See Balkan, 'Charlie Hebdo and the Politics of Mourning'.
42. According to Ibn Hazm, a Spanish-born Arab theologian and jurist who is considered a leading exponent of the Zāhirī (Literalist) school of jurisprudence, the '[f]uneral prayer should be offered for all Muslims, whether good or bad, including those sentenced to death and those that die fighting or in revolt. The imam, or anyone other than him, may lead the funeral prayers. Likewise, funeral prayers should be said for an innovator, provided his innovation does not become blasphemy, and prayer may be said for one who commits suicide or kills someone else. A funeral prayer may be offered in all such cases even though the deceased might have been the most evil person on the face of the earth.' See *Fiqh-us Sunnah, Vol. 4: Funerals and Dhikr*.
43. Quoted in 'Avukat Keskin: Hainler mezarlığı gömme-gömülme hakkına aykırı'.
44. See <http://www.turkeypurge.com> (last accessed 28 May 2019).

Bibliography

Anderson, Benedict, *Imagined Communities: Reflections on the Origins and Spread of Nationalism* (New York: Verso, 1983).

Arango, Tim, and Ceylan Yeginsu, 'Turks Can Agree On One Thing: US Was Behind Failed Coup', *New York Times*, 2 August 2016, <https://www.nytimes.com/2016/08/03/world/europe/turkey-coup-erdogan-fethullah-gulen-united-states.html?_r=0> (last accessed 21 October 2018).

Associated Press, 'Turkey Builds Traitors' Cemetery for Insurgents Who Died in Failed Coup', *The Guardian*, 28 July 2016, <https://www.theguardian.com/world/2016/jul/28/turkey-builds-traitors-cemetery-for-insurgents-who-died-in-failed-coup> (last accessed 21 October 2018).

'Avukat Keskin: Hainler Mezarlığı Gömme-Gömülme Hakkına Aykırı', *Birgün*, 27 July 2016, <https://www.birgun.net/haber-detay/avukat-keskin-hainler-mezarligi-gomme-gomulme-hakkina-aykiri-121746.html> (last accessed 22 October 2018).

Balkan, Osman, 'Charlie Hebdo and the Politics of Mourning', *Contemporary French Civilization* 41, no. 2 (2016): 253–71.

Bargu, Banu, 'Another Necropolitics', *Theory & Event* 19, no. 1, January 2016.

'Başbakan Açıkladı: Kaç Darbeci Öldürüldü', *Ihlas Haber Ajansı*, 17 August 2016, <http://www.iha.com.tr/haber-basbakan-acikladi-kac-darbeci-olduruldu-580952/> (last accessed 21 October 2018).

'Binbaşı Mehmet Akkurt'un Cenazesi Toprağa Verildi', *Habertürk*, 18 July 2016, <https://www.haberturk.com/gundem/haber/1268440-binbasi-mehmet-akkur-tun-cenazesi-topraga-verildi> (last accessed 22 October 2018).

Bozdoğan, Sibel, *Modernism and Nation Building: Turkish Architectural Culture in the Early Republic* (Seattle: University of Washington Press, 2002).

'Darbeci Askerler Vatan Hainleri Mezarlığına Gömülsün', *NTV*, 20 July 2016, <https://www.ntv.com.tr/turkiye/darbeci-askerlervatan-hainleri-mezarligina-gomulsun,uBU99Imkwk6qnOYJFf1_MA> (last accessed 21 October 2018).

'Darbeci Astsubay'a Mezar Yeri Verilmedi', *Vatan*, 19 July 2016, <http://www.gazetevatan.com/darbeci-astsubaya-mezar-yeri-verilmedi-968154-gundem/> (last accessed 22 October 2018).

'Darbeci Binbaşının Cenazesi Camiye Alınmadı', *YouTube*, 18 July 2016, <https://www.youtube.com/watch?v=zjkRnMzX9hg> (last accessed 22 October 2018).

'Darbeci diye Öldürülen Er Burak'ın Ailesi "Şehitlik" İstedi', *Doğan Haber Ajansı*, 8 August 2016, <https://www.dha.com.tr/haber-arsiv/darbeci-diye-oldurulen-er-burakin-ailesi-sehitlik-istedi/haber-1298165> (last accessed 22 October 2018).

'Darbeci Subay Şen'e Mezar Yeri Verilmedi, Cenaze Tarlaya Gömüldü', *CNN Türk*, 19 July 2016, <https://www.cnnturk.com/turkiye/darbeci-subay-sene-mezar-yeri-verilmedi-cenaze-tarlaya-gomuldu> (last accessed 22 October 2018).

'Darbeciler İçin "Vatan Hainleri Mezarlığı"', *Rudaw*, 20 July 2016, <http://www.rudaw.net/turkish/middleeast/turkey/200720163> (last accessed 22 October 2018).

Dilmaç, Julie Alev, 'Martyrs Never Die: Virtual Immortality of Turkish Soldiers', *Omega: Journal of Death and Dying* (January 2017): 1–17.

'Diyanet: Öldürülen Darbecilere Din Hizmeti Verilmeyecektir', *Bir Gün*, 19 July 2016, <https://www.birgun.net/haber-detay/diyanet-oldurulen-darbecilere-din-hizmeti-verilmeyecektir-120632.html> (last accessed 21 October 2018).

'Erdoğan, Erol Olçak'ın Cenaze Töreninde Gözyaşlarını Tutamadı', *CNN Türk*, 17 July 2016, <https://www.cnnturk.com/turkiye/erdogan-erol-olcakin-cenaze-toreninde-gozyaslarini-tutamadi> (last accessed 21 October 2018).

'Erzincan'da "Semih Terzi" Krizi', *Cumhuriyet*, 6 October 2016, <http://www.cumhuriyet.com.tr/haber/turkiye/610987/Erzincan_da_Semih_Terzi__krizi.html> (last accessed 22 October 2018).

Fiqh-us Sunnah, Vol. 4: Funerals and Dhikr, <http://hadithcollection.com/fiqh-ussunnah/385-Fiqh-us%20Sunnah%20Section%2062.%20Funeral%20Prayers%20(Salatul%20Janazah)/21434-fiqh-us-sunnah-volume-004-funerals-and-dhikr-fiqh-4049a.html> (last accessed 22 October 2018).

Gal, Susan, 'Bartók's Funeral: Representations of Europe in Hungarian Political Rhetoric', *American Ethnologist* 18, no. 3 (August 1991): 440–58.

Glastonbury, Nicholas (2015), 'What Does the State Want from Dead Bodies? Suruç and the History of Unmournability', *Jadaliyya*, 7 August 2015, <http://jadaliyya.com/Details/32347/%60What-Does-the-State-Want-from-Dead-Bodies%60-Suru%C3%A7-and-the-History-of-Unmournability> (last accessed 21 October 2018).

Glyptis, Leda, 'Living Up to the Father: The National Identity Prescriptions of Remembering Ataturk; His Homes, His Grave, His Temple', *National Identities* 10, no. 4 (2008): 353–72.

'Hainler Mezarlığı'ndan Kurşun Sesleri . . . Ve Tabela Kaldırılıdı', *Cumhuriyet*, 29 July 2016, <http://www.cumhuriyet.com.tr/haber/turkiye/576114/_Hainler_Mezarligi_ndan_kursun_sesleri..._Ve_tabela_kaldirildi.html> (last accessed 21 October 2018).

Hersh, Seymour, *The Killing of Osama Bin Laden* (New York: Verso, 2016).

'Kahraman Asker Ömer Halisdemir'in Mezarını 100 Bin Kişi Ziyaret Etti', *Haber Türk*, 13 August 2016, <https://www.haberturk.com/gundem/haber/1281330-kahraman-asker-omer-halisdemirin-mezarini-100-bin-kisi-ziyaret-etti> (last accessed 21 October 2018).

'Kadir Topbaş: Hain Lafını Hak Ediyorlar', *Hürriyet*, 26 July 2016, <http://www.hurriyet.com.tr/gundem/kadir-topbas-hain-lafini-hak-ediyorlar-40171039> (last accessed 21 October 2018).

Mbembe, Achille, 'Necropolitics', trans. Libby Meintjes, *Public Culture* 15, no. 1 (Winter 2013): 11–40.

Stepputat, Finn (ed.), *Governing the Dead: Sovereignty and the Politics of Dead Bodies* (Manchester: Manchester University Press, 2014).

US Department of State, 'Daily Press Briefing', 29 July 2016, <https://2009-2017.state.gov/r/pa/prs/dpb/2016/07/260680.htm> (last accessed 22 October 2018).

Verdery, Katherine, *The Political Lives of Dead Bodies: Reburial and Post-Socialist Change* (New York: Columbia University Press, 2000).

Wilson, Christopher, *Beyond Anıtkabir: The Funerary Architecture of Ataturk and the Construction and Maintenance of National Memory* (Burlington, VT: Ashgate, 2013).

Weber, Max, 'Politics as a Vocation', in David Owen and Tracy B. Strong (eds), *The Vocation Lectures* (Indianapolis: Hacket Publishing Company, 2004), pp. 32–94.

Zengin, Aslı, 'Mortal Life of Trans/Feminism: Notes on "Gender Killings" in Turkey', *TSQ: Transgender Studies Quarterly* 3, no. 1–2 (May 2016): 266–71.

TWELVE

Nightmare Knowledges: Epistemologies of Disappearance

Ege Selin Islekel

Between August 2015 and August 2016, 114 round-the-clock curfews were declared in eastern regions of Turkey. One of the longest of these took place in Silopi, where the residents could not leave their houses for a period of twenty-three days.[1] During the curfew, Taybet İnan, a fifty-seven-year-old mother of twelve, was shot in front of her house while she was returning from her neighbour's home. She was alive for about twenty hours afterwards before dying in the street, where her body remained for the following seven days. During this period, her family was not able to leave the house to retrieve her body or come to her aid while she was still alive.[2] At the end of seven days, İnan's body was first taken to the Şırnak Public Hospital, and then she was buried by local authorities at midnight.[3] According to the local authorities, there are no records of any calls made to remove her body during those seven days, and officials were only made aware of the incident after these seven days had passed. In a letter, however, İnan's son wrote that there must be some records, as he distinctly remembers that no one in the house was able to sleep during that time, for they were all worried that birds might prey upon her corpse.[4]

Even though her family was not allowed to attend the burial, İnan's case is considered an official burial by the state, with a designated gravesite. However, the relatives of those who are buried by the state do not always get any acknowledgements of the burial process or have information on the whereabouts of the burial site.[5] The Saturday Mothers, as mothers of the disappeared in Turkey have come to be known, have been meeting on Istiklal Street in Istanbul on Saturdays for the last 704 weeks at the time of writing this chapter. The oldest member of the Saturday Mothers,

Berfo Kırbayır, died at the age of 105 after thirty years of looking for her son Cemil Kırbayır, who was called in to a police station in 1984 'for five minutes'. During the thirty years that she was looking for her son, Kırbayır refused to lock her doors or close her windows in case her son might come back one night.[6] Kırbayır was one of the many Saturday Mothers who insisted that their disappeared relatives are present to them. Another one of the Saturday Mothers describes the presence of her son by saying: 'He is there before my eyes, and he will always remain. For instance, when I am alone, the neighbours visit in the evening, we sit and chat, but when they leave, I am left alone here. Until twelve o'clock, or eleven o'clock. Then he suddenly comes and sits beside me. "I see him now," I say to myself, "he is here."'[7]

Even though virtually all of the mothers insist on the presence of the disappeared, their remains are mostly absent. Very few people have been able to retrieve the bones of their disappeared relatives, or been informed as to where such remains might be. The remains were often reported to be in unofficial mass graves, such as unused wells, empty lots or trash disposal areas, and only later found by chance encounters.[8] *Newala Qaseba*, 'the River of Butchers', is one of these mass burial sites in Siirt, another town in eastern Turkey. While the remains of over 300 people are estimated to be here, the families of ninety-three people know with certainty that their relatives were thrown there. One of them states that, ever since, they have been going to *Newala Qaseba* to 'talk to the river'.[9] Despite its name, there is no river in *Newala Qaseba*, and what is called the 'River of Butchers' is but a large trash disposal area where civilians' entrance is not permitted.

This chapter works on discourses that are strange or that do not 'make sense', that emerge in the context of improper burial practices, such as the worry of Inan's family about birds landing on her body, the Saturday Mothers' insistence on the presence of their disappeared relatives or the families in *Newala Qaseba* talking to the river. I aim to understand how and why such discourses emerge, and specifically, what kind of resistant capacities these discourses carry in necropolitical spaces where life and the living are subsumed under the active production, regulation and optimisation of death. To this end, the chapter is divided into three parts: the first part analyses the relation between necropolitics and knowledge production in order to establish necropolitics not only as a political technology but also an epistemic one. The second part investigates the specific techniques of knowledge deployed in necropolitics. These techniques, which are here called 'necro-epistemic methods', target the temporal and logical coherence of memory in necropolitical spaces. The last part focuses on the practices of epistemic resistance, which work through mobilising perplexing realities in order to instigate counter-discourses that challenge official narratives about death. Overall, I argue that necropolitics is a power/knowledge assemblage, infused with technologies that work on memory and coherence, which function to produce unstable knowledges around death. These same knowledges, which I here call 'nightmare knowledges', however, can be politicised, insofar as they constitute instances of collective epistemic agency, where memory and grief are mobilised to challenge necropolitical rationalities.

Necropolitical Assemblages, Frames of Death

According to Michel Foucault, contemporary politics is defined not by traditional modes of sovereignty but rather by a kind of power that works to optimise life, which he calls biopolitics. For Foucault, sovereignty is primarily a model of power defined by its relation to laws and borders; as such, it is invested in life only through its threat to take life in the instances where borders are crossed or laws are broken. 'Sovereign power's effect on life is exercised only when the sovereign can kill.'[10] Such killing is done in the name of the sovereign, and therefore the punishment reflects both the sovereign decision and sovereign power.[11] Thus, the height of sovereign power, Foucault argues, is the moment in which life is taken, and therefore it must prolong and spectacularise that moment. In contrast to sovereignty, biopolitics takes life as its object, its main role is to 'to ensure, sustain and multiply life'.[12] For this reason, the methods of biopolitics are much more discreet, as it works through a normalising impulse on behalf of life. Thus, Foucault famously states, while sovereignty is shaped by a power to 'take life or let live', biopolitics works as a power to 'make live or let die', steeping its technologies in the midst of life.[13] Insofar as it is invested in life, death is 'embarrassing' to biopolitics.[14]

Various scholars after Foucault have indicated that the politics of life does not mean that there is no death involved in biopolitics. 'Life can be a threatening force,'[15] as Rosi Bradiotti asserts; as much as the principal goal of biopolitics is to optimise life, such optimisation is made possible through the regulation of death, as well as life. Achille Mbembe argues that biopolitics is inseparable from the presence of a yet another technology that he calls 'necropolitics', which dovetails with biopolitics and consists in the government of death and the dead. In necropolitics, the sovereign right to kill has found a normative basis in biopolitics and, therefore, now works in the production of 'death-worlds', where entire populations are positioned as having a close affinity with death.[16] Round-the-clock curfews, such as the one during which İnan died, are an example of such death-worlds, where sovereign killing is distributed beyond the purview of sovereignty, and is executed beyond its relation to laws and borders. As a result, death dealing is neither spectacular nor punitive. Instead, killing is normalised, and the occurrence of death within a curfew becomes the expected state of affairs.

Death-worlds, for Mbembe, are primarily spaces of normalised exceptionality, where life is subsumed under the powers of death. These are, in his words, 'new and unique forms of social existence in which vast populations are subjected to conditions of life conferring upon them the status of *living dead*'.[17] Necropolitics in this sense has a mobile relation to space: a necropolitical space refers not to a concrete geography (such as a city or a country), but to spaces of exceptionality. Curfew zones, prisons, mass burial sites or temporary detention centres transformed from parking lots or schools constitute necropolitical spaces, not because of their location, but precisely because of their detachment from their location. Mbembe asserts that politics is a 'work of death': if the death of İnan attests to this, it is not only because it demonstrates an exceptional form of sovereign killing, but rather shows the normalisation of sovereign killing to such an extent that all forms of life in these spaces are shaped by their relation to death.[18] As such, necropolitical spaces are spaces where not only the possibility of living, but also the entire content and fact of living, constituted by the ethical, political and epistemological conditions of life, are subsumed under death.

When it comes to death-worlds, the questions of how knowledge is produced, how information is distributed, the normative frames through which it is made available, the kinds of logics that are used and the value of truth attributed to knowledge are all central. Foucault argues that power and knowledge are never separable from each other, and, instead, he refers to 'power/knowledge assemblages' where 'the exercise of power perpetually creates knowledge and, conversely, knowledge constantly induces effects of power . . . It is not possible for power to be exercised without knowledge, it is impossible for knowledge not to engender power.'[19] Technologies of power are not inseparable from methods deployed in the field of knowledge. Relations of power that traverse the social body are indeed 'indissociable from a discourse of truth, and they can neither be established nor function unless a true discourse is produced, accumulated, put into circulation, and set to work.'[20] Similarly, in necropolitics, both the tactics that are deployed and the modes of knowledge that are produced, practised and distributed are shaped through the normalisation of death.

Invaluable work has been produced on normative knowledge production and information distribution around death in necropolitical spaces. Jasbir Puar, for example, argues that the necropolitical work of death is not separable from a normative impulse to protect and optimise a certain *kind of life*. For Puar, discourses such as that of the 'war on terror' attest to how necropolitics disguises itself by promoting the kinds of life that are normatively deemed acceptable.[21] Thus, Puar argues, what is at stake is a 'bio-necro collaboration' where the 'latter (necropolitics) makes its presence known at the limits and through the excess of the former; the former masks the multiplicity of its relationships to death and killing in order to enable the proliferation of the latter'.[22] The work of necropolitics, in this sense, would be known only in the cases where lives that are deemed normal and acceptable are endangered; promoting the wellbeing of these kinds of lives would entail actively hiding the necropolitical work of death.

This normative impulse can also be thought of in relation to what Judith Butler calls 'framing', where certain parts of the population, and even entire populations, can be positioned as 'deadly' or 'prone to death'.[23] The act of framing works on political and epistemological levels and refers to the destruction of parts of the population by considering them both political agents and objects of knowledge. İnan's death during the curfew and the general silence of the press regarding this death would be an example of such a frame, where the entire population of Silopi is positioned as akin to death, such that the actual dying that takes place is not an object of knowledge to be registered, known or distributed. Frames, in Butler's account, provide a general coherence for events that would otherwise be unrelated or incoherent. Normative production of these frames, moreover, works to regulate the very possibility of knowledge regarding the work of necropolitics.

However, knowledge of death is not limited to how it is reflected 'outside' of such death-worlds. People in the curfew zones know, for example, that going out on the street when they are not allowed to do so results in death, or that there would be records of dead bodies lying on the street and that those records would be buried or erased. If we are to take the question of knowledge in necropolitics seriously, it is necessary to discuss not only the knowledge *of* necropolitics, but also the knowledge produced *in* necropolitics. This would require an investigation regarding how information on the work of necropolitics is distributed as well as the knowledge production practices deployed in and through necropolitical mechanisms, where the inhabitants of death-worlds do not only constitute objects of knowledge but are also subjects thereof.

Necro-Epistemic Technologies: Memory and Coherence

In *'Society Must Be Defended'*, Foucault discusses what he calls 'subjugated knowledges', knowledges that emerge from interactions with power. There are two modes of subjugated knowledges that he mentions: the first one is the kind where the contents have been actively disguised in relation to political practices, 'buried and disguised in a functionalist coherence or formal systematisation', and second, 'the kinds of knowledges that have been disqualified from counting as knowledge'.[24] The former are the kinds of knowledges whose contents do not match the official or dominant discourse. These are, in other words, the kinds of knowledges that encounter active dismissal and denial and get buried in the archive. The archive of enforced disappearances is an example of this first mode of knowledge subjugation: consisting of names that were recorded or deleted many times or names that did not make it into the archive at all, numbers that are vague or shifting and discursive shortcuts used to obscure the facts. Thus piecing out the 'who/what/where' becomes difficult, if not impossible. The archive becomes obsolete, and its contents are buried. They may or may not be revealed at another time.

The second set of subjugated knowledges is a 'whole set of knowledges that have been disqualified as inadequate to their task or insufficiently elaborated'.[25] These are a whole set of 'localised knowledges' that do not rise to the threshold of official knowledge, where the agent is dismissed from credibility.[26] This kind of subjugation of knowledge is what Miranda Fricker calls 'epistemic injustice', where the agent is subjected to games of power that question 'their capacity as a knower'.[27] These modes of subjugated knowledges suggest that power works on knowledge in more ways than impacting the relation between what is said and how it is recorded.

What are the apparatuses of knowledge operative in necropolitical spaces? I argue that the epistemic techniques of necropolitics work not only on the documentation or suppression of memory, but also in shaping, producing and organising a collective memory of necropolitical death. These methods, which I refer to here as 'necro-epistemic methods', target the temporal and logical coherence of memory by impacting the credibility of the knower and blocking lucidity regarding the event. These methods involve targeting the coherence of temporality, the erasure of memory and the gendered hysterisation of the relatives of the disappeared.

One of the earliest descriptions of enforced disappearance, proposed by the UN Working Group on Enforced or Involuntary Disappearances (WG), states three main characteristics: (a) deprivation of liberty against the will of the person concerned; (b) involvement of government officials, at least indirectly by acquiescence; (c) refusal to acknowledge the detention and to disclose the fate and whereabouts of the person concerned.[28] In most cases of enforced disappearances in Turkey, the scenario follows these characteristics: a person is taken in with the direct or indirect involvement of state officials, yet the involvement is denied by the state. In many of the cases, the refusal to acknowledge the detention of the person is accompanied by the production of a temporal lag between the official account and the experiential one, where those who seek to find the missing person are given varying temporal explanations with no concrete reference to the experiential reality of the event. The case of the three people disappeared in the Doruklu village of Silopi is a typical example of this: on New Year's Eve, three people drive their own car to the Silopi District Gendarmerie Central Station, in order to bring a turkey to the soldiers, which they had demanded. When others in the village go to the gendarmerie asking after these three people when they have yet to return home, the answer they receive is that 'they left ten minutes ago', although those three people were never seen again.[29] Answers such as 'they left ten minutes ago' are most common in the cases where a disappeared person had gone to the government building voluntarily. In the cases of public detentions, on the other hand, the temporal lag in the accounts is much larger. In these cases, those seeking their relatives are told that the relatives have been released 'a long time ago' even though the person has disappeared just a day before.[30]

This temporal lag is often shaped along the lines of what Fricker calls 'testimonial injustice', where the testimonies of the individuals searching for the disappeared are not afforded credibility. One necro-epistemic method, then, is to create a temporal displacement where the experiential temporality is replaced by official temporality, but the official temporality does not constitute a coherent whole. This is perhaps most conspicuous in cases of 'unofficial public detentions', where the person is taken into detention from a public place such as a post office or a patisserie, when they were likely by themselves, by individuals that look like civilians, who are not in uniform.[31] While the witnesses describe the situation as 'abduction by unknown people', the relatives searching for the disappeared are told that the person was afterwards seen here and there, continuing to run errands. Ramazan Bilir, for example, searched for his brother for three years, pursuing a variety of claims made to him by officials about his brother being seen in various cities, and he himself finally disappeared after pursuing someone who told him that his brother was last seen in Mardin. The impact of such discordant narratives is to discredit the experiential memories of the relatives or the searchers by crowding them with conflicting information and thereby actively producing temporal discontinuities.

It is not only the possibility of temporal coherence that is targeted in necro-epistemic methods, however. It is also the logical coherence of events. Fricker, discussing epistemic injustice, describes another mode, which she names 'hermeneutical injustice', where the experiences of the knower become obscure to themselves, such that the means of making sense of the experience are made unavailable to the knower and the knower is left with a vague series of memories that consist of silences, unanswered questions and answers that do not make sense. In Fricker's words, hermeneutical injustice is an experience one encounters 'when a gap in the collective interpretative resources puts someone in an unfair disadvantage when it comes to making sense of their own experience'.[32] As another prominent necro-epistemic method, this gap is often times shaped along gendered dynamics between the relatives of the disappeared and the state. Take, for example, the Saturday Mothers as a specifically gendered group, consisting not only of mothers but also the sisters and wives of the disappeared. For many of them, the process involves both being sexualised as widowers and being hysterisised as grieving women. Many of them recall sexual advances enacted by the officials at one point, and being told that the disappearance is their own fault at other points. Being told that they are 'crazy' for still expecting the relatives to return is a common experience for many, as is being told that all they need is a husband.[33] Hermeneutical injustice refers to the insufficiency of one's own hermeneutical resources to make sense of the events unfolding; between the silences, requests for sexual favours, and being held accountable for the continued absence of the disappeared, many of the women indeed refer precisely to 'not understanding' what is happening, or why it is happening.[34]

Such a lack of understanding or events 'not making sense' is not a peripheral but rather a fundamental aspect of enforced disappearances. Many of the elements that make up the organised system called 'enforced disappearance' are unbelievable themselves. As Avery Gordon states, 'secret arrest, transportation under cover of darkness, the refusal to give information as to the person's whereabouts, and the belief that "deterring" resistance could be best accomplished by people vanishing "without a trace" are the elements that refigure the system of repression known as "disappearance"'.[35] From secret detention centres to unrecorded torture locations to random mass burial sites, what makes up the system of enforced disappearance is its improbability, where the possibility of corroborating information is blocked at each and every step, and even when it is corroborated and concrete, it does not become any less difficult to 'believe'. Not understanding, in many of these cases, can remain even when the relatives learn of minor or major aspects of the whereabouts of the disappeared. For example, the relatives of victims in *Newala Qaseba*, some of whom were told at some point that the remains of their loved ones are there in the pile of trash, report waking up some mornings utterly convinced that the whole thing 'was a dream and nothing more' and still can't believe that it is true.[36]

The last necro-epistemic method targets memory altogether and makes the event unmemorable, where the event or the possibility of the event is taken away, and those who remain are left with blocks of absences in the epistemological web. As Antonious Robben states, 'the anonymous burial of the executed and the disappeared entailed their physical, social, political, legal and spiritual eradication'.[37] In most of the cases of disappearance, there are no records of the person disappeared: no records of death or funeral, but also no record of detention, court orders, and, in many cases, no records of birth, either. The name of the disappeared may become a forbidden subject, where uttering the name in public might put the speaker at risk of detention.[38] Erasure involves the eradication of the possibility of remembering, where those who remember can also disappear.[39] In the absence of records, there is no person, no body, no one to disappear in the first place; in the absence of utterances, there is no loss, nothing to grieve and nothing to remember. Banu Bargu calls this process 'invisibilisation', which 'renders bodies, history and violence invisible'.[40] This invisibilisation erases not only the person disappeared, but also the world in which the possibility of this person existed, and the world to which the person has disappeared.

Rendering invisible is inseparable from rendering unmemorable: the collective oblivion of necropolitics is the effect of such an act of rendering unmemorable. During the curfews when İnan died, Ahmet Davutoğlu, the prime minister at the time, gave multiple speeches where he argued that there is 'not a single dead civilian' in the towns with curfews.[41] In the case of enforced disappearances, many were attributed by the state to counter-guerilla activity.[42] The families of *Newala Qaseba*, on the other hand, were repeatedly told that there are only animal bones and random clothes there, because it is a trash disposal area after all, and the things they see there are trash, and nothing more.

María del Rosario Acosta refers to 'oblivion in collective memory', where the traces of violence can be erased in such a way that the remainders of memory do not make sense beyond inducing horror.[43] Similarly, disappeared people, unburied bodies and trash disposal areas where dogs dig up human bones become, in the oblivion of collective memory, nothing more than tales that are told. For these tales there is little to no evidence beyond instances of women who were told their husbands purposefully left them without any logical rationale for their supposed 'actions', people who disappear while looking for their disappeared relatives and images of dead bodies that are hard to imagine in the first place. What these tales leave behind is, as Gordon says, 'a society filled with ghosts', inundated with uncorroborated memories, illogical statements, disappeared people who have never existed and disjointed temporalities consisting of official and unofficial moments.[44]

Nightmare Knowledges and Epistemic Resistance

As Foucault says, 'Where there is power, there is resistance.'[45] There is no method of power that works only in a unilateral form, in the mode of domination. Instead, power permeates life and death, and so does resistance. In *Starve and Immolate*, Bargu refers to the ways in which life and death emerge in contemporary politics not only as objects of power, but also as objects of resistance.[46] Insofar as the biopolitical infusion of life is inseparable from the necropolitical work of death, resistances that work in the name of life are also coupled with those that weaponise life. Bargu refers to this form of resistance as 'necroresistance', which 'negates life and turns death against the power regime'.[47] Just as life and death are not solid categories that are separate from the field of power relations, so are they intimately linked in practices of resistance: if power can work on death, so too can death be politicised against power.

Necropolitics, however, is not only a mechanism of power that works to produce and regulate death. It rather is a power/knowledge assemblage, where the production and regulation of knowledge constitute a fundamental aspect of its work. As such, it is necessary to see not only death itself, but also the knowledge of death as a possible site of resistance. An analysis of death as an object of politics thus requires us to pay attention to resistant knowledge production practices that are played out around death and the knowledges established through such resistances, which expose the incoherence of necro-epistemic methods and make space for counter-memories and counter-discourses.

How can the knowledge of death be taken up and politicised in order to challenge necro-epistemic methods? Such resistance depends on what I call 'nightmare knowledges', knowledges that are born out of necro-epistemic techniques and yet work to politicise the knowledge of death in response to these techniques. If necro-epistemic methods target the coherence and continuity of memory, nightmare knowledges demonstrate modes of epistemic resistance precisely because they work to mobilise perplexity by underlining the incoherence born out of these methods, and making space for counter-memories that challenge the official discourse.

José Medina states that epistemologies of resistance are built on the premise that the subjects of epistemic injustice are not solely subjected to injustice but are also endowed with the epistemic capacity to survive, build relations and resist in the context of such injustice.[48] Insofar as power is not only exercised from a single locus of domination, resistance does not only mean opposition. 'Points of resistance are everywhere in the power network ... producing cleavages in a society that shifts about, fracturing unities and effecting regroupings, furrowing across individuals themselves, cutting them up and remolding them, marking off irreducible regions in them.'[49] Resistance takes on multiple shapes in forming subjects and knowledge while destabilising and fracturing relations of power. In resistant epistemologies, locating resistance requires investigating those cuts, moulds and cleavages, in individuals and collectives, memories and forgettings.

Medina asserts that one way epistemic resistance can be experienced is through 'perplexity', where, instead of a directly oppositional movement, resistance is experienced as 'more like being pulled in different directions from the inside' or 'like feeling a rupture'.[50] The knower is perplexed insofar as their experiential memory is disjointed from the dominant discourse, and yet the dominant discourse itself does not constitute a coherent whole. Mobilising perplexity as epistemic resistance entails two aspects: first, challenging the dominant discourse by pointing to the incoherencies of the official discourse, and second, claiming experiential memory in order to reveal the ways in which what is recorded is no more credible than what is experienced. In necropolitical spaces, perplexity is produced precisely by necro-epistemic methods, which target the temporal and rational coherence of memory by discrediting the agents and erasing their experiences. Nightmare knowledges, on the other hand, mobilise this perplexity by pointing to the incoherencies of the official discourse and challenging the boundaries of necropolitical rationalities, such as the boundaries between dream and reality, memory and imagination or reason and unreason.

Many of the Saturday Mothers, when asked to explain their experiences for the last thirty years, describe these years as a series of dreams. One of them describes a recurring dream in which: 'I see him in my sleep. "Ayşe", he calls out to me, I look up, and I see my deceased son next to him, too. He asks me, "Ayşe, do your eyes still see?" and "Yes," I reply. "Do you see the white rock over there?" he asks me, "Yes, I do," I reply. "Go there, you will find my clothes," he says. There is a hill, a very high hill.'[51] As much as this is a recurring dream for her, it does not belong singularly to her. Many of the Mothers have similar dreams, dreams where they find the person, dreams where they sort through cadavers, trying to dig out the one that is theirs, or dreams where they come to the verge of finding the clue to the disappearance of the person. Some describe the last time they saw the person as the recurring dream that they have, where they put the person 'in a white car and leave'.[52] The white car that they see is a white Toros, a station wagon Renault, the type of car that was used by the Gendarmerie Intelligence and the pro-state militia throughout the 1980s and 1990s.[53] Many of them describe the experience of Berfo Kırbayır, where the disappeared person comes and sits with them and looks at them, long and hard. All too often, the person who comes and sits with the mothers is wearing pyjamas, as they did when they were taken away.[54]

In the consistent repetition of these dreams or in Berfo Kırbayır's conviction to not lock her doors or windows, the perplexities involved in the experience of disappearance become clear: the perplexity regarding the unknown fate of the disappeared person, which is all too often simply death, and even more so, the perplexity that comes out of questioning whether a person can actually vanish in the first place. As one of the Mothers says, a person is *not* a bird that flies away; after all, one cannot just disappear into the abyss. Amnesty International states that 'disappearance is a misnomer. Many prisoners who have "disappeared" may well, at worst, have ceased to be. None, however, is lost or vanished. Living or dead, each is in a very real place.'[55] Mobilising this perplexity by referring to dreams reveals that a world in which people vanish into thin air is no less unbelievable or fantastic as it stands than the dreams that their relatives have. Indeed, the dreams of the pyjamas or the white car all too often continue to haunt those who remain. These dreams serve as a reminder that what is real and not a dream forms a thin thread that ties together nothing other than unbelievable facts. As Gordon says, 'Spiraling between unbelievable facts and potent fictions, the knowledge of disappearance cannot but be bound up with the bewitching and brutal breaks and armature of disappearance itself.'[56] Nightmare knowledges mobilise perplexity by reminding that what is official is not any more realistic than dreams and no more credible than memories.

Perplexity is not an impasse. Rather, it is accompanied by a certain lucidity regarding incredulity not only towards the official discourse, but also towards the event itself and the cognitive attitudes that underlie necro-epistemic methods. Medina calls such lucidity 'meta-lucidity', which 'involves not just lucidity about the social world, but about the cognitive attitudes, cognitive structures, and cognitive repertoires of those who navigate the social world'.[57] This is the kind of lucidity that arises from a 'double consciousness', from looking inward and outward at the same time. It looks inwards 'insofar as it recognizes, through the internal friction of the perspectives available to itself, the limitations and obstacles of cognitive elements'.[58] In this sense, nightmare knowledges emerge out of 'looking inwards', as much as they refer to a certain knowledge that understands the limitations of the accounts offered in the official discourse because they can have access to both the official discourse and the experiential and collective memory. People in *Newala Qaseba* know, for example, that the bones that they see are not actually animal bones; or İnan's family knows that there have been calls to report her body on the street, that what is nightmarish about what is real lies precisely in that blank space between the said and unsaid. At the same time, nightmare knowledges are products of 'looking outwards' insofar as they come with the realisation that what is taking place is not singularly their experience, or that necro-epistemic methods work not only on particular subjects, but also on groups, on entire parts of the population. If dreams take up such space in their accounts, it is precisely because they know that these dreams are not products of singular psychic processes but, rather, of collective experiences. Nightmare knowledges mobilise this knowledge to remember that nightmarish gap between uncorroborated memories and unbelievable facts.

Meta-lucidity ensures that the resistance of nightmare knowledges is not born only in oppositional terms, but in perplexities that work to mobilise the gap between dream and reality, memory and forgetting. Nightmare knowledges are the results of what Medina calls 'guerrilla pluralisms' insofar as they work to multiply both the sources and methods of knowledge by shifting the space of credible knowledge from written word to memory. 'Resistance is not simply something that happens to us, but rather is something we do (or fail to do)'; resistance is, indeed, a product of active remembering, mobilising memory and mobilising the perplexity of the divide between the real and the surreal.[59]

Gordon states, 'Disappearance is an exemplary instance in which the boundaries of rational and irrational, fact and fiction, subjectivity and objectivity, person and system, conscious and unconscious, knowing and unknowing, are constitutively unstable.'[60] Just as these divides become unstable, so does the distinction between complete and incomplete memories, corroborated and uncorroborated remembrances: one of the ways in which resistant memories function is to remember and to remind others that what took place is impossible to remember. The insistence of the Saturday Mothers and the relatives of *Newala Qaseba* in remembering the details, the colour of the pyjamas that the person was wearing, the exact words that they said, the white car that took them, is a work of making memory from its absence. The act of remembering when there are no corroborating memories is a collective act of mobilising memory as a resistance mechanism. Take the emphasis on the uniqueness of each individual: virtually every relative discusses the person lost as a 'wonderful person', as a 'person that everyone loved', as a person 'who had never even hurt an ant in their lives'.[61] In the absence of dead bodies or disappeared persons, this emphasis weaves a person out of memory, in order to produce an alternative frame than can displace the official discourse. As Acosta Lopez states, 'memory can make history precisely by erasing it'.[62] Collective memory practices in *Newala Qaseba* and of the Saturday Mothers attest to such a work of actively erasing the official history, insofar as they produce frames that challenge this discourse through the 'unresolvable excess' that emerges in the death-worlds of necropolitics.[63]

Prolonged grief, on the other hand, mobilises memory in order to disrupt necro-epistemic temporalities: it functions as a method of claiming another temporal regime than the fractured one of necropolitical time. One of the mothers of *Newala Qaseba* says that she turned her home into a 'funeral house' thirty years ago, even though her son never had a formal funeral. As funeral houses are houses of grief, her house never leaves the state of mourning, she has been 'crying for thirty years', and she will do so until she dies.[64] Many of the Saturday Mothers recall being told to 'move on', some being told to find a new husband, and others to devote themselves to their children.[65] Instead, they all declare their commitment to not stop grieving, no matter how much time passes, and state that they will 'never forget'. Active remembering reminds us that grief is not simply a personal process but a collective one, one that is shared in funeral houses where there are no bodies or in weekly activist meetings that are regularly disrupted by the police. The insistence on collective prolonged grief reveals itself as a method of politicising grief by disrupting the necropolitical temporal order. If the collective oblivion of necropolitics proposes a temporality that is composed of fractured moments and replaced memories, prolonged grief opens up counter-temporalities that extend over time, which work through adding together ruptured memories, by ceaselessly remembering and sharing what is meant to be forgotten a long time ago.

Nightmare knowledges denote modes of political-epistemic agency, which can produce modalities of coherence out of the absence of temporal consistency. This agency can also produce memories within the impossibility of remembering as such and work to create 'counter-discourses' that are not only in opposition to necro-epistemic discourses but also revealing of the incoherence that is rooted in these discourses. The world of necropolitics is 'filled with ghosts', as Gordon says, so the work of nightmare knowledges is to 'recognise the world that the ghost conjures up'.[66] Such conjuring requires resistance that resembles Medina's 'guerrilla pluralism', which consists in developing counter-discourses, weaving words out of silences and memories out of forgettings. Nightmare knowledges comprise precisely such work, a collective epistemic agency that is born out of the weavings of dreams and reality, told and untold statements and uncorroborated memories. The work of nightmare knowledges is a work of conjuring up ghosts, insofar as these apparitions present the possibility of another kind of discourse and another kind of memory.

Nightmare Knowledges: Necropolitics of Knowledge

Power, as Foucault says, does not function without relation to knowledge: instead, it works to infiltrate knowledge, mould and bend it, work in and through it. If necropolitics is a kind of power that works to subsume life and the living under the overwhelming presence of death, such work does not take place without thoroughly investing itself in epistemic methods. These 'necro-epistemic methods' transform the knowledge of death itself into an object of power. They work on the political and epistemic agency of the subjects by targeting their agency as knowers through methods of epistemic injustice.

The experience of mass graves and enforced disappearances points us to such a work of epistemic injustice, where disappearance shows itself in the destabilisation of temporal coherence, testimonial injustice through gendered hysterisisation, and erasure of memory. These methods imply both testimonial and hermeneutical injustice, insofar as they both rely on the erasure of credible epistemic agents and the targeting of their memories. Necro-epistemic methods work on the knowledge of death, knowledge consisting in not only what is known of death, but also what is knowable and what is thinkable in relation to death.

On the other hand, methods of power do not exist in the absence of resistance. Just as death is an object not only of power but also of resistance, so is the knowledge of death, which is contested and politicised. Necro-epistemic methods do not work as a unilateral vector without obstruction: instead, they open up cleavages of memory and forgetting, gaps between dreams and concrete reality, a world where living is not simply subsumed under death but is rather haunted by the dead. What emerges in and through necro-epistemic methods are nightmare knowledges, knowledges that do not fit within the proposed rationalities of death and dying.

Nightmare knowledges are products of epistemic resistance, which challenge the proposed lucidity of the official discourse through mobilising perplexities, blurring the distinction between dreams and reality in order to reveal what is not realistic in official knowledge. If necropolitics works through the production of an official knowledge that is shaped by oblivion, by rendering testimonies incredible and experiences incomprehensible, nightmare knowledges work precisely to mobilise perplexity. In Berfo Kırbayır's insistence on not locking her doors, the families of *Newala Qaseba* visiting the trash disposal area in order to talk to the river, and İnan's family's worry that birds may have preyed on her body when she remained on the street, what is at stake is the production of another discourse – a counter-discourse that consists of weaving together unsaid statements, incomplete moments and memories that reveal an arsenal of nightmare knowledges that attest to the possibility of epistemic agency in the death-worlds of necropolitics.

Notes

1. Türkiye İnsan Hakları Vakfı, '16 Ağustos 2015–16 Ağustos 2016 Tarihleri Arasında Sokağa Çıkma Yasakları ve Yaşamını Yitiren Siviller Bilgi Notu', 20 August 2016.
2. Şeyhmus Çakan, 'Turkish "Cleansing" Operation Rocks Southeastern Cities', *Reuters*, 25 December 2015.
3. 'Taybet Inan 23 Gün Sonra Defnedildi', *T24*, 11 January 2016.
4. *7 Roj 7 Sev*.
5. Unlike many others mentioned in this chapter, Taybet Inan was given a burial, even though her family was not allowed at the funeral, and she has an official burial site.
6. Özgür S. Göral, Ayhan Işık and Özlem Kaya, *Unspoken Truth*, p. 96.
7. Ibid.
8. This information was taken from <http://www.ihddiyarbakir.org/Map.aspx> (last accessed 11 March 2017). The website provided a complete map of reported mass graves in Turkey and their specifics. However, it is no longer functional, as a number of the organisers have since been arrested. For information on the map, see Felat Bozarslan and Serdar Sunar, 'Toplu Mezarlarda 4201 Ceset Var', *Radikal*, 16 December 2014, and Mahmut Oral, '348 Mezar, 4 bin 201 Ceset', *Cumhuriyet*, 16 December 2014.
9. *Mirî û jî sax/Dead and Alive*.
10. Michel Foucault, *'Society Must Be Defended'*, p. 240.
11. Michel Foucault, *Discipline and Punish*, p. 47.
12. Michel Foucault, *History of Sexuality*, p. 138.
13. Ibid.
14. Ibid.
15. Rosi Braidotti, 'Bio-Power and Necro-Politics', p. 19.
16. Achille Mbembe, 'Necropolitics', p. 12.
17. Ibid. p. 40.
18. Ibid. p. 16.
19. Michel Foucault, 'Prison talk', pp. 51–2.
20. Ibid.

21. Jasbir Puar, *Terrorist Assemblages*, p. 35.
22. Ibid. p. 36.
23. Judith Butler, *Frames of War*, p. 34.
24. Foucault, *'Society Must be Defended'*, p. 6.
25. Ibid.
26. For Foucault, discourses are formed through multiple sources, which are at times in conflict with each other. Similarly, what I refer to as 'official discourse' here is constituted through the words of state officials, records in the state archives and the mainstream media. The role of oppositional media, however, is quite varying, insofar as there is not a unified identity for such media. Forms of oppositional media take different roles in corroborating the official discourse at some points and challenging it at others. It is important to note that a large number of journalists from the oppositional media, reporting on the curfews, have been arrested and imprisoned. For more information on journalists' detentions, see 'Turkey' in Amnesty International, *Report 2017/2018*. For more on discourse formation, see Foucault, *Archeology of Knowledge*.
27. Miranda Fricker, *Epistemic Injustice*, p. 19.
28. Mária Fernanda Perez Solla, *Enforced Disappearances*, p. 8.
29. Göral, Işık and Kaya, *Unspoken Truth*, p. 38.
30. Ibid. p. 42.
31. Gökçen Alpkaya, 'Kayıplar Sorunu ve Türkiye', p. 48.
32. Fricker, p. 1.
33. *Holding Up the Photograph*.
34. Ibid.
35. Avery F. Gordon, *Ghostly Matters*, p. 72.
36. *Mirî û jî sax/Dead and Alive*.
37. Antonius C. G. M. Robben, 'Exhumations, Territoriality, and Necropolitics in Chile and Argentina', p. 57.
38. Alpkaya, 'Kayıplar Sorunu ve Türkiye', p. 48.
39. Banu Bargu, 'Sovereignty as Erasure', p. 61.
40. Ibid.
41. 'Davutoğlu: Cizre'de Tek Bir Sivil Kayıp Yok', *BBC News*, 10 September 2015.
42. Gökçen Alpkaya, İlkem Altındaş, Öznur Sevdiren and Emel Ataktürk Sevimli, *Enforced Disappearances, Conduct of the Judiciary*, p. 39.
43. María del Rosario Acosta López, 'One Hundred Years of Forgottenness', p. 6.
44. Gordon, *Ghostly Matters*, p. 78.
45. Foucault, *History of Sexuality*, pp. 95–6.
46. Bargu, *Starve and Immolate*, p. 54.
47. Ibid. p. 85.
48. José Medina, *The Epistemology of Resistance*.
49. Bargu, *Starve and Immolate*, p. 85.
50. Medina, *The Epistemology of Resistance*, p. 6.
51. Göral, Işık and Kaya, *Unspoken Truth*, p. 78.
52. *Holding Up the Photograph*.

53. Göral, Işık and Kaya, *Unspoken Truth*, p. 78. For more information on the white Toros and its role in collective memory, see Caleb Lauer, 'The Long Read: Where Are Turkey's Disappeared?' *The National*, 21 May 2015.
54. Göral, Işık and Kaya, *Unspoken Truth*, p. 87.
55. Gordon, *Ghostly Matters*, p. 87.
56. Ibid. p. 76.
57. Medina, *The Epistemology of Resistance*, p. 196.
58. Ibid.
59. Ibid.
60. Gordon, *Ghostly Matters*, p. 102.
61. Göral, Işık and Kaya, *Unspoken Truth*, p. 75.
62. Acosta López, 'One Hundred Years of Forgottenness', p. 12.
63. Ibid.
64. *Mirî û jî sax/Dead and Alive*.
65. *Holding Up the Photograph*.
66. Gordon, *Ghostly Matters*, p. 66.

Bibliography

7 Roj 7 Şev, short film, directed by Ali Bozan (Turkey, 2017).
Amnesty International, 'Journalists in Turkey', *The State of World's Human Rights: Report 2017/2018*.
Amnesty International, 'Turkey: For Journalists Turkey Has Become a Dungeon', *Amnesty International*, 3 May 2018, <https://www.amnesty.org/en/latest/news/2018/05/turkey-for-journalists-turkey-has-become-a-dungeon/> (last accessed 13 November 2013).
Acosta López, María del Rosario, 'One Hundred Years of Forgottenness', in *Philosophical Readings* (2018, forthcoming).
Alpkaya, Gökçen, İlkem Altındaş, Öznur Sevdiren and Emel Ataktürk Sevimli, *Enforced Disappearances, Conduct of the Judiciary*, ed. Murat Çelikkın, Gamze Hızlı, trans. Fethi Keleş (Istanbul: Truth, Justice and Memory Center, n.d.)
Alpkaya, Gökçen, 'Kayıplar Sorunu ve Türkiye', *Ankara Universitesi Siyasal Bilgiler Fakultesi Dergisi* 50, no. 3 (1995): 35–61.
Bargu, Banu, 'Sovereignty as Erasure: Rethinking Enforced Disappearances', *Qui Parle: Critical Humanities and Social Sciences* 23, no. 1 (2014): 35–75.
Bargu, Banu, *Starve and Immolate: The Politics of Human Weapons* (New York: Columbia University Press, 2014).
Bozarslan, Felat, and Serdar Sunar, 'Toplu Mezarlarda 4201 Ceset Var', *Radikal*, December 16, 2014, <http://www.radikal.com.tr/turkiye/toplu-mezarlarda-4201-ceset-var-1252618/> (last accessed 13 November 2018).
Braidotti, Rosi, 'Biomacht und nekro-Politik. Uberlegungen zu einer Ethik der Nachhaltigkeit', *Springerin, Hefte fur Gegenwartskunst* 13, no. 2, Fruhjahr, 2007.
Butler, Judith, *Frames of War: When is Life Grievable?* (New York: Verso, 2010).

Çakan, Şeyhmus, 'Turkish "Cleansing" Operation Rocks Southeastern Cities', *Reuters*, 25 December 2015, <https://www.reuters.com/article/us-turkey-kurds-idUSKBN0U80FQ20151226> (last accessed 13 November 2018).
'Davutoğlu: Cizre'de Tek Bir Sivil Kayıp Yok', *BBC News*, 10 September 2015, <https://www.bbc.com/turkce/haberler/2015/09/150910_davutoglu_cizre> (last accessed 13 November 2018).
Foucault, Michel, *The Archeology of Knowledge and The Discourse on Language*, trans. A. M. Sheridan Smith (New York: Pantheon Books, 1971).
Foucault, Michel, *The History of Sexuality, Volume 1: An Introduction*, trans. Robert Hurley (New York: Vintage Books, 1978).
Foucault, Michel, 'Prison talk' in *Power/Knowledge: Selected Interviews and Other Writings*, trans. Colin Gordon, ed. Colin Gordon, Leo Marshal, John Mepham, Kate Sopher (New York: Pantheon, 1980).
Foucault, Michel, *'Society Must Be Defended': Lectures at Collège de France 1975–1976*, ed. Mauro Bentani and Alessandro Fontana, trans. David Macey (New York: Picador, 1997).
Fricker, Miranda, *Epistemic Injustice: Power and the Ethics of Knowing* (Oxford: Oxford University Press, 2007).
Gordon, Avery F., *Ghostly Matters: Haunting and the Sociological Imagination* (Minneapolis and London: University of Minnesota Press, 2008).
Göral Özgür Sevgi, Ayhan Işık and Özlem Kaya, *Unspoken Truth: Enforced Disappearances* (Istanbul: Truth, Justice and Memory Center, 2013).
Holding Up the Photograph, documentary (Istanbul: Truth, Justice and Memory Center, 2014).
Lauer, Caleb, 'The Long Read: Where Are Turkey's Disappeared?' *The National*, 21 May 2015, <https://www.thenational.ae/arts-culture/the-long-read-where-are-turkey-s-disappeared-1.122645.> (last accessed 13 November 2018).
Mbembe, Achille, 'Necropolitics', trans. Libby Meintjes, *Public Culture* 15, no. 1 (Winter 2003): 11–40.
Medina, José, *The Epistemology of Resistance: Gender and Racial Oppression, Epistemic Injustice, and Resistant Imaginations* (Oxford: Oxford University Press, 2013).
Mirî û jî sax/Dead and Alive, documentary, directed by Bilge Demirtaş, Alper Elitok, Can Gündüz, Murat Kocaman and Osman Şişman (Turkey, 2015).
Oral, Mahmut, '348 Mezar, 4 bin 201 Ceset', *Cumhuriyet*, 16 December 2014, <http://www.cumhuriyet.com.tr/haber/turkiye/163719/348_toplu_mezar__4_bin_201_ceset.html.> (last accessed 13 November 2018).
Perez Solla and Mária Fernanda, *Enforced Disappearances in International Human Rights* (Jefferson and London: McFarland & Co. Inc., 2006).
Puar, Jasbir K., *Terrorist Assemblages: Homonationalism in Queer Times* (Durham, NC and London: Duke University Press, 2007).
Robben, Antonious C. G. M., 'Exhumations, Territoriality, and Necropolitics in Chile and Argentina', in Francisco Ferrándiz and Antonious C. G. M Robben (eds), *Necropolitics: Mass Graves and Exhumations in the Age of Human Rights* (Philadelphia: University of Pennsylvania Press, 2015).

Taussig, Michael, *The Nervous System* (London and New York: Routledge, 1992).

'Taybet Inan 23 Gün Sonra Defnedildi', *T24*, 11 January 2016, <http://t24.com.tr/haber/taybet-inan-23-gun-sonra-defnedildi-esi-ve-cocuklari-izin-verilmedigi-icin-cenazeye-katilamadi,323748> (last accessed 13 November 2018).

Türkiye İnsan Hakları Vakfı, '16 Ağustos 2015-16 Ağustos 2016 Tarihleri Arasında Sokağa Çıkma Yasakları ve Yaşamını Yitiren Siviller Bilgi Notu', 20 August 2016, <http://tihv.org.tr/16-agustos-2015-16-agustos-2016-tarihleri-arasinda-sokaga-cikma-yasaklari-ve-yasamini-yitiren-siviller-bilgi-notu/> (last accessed 13 Novemeber 2018).

United Nations Human Rights Office, 'International Convention for the Protection of All Persons from Enforced Disappearance (ICCPED)', *United Nations Human Rights Office of The High Commissioner*, 1980, <http://www.ohchr.org/EN/HRBodies/CED/Pages/ConventionCED.aspx.> (last accessed 15 April 2016).

INDEX

15 July 2016, 12, 18, 29, 46, 49, 53, 57, 64, 232, 237–8, 240, 247; *see also* failed coup; coup d'état
1980 coup, 10, 140, 143, 209–10, 219, 238

Academics for Peace, 89n24, 90; *see also* Peace Petition
Agamben, Giorgio, 5, 6, 50, 224n19
Alagöz case, 166–7, 178
alterisation, 18, 216
Anıtkabir, 236
assemblage
  biosovereign, 130
  medico-political, 15, 118–19, 127, 129–30
  necropolitical, 255
  power/knowledge, 19, 255–6, 262
  see also network; Deleuze and Guattari
autonomy
  and self-defence, 74, 79
  democratic, 74, 226n51
  female, 120

illusion of, 165
politics of, 79
sexual, 120
struggle for, 75–6, 78, 84, 87, 122
woman's, 120

bare life, 134, 224n19, 233
Bargu, Banu, 33, 78, 148, 162, 233, 235, 261–2
biological citizenship, 110
biopolitics
  and death, 255
  and necropolitics, 5, 15, 46, 64, 98, 111, 160, 165, 255
  and sovereignty, 4, 162, 255
  and welfare state, 179
  ends of, 6
  governmentality of, 161
  instruments of, 163
  of disposability, 8
  see also biopower; biosovereign; Foucault, Michel
biopower, 4, 72, 82, 87, 98, 122, 130, 161–3; *see also* biopolitics; biosovereign; Foucault, Michel
biosovereign, 9, 130, 140, 143; *see also* biopolitics; sovereignty

blood money, 16, 160, 164–6, 169
  acceptance of, 175, 178, 185, 186
  and media, 160, 167, 169, 173, 177–8
  and necrodomination, 172–3, 175, 178–82,
  and qisas, 167
  and Turkey's judiciary system, 168–9, 175, 181
  bargaining, 160–2, 167–8, 171, 178–81
  political use of, 177–8, 181
  rejection of, 171, 174, 182
  see also compensation claims
boundary-making, 48–51, 53, 61, 63, 220
burial, 2, 9, 48–9, 85, 139, 212, 215, 220, 232, 245, 253
  and reburial, 49, 51
  ground, 18, 62, 232, 243
  right to, 244, 247
  rites of, 242, 244, 246
  robes, 240
  sites, 18, 213, 253–4, 256
  see also grave; mass burial
Butler, Judith, 8, 50, 118, 162, 219–20, 257

Cemetery of Traitors, 18, 232–3, 238, 243, 246
Çetin, Sinan, 167
chastity, 18, 217; see also virginity
civil dissent, 141, 149, 152; see also civil resistance; resistance
civil resistance, 152; see also resistance
civilian, 11–13, 16, 18, 26–34, 38–39, 47, 59, 72–4, 76–7, 79, 83–4, 150, 190, 201, 210–11, 214–15, 219, 233, 239, 241, 246, 254, 259, 261; see also combatant

civilian court, 188, 191–6, 198, 202, 203
Cizre, 13, 71–87, 157, 169, 172
class, 8, 16, 132, 148, 171–2, 178, 212
  differences, 177
  domination, 163, 172, 180
  inequalities, 164
  hierarchy, 178, 180
  war, 182
collective memory, 5, 17, 19, 50, 53, 258, 261, 265–6; see also counter-knowledges
combatant, 11, 13, 72–4, 76–7, 79, 82–3, 85–7, 245; see also civilian
commemoration, 9, 18, 29, 49, 142, 213, 215, 233, 236
compassion, 73, 79, 81, 82
compensation claims, 16–17, 188
  and border killings, 189, 190, 192, 202
  court-processed, 194–5, 202
Constitutional Court, 81, 171, 174
corpse, 17–18, 51, 52, 212, 214–15, 232–6, 242–4, 253; see also dead body
Council of Forensic Medicine, 97, 101, 103–6, 108–9
counter-knowledges, 17, 19
counterinsurgency, 5, 10, 11, 13, 15, 27–8, 30–1, 34, 36, 218; see also guerrilla: warfare
coup attempt see 15 July 2016
coup d'état, 10, 11, 140, 209–10, 219; see also failed coup; 1980; 15 July 2016; postmodern coup
curfew, 71, 75–7, 79, 81, 83–4, 139, 211, 247, 253, 256–7, 261

dead body, 9, 17-19, 48-53, 75, 78, 83-4, 86, 195, 214-18, 220, 233-5, 239, 242, 268; *see also* corpse
death
  bare death, 224
  controlling the narrative of, 26, 36-38
  depoliticisation of, 26, 34-5
  logic of, 17, 119, 123, 130, 134
  management of, 12, 25, 39, 163
  metaphorical, 51, 118, 120, 123, 131, 134
  normalisation of, 26, 31-3, 256
  premature death, 97, 99, 102, 106
  relativisation of, 32
  slow death, 7, 109
  social death, 8, 9, 10, 14, 120, 124, 130, 133
  symbolic, 120
  see also homicide
death squads, 144
death-logics, xiii, 2, 10
death-making, 1, 4, 6, 9, 100, 111-12, 146, 148-50, 212-13, 222
death-worlds, 7, 122, 124, 255-7, 268
debilitation, 6, 9
Dedeman, 175-7, 179
Deleuze & Guattari, 127
democracy, xii, 1-7, 10, 19, 38, 40n8, 49, 51, 58-9, 63, 74, 145, 232, 239, 247
denuding, 18, 148, 213-14, 216, 220; *see also* corpse; dead body; desecration
desecration, 2, 18, 139, 148, 213, 216-17, 233, 235; *see also* corpse; dead body
dignity, 52, 151, 217, 245

Directorate of Religious Affairs, 33, 242-3, 246, 248n28
dirty war, 144, 213, 218
disappearing, 144; *see also* enforced disappearance
disposability, 2, 8, 48

economic subjugation, 189, 190, 195, 198, 201-3
ECtHR, 76, 81, 83, 86, 89n39, 89n40
election, 16, 37, 40n8, 51, 54, 174, 209-22, 219, 247
Encü, Ferhat, 171, 174
enemy, 11, 18, 50, 123-4, 170-1, 216-17, 245; *see also* enmity
enemy criminal justice, 170-1
enforced disappearance, 5, 9, 10, 17, 19, 213, 218, 258-61, 267
enmity, 18, 124, 213, 216, 222, 225n3; *see also* enemy
Erdoğan, Recep Tayyip, 25, 30-5, 37, 47, 57-9, 75, 147, 154n9, 169, 171, 209-10, 232, 238-41, 247
European Court of Human Rights, 76, 141, 155n23, 173, 204n10; *see also* ECtHR
exception, 5, 50, 87
  geographies of, 148, 212
  space of, 148, 212
  state of, 6, 7, 17, 124
  see also exceptional; exceptionality
exceptional
  corpses, 234
  figure, 236
  moments, 6
  powers, 5
  spaces, 10, 48
  violence, 113, 256
  see also exception; exceptionality

exceptionality, 5, 6, 219, 256
exposure, 2, 7, 15, 72, 139, 212, 214, 220
extrajudicial killing, 198, 218

failed coup, 1, 12, 18, 29, 37, 47, 49, 63, 154n9, 239; *see also* 15 July 2016
Fassin, Didier, 79
femicide, 25, 217
feminisation, 216
forensic, 11, 13
  documents, 73
  experts, 82
  regime of truth, 83, 85
  reports, 83, 85, 108, 176
  science, 83, 87, 97
  tests, 86
Foucault, Michel, 4, 5, 7, 19, 39, 83, 98, 148, 161–2, 212, 234, 255–6, 258, 262, 267, 269n26
funerals, 17, 18, 30, 31, 35, 47, 142, 233, 237–9, 241–3; *see also* commemoration; funerary rites
funerary rites, 242, 244–6; *see also* funerals

gender regime, 15, 118–20, 122–33
governmentality, 160–3, 179
  neoliberal, 16, 164, 212
grave, 17–19, 51, 53, 62, 72, 83, 148, 157, 212, 215, 232–3, 235, 239, 242–3, 245, 253–4, 267
guerrilla
  attacks, 73
  camps, 73–4
  pluralism, 265, 266
  resistance, 72
  warfare, 13, 73–4, 87, 212

guerrillas, 74–5, 144, 148, 153n1, 214, 216–17; *see also* PKK
Gülen, Fethullah, 29, 37–8, 46–7, 154n9, 239–41

harm, 1, 2, 9, 89n39, 147, 151, 153, 221, 235; *see also* violence
HDP (Peoples' Democratic Party), 73, 209–11, 215
  deputy/deputies, 77–82
  report, 82
  see also Kurdish political movement
homicide, 160, 163–5, 169, 171–2, 175
honour killings, 15, 120–4, 130, 135n20
human rights
  activism, 83
  activists, 98, 104, 108–11, 113, 179, 189, 246
  advocates, 78, 82, 87
  association, 103, 106, 109
  defenders, 14, 176, 177
  groups, 97, 183n35
  lawyers, 106, 174, 189
  organisations, 15, 102, 156n32, 173, 214
  slogans, 103
  violations, 9, 39, 171, 194, 223n5
human shields, 84, 215
humanitarian, 13, 33, 80, 102–3, 109, 112
  aid, 87
  campaigns, 77
  crisis, 75, 78
  ethics, 79
  laws, 97, 101, 103, 113
  mission, 76
  see also humanitarianism

humanitarianism, 78, 80
humiliation, 18, 120, 139, 217
hung parliament, 17, 210
hunger strike, 10, 78, 98, 100–2, 218
hush money, 169, 171
hymen, 15, 118–21, 123, 125–31, 133–4
hymenoplasty, 14, 15, 119–20, 125–34

ideal citizen, 11
identity, 8, 13, 16, 18, 50, 53, 85, 119, 130–1, 139, 142, 163–4, 172, 175, 179–82, 216, 218, 232, 235, 246
ill prisoners, 14, 97–100, 102–4, 106–9, 111–13
illness article, 101–2, 106, 108, 110–11, 114n32
impoverishment, 2
impunity, 86, 173–4, 176, 188, 193–4
inequality, 2, 132, 178
injury, 1, 2, 6, 98–9, 166, 168, 198; *see also* harm; violence
insecurity, 8, 57, 213, 222
insurgents, 5, 31, 134, 139

Kazanhan, 169–70, 172, 174, 176–7
Kurdish political movement, 28, 32, 37, 103, 173; *see also* HDP

laboratory, 2
legitimation, 3, 6, 11
life-logics, 4, 8
living dead, 7, 9, 49, 98, 106, 122, 189, 213, 233–5, 256

Malkki, Liisa, 80
martyr, 27–8, 31, 33, 39, 40n20, 51–2, 57–8, 60, 62, 142–3, 217–18, 236, 244
martyrdom, 1, 5, 9–13, 15, 18, 26–31, 33–4, 36, 51–3, 56–8, 60, 63, 64, 139–46, 149–53, 218, 220, 236–7
  civilian, 27–9
  Islamic, 15–16, 146–51
mass burial, 9, 254, 256, 260; *see also* burial; mass grave
mass grave, 19, 72, 83, 148, 235, 254, 267; *see also* grave
Mbembe, Achille, 2, 4–7, 10, 48–50, 63, 82, 98, 122, 148, 161–3, 188, 212, 234, 255–6
Mecidiyeköy, 168
medical reports, 98, 102, 105
memory, 52–3, 58, 177, 180–1, 211, 237, 254–5, 261–3, 266–7; *see also* collective memory
mourning, 2, 9, 30, 39, 50, 67, 219–20, 222, 235, 237, 244, 266
Muslim conscientious objection, 140, 145, 153

necro-epistemic methods, 254, 260, 262–3, 265, 267
necrodomination, 164, 172, 175, 178–80, 182
necrogeopolitics, 13, 48, 56–7, 62
necropolitical
  agent, 12, 38
  episteme, 19
  discourse, 33, 53, 64
  domination, 16
  gender regime, 15, 118, 123, 131
  hierarchy of documents, 99, 107, 110–11

necropolitical (*cont.*)
  imaginary, 50
  intervention, 120
  logic, 8, 108, 149
  power, 46–50, 53, 56–7, 62, 112, 122, 127
  problematic, xii, 3, 10
  rationalities, 255, 263
  repertoire, 11, 14
  resistance, 134
  sabotage, 133–4
  setting/site, 188, 195, 198, 201, 202
  space, 46–9, 53–7, 62–4, 254, 256, 258, 263
  spatialisation, 49, 63
  time/temporality, 266
  undercurrent, 2, 140
  violence, 15–17, 98–9, 109, 112–13, 139–40, 148–50, 212–13, 215–19, 221–2, 233, 235, 242
  violence of documents, 106–7, 110
  see also necrodomination; necropolitics; necroresistance
necropolitics, 1–19, 31, 39, 46, 48–9, 62–4, 72, 98, 111–13, 119–24, 130, 134, 140, 148, 151–2, 160–3, 165, 188, 212–13, 215, 220, 222, 233–5, 247, 254–8, 261–2, 266–8; *see also* biopolitics; necropolitical; necropower; sovereignty
necropower, 63, 72, 76, 78, 82–3, 87, 148–9, 164, 172, 188–90, 202, 212
necroresistance, 73, 78, 87, 130, 262; *see also* resistance

neglect, 7–8, 10, 14, 18, 35, 99, 166, 212, 234–5
Neocleous, Mark, 163
neoliberal
  economy, 132
  governmentality, 16, 164, 212
  judicial system, 160, 179
  logic, 128, 165
  securitization, 163
  state, 180
neoliberalism, 8, 16, 128, 163
network, 47, 57, 127, 129, 167, 169, 171, 176, 263
Newala Qaseba, 254, 261, 265–6, 268
NGOs, 173, 175–8
nightmare knowledges, 19, 255, 262–8
nudity, 216

Öcalan, Abdulah, 74, 153n1, 157n38
overkill, 9–10

Peace Petition, xiii
peace process, 17, 30, 103, 111, 153n1, 210–11; *see also* Kurdish political movement
PKK (Kurdistan Workers' Party), 25–7, 30, 34–5, 71–4, 86–7, 139, 141, 148, 153n1, 155n13, 156n37, 157n38, 187, 190, 199, 203n1, 210–12, 214, 237; *see also* guerrilla: warfare; guerrillas
political prisoners, 98–102, 108–10, 112, 114n17
post-modern coup, 238
precariousness, 8, 36

precarity, 5, 8, 17, 234
prisoner rights, 14, 99, 100, 103, 109, 111–13
prisons, 5, 8, 11, 13–4, 76, 97–101, 106, 109, 218–19, 256

racial, 162–4, 172, 175, 179–80
racialisation, 7, 18, 216
racism, 4, 153, 162, 212
resistance, 3, 9–11, 13–5, 18–19, 63, 72–3, 77, 81, 110, 119–20, 123, 126–7, 130–1, 133–4, 144, 146, 150–2, 172, 174, 177–8, 180–2, 214–15, 220, 233, 255, 260, 262–3, 265, 267
  and resilience, 19, 120, 129, 131
  necroresistance, 73, 78, 87, 130, 262
right to kill, 6, 48–9, 73, 162, 172, 180, 194, 201–3, 212, 255
Roboski, 27, 32–3, 38, 171, 174, 176–7, 187, 190

sabotage, 130–1, 133–4
Sarıyıldız, Faysal, 77–9
Saturday Mothers, 38, 157, 253–4, 260, 263, 265–6
security-state nexus, 163
self-defence, 13, 73–5, 79, 84, 87
self-destruction, 10, 134
self-harm, 10
sexualisation, 18, 216–17
Siirt, 173, 254
Şırnak, 75–6, 85, 157, 171, 174, 215, 253
slow death *see* death
social death *see* death

sovereign, 3, 46–53, 59–60, 63, 81, 122, 124, 142–3, 150, 163–6, 171, 180, 216, 244
  boundary-making, 220
  erasure, 19
  power, 10, 130, 140, 151–2, 161–2, 170, 218, 233–5, 241, 246, 255
  right to kill, 162, 172
  subjects, 78, 81, 118–19, 123
  violence, 1, 3–5, 8–9, 11, 17, 212, 224n19, 256
sovereignty, 3–6, 8–9, 14–15, 26, 73, 76, 101, 118, 122–4, 130, 140, 146–8, 150–2, 161–2, 164, 166, 170–1, 180–1, 212, 217, 219–22, 226n51, 234–5, 255–6; *see also* biosovereign; sovereign
Söylemez gang, 175
state of emergency, 6, 37, 55, 211, 213, 219, 232, 247
subjects, 7–9, 11–13, 16, 46, 48, 51, 53, 57, 59, 63, 72, 78, 82, 101, 119, 122–4, 129–30, 133, 141, 149, 190, 216, 235, 257, 263, 265, 267
surrogation, 217, 222, 225n40

techno-science, 73, 83, 87
temporality, 7, 14, 258–9, 266
terror formation, 4
Torunlar, 168–9, 178
trench, 74–5, 84, 211
Tunç, Mehmet, 79–81, 87
Turkish Medical Association, 102

ungrievable lives, 123, 130, 135n24, 162, 220, 225n49, 244; *see also* Butler, Judith

village guard, 27, 41n26, 148, 173–74, 177, 183n35
violence, 1–5, 7–12, 14–19, 26–8, 31, 34–5, 37–8, 72–4, 77, 79, 98–9, 106–7, 109, 112–13, 124, 139–40, 142–3, 145–53, 162, 165, 195, 210–22, 233–6, 242, 245–6, 261
  epistemic, 2, 19, 254, 261
  infrastructural/structural, 2, 7, 10, 15, 148
  postmortem, 9–11, 17, 19, 213–14, 216
  psychic, 2, 218, 220
  slow, 6, 7, 10, 14, 56, 98, 103, 109, 124
  symbolic, 1, 2, 7, 9, 17, 19, 124, 235, 237, 246
  wide spectrum of, 2, 4, 5
  see also injury; harm; necropolitical

virginity, 16, 118–23, 125, 128–31, 133–4
  medical examinations of, 15, 121–2, 134n10, 135n12
  performance of, 126, 130
vulnerability, 2, 8, 50, 148, 219–21, 224n19

war on terrorism, 160, 163, 165, 170, 179, 181
weaponisation, 130–1
weaponise
  body, 51, 100
  life, 10, 262
Wernicke-Korsakoff, 101, 114n17

YDG-H (Revolutionary Patriotic Youth Movement), 71, 86, 211

EU representative:
Easy Access System Europe
Mustamäe tee 50, 10621 Tallinn, Estonia
Gpsr.requests@easproject.com

www.ingramcontent.com/pod-product-compliance
Lightning Source LLC
Chambersburg PA
CBHW071829230426
43672CB00013B/2797